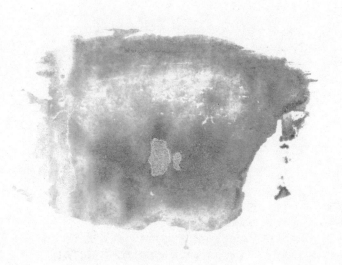

Assertive Behavior

Assertiveness Training (AT) has been widely researched and extensively applied for over two decades. Although some have claimed that it is an over-valued concept, too often applied when inappropriate, there is still an abundance of AT courses and therapists practising throughout the industrialized West.

But despite such activity and debate, the field lacks any attempt to draw together the available material into a comprehensive and realistic appraisal of AT. *Assertive Behavior* is the first book to provide this critical review. Richard Rakos places AT in its social and cultural context, from the socially and politically activist 1960s, to the more individualist 1980s, showing how the therapy has become an increasingly relevant option in today's society. Yet, it is not enough to regard AT as a 'pop' psychology panacea for post-modern troubles – Rakos describes a complex intervention requiring clinical expertise.

As well as providing a critical analysis of the concept of AT, *Assertive Behavior* contains a comprehensive summary of the theoretical and empirical literature. Rakos also draws conclusions from his own empirical research, and suggests techniques for intervention, as well as identifying issues requiring further research and debate.

Richard F. Rakos is internationally known in the field of Assertiveness Training, and has been involved in the research and practice of AT for over a decade. He is currently Associate Professor of Psychology at Cleveland State University, and has a private practice in behavior therapy.

International Series on Communication Skills

Edited by Owen Hargie
Head of the Department of Communication
University of Ulster

Assertive Behavior
Theory, Research, and Training

Richard F. Rakos

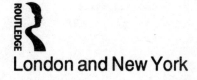
London and New York

First published 1991
by Routledge
11 New Fetter Lane, London EC4P 4EE

Simultaneously published in the USA and Canada
by Routledge
a division of Routledge, Chapman and Hall Inc.
29 West 35th Street, New York, NY 10001

© 1991 Richard F. Rakos

Typeset by LaserScript Limited, Mitcham, Surrey
Printed and bound in Great Britain by Mackays of Chatham PLC, Kent

British Library Cataloguing in Publication Data

Rakos, Richard F. *1950*
Assertive behavior, research, and training.
  1 Interpersonal relationships. Communication. Assertive behaviour.
  I. Title
  302.2

Library of Congress Cataloging in Publication Data

Rakos, Richard F., 1950–
    Assertive behavior : theory, research, and training / Richard F. Rakos.
        p.   cm. – (International series on communication skills)
    Includes bibliographical references.
    1. Assertiveness training.   2. Assertiveness (Psychology)
    I. Title. II. Series
    RC489.A77R35 1991   90-33163
    158′.2–dc20   CIP

    ISBN 0-415-00041-6
    ISBN 0-415-00042-4 (pbk)

To Kennee, Rhoni, Mikaela

Contents

List of figures

Editorial introduction

International Series on Communication Skills

In recent years increasing attention has been devoted to the analysis of social interaction in terms of the communicative competence of the participants. In particular, the conceptualization of interpersonal communication as skilled performance, has resulted in a veritable flood of empirical, scientific, and descriptive publications regarding the nature of social skills. However, these publications have been disseminated over a wide spectrum of discipline areas including psychology, communication, sociology, education, business, and counselling. As a result, there is a need for a new series of books designed specifically to draw together this material, from disparate sources, into a meaningful evaluation and analysis of a range of identified communication skills.

Each book in this series contains a blend of theory, research, and practice pertaining to a particular area of communication. However, the emphasis throughout the series is upon the practical application of communication skills to social interaction *per se*. The books are written by authors of international repute, chosen specifically for their depth of knowledge, and extensive publications, in the specific topic under consideration. As such, this series will make a significant contribution to the rapidly expanding field of interpersonal communication.

The books in this series therefore represent a major addition to the literature and will be of interest to students and researchers in psychology, communication, and other disciplines. They will also prove invaluable to the vast range of people in the 'interpersonal professions' (doctors, nurses, therapists, social workers, and so on), whose day-to-day work so much depends upon effective communication skills.

Taken as a whole, this series represents an encyclopaedia of information on the current state of our knowledge of skilled communication. It is certainly the most comprehensive attempt to date to chart the existing state of this field of study. As such, it is both a privilege and a pleasure to have been involved in the conception and execution of this series.

Assertive Behaviour: Theory, Research, and Training

The study of the nature, functions, and outcomes of assertive behaviour has attracted considerable interest within psychology and communication during the past fifteen years. A voluminous number of papers, articles, book chapters, and, indeed, books have been devoted to the topic of assertiveness. However, up until the publication of the present text, there would seem to have been no concerted attempt to draw together the many and diverse strands associated with this area. This book, by Richard Rakos, is therefore very timely, representing as it does a comprehensive analysis and evaluation of the many facets of assertiveness.

The book itself is divided into two coherent parts. Part one presents a conceptualization of assertiveness, including clear definition of terms, delineation of the subject area, theoretical perspectives, identification of overt and covert dimensions, and the study of this topic within a wider social context. Part two builds upon this foundation to examine the training implications of assertiveness in terms of assessment, training methods, relevant target populations, and general clinical issues. Throughout both parts, Rakos leaves no stone unturned, and provides the reader with a wealth of research material to underpin his presentation.

Richard Rakos has acquired an international reputation as a result of his publications in the field of assertiveness for over a decade, and his mastery of the subject is clearly evident. He has produced a thought-provoking text, which will be relevant to academics and practitioners alike. He grasps the nettle regarding the issue of the extent to which assertion is now an outmoded, over-stated, and over-valued concept, and proceeds to present a convincing argument which tempers optimism with reality concerning the utility of the concept *per se*, and of assertiveness training as a therapeutic medium.

Overall, the content of this book provides the most detailed, informed, and informative account to date of research, theory, and practice in assertiveness. Since this is an area of study which is of interest in a wide range of settings, the information presented will be of relevance, and benefit, to academics and professionals in many contexts. The theoretical and research material covered results in a fine balance of academic and applied perspectives on the study of assertiveness. The book is, in every sense, comprehensive.

Owen Hargie
Head of Department of Communication
University of Ulster

Preface

When Owen Hargie asked me, in May 1987, to write a book on assertiveness training for a series on communication skills that he was editing, I jumped at the opportunity. Assertiveness training had been around for almost twenty years and was a popular clinical and personal growth intervention, yet there was no comprehensive review and summary of its huge scholarly literature. The end of the eighties seemed to be the right time for such an endeavor, particularly since research and lay interest has abated to a significant degree. In fact, many prominent researchers believe the whole concept of assertion has outlived its usefulness and should be abandoned. As is evident in this book, I do not share this perspective. To me, it is clear that assertiveness training is firmly entrenched as a mainstream behavioral intervention; and like other empirically validated techniques, it is quite effective when used appropriately. The decline in assertiveness training's (unwarranted) popularity among both lay people and clinicians is welcome; now, assertiveness training can simply take its place beside systematic desensitization, participant modeling, and token economies in the behavioral arsenal.

This book has two purposes: first, to review the published literature on assertion and assertiveness training and, second, to distill empirically based clinical implications from the research. To accomplish these in a relatively short book, and to maintain the interest of practitioners as well as researchers, I decided to avoid detailed methodological critiques in most instances. Instead, I point out such problems in a general way, note contradictory or inconclusive data, and indicate areas needing additional research.

This book could not have been written without the support of many people. Kennee, my wife, tolerated my long hours of work and unpredictable distractions, and, moreover, offered valuable suggestions and constant encouragement. Rhoni, now three, helped me retain my sense of humour and my perspective as to what is really important in life. Mikaela, though only recently born, was still a real presence through much of the writing process, and provided comfort, perspective, excitement, and hope for the future. At Cleveland State University, Lynn Viola incessantly prodded me to give her drafts to revise or print; her genuine desire to help me complete the manuscript, and her gracious acceptance of work that resulted from my errors or carelessness, made the whole process so much easier for me. My Research Assistants, Sonia Minnes and Tava Slone, spent hours in the library, at the computer, or with draft copies of the manuscript; they did much of the unrewarding but essential work that contributes to a finished product of the magnitude of a book. In addition, Cleveland State University granted me six months professional leave to work on this book; without such relief from my normal academic duties, I doubt I could have devoted to this project the time it demanded. Finally, throughout the writing process, Owen Hargie's support, encouragement and feedback, and understanding of missed deadlines has been deeply appreciated.

Cleveland
February 1990

Part one

Assertive Behavior

Chapter one

Assertive behavior in societal context

Assertiveness training ascended to prominence as a behavior therapy technique and pop psychology in the mid-seventies, and has, to a large extent, maintained its popularity throughout the 1980s. Its rise was dramatic. In research programs, assertiveness training displaced desensitization as the most researched behavioral intervention; college sophomores suddenly were no longer snake, rat, height, and speech phobic, but now were inappropriately timid and inhibited. Clinically, assertiveness training (AT) was prescribed for almost all clients, but often implemented in rigid formats that taught individuals to cope with personally trivial or irrelevant situations (Emmons & Alberti, 1983). Professionals popularized the AT model in books, tapes, and workshops for lay people by presenting AT as a panacea for much, if not all, human distress. The concept of assertion was simplified to saying 'no' and 'getting your own way' (Smith, 1975) or to 'stand[ing] up for your rights' and 'get[ting] where and what you want in bed, at work, on the social scene, and at home' (Baer, 1976).

These widely disseminated materials had a strong impact on a society in the process of turning from the political and social consciousness of the sixties and early seventies to the introspection, narcissism, and self-improvement that characterized the late seventies and eighties. A product – AT – was created that tapped into an unexploited market. The result was an explosion in the popularity of AT, the development of dozens of self-help books and tapes (Heimberg, Andrasik, Blankenberg, & Edlund, 1983; Kelly, 1979), and the promulgation of countless one-shot, 3-hour AT 'sessions' offered by individuals who had little or no training in the sophisticated provision of clinical services.

AT as a fad, however, seems unlikely to survive past the eighties. The reason partly resides in market mechanisms – after all, how many people can enrol in endless 'courses'? However, the integrity of the scientific underpinnings of AT may also have played a role in the depopularization of AT. The early deluge of studies that showed AT effectively taught the basic response components of assertion has been followed by more sophisticated research that has clearly demonstrated the complexity of assertiveness. For example, consideration of the social and cultural context is now recognized as an essential foundation of a functionally useful assertive response. Responsible assertiveness trainers

1

understand that they must conduct careful assessments, introduce interventions in a thoughtful manner, and provide comprehensive services that meet the real needs of clients. Today, AT is viewed by the scientific and professional communities as a powerful but limited technique that can be of tremendous benefit to individuals when used by well-trained clinicians who are cognizant of the complexities involved in helping people achieve their behavior-change goals.

The emergence of the concept of assertive behavior and the strategies to teach the skills were facilitated by – and perhaps required – the *Weltanshauung* guiding the United States, and, to a lesser extent, the other industrialized Western societies. Four key elements of the predominant world view are intrinsic to the notion of assertive behavior: rationality, activism, ethical relativism, and pragmatism.[1]

The importance of the rational philosophical underpinnings of assertive behavior cannot be underestimated. AT clearly values reason over emotion, despite its *raison d'etre* of expressing feelings and desires. The key element in all contemporary definitions of assertive behavior, as we shall see in the next chapter, is the *appropriate* expression of emotion. However, the ability to produce such a response is dependent upon accurate discrimination of situational cues, effective decision-making skills, and the emission of acceptable interpersonal behavior, all of which are produced by rational rather than emotional processes. AT, therefore, embodies rationalist philosophical tenets.

Socrates, an early, extreme rationalist, argued that all voluntary acts were rational, in the sense that the person had good reasons for the action, and that it was impossible for a person to respond voluntarily in ways antagonistic to good reasons (Wadia, 1986). This is known as the Socratic Paradox and has at its center the proposition that virtue is knowledge (Santas, 1979), with self-knowledge assuming a particularly prominent position ('the unexamined life is not worth living'). For Socrates, knowledge provides morality *and* the ability to act morally (rationally) in the face of emotional stress (Vlastos, 1971) – in other words, it provides both the ends and the means for the emission of appropriate behavior. The Socratic position clearly has glaring weaknesses, such as the assumption that knowledge alone is both necessary and sufficient for moral goodness (Vlastos, 1971) and the omission of the concept of choice as an intervening process between knowledge and action (Wadia, 1986). However, the knowledge Socrates valued was concerned mainly with information processing, deduction, and decision making rather than empiricism and facts (Vlastos, 1971), and it is that type of knowledge that has become the focal point of contemporary AT, conceptually surpassing molecular skill training in importance and functionally surpassing it in utility. Thus, while AT does not view humans as perfect rational machines, as did Socrates (Wadia, 1986), it does see humans as having the potential to control emotions via a rational reasoning process that is a product of certain types of knowledge.

Today, rationalist philosophy can be applied to three domains (Irani, 1986). First, rationality is involved in deductive inference, empirical confirmation judgement, and decision making. Second, it is the means by which we comprehend and judge the behavior of others. And third, it provides explanations for the events that we experience and hence further understanding of the environment in which we live. All three domains assume critical roles in the guidance of behavior in the modern world – one characterized by a decreasing influence of traditional, stable sources of behavior control, such as family, community, church, and government. In our technological and scientifically oriented society, rationality is therefore highly valued (Habermas, 1973), very functional (Nisbet, 1976), and, not surprisingly, an integral part of therapies, such as behavioral ones, spawned by 'the ideology of modernity' (Woolfolk & Richardson, 1984). And few behavioral techniques rely on rationality more than AT does, both philosophically and pragmatically. The *process* and the *content* of assertive responding are both based in a rational philosophical approach to human interactions.

The rational underpinnings of AT were not clearly evident in its historical development, as iconoclasm was the more prominent motivating force. Salter (1949) was the first to introduce AT in *Conditioned reflex therapy*, his polemical diatribe against psychoanalysis. He described 'excitatory' exercises such as feeling talk, facial talk, expression of contradictory opinions, use of the pronoun 'I', acceptance of compliments, and improvisation. His training strategy combined the excitatory exercises with exhortation and prompting to behave more assertively (Rimm & Masters, 1979). Though Salter's impact on behavior therapy was minimal, his writings encouraged Wolpe (1982), whose dissatisfaction with psychoanalytic therapy also prompted a search for alternative intervention strategies based on conditioning theory. Wolpe viewed assertive behavior as 'the appropriate expression of any emotion other than anxiety toward another person'(1982, p. 118). He developed the first training techniques consistent with a view of assertiveness as a situation-specific response that required sensitivity to social consequences (Rimm & Masters, 1979). Other historical contributions to the foundations of AT include Moreno's psychodrama, Kelly's fixed-role therapy, and Ellis's rational-emotive therapy, which all developed in the 1950s and early 1960s (Rimm & Masters, 1979). These approaches also challenged the hegemony of traditional psychoanalysis, sometimes quite vociferously (eg Ellis, 1962).

While the intellectual roots of AT were being nurtured, the social and political activism of the 1960s provided a cultural impetus for the development of techniques that promoted direct personal influence and expression. The sixties were characterized by the rejection of arbitrary authority and, simultaneously, by the expression of nonconformist behaviors, beliefs, and desires. These phenomena could be observed on an individual behavioral basis (long hair, 'free sex', drug experimentation) as well as on a social scale that included both verbal and behavioral expression (civil rights, anti-war, feminist, and environmental movements). The cultural toleration, and even acceptance, of these challenges to existing conventions provided a natural foundation for the introduction of a

3

qualitative shift in the nature of individual verbal expression that would nevertheless be judged to be socially acceptable. The previous development of the component techniques of AT, and the humanistic, iconoclastic, and egalitarian values promoted by behavior therapists in general (Woolfolk & Richardson, 1984), meant that the ends had a means, or the means had an end, or both: a happy marriage.

The early AT books reflected this 1960s activist stance. Alberti & Emmons (1970), in the first AT book written for a lay audience, discussed how social structures perpetuate the myth of social inequality; how family, education, business, and religion inhibited open expression of feelings; how women, children, and ethnic minorities were taught assertion is reserved for the white male; and how the 'haves' fail to acknowledge the human rights of the 'have nots'. They advocated adherence to the UN Universal Declaration of Human Rights, and argued that powerful political, corporate, and labor establishments control and exploit the average citizen. Smith (1975), in an early, popular self-help book, presented a bill of assertive rights, declared morals and laws to be arbitrary controls on behavior, described a police officer who gave him a ticket as a 'pot-bellied centurion', and asserted that conscientious objectors to the draft (during the Vietnam War) were subjected to the emotional application of law, a practice he saw as incompatible with democracy. These authors correctly perceived the time was right for the widespread acceptance of a concept and strategy promising personal empowerment at the expense of establishment institutions that had fallen out of favor.

Over the past two decades, the social and political activism that provided the initial impetus to the AT movement has given way[2] to various forms of individual activism that are, nevertheless, still consistent with the concept of assertiveness as a means toward personal power. Thus, consumerism, litigiousness, and attempts to develop personal fitness, healthy lifestyles, and attractive personal environments all can be facilitated by the use of appropriate assertive skills.

A third element that helped AT gain prominence was the rejection of absolute standards of morality, which was, in reality, a corollary of the discreditation of societal establishments. Patriotism no longer meant 'my country right or wrong', and faith no longer referred exclusively, if at all, to belief in a deity. Ethical relativism emerged as an explicit characteristic of behavior therapy (Woolfolk & Richardson, 1984) and as a *sine qua non* of AT. Indeed, Smith (1975) insisted that each person's prime assertive right is the right to judge one's own behavior. For many people, the secular sources of morality seemed much more relevant to the requirements of modernity than the traditional Judeo-Christian foundation. As an example, consider the following passages from Chapter 5 of Matthew:

Blessed are the meek: for they shall inherit the earth.

(Matt. 5:5)

Ye have heard that it hath been said, An eye for an eye, and a tooth for a tooth: But I say unto you, That ye resist not evil: but whosoever shall smite thee on thy right cheek, turn to him the other also. And if any man will sue thee at the law, and take away thy coat, let him have *thy* cloke also. And whosoever shall compel thee to go a mile, go with him twain. Give to him that asketh thee, and from him that would borrow of thee turn not thou away.

(Matt. 5:38–42)

Clearly, these are not beliefs that, if profoundly adhered to, will facilitate assertive responding! Though Jesus evidenced little concern for logical consistency and presented his messages in signs and symbols (Jaspers, 1957), many religious individuals understand his concrete messages in very literal terms and many others find them far removed from the exigencies of modern life. AT, therefore, like behavior therapy (London, 1984; Woolfolk & Richardson, 1984), captured the attention of practitioners and clients who adhered to a secular value system for everyday guidance. Though AT has been adapted for work with religious Christians (eg Augsberger, 1979; Emmons and Richardson, 1981; Sanders and Malony, 1982), its popularity in a technological and rapidly changing world is strongly embedded in the attractiveness of its secular humanism.

The final element intrinsic to AT is pragmatism, a philosophy best articulated by Dewey (1957). Indeed, if there is one philosophy that seems most accurately to characterize Americans, it is the notion that what works is much more important than dogmatism or ideology. This metaphysical orientation nurtured the development and expansion of the behavioral therapies (Rakos, 1980; Woolfolk & Richardson, 1984), as Americans sought treatments that promised efficient and efficacious relief rather than illumination of underlying, but not immediately relevant, historical sources or existential meanings of distress. Consistent with these desires, AT stresses that a pragmatic appraisal of each situation must be conducted, and, based on that assessment, the choice between behavioral options should be guided by the probable outcomes of each of the possibilities; the response that is selected should, overall, provide the maximum amount of positive reinforcement, however that is defined by the individual.

Thus, AT emphasizes that assertive behavior is only one option for coping with difficult or problematic circumstances, and in many instances it may not be the preferred one. In other words, there is no ideological mandate always to respond assertively! Such pragmatism is, of course, highly adaptive in our modern world, with its shifting value systems, complex and ambiguous situations, and increasing cultural and social heterogeneity. Thus, it comes as no surprise that AT was rapidly and widely embraced throughout the industrialized nations, particularly Canada (Lefevre & West, 1984), Australia (Smith, 1985; Wilson, 1975), the Netherlands (Kienhorst, Van Ijzendoorn-Schmitz, & Diekstra, 1980), France (Viala & Riviere, 1976), Germany (Borgart, 1985), and Japan (Maeda, 1985).[3] And, despite a shakier history of democratic politics, and less reliance on relativism, members of the Second World, such as Czechoslovakia

(Ferjencik, 1979), and the Third World, such as Latin America (Riso, 1984) and India (Bhargava, 1983; Kumaraiah, 1979), also found AT's pragmatism attractive.

AT has proven to be a resilient intervention over the past two decades. The concepts and training strategies developed by behaviorists aligned with liberal reformist values have proved to be equally well suited for the societal shift toward conservative philosophies, centered on material gain and personal self-improvement, that was prompted by the social and political climate in the West in the eighties. Thus, we have a concept and set of techniques that promote an activist, but pragmatic, orientation toward coping with our post-industrial, information-driven society. They can be applied toward altering or maintaining the status quo, rely on ethical relativism to determine the ends, and utilizing rationality to provide the means. AT is really a prototypical intervention for the modern world, one that, while unnecessary in earlier times, dramatically meets the needs of people in today's technological, chaotic, and unstable environment.

Chapter two

Conceptualizing assertive behavior

Definitions of assertion

The pragmatism inherent in the behavioral approach to therapy has proved its value repeatedly: an intervention is accepted as valid when research demonstrates it effects desired changes (O'Leary & Wilson, 1987). However, this atheoretical approach can at times have drawbacks, most notably in the frequent absence of a general organizational scheme in which to place the intervention. The lack of such a conceptual framework can hinder efforts to generalize the application of the technique to different problems and/or clinical populations as well as to identify the limits within which the technique must be expected to operate. The development of AT provides an excellent example of this phenomenon: the training package was empirically validated before the concept of assertiveness was defined with any precision whatsoever. The result was an intervention applied without proper assessment, since it was so unclear as to what exactly was to be evaluated! Perhaps that is part of the reason why AT was trumpeted as a panacea for remediating the interpersonal difficulties experienced by many, if not most, people.

A striking demonstration of the lack of conceptual clarity characterizing assertiveness is provided by St. Lawrence (1987), who identified more than 20 distinctly different definitions presently used in research and training. Galassi, Galassi, and Vedder (1981) observed that the definitions formulate assertion in terms of one of the following: a) basic human rights; b) honest and/or appropriate emotional expression; c) rights and emotional expression; d) rights, emotional expression, and theoretical assumptions; e) specific response classes; or f) content-free, functional properties of the response. The variability inherent in the conceptualization of the assertive response can be further appreciated through the provision of specific examples of each category.

Smith (1975), as noted earlier, views assertive behavior as a fundamental right of each individual. His conception of human rights appears to embody libertarian assumptions to a much greater extent than it does social democratic philosophy: 'You have the right to judge your own behavior, thoughts, and emotions, and to take responsibility for their initiation and consequences upon yourself' (p. 28).

Rakos (1979) criticized definitions based on rights alone for their failure to acknowledge that the expression of rights by an individual acting in a social context entails functionally related antecedent and subsequent responsibilities. An emphasis on individual rights at the expense of both societal rights and individual responsibilities imbues the concept of assertion with the aura of selfishness and narcissism, and contributes to public confusions that erroneously assume books with titles like *Looking out for #1* (Ringer, 1977) are about assertive behavior.

Several definitions focus on emotional expression as the key element in assertion. Wolpe (1982), for example, conceptualizes assertion in terms of '… the proper expression of any emotion other than anxiety toward another person' (p. 118). The introduction of the idea of a 'proper' type of expression is too vague to be of much practical use, but still probably superior to the kind of expressive definition that omits any recognition of social context: 'Assertiveness [is] expressing one's opinions and wishes directly' (Eisler & Frederiksen, 1980, p. 185). The best definition of this general type is suggested by Rimm and Masters (1979): 'Assertive behavior is interpersonal behavior involving the honest and relatively straightforward expression of thoughts and feelings [that is] socially appropriate [and in which] the feelings and welfare of others are taken into account' (p. 63). As the authors themselves note, the definition is intended to convey a sense of the concept, and is not offered as an operational prescription for assertive responding.

The third type of definition relies on both rights and emotional expression. Lange and Jakubowski's (1976) contribution is of this kind: 'Assertion involves standing up for personal rights and expressing thoughts, feelings, and beliefs in *direct, honest,* and *appropriate* ways which do not violate another person's rights' (p. 7). Theoretical assumptions are included with rights and expressiveness in the fourth type of definition, exemplified by Alberti and Emmons (1970): 'Behavior which enables a person to act in his own best interests, to stand up for himself without undue anxiety, to express his honest feelings comfortably, or to exercise his own rights without denying the rights of others we call assertive behavior' (p. 2).

Lazarus (1973) was the first to identify specific response classes by which assertive behavior could be defined: 'the ability to say "no", the ability to ask for favors or to make requests, the ability to express positive and negative feelings, the ability to initiate, continue, and terminate general conversation' (p. 697). Galassi and Galassi (1977a) expanded these to nine categories: giving and receiving compliments, making requests, initiating and maintaining conversations, standing up for rights, refusing requests, and expressing personal opinions, displeasure, anger, and positive feelings. More recently, Christoff and Kelly (1985) have conceptualized assertion as simply refusal, request, or commendatory responses.

Finally, several functional definitions have been offered in the literature. Heimberg, Montgomery, Madsen, and Heimberg (1977) suggested that 'assertive behavior be conceptualized as "effective problem solving"'(p. 954). Rich and Schroeder (1976) proposed that assertive behavior is 'the skill to seek, maintain, or enhance reinforcement in an interpersonal situation through the expression of feelings or wants when such expression risks loss of reinforcement or even punishment ... The degree of assertiveness may be measured by the effectiveness of an individual's response in producing, maintaining, or enhancing reinforcement' (p. 1082). A third example is St. Lawrence's (1987) broadening of the assertive concept to 'the learned skill to adapt one's behavior to the requirements of an interpersonal situation' (p. 157) so that positive consequences are maximized and negative ones minimized.

As noted by Galassi et al. (1981), each of the approaches has particular difficulties associated with it. Definitions based on rights can be subjective, arbitrary, and socially irresponsible, while those based on emotional expressiveness are too vague. Definitions that rely on theory are constricted by current research findings. Response-class definitions may be too specific and fail to encompass the entire construct. Functional definitions allude only to the social context and thereby fail to differentiate assertion from aggression (cf. Rakos, 1979). Furthermore, broad functional definitions such as those of St. Lawrence (1987) and Heimberg et al. (1977) seem to encompass almost any behavior and therefore have little utility for identifying assertive behavior *per se*. They describe the function of numerous social skills, including assertion, but fail to specify the unique qualities, attributes, or elements of the response that distinguish it from other effective interpersonal competencies (eg active listening skills). Thus, after almost 20 years of intense activity in the area, we still lack an adequate conceptualization of what exactly we are teaching to our clients.

Though the existing definitions are problematic, they still make clinically useful contributions to the conceptualization of assertive behavior. An emphasis on rights permits the clinician to lay the foundation for the acceptance of assertion as a legitimate option. Rights in democratic nations are central concepts with tremendous impact. But their utility is tempered by the potential for misuse (Rimm & Masters, 1979), and the clinician must present them in a balanced fashion. A focus on appropriate emotional expression succinctly captures the essence of assertiveness, as Rimm and Masters (1979) note. Clarification of response classes provides a framework for organizing and expanding a behavioral repertoire. Finally, functional definitions specify the goals of assertive behavior and elucidate the abstract, contentless elements that comprise the response.

The functional definition offered by Rich and Schroeder (1976) is particularly useful in concisely operationalizing the elements so that five essential performance implications are salient to the client. First, assertion is a learned *skill* that is a function of the situation and the interaction of the person and situation.[1] It is not a function of intrapersonal cross-situational dispositions or traits that a person 'has' or 'lacks' (Galassi, Galassi, & Fulkerson, 1984; Galassi et al. 1981; Heimberg & Becker, 1981; Schroeder & Rakos, 1983). In fact, the influence of situational variables expands as the task increases in complexity (Chiauzzi, Heimberg, & Doty, 1982). This does not mean that there is no consistency in the assertive behavior of individuals. However, stability is generally obtained only when multiple responses are measured over long periods of time and then summed (Deluty, 1985a). But even such 'behavioral aggregates' are sensitive to immediate environmental stimuli: '... there was much consistency in interpersonal behavior across situations that varied (but not highly) in structure and permitted activity; as long as the situational cues and constraints ... were fairly constant, interpersonal behavior ... was quite consistent' (Deluty, 1985a, p. 1064). Furthermore, even persons who are generally assertive or passive are influenced by contextual stimuli (Kirschner & Galassi, 1983). Thus, an individual's performance of assertive behavior is likely to vary from situation to situation.

Rich and Schroeder's formulation further clarifies assertion as an *expressive* skill, composed of verbal and nonverbal response components, that is performed in an *interpersonal* context in which there is some *risk* of a negative reaction by the recipient. Finally, the extent of assertiveness is measured by *outcome*, which is commonly considered to be the 'ultimate criterion for evaluating performance' (McFall, 1982, p. 17).

The functional definition's emphasis on outcome highlights one important way to measure assertiveness, but ignores other essential criteria that make independent contributions to the evaluation of the response. First, since assertion involves risk, it follows that even technically proficient behavior may fail to produce reinforcement in any given instance. However, the *technical criterion*, while critical for effective skill training in clinical and research settings, is not fully appreciated by trainees, who tend to judge assertiveness solely through outcome effectiveness, without consideration of response quality (Heimberg & Etkin, 1983). Second, appropriate assertion may achieve its immediate goals but significantly injure the relationship; assertion may 'work' but only in a limited way, and the 'net' effect of the response must be determined by a *cost–benefit criterion*. Since assertiveness is conceptualized to be a self-enhancing skill (Alberti & Emmons, 1970; Rimm & Masters, 1979), an unfavorable balance would rarely characterize an assertive response. Finally, behavior must have social validity (Kazdin, 1977; Wolf, 1978), which, at its most fundamental level, is concerned with legitimacy through social acceptability. Behavior that is consensually judged to be unskilled (eg crazy talk, Curran, 1979) or antisocial (eg physical assault, Arkowitz, 1981) may in fact be reinforced; the interpersonal behavior must somehow be judged to be socially appropriate by a *cultural criterion*. Thus, objective effectiveness of the response in producing reinforcement is a very limited way to measure assertiveness. In fact, in clinical work, most trainers emphasize technical expertise, net benefit, and cultural appropriateness far more than they stress actual interpersonal impact as the standards by which to evaluate social skill (cf Heimberg & Etkin, 1983).

The impediment to obtaining a consensually agreed upon definition of assertive behavior clearly does not lie with a lack of creativity by the researchers. Rather, the difficulty resides in the nature of the response itself: it is a social skill (Schroeder & Rakos, 1983) that contributes to social competence (St. Lawrence, 1987). But social competence is a construct that, by definition, must be analyzed within the social and cultural community in which it occurs. Because of this, researchers periodically contend that the assertion construct has outlived its usefulness and should be abandoned (Galassi et al., 1981; Galassi et al., 1984; Gervasio & Crawford, 1989; Montgomery & Heimberg, 1978).

However, despite these repeated pleas, the construct lives on and even flourishes, suggesting that, despite its flaws, it is both appealing and useful. Thus, rather than dispatching assertion to the crowded psychological graveyard, its conceptualization should be expanded in breadth, depth, and specificity. In this regard, Pepper's (1942) distinction between mechanistic and contextualistic world views is helpful. The mechanistic perspective, which adheres to the machine as its root metaphor, proposes that the discrete parts have primacy over the whole, and that the parts do not change their nature whether viewed separately or together. The parts are discovered, not constructed. Furthermore, there is a force that propels the system toward theoretically predictable outcomes. Finally, truth resides in demonstrating that predictions are corroborated by observation (Hayes, 1988; Hayes, Hayes, & Reese, 1988). The history of AT suggests it adopted the mechanistic world view to a large extent: component responses have been stressed as universally important and subsequently identified through factor-analytic studies, a 'force' exists in the notion of expression of rights, and AT is observed to 'work' when individuals emit the desired responses. Only in basing prediction on common sense and pragmatism, rather than theory, has AT diverged from mechanism. Contextualism, on the other hand, has as its root metaphor the ongoing act in context. The response has no meaning when divorced from the setting in which it occurs. The parts are derived from the whole, but have no meaning apart from the whole, and the whole, therefore, has primacy over the parts. Finally, the truth criterion of contextualism is successful working, or pragmatism (Hayes, 1988; Hayes et al., 1988). Except for the pragmatic truth criterion, the definitions of AT and much of the research on it have failed to adopt the contextualistic position. However, clinical work always has, for if it did not, skill acquisition would be meaningless: an individual would be unable to integrate the assertive competencies within the previously acquired behavioral repertoire and would fail to cope adequately with the ambiguous and fluid situations that arise in specific, often unique, contexts. In fact, the influence of contextual variables is increasing rapidly within behavioral assessment and treatment (eg Dumas, 1989). Perhaps in recognition of the clinical realities, AT research has finally begun to incorporate the broader context within which the assertive response is emitted (see Chapter 5). The contextualistic perspective has also been advocated by researchers addressing themselves to the more general area of social skills. Two major theoretical proposals will be briefly reviewed.

Trower (1982) suggested a *generative model* of social skills. In this perspective, *social skills* are the discrete, overt response components (eg eye contact) embedded in an interactive behavioral sequence. *Social skill* comprises the production, or generation, of skilled, purposive behavior, while *social competence* consists of the ability to emit social skills *and* the social skill of generation (of skilled behavior). Cognitive behaviors and information-processing skills are essential for social competence, since they articulate the meaning of the situation, and hence the purpose to which the overt skills are addressed. Meaning, however, can only be ascertained within the situational context of 'naturally occurring chunks [of behavioral interactions] that have identifiable internal structures' (Trower, 1980, p. 412) consisting of a beginning, an end, and an identifiable goal.

A second contextualist model, proposed by McFall (1982), can be termed the *dual model*. One element involves *social competence*, which is an evaluation of the response by another, rather than an inherent feature of the behavior. *Social skills*, on the other hand, are the 'specific abilities that enable a person to perform competently at particular social tasks' (p. 23). The entire skill is greater than the component behaviors, which include decoding skills, cognitive decision skills, and encoding skills. Emission of the overt response and evaluation of the outcome are considered to be part of the encoding capabilities. Social skills are emitted in the context of tasks, which involve the 'chunking [of] events into some kind of units'. The *task analysis* specifies the purpose of and constraints on behavior, the setting and relevant social rules, and the evaluative criteria by which behavior will be judged, all within a systems perspective that places behaviors in a complex interrelated matrix.

These models, and other similar ones (eg Bellack, 1979a, b; Gambrill & Richey, 1986; Meichenbaum, Butler, & Gruson, 1981; Morrison & Bellack, 1981), have been termed interactive (Schroeder & Rakos, 1983) to highlight the orientation of the conceptualization. Specifically, interactive models assess consequences and social evaluations of behavior, expand the focus of skilled performance beyond overt responses by placing covert behaviors and/or cognitive processes in a central role, and embed behavior in a specific and elaborate context that provides goals for, and meaning to, the component responses. However, in recognizing the complexity of even the simplest social situation, models such as Trower's and McFall's sacrifice specificity in the identification of component responses and evaluative criteria.[2] Nevertheless, interactive conceptualizations possess significant heuristic and practical value. They enlarge and shift the focus of social skill from narrowly defined, environmentally determined overt responses to a complex of overt and covert skills that functionally provide the person with an internal source of action directed toward a goal that can only be ascertained by analyzing the context in which the act occurs.

The interactive emphasis on behavioral sequences provides a challenge to researchers that is only now being confronted, ie the identification of the 'natural units' or 'chunks' of behavior existing within a particular situational context. Currently, there is no 'task catalog', and hence no real method by which to assess empirically the situational requirements in any particular instance (Schroeder & Rakos, 1983). However, research on situational parameters has been initiated. For example, Rudy, Merluzzi, and Henahan (1982) found that intimacy with and status of the other person, and formality and location of the setting, were salient dimensions affecting an individual's construal of various assertion situations. Furnham, Argyle, and their colleagues determined that social situations have approximately 65–90 main elements (Argyle, Furnham, & Graham, 1981), universal and specific rules (Argyle, Graham, Campbell, & White, 1979), and clearly identifiable goals (Graham, Argyle, & Furnham, 1980). Schlundt and McFall (1987) developed meaningful taxonomies of college-based social situations from cluster analyses of stimulus features, behavioral profiles, and perceptual similarities. Obviously, much more work needs to be done, probably utilizing time-consuming and unfamiliar descriptive methodologies (eg ethology, Boice, 1982) and incorporating knowledge from diverse disciplines such as sociology (Goffman, 1956; Schur, 1971) and anthropology (Maretzki, 1981). The necessity for this kind of comprehensive approach to social skill is exemplified by the cultural determinants of appropriate assertion, a topic with a modest research history, to which we now turn.

Culture and assertion

AT, as noted earlier, is in part a product of America's enduring allegiance to individual freedom. Throughout its history, the US has been a nation concerned with protection of individual rights, often at the expense of communal interests. Thus, even early observers of the AT movement recognized the cultural assumptions inherent in the advocacy and expression of personal desires:

> ... the concept of assertiveness is culture bound, and particularly North American. In many other cultures, asserting oneself in the way that is normative in North America and parts of Europe is neither encouraged nor tolerated. Humility, subservience, and tolerance are valued above assertiveness in many other cultures, especially for women. Furthermore, the lack of assertiveness is not necessarily a sign of inadequacy or anxiety, though in instances it may be.

(Furnham, 1979, p. 522).

However, more specifically, the concept of assertiveness is a manifestation of the *dominant* American value system that guides the behaviors of *whites*. In fact, studies with diverse cultural groups generally find the normative level of self-reported assertive behavior approaches that of white Americans as the group's sociocultural similarity to mainstream American norms and values increases (Furnham, 1979; Hall & Beil-Warner, 1978; Kipper & Jaffe, 1976; Margalit & Mauger, 1984, 1985; McCormick, 1982).[3] In the US, minorities that report being less assertive than whites tend to be those with strong cultural identities, such as Mexican-Americans (Hall & Beil-Warner, 1978), Japanese-Americans and other Asian-Americans (Fukuyama & Greenfield, 1983), and Chinese-Americans (Sue, Ino, & Sue, 1983). And when self-reports achieve white norms, as they appear to for Native American Indians, factor analyses of the responses yield unique factors (LaFramboise, 1983).

Interestingly, these self-reported assertion deficits may not reflect actual skill deficits. Hupkens, Verhoeven, and Boon Van Ostade (1975) failed to obtain differing levels of assertiveness in Indonesian as compared to Dutch psychologists. It is possible that in this case role requirements obscured cultural variance. However, Sue, Ino, and Sue (1983) found that the Chinese-Americans who reported less assertive behavior than Caucasians were able to behave as assertively as the Caucasians in role-play situations. These data strongly suggest that at least some of the differences in assertiveness among cultural groups are fundamentally due to cognitive variables stemming from cultural values and norms and only secondarily from skill deficits. Indeed, for many nonwhite subcultures, assertive behavior has very specific situational guidelines for its emission. Assertion may be discouraged toward members of the dominant (white) culture, elders and family members, and authority figures, or toward males by females (Sue, 1981). It may be constrained by specific conceptualizations of social interaction, as in the Puerto Rican emphasis on *personalismo*, the personal and repeated contact with shopkeepers, service people, and professionals (Comas-Diaz, 1985).

Since cultural groups adhere to varying conceptions of appropriate social behavior, evaluative criteria, definitions of particular skills (Galassi & Galassi, 1978a), and normative levels of skill performance, assertion can only be understood within the context of the relevant cultural variables. Thus, members of minority groups in the US have repeatedly stressed that the assertion construct must be modified to be consistent with cultural values before it can be employed with nonCaucasians (blacks: Caldwell-Colbert & Jenkins, 1982; Cheek, 1976; Minor, 1978; hispanics: Comas-Diaz & Duncan, 1985; Southeast Asians: Fukuyama & Greenfield, 1983; Hwang, 1977; Native American Indians: LaFramboise & Rowe, 1983; Mexican-Americans: Grodner, 1977). These issues will be discussed in greater detail in Chapter 5.

Clarification of the assertion concept

The specification of response classes

Assertive behavior is a situation-specific, learned skill comprised of a number of partially independent response classes. Individuals may emit behaviors of one class but not of another (Galassi et al., 1981), strengthening the behavioral interpretation and further weakening trait conceptualizations. The specific response classes that have been identified depend to some extent on the methodology utilized, but an extensive review of the literature (Schroeder, Rakos, & Moe, 1983) coalesced the findings into seven categories that appear to have suitable comprehensiveness, flexibility, and utility. Four 'positive' response classes consistently emerged: a) admitting personal shortcomings; b) giving and receiving compliments; c) initiating and maintaining interactions; and d) expressing positive feelings. Three 'negative' or conflict response classes were specified: a) expressing unpopular or different opinions; b) requesting behavior changes by other people; and c) refusing unreasonable requests. It is important to recognize that the above is a useful organizational scheme, not a statement of fact.[4] As noted by Galassi et al. (1981), response class delineation is to some extent arbitrary and limited in scope. Nevertheless, such categorization provides a consensually validated means by which to discuss and train different types of assertive behaviors.

The conflict response classes have received the bulk of the research and clinical attention, but that is probably a reflection of social and historical factors (such as the dominance of male values) rather than scientific or clinical ones. Indeed, many individuals are frustrated in their desire to speak in groups, express caring and love, share complimentary perceptions, and comfortably accept praise. Nevertheless, the focus on conflict skills is not entirely misplaced, as numerous individuals are unable to deal with confrontation in a constructive manner, and many clinical syndromes appear to include an inadequate conflict assertion repertoire (Rakos, 1986). Clearly, a recognition that assertiveness comprises interpersonal expressiveness in both positive and negative contexts is necessary.

Distinguishing assertive behavior from aggressive behavior

Assertive behavior is most frequently conceptualized as representing the midpoint on the continuum between nonassertive and aggressive behavior. Research has generally supported this approach, finding little support for independent assertive, aggressive, and nonassertive dimensions (Galassi et al., 1981). The single continuum highlights the appropriateness of AT for both passive and aggressive individuals but, in viewing the differences as essentially quantitative (intensity) rather than qualitative (kind), it also exacerbates defini-tional problems. In particular, a lively debate has ensued concerning the differen-tiation of assertion from aggression. This is a critical distinction since the lay population may fail to distinguish between the two styles of responding (Hess, Bridgewater, Bornstein, & Sweeney, 1980), describe assertion as pushy, rude, and insensitive (Elkins, Osborne, & Saltzberg, 1983), and often label conflict assertion as aggressive behavior (Hull & Schroeder, 1979).

Most attempts to distinguish the two concepts have utilized the notion of 'social acceptability'. Both Alberti and Emmons (1970; 1986b) and Lange and Jakubowski (1976) stress that appropriate conflict assertion, unlike aggression, respects the other person's rights and dignity through the use of nonhostile verbal content and vocal characteristics. Assertion is expected to result in a stronger relationship and a minimalization of negative emotion, whereas aggression is predicted to produce a strained relationship with, and an exacerbation of the hurt, anger, and/or humiliation experienced by, the recipient of the communication. Hollandsworth (1977) criticized these formulations for establishing distinguishing criteria in terms of the consequences of the response instead of objective behaviors. He proposed instead that aggressive responses were defined by their use of coercive content. Coercion includes verbal disparagement and name calling, as well as the use of a verbal threat specifying the future delivery of some physical or social punishment (noxious stimulation). This definition raised other objections. Alberti (1977) asserted that the distinctions cannot be based solely in the content of the response, but must also acknowledge intentions, consequences, and context. Rakos (1979) argued that both the consequences of the response and the specific content (ie threats) suggested by Hollandsworth constituted inadequate criteria. He noted specification of threats may be appropriate after repeated nonthreatening assertions have failed, since the process of 'escalation' (Rimm & Masters, 1979) is an essential component of effective conflict resolution. Thus it would not be unreasonable to threaten to initiate legal action or refuse further cooperation as part of the escalation process.[5]

Functional definitions, such as Rich & Schroeder's (1976), also are unable to distinguish between assertion and aggression because they fail to specify any content (social values, particular goals, appropriate behaviors). However, Rakos (1979) suggested that the functional definition can serve as the basis from which other functionally related behaviors with specified but general content can be identified. Assertion, which is generally viewed as a discrete behavior and a personal right, should instead be considered as a chain of overt and covert responses encompassing rights (actually, rights behaviors) and their functionally related antecedent and subsequent responsibilities (obligation behaviors). Verbalization of only the assertive right or feeling, without the attendant social obligation behaviors, is 'expressive behavior', and, by itself, aggressive. Conflict assertion, as opposed to aggression, requires the emission of the following social responsibilities (Rakos, 1979).

Antecedent (emitted prior to expressive behavior):
1. Engaging in sufficient overt and covert behavior to determine the rights of *all* participants;
2. Developing a verbal and nonverbal response repertoire that is intended to influence the other person's offending behavior but not the evaluation of his or her 'self-worth';
3. Considering the potential negative consequences the other person may experience as a function of expressive behavior.

Subsequent (emitted after expressive behavior):
1. Providing a brief, honest, but nonapologetic explanation for the expressive behavior;

2. Providing clarifying interpretations of the expressive behavior, and empathic communications concerning its implications, in an attempt to minimize any hurt, anger, or unhappiness experienced by the other person as a consequence of the expressive behavior;

3. Protecting the other person's rights if that person is unable to do so;

4. Seeking a mutually acceptable compromise when legitimate rights of both parties exist and are in conflict.

Rakos suggested that the antecedent obligations are necessary prerequisites to expressive behavior in all conflict interactions, while the subsequent ones are critical elements of assertion only when the relationship is an important, continuing one.[6] From this perspective, assertion is characterized by the emission of obligation behaviors as well as expressive ones, whereas aggressive behavior involves only the expression of rights. Thus simply saying to your boss, 'Marilyn, I'm sorry, but I can't work late tonight' – which is an assertive response according to Hollandsworth and, if it "works", Rich and Schroeder – would be classified by the chain definition as an expressive response, and by itself, aggressive. In a continuing relationship with a boss, the antecedent and subsequent responsibilities also define appropriate assertion. The chain of responses might be as follows.

Antecedent obligations:

1a. Asking: 'When did this work come in?' and 'When does the paperwork have to be completed?' (The boss has more legitimacy to her request if the work is of an 'emergency' nature.)

1b. Thinking: 'The boss has the right to ask me to stay, since this is an emergency. Also she is very considerate of my personal needs, lets me work flexible hours, and understands when I have to come in late like I did yesterday. But I still have the right to say no in any particular instance. So conflicting rights are present.'

2. Thinking: 'Let me rehearse exactly what I want to say so I do not sound attacking, demeaning, or inconsiderate.'

3 Thinking: 'I must also decide if my desire to say "no" is important enough to me so that I am willing to allow the boss to have problems. If it is important enough, in relation to the problems it will cause, then I will say no.'

Rights behavior (expressiveness):
Saying: 'Marilyn, I'm sorry, but I can't work late tonight.'

Subsequent obligations:

1. Saying: 'I have dinner reservations and theatre tickets for tonight. These plans were made weeks ago to celebrate my wife's birthday.'

2. Saying: 'I know you need to get these materials in the mail as soon as possible and that I'm the person with the experience to do it correctly, but tonight is just a very inconvenient night for me. I hope you understand my position.'

17

3. Saying (since conflicting rights are present): 'I think I have a possible solution though. If I came in a couple of hours early tomorrow, I'm certain I could have the papers prepared by noon. Then we could have a delivery boy take them over immediately. How does that sound?'

When assertive behavior is conceptualized as a chain of responses rather than as a discrete behavior, attention is necessarily directed to the context in which the conflict occurs. Thus, the chain perspective is contextualistic: it specifies components that contain a general, flexible content that is expected to vary according to situational, social, and cultural norms and values. The components themselves, therefore, have little meaning apart from the chain. Nevertheless, competent emission of the individual components can be reliably trained and then effectively generalized to the natural environment, despite the variability in specific content and the reliance on context (Rakos & Schroeder, 1979).

Assertive responses as communication behaviors

I noted at the beginning of this chapter that the conceptualization of assertion has been largely atheoretical. The literature reviewed up to this point has relied on face, content, and social validity, as well as on statistical procedures such as factor analysis, to clarify the behaviors encompassed by the term 'assertion'. Recently, however, several writers have attempted to place assertion within the theoretical propositions of communication and speech theory. These initial formulations deserve comment because they lead to the generation of empirical as well as clinical hypotheses.

Boisvert, Beaudry, and Bittar (1985) proposed that assertive behavior be conceptualized within the general human communication theory proposed by Dittman (1972). In this model, five key elements emerge: the sender, the channel of transmission, the message itself, the receiver, and feedback to the sender. Each of these components of communication is germane to the assertive expression of needs, desires, and opinions. The sender produces the message by encoding it in an understandable system (eg the dominant language of the cultural milieu). The intention of the message must be clearly communicated, necessitating that the sender have a good understanding of his or her desires and purposes. Boisvert et al. therefore emphasize that AT must teach strategies for identifying intentions. Furthermore, clients as senders of messages must be aware that their communications are modified by their cultural frame of reference and by their anticipation of negative consequences, both of which are incorporated within the AT literature from behavioral perspectives.

The channel of transmission refers to the behavioral repertoire that transmits the message. For assertion, the primary channels are auditory (language) and visual (nonverbal responses). The parameters of these channels are discussed in detail in Chapter 3, but the interesting contribution of communication theory is that each channel has a limited capacity to transmit information (Dittman, 1972).

The speed of delivery and complexity of information determine the capacity of a channel. Thus, the asserter must express his or her ideas and emotions more slowly when the content is complex but, in the interests of efficiency, more rapidly when the message is simple. The AT literature, as we shall see in the next chapter, has not investigated the paralinguistic elements of an assertive response as a function of message complexity. Boisvert et al. also suggest redundancy of the message will facilitate communication when the message is complex, but will be inefficient when the message is simple. However, regardless of message characteristics, AT does not emphasize redundancy prior to the reply by the recipient. The possibility that assertive desires could be communicated more effectively if they were presented in greater detail and with examples has not been empirically assessed. Finally, Boisvert et al. note that some channels (eg body gestures) cannot transmit complex messages as well as other similar channels (eg facial expressions). The communication literature they cite is consistent with the research on the nonverbal aspects of assertion (see Chapter 3).

The message, to communicate information effectively, must be sent in a code that is mutually understood by sender and receiver. Assertive behaviors rely on both verbal and nonverbal codes. In many instances, language and nonverbal behaviors have clear referents and implications, but cultural and situational variables will often obfuscate the clarity of the code. AT has been cognizant of this impact on the assertive message, though not always to the degree necessary or desirable (see Chapter 5). The message also has a form. This includes content, which has been extensively studied (see Chapter 3), as well as grammar and syntax, which have been the subject of only two studies to date. Gervasio (1988; Gervasio, Pepinsky, & Schwebel, 1983) found that assertive messages are stylistically complex and contain fewer 'feeling' verbs than predicted by the literature. Thus, assertive responses utilize 'I feel', 'I want', etc, less than the training manuals advocate and rely on 'cognitive' verbs ('I think', 'I believe') to a greater extent than suggested.

The receiver must perceive the message accurately, ie recognize that a message has been sent, attend to the correct channel, and understand the code in which the message has been sent. In turn, the asserter must be able to assess the extent to which the receiver has indeed understood the message. Social perception skills that involve active and passive listening may need to be taught to asserters deficient in these abilities.

The feedback involves information sent by the receiver to the sender that has the intention of somehow impacting upon, or regulating, the behavior of the sender. Feedback can be systematic or unsystematic, verbal or nonverbal. Boisvert et al. note that without feedback communication does not occur, though information may be transmitted. The sender of an assertive message, however, *always* has feedback from the receiver: even no response is feedback. Thus, an additional social perception skill that is necessary for effective assertion is the ability to discern the reaction of the recipient and to modify subsequent responses accordingly. Clients must be able to ask for additional feedback when the initial reaction is unclear.

The placement of assertive behavior within the more general field of human communication introduces a challenging new perspective. Boisvert et al. (1985) are able to identify several interesting clinical suggestions from their rudimentary analysis, and further work in this area will yield increasingly useful research and treatment insights.

A second recent theoretical proposal is that of Gervasio (1987), who provides a relatively narrow conceptualization of assertive responses as 'performance speech acts' possessing similarities and differences with ordinary language in both structure and rules. She relies on the work of Searle (1969), who proposed that 'speech acts' (ie the varied linguistic forms utilized in conversation) are not simply words, but also are often deeds. 'Performatives' are specific speech acts that exist only because they have been linguistically emitted. 'For example, one can make a crude request by pointing to an item, but one cannot make a promise except by stating, "I promise." Similarly, the acts of christening a ship, marrying, and declaring war involve the performance of specific linguistic utterances' (Gervasio, 1987, p. 108). Performative speech acts follow constitutive rules that create or define behavior: particular combinations of words in specific situations compose different speech acts (questions, statements, greetings, warnings, etc.). Assertive speech, argues Gervasio, 'may be thought of as a series of performance speech acts following constitutive rules of the form "A string of sentences X counts as Assertive Technique Y"'(p. 109). This formulation of assertive behavior is clearly derived from definitions that rely on rights, emotional expressiveness, or virtually any content; it does, however, exclude propositions based on function (eg Rich & Schroeder, 1976). Gervasio then draws on the theoretical work of Labov and Fanshel (1977) to analyze the rules of conversation that govern the emission of requests and refusals, two specific, common assertive speech acts (or response classes in our earlier discussion).

Requests can be either direct or indirect, with the latter the norm of polite everyday conversation. A direct request is in the form of an imperative, such as 'Would you please cook dinner tonight', while an indirect request might take the form 'I wonder if you would mind cooking dinner tonight'. As Gervasio (1987) notes, indirect requests are categorized as nonassertive in the AT literature. Requests can also be 'mitigated' or 'aggravated', that is, made more polite or more threatening. References to needs and abilities are seen to be mitigating while references to rights and obligations are proposed to be aggravating. Finally, Gervasio suggests that any request contains an implicit or explicit challenge to the competence of the person to whom it is directed, but one that can be moderated by greater diversity in the surface structure of the request.

Refusal of a request can occur with or without an accounting (a reason or explanation). Provision of an accounting implies that the request might be accepted if certain conditions are met. Refusals lacking accountings are hypothesized to institute conditions that can lead to a break in social relations.

Furthermore, Gervasio asserts that refusing a request is less socially acceptable than 'putting it off' by requesting more information or investigating the needs or rights that prompted the request.

The rules governing ordinary conversational requests and refusals are frequently at odds with the content and structure of recommended assertive responses. Trainees are taught to be direct, which may be perceived as less polite. They are urged to emit refusals without accounting, which may disrupt social interaction. Invariant repetition of assertive verbalizations may escalate the perceived challenge to the recipient's competence to the point that the assertion is experienced as aggression. Generally, putting off a refusal is strongly discouraged in AT, though it may be the norm in everyday social discourse. Only the training emphasis on reference to needs and desires, rather than to rights and obligations, is consistent with conversational norms. These differences between social conventions and assertive prescriptions may underlie the perception that assertive behavior is aggressive (see Chapters 3 and 5), or at least stilted and unnatural, and lead to the reluctance of some trainees to emit the behavior under natural conditions. However, as Gervasio (1987) notes, the concept of the empathic assertion, to be discussed in detail in the next chapter, addresses these issues quite directly. Empathic assertions include more accountings, content, and variety in surface structure, and are generally less direct (though definitely not indirect) when compared to the standard and popularized conception of assertion.

Gervasio also proposes that effective communication requires that the listener and speaker share common assumptions about the interaction. These 'conversational postulates' (Grice, 1975) include sufficiency of information, evidence to back up the statement, relevancy and nonredundancy, and consistency with the norms of clarity, brevity, and politeness. Standard assertive verbalizations do introduce information in a clear manner, but one that, in some cases, may be *too* brief, and hence socially inappropriate (Gervasio & Crawford, 1989). Furthermore, perhaps due to excessive brevity and content restriction, assertions are often inappropriately redundant (particularly in simple situations; cf Boisvert et al., 1985), impolite, or lacking in adequate information and evidence, characteristics that may have repercussions on the long-term relationship even though short-term desires may be achieved. For example, assertive responses often rely on opinions and feelings, rather than facts, as evidence to support statements (Gervasio, 1987). Such 'arbitrary justifications' (Hassan, 1973) for action are generally insufficient to validate the statement in ordinary discourse.

Opinions, as well as the absence of accountings, also imply an individualistic approach to social relations that dismisses communal obligations such as negotiation and sharing (Schur, 1976). This individualism is reinforced at the syntactic level by the common strategy of teaching trainees to use 'I statements' rather than 'we statements' or 'I and you statements' (see Chapter 3). As Gervasio notes, 'If "we-ness" occurs more in ordinary conversation than I-me language, then it may be difficult for speakers to adopt this new language at the behavioral level and to justify it cognitively, even when I-me language may be the only effective one' (p. 116–117). The individualism inherent in assertive behavior has already been discussed from a social and political perspective, and here finds corroboration at the psycholinguistic level. Gervasio suggests, therefore, that standard assertive behaviors will have little utility in intimate relationships or in situations that present ongoing and complex issues. On the other hand, they will be useful in simple, noncontinuing situations, in instances of isolated contact, and in relationships that involve strangers or formal roles (eg customer–salesperson). Her linguistic analysis provides important theoretical support for the development of the concept of the empathic assertion and for the content distinctions between aggressive and assertive replies (ie the obligation verbalizations) proposed by Rakos (1979).

Clinical implications and recommendations

1. The absence of a clear definition of assertive behavior necessitates that clinicians utilize AT procedures in a restrained fashion. Many clients will manifest apparent deficits in the skill, but before AT is selected as the appropriate intervention, a careful assessment must be conducted (see Chapter 6). The assertive deficits may not be the central problem, though they may be functionally related to it. This caveat increases in importance since the popularity of AT leads many clients to describe a lack of assertiveness as the presenting complaint and to request AT. Many clinicians also suggest AT as an adjunct to the treatment they are providing, but these referrals are frequently based on popular misconceptions of the procedure as a simple, universally appropriate treatment (Emmons & Alberti, 1983). The success of AT relies on the same careful comprehensive, functional analysis (Kanfer & Saslow, 1969) of behavioral excesses, deficits, and assets and their relationship to environmental variables that all behavioral interventions require.

2. Should AT be determined to be an appropriate intervention for a client, the clinician must begin treatment with a discussion of the current understanding of the concept of assertive behavior as well as a brief overview of the process of the training regimen, including its benefits, limitations, and likely effect – both positive and negative – in the client's life. This information is necessary for the client to adopt appropriate treatment expectations and provide informed consent, issues that will be discussed extensivelyin Chapter 9.

The presentation of the concept of assertive behavior should ensure that the following specific points are clearly conveyed to, and understood by, the client:

a) Assertive behavior is a *situation-specific, learned skill* comprised of several response classes. As with any skill, achievement of behavioral competency requires gradual acquisition (shaping), repeated practice, feedback, and accurate evaluation of the response.

b) Assertive behavior is an *interpersonal skill that is emitted in a situation involving some risk*. Clients must understand, however, that part of the goal of

AT is to teach them to accurately assess the risks, discriminate when the risks are worth taking, and determine whether to enact or withhold the response (Rakos & Schroeder, 1980). They must recognize that the existence of the *right* to be assertive does not constitute a *mandate* to always behave in such a manner (Alberti & Emmons, 1970; Lange & Jakubowski, 1976; Rimm & Masters, 1979).

c) The objective impact of the assertive response is not the central concern of the training regimen. Technical proficiency, net cost–benefit assessment, and cultural appropriateness should be emphasized as the primary means by which the assertive response is measured. In general, if response quality and social validity are high, the objective impact of assertion can be expected to be positive in a large proportion of situations.

d) The concept of the right to be assertive must be introduced in a balanced manner. Most AT programs validate assertion as an appropriate behavior by appealing to rights. As noted earlier, the concept of rights strikes a resonant chord in the Western democracies, especially in the US. However, Rimm and Masters (1979) suggest that the use of rights to legitimize assertion has significant disadvantages. First, they observe that in the inevitable instances when assertive behavior fails to achieve its desired impact, the client will experience increased frustration since the behavior was motivated, at least in part, by a sense of righteousness. Second, the relativistic nature of assertion is logically inconsistent with any suggestion of assertion as an absolute right. And third, an emphasis on assertion as a right may lead many clients to assume they should always behave in an assertive fashion, which, as noted above, is definitely not the philosophy or intent of AT. Clients who rigidly adhere to a rights conception are likely to react negatively when, at some point, they inevitably fail to emit the assertive response in a situation that seemingly is appropriate for it. For these reasons, Rimm and Masters conclude that 'the risks associated with presenting assertiveness as a *right* far outweigh the therapeutic or motivational value' (p. 71) of the concept. They suggest an alternative introductory approach emphasizing assertion as self-enhancing and its lack as self-defeating.

However, in my experience (in the US), the acceptance of a 'right' to behave assertively is a fundamental and essential initial step in the behavior change process, since most clients either do not believe they have the right to express themselves, or believe in the right in only the most abstract, intellectual sense. Without some real understanding that they do indeed have this right, presentation of assertion as self-enhancing is often clinically meaningless, since many non-sanctioned responses may also be self-enhancing (eg aggressive, illegal, selfish, and cheating behaviors). Assertion must be clearly and concretely distinguished from these other behaviors; without some way to discriminate assertion as fundamentally different, the powerful conditioned beliefs and attitudes that support a widely generalized compliant and passive behavioral pattern cannot be effectively challenged, and assertive behavior will not be accepted as a legitimate option. The presentation of rights, of course, can be sensitive to the concerns raised by Rimm and Masters.

e) The introduction of AT must also stress that assertion is *not* aggression; as alluded to above, the effective communication of this distinction is a prerequisite for the client's acceptance of assertive behavior as a socially valid response alternative (Rimm & Masters, 1979). I teach clients this discrimination by first presenting various nonspecific distinctions that have been offered in the literature (eg Lange & Jakubowski, 1976). I then present my more operationalized chain conceptualization of assertion (Rakos, 1979) and discuss its implications in detail and with numerous examples. The advantages of the chain definition – specificity with flexibility, common sense yet analytical – are reflected in trainees' rapid intellectual acceptance and understanding of the distinction between assertion and aggression. Finally, I will often ask clients to complete a written exercise on the discrimination of assertive, aggressive, and passive behaviors (Lange & Jakubowski, 1976). The goal at this early point in intervention is to help the client acknowledge that assertion and aggression are distinguishable; I do not expect clients to have mastered the distinction until much later in treatment when role plays and real life experiences are discussed and analyzed.

f) Teaching clients to assess the risks attendant on assertion accurately is an important part of AT. The process is facilitated by reviewing the substantial amount of data suggesting that the potential adverse consequences are usually overestimated by nonassertive clients. Thus, the conclusions of this significant body of literature (see Chapters 3 and 5) should be shared with the client in some detail.

3. The concept of assertiveness should be presented in the interactive or contextualistic framework. Clients must understand that while basic, concrete, and discrete skills will be taught, the effective performance of assertive behavior requires both the integration of individual responses and an appreciation of the particular context in which it is to occur. AT, therefore, emphasizes generative abilities (Trower, 1982) that require the acquisition of numerous cognitive skills (Chapter 4) as well as overt ones (Chapter 3). There is no *a priori* correct assertive response, though there are general behavioral guidelines for effective expression of feelings and desires. The overt behaviors are the means by which assertion is appropriately demonstrated, but the more important part of training involves the acquisition of the covert skills necessary to produce the overt components in an adaptive, flexible manner.

Finally, clients must also appreciate the role played by conventions governing human communication. Assertive behavior will be most effective when norms are not violated and the parameters of the process are well understood. Similarly, cultural norms and values must be considered when developing a conflict resolution strategy. Responses that simply don't 'feel' right to a client after extensive cognitive and performance skill training are probably inconsistent with contextual expectations. In such cases, a re-examination of the situation, response, and alternative options is obviously indicated.

Chapter three

Conflict assertion: overt behavioral components

Assertiveness training, like its parent discipline of behavior modification, developed with a primary concern for publicly observable responses. Researchers, clinicians, and popular self-help books emphasized discrete molecular behaviors and conveyed the impression that assertion was principally a simple response such as saying 'no'. This early understanding has evolved into an appreciation of overt components as important but limited parts of effective assertion; covert components, to be discussed in detail in Chapter 4, are additional essential ingredients. Furthermore, the overt behaviors identified as components of assertion are not absolutes. There is rarely, if ever, one right way to assert in any particular situation; just as there are numerous counterproductive ways to cope with a conflict situation, there are also various adaptive ways to resolve the problem or come to terms with unfavorable circumstances. Effective assertion requires the ability to emit flexible responses that are sensitive to the unique circumstances manifested in each particular conflict situation.

Words such as 'flexible' and 'sensitive' suggest that covert behaviors are integrally involved in the selection of the overt responses, and the idea of selection implies that overt responses will vary across situations. Therefore, the research, rather than articulating prescriptions or directives, only provides guidelines for the development of a diverse repertoire. It really cannot be any other way: the conceptualization of assertion as a situation-specific learned skill places the interpersonal context in the position of the central determinant of the behavior. When the components are discussed without the specific context, only very general, though useful, guidelines can be delineated.

With this caveat in mind, the overt response components can be categorized in the following manner:

1. *Content*: the verbal behavior of the asserter, or what the individual *says* to the other person(s).

2. *Paralinguistic elements*: the vocal characteristics of the verbal behavior, or how the asserter *sounds*.

3. *Nonverbal behaviors*: the body movements and facial expressions that accompany the verbal behavior, or how the asserter *appears*.

4. *Social interaction skills*: the timing, initiation, persistence, and stimulus control skills that enhance the impact of the verbal behavior, or how the asserter behaves in the *process* of the interaction.

As each of these skill components is discussed in detail below, the reader will notice that the majority of the references are at least several years old. An exhaustive literature search of approximately 1800 journal articles and dissertations confirmed that assertiveness investigators have turned their attention from overt behaviors to either covert responses or contextual issues. However, the validity of these relatively early studies has remained robust, for it is rare for social, cultural, and psychological variables to change within a matter of a few short years!

Overt components

Content

The verbal content of conflict assertion can be divided into two major response categories: the expression of the assertive right and the emission of 'elaborations', the functionally related obligations that address the context in which the expression of the right is emitted (Rakos, 1979; 1986).

Expression of rights

The expression of rights is the core of any assertion, its *raison d'être*; it is necessary but insufficient to maximize long-term as well as short-term positive consequences. The specific content of the rights statement, while varying as a function of the response class and the particular circumstances of the situation, will always contain a verbalization of desire, affect, or opinion (Kolotkin, Wielkiewicz, Judd, & Weiser, 1984; Romano & Bellack, 1980). For example:

Refusal: 'No, thank you, I am not interested in contributing at this time.'

Behavior change request: 'I feel that I am doing more than my share of the housework' (statement of affect). 'I would like you to do more of it' (request for new behavior).

Expression of unpopular or different opinion: 'I don't agree with you. I think I am doing my share of the housework.'

These statements exemplify important topographical features of the expression of rights. They employ 'I statements' that localize responsibility for the affect, desire, or opinion with the asserter. Such statements are contrasted to 'you statements' that attempt to place responsibility for personal feelings on the other person (Lange & Jakubowski, 1976; Hewes, 1975). For instance, 'You make me angry when you don't do your share of the housework' constitutes a very different communication to the recipient than 'I am angry because I feel you don't do your share of the housework'.

'I' and 'you' statements present the problem in differing terms: the former offers a *perception* and the latter articulates a *statement of fact*. While every perception is legitimate, in the sense that a person is entitled to his or her interpretation of events, any particular one may nevertheless fail to be confirmed by the social environment. When perspectives are not consonant, an 'I statement' permits the recipient to offer an alternative interpretation without denying the validity of the other's perception, but a 'you statement' requires the acceptance of that which appears to be an incorrect fact.

Furthermore, 'you statements' shift the responsibility for a 'factual' event onto the recipient, inadvertently (or deliberately) *blame* him or her for producing the negative feelings, and fail to recognize that the experience of anger in a social situation requires a contribution from the dissatisfied person. The perception and interpretation of a situation contribute greatly to its phenomenological impact (Ellis, 1962); after all, many individuals would not get angry if they felt they were doing more than their share of the housework, and anger is therefore not an inevitable consequence of the situation. The blaming character of 'you statements' increases the probability that the recipient will react defensively and nonconstructively in terms of the real issue; for example, it would not be surprising if the recipient retorted, 'Well, you make me angry when you work late and don't telephone to let me know.' The original expression of concern over household chores has nothing to do with failing to phone when late, yet the two issues are suddenly intertwined. Alternatively, 'you statements' may also lead to an aggressive reply, such as 'You have your nerve. The work you do is sloppy and I have to fix it up!' Clearly, this is not the intent of an assertion!

It is, therefore, not surprising that the 'I statement' is strongly related to judgements of overall assertion while 'you statements' are associated with aggressiveness (Kolotkin et al., 1984). Furthermore, 'I statements' can minimize the possibility of negative reactions such as anger (Hollandsworth & Cooley, 1978). Gervasio (1987) suggests, however, that 'I statements' are not characteristic of ordinary conversation and may be difficult for trainees to adopt. Their explicit individualistic nature contrasts sharply with the social norm of collaborative 'we statements'. Unfortunately, no research has compared these two styles of speech in terms of their ease of emission or social impact. 'I statements' may indeed be perceived as selfish as well as assertive, but 'we statements' may be perceived as demanding, coercive, or manipulative under certain circumstances. For example, 'we need to come up with a better way to divide household chores' may or may not be seen as a cooperative overture. The social impact of 'I' and 'we' statements may be largely dependent upon the paralinguistic and verbal features and empathic elaborations of the assertion. Since there are no empirical guidelines as yet, the clinician must rely heavily on clinical experience and client preferences. In most cases, an increase in the frequency of 'I statements' is usually warranted, though an exclusive reliance on them is probably unnecessary and undesirable.

Expressions of rights are also direct, specific, and respectful. A *direct* expression avoids the use of blatant lies, subtle dishonesty, or exaggerated excuses. Instead, it contains a clear, succinct statement describing one's perceptions, feelings, desires, or opinions. However, brevity should not violate conversational rules; thus, compound sentences joined by 'and' or 'but' should be used (cf Gervasio & Crawford, 1989). Furthermore, an introductory 'orienting statement' that signals the topic to be discussed is usually indicated (Kolotkin et al., 1984), as in the following behavior change request: 'I would like to discuss some concerns I have about our agreement for dividing up the housework. I feel that I am doing more than my share of it, and this was not the intent of the agreement. I would like us to redivide the chores to equalize our responsibilities.'

A direct statement avoids the use of explanations or apologies; though these may be appropriate elaborations (see p. 31), when intertwined with the rights statement they tend to obscure the focus, convey insecurity, and reduce the impact of the message. Compare the following with the previous example:

'I hate to bother you, but I have some concerns about our agreement for dividing up the housework. I know you are very busy, but so am I, and I feel that I am doing more than my share of the work. I'm sorry to add to your pressures, but I really would like you to do more of it.'

There is nothing inappropriate about this assertion (cf Gervasio, 1987), and in some contexts it may be the best choice. Nevertheless, its message tends to get diluted in apologies and explanations. Those may be necessary, but they can – and should – be stated after the expression of rights.

An assertion is *specific* when the statement clearly delineates the central issue and avoids generalizations. 'I have concerns about the way we divide the housework' is much more specific than 'I have concerns about the way we divide our responsibilities'. *If* housework is the *only* contention, then there is no reason to introduce other issues (child care, financial duties, yard work, etc.) that can only confuse the discussion, dilute the focus, increase the perceived demands, and hinder problem solving.

A *respectful* expression adheres to norms of politeness (eg appropriate use of 'please', cf Gervasio & Crawford, 1989) and shares concerns without labeling, blaming, attacking, or demeaning, or making motivational assumptions about, the other person. A subtle part of conveying respect, and thereby reducing the likelihood of a negative reaction, resides in the choice of language. For example, 'I feel I am doing an unfair amount of the housework' conveys something very different than 'I feel I am doing more than my share of the housework'. The word 'unfair', while not used as a direct label (as in 'I feel you are unfair'), still implies the other person is behaving in a way that maintains or promotes inequity, and therefore increases the likelihood that the recipient will assume a defensive posture. The fundamental issue, after all, really has nothing to do with fairness, however that may be construed by the participants; it is only concerned with the division of household responsibilities. In most instances, such issues have little to do with the moral implications of fairness: agreements made in good faith may now be inadequate for changed (or even original) circumstances. Even in those cases where the other person is deliberately avoiding the work, and hence acting

'unfairly', the label will still introduce impediments that will hinder the resolution of the conflict.

Thus, a direct, specific, and respectful behavior change request simply
describes the offending behavior and then politely asks for a behavior change.
The expression of an unpopular opinion is similarly constructed. It is one thing to
assert that 'I believe that the Prime Minister is completely unconcerned about the
plight of the poor and the working class', but quite another to say 'Anyone who
supports the Prime Minister is selfish and protecting his cheque book'. The first
statement is an honest and succinct opinion that may elicit disagreement but is
unlikely to arouse defensiveness. The second one, however, generalizes
('anyone'), labels ('selfish'), and makes motivational assumptions ('protecting
his cheque book'). The refusal of unreasonable requests also incorporates these
three characteristics. 'No thank you, I'm not interested' is much superior to an
indirect refusal replete with apologies, excuses, lies, and explanations, or a direct
one that is offensive, such as 'No way. That brand is terrible and not worth half
of what it costs.' This reply, even if 'true' in some sense, generalizes (the whole
brand), labels (it's terrible), and implies that the salesperson is at some level less
than honest (the product is not worth the cost).

The importance of employing a direct, specific and respectful statement that
simply describes the problem behavior or issue and avoids generalizations,
labels, and motivational assumptions about the other person should not be
underestimated. Statements that lack directness are likely to be viewed as
nonassertive, those lacking respect as aggressive, and those lacking both as
passive-aggressive. Lack of specificity characterizes all three alternatives to
assertion, though some instances of aggression will be highly specific.

Several comments concerning the particular content of behavior change
requests and refusals are necessary. Behavior change requests are conceptualized
as comprised of two components: a statement of feeling *and* a specific request to
modify the offending behavior. Indeed, the specific request for altered behavior
is judged to be characteristic of assertive individuals (Eisler, Miller, & Hersen,
1973; Pitcher & Meikle, 1980) and contributes to assessments of assertion by
trained observers (Bordewick & Bornstein, 1980; Kolotkin et al., 1984).
However, untrained judges evaluate it as bordering on aggressiveness (Rose &
Tryon, 1979) while adding little impact to the conflict or feeling statement
(Mullinix & Galassi, 1981). These conflicting data suggest that the specific
request statement may be most appropriate and useful when a desired response to
the conflict statement alone is not forthcoming. This will be discussed further
when persistence and escalation are addressed. For the initial assertion,
particularly in a continuing relationship, a better alternative may be to state the
perceived problem and solicit the other person's reaction via an open-ended
question. In this way, a constructive problem-solving dialogue is initiated: 'I
would like to discuss some concerns I have about our agreement for dividing up
the housework (orienting statement). I feel that the way things have worked out,

I am doing more than my share (statement of concern). What is your feeling about this?'

Finally, the stereotypical 'no' is indeed an important response component in refusing unreasonable requests. Noncompliance is characteristic of assertive individuals (Eisler, Miller, & Hersen, 1973; Pitcher & Meikle, 1980) and is highly correlated with judgements of overall assertion (Bordewick & Bornstein, 1980). Nevertheless, its verbalization is often difficult, particularly in continuing relationships, for at least two reasons. First, it may be socially awkward, especially when the issue is an important one for the requester. For example, a wife asks her husband, 'Could we go to this play I've been dying to see?' A reply of 'No, it's just not the type I appreciate. I know you want to see it badly but let's pick one we'll both enjoy', while superficially appropriate since the obligation components are included, will probably seem unnecessarily forthright. Rules of conversational and social convention have been breached (cf Gervasio, 1987). An assertion of 'Honey, I know how much you want to see that play, but I know I will really dislike it. I'd rather find one that we will both enjoy', in which noncompliance is embedded within the elaboration components, is likely to be more comfortable for both parties. Second, some requests will be structured in a way that precludes the use of 'no'. These situations implicitly present an unreasonable request through the verbalization of expectations derived from previous interactions. Thus, a friend who contributed minimally to earlier study groups may say, 'I hope you're ready for our all-night sessions this term' (rather than 'Will you study with me this term?'). Obviously, noncompliance to the first statement will be best communicated without the use of 'no'.

The expression of rights alone, without the elaboration components to be discussed below, has been termed *standard assertion* (Rakos, 1986). Numerous studies have investigated the social reaction to such expressiveness, and a consistent pattern has emerged: standard assertion is judged to be equally potent to, and more desirable than, aggressive behavior (Epstein, 1980; Frisch & Froberg, 1987; Hull & Schroeder, 1979; McCampbell & Ruback, 1985; Mullinix & Galassi, 1979; Woolfolk & Dever, 1979). However, it is also perceived to be *distinctly less likeable*, though more socially competent, than nonassertive behavior (eg Hull & Schroeder, 1979; Kern, Cavell, & Beck, 1985).[1] Furthermore, standard assertion is judged to be less likeable and more unpleasant than ordinary nonconflict conversation (Wildman & Clementz, 1986) and expression of positive feelings (commendatory assertion) (Cook & St. Lawrence, 1990).

The reaction to standard assertion is consistent with common negative connotations of the term (Elkins et al., 1983; Hull & Schroeder, 1979) and appears to introduce clearly identifiable risks. However, it is apparent that situational variables may moderate the perception. Some of these involve the characteristics of the recipient. For example, highly competitive (Levin & Gross, 1987) and socially skilled (Frisch & Froberg, 1987) undergraduates preferred standard assertion to nonassertion as a means to deal with conflict. Additionally, occupational settings, such as the corporation (Solomon, Brehony, Rothblum, & Kelly, 1982) and the psychiatric hospital (Dura & Beck, 1986), may produce judgements of standard assertion that are superior to those of nonassertion. Other, currently unspecified factors probably account for Heisler and McCormack's (1982) finding that standard assertion was viewed as a more positive way than passivity to improve a relationship.

Expression of elaborations

It has always been clear to clinicians implementing AT that the expression of rights, in and of themselves, constitutes an inadequate assertive response: the social context, cultural norms, and the long-term growth of the relationship are not addressed by such expressiveness. Several writers presented early models of assertion that included verbalizations directed toward maintenance of the relationship (Heisler & Shipley, 1977; Winship & Kelly, 1976), but researchers did not address themselves to the elaboration components until the late 1970s. Woolfolk and Dever (1979) produced the first data comparing the social perception of standard assertion with what they called 'assertion plus extra consideration'. The 'extras', which included a short explanation and an acknowledgement of the other person's experience, were found to enhance the evaluation of assertion without reducing its effectiveness. These data were supported by other studies published shortly thereafter. Romano and Bellack (1980) found that offering compromises and alternatives, acknowledging the feelings of the other person, and providing reasons for the assertion were judged to be important aspects of socially skilled refusal behavior. Pitcher and Meikle (1980) observed that assertive individuals used more praise and apologies in conflict situations than did nonassertive persons. Twentyman, Zimering, and Kovaleski (1981) determined that refusals containing an explanation and apology were judged to be effective and socially acceptable. These elaborations are strikingly similar to the 'obligations' that Rakos (1979) proposed must accompany the expression of rights if assertion is to be distinguished from aggression.

Subsequent research confirmed that the elaboration verbalizations are key elements for minimizing a negative social reaction to conflict assertion. Assertions that contain explanations, acknowledgements of feelings, compromises, and praise have been termed *empathic assertions* (Rakos, 1986), and are judged to be as potent as *standard assertions*, yet more likeable, desirable, and appropriate (eg Hrop & Rakos, 1985; Levin & Gross, 1987; Rakos & Hrop, 1983).[2]

Empathic assertions are judged favorably in comparisons with other styles of behavior as well. They provoke less anger than, yet are as effective as, aggressive responses (Hollandsworth & Cooley, 1978), and are comparable or superior to nonassertion in terms of likeability and desirability, but, of course, more efficacious (Heisler & McCormack, 1982; Kern, 1982a; Kern et al., 1985; Levin & Gross, 1987; Solomon et al., 1982; Woolfolk & Dever, 1979; Zollo, Heimberg, & Becker, 1985). In addition, empathic assertions are equivalent to neutral, nonconflict conversations in terms of likeability and unpleasantness (Wildman & Clementz, 1986), and much more characteristic of popular than unpopular boys (Weist & Ollendick, 1989). The empathic assertion combines power with social and linguistic appropriateness, and utilizes components that can be easily operationalized and reliably assessed (Bruch, Heisler, & Conroy, 1981; Rakos & Schroeder, 1979) as well as successfully trained (Rakos & Schroeder, 1979). Thus, the empathic assertion has emerged as the preferred verbal response goal of AT, particularly when maintenance or enhancement of a continuing relationship is important. The specific elaboration components can be categorized as follows (Rakos, 1986):

1. A short, truthful, nondefensive explanation for the expression of rights.

2. A statement conveying understanding of the effects of the expression of rights on the other person.

3. Praise or another positive comment directed toward the other person.

4. A short apology that is clearly directed toward the inconvenience or disappointment that will result from the expression of rights ('I am sorry that the work will pile up'). The apology should not address itself to the necessity for, or the fact of, the expression of rights ('I am sorry I have to say no').

5. An attempt to achieve a mutually acceptable compromise when legitimate rights conflict, recognizing that such a compromise may not always be identifiable or achievable. The determination of legitimate rights involves covert response components to be discussed in Chapter 4.

The evolution of the AT research from a focus on standard assertion to an emphasis on empathic assertion has enabled empiricism to catch up with clinical application. The training implications of the empathic assertion will be discussed in detail at the end of this chapter.

Paralinguistic components

The verbal characteristics of an assertive communication have been the focus of a great deal of research. Although paralinguistic variables are usually considered to be a subset of nonverbal behaviors (eg Knapp, 1972), AT research and intervention has generally investigated vocal dimensions of the response separately from the other nonverbal aspects such as gestures, facial expressions, etc. Attention has centered primarily on voice volume, firmness and intonation, and response latency, duration, and fluency.

Response latency

Observation of the hesitancy and passivity of nonassertive individuals probably accounts for the early presumption that a short response latency is an important characteristic of assertion. However, the research has failed to consistently confirm this hypothesis. Some studies found short response latency was an important criterion variable (Eisler, Miller, & Hersen, 1973; Kolotkin et al., 1984; Pitcher & Meikle, 1980; Rose & Tryon, 1979), but others did not (Bourque

& Ladouceur, 1979; Romano & Bellack, 1980). Furthermore, latency is greater in conflict situations than in positive ones (Eisler, Hersen, Miller, & Blanchard, 1975; Hersen, Bellack, & Turner, 1978; Pitcher & Meikle, 1980) and is influenced by sex of the participants (Pitcher & Meikle, 1980; Rose & Tryon, 1979; Skillings, Hersen, Bellack, & Becker, 1978). Pitcher & Meikle, for example, found that conflict assertions to males produced the greatest latencies.

The contradictory data may be due to methodologies that failed to isolate situational variables (Galassi et al., 1981). The speed with which a person responds will very appropriately be moderated by the particular circumstances of the conflict. The decision to emit an assertive response and the determination of the desired content require the utilization of covert skills to process the relevant contextual information. In some instances, this processing may be very rapid, but other circumstances may require a greater amount of integration and reflection. Thus, it is likely that response latency will vary from virtually nonexistent to moderately short (a few seconds). Clinically, it appears that a short latency is less important for effective conflict assertion than is the avoidance of a very long latency; if the desired response is difficult to determine or absent from the current behavior repertoire, then the appropriate assertive reply – with modest latency – would be one that firmly requests more time for an answer or sets up a specific time for further discussion. These 'assertions for time' are discussed later in this chapter and again in Chapter 5.

Response duration

The empirical status of response duration is similar to that of response latency. Originally, researchers assumed that a short duration is characteristic of assertion, since nonassertive individuals tend to include long explanations, excuses, lies, and apologies in their responses. However, since the most socially acceptable style of conflict assertion is the empathic variant, which by definition includes elaborative verbalizations, it is predictable that short response duration has emerged as a criterion feature of assertive behavior in only one study (Kirschner & Galassi, 1983) but failed to in two others (Bourque & Ladouceur, 1979; Pitcher & Meikle, 1980). In fact, response duration of assertive replies may be greater than nonassertive ones (Gervasio, 1987). Nevertheless, short response duration is utilized by lay people to evaluate conflict assertion (Romano & Bellack, 1980) and is consistently correlated with ratings of overall assertiveness (Bordewick & Bornstein, 1980; Kolotkin et al., 1984). Duration is longer in conflict situations than in positive ones (Eisler et al., 1975; Hersen et al., 1978; Pitcher & Meikle, 1980; Skillings et al., 1978) and when the recipient of the assertion is a male (Pitcher & Meikle, 1980). This pattern is identical to the one found for latency, and here too highlights the importance of the situational context. There is no mandate for an assertive response to be short: it must be sufficiently long to deal with the situation in an appropriate manner (cf Boisvert et al., 1985). As a matter of fact, Heimberg, Harrison, Goldberg, DesMarais, and Blue (1979) obtained a curvilinear relationship between assertiveness and duration: moderately assertive individuals emitted responses of significantly shorter duration than either highly assertive or nonassertive persons. On the other hand, excess duration will not be likely to help the response achieve greater impact, but will increase the chances for confusion, diversion, and irrelevancy. Therefore, the guideline here is similar to that for latency: response duration should be flexible so as to meet the demands of unique situations. Baseline behavior and situational requirements will determine whether duration should be increased, decreased or accepted as is.

Response fluency

Fluency is frequently considered to be an important feature of conflict assertion (eg Eisler & Frederiksen, 1980; Lange & Jakubowski, 1976; Rakos & Schroeder, 1980), yet it has been poorly investigated. Skillings et al. (1978) found fluency did not vary with assertive skill level, and Kolotkin et al. (1984) found it only weakly related to evaluations of overall assertiveness. Pitcher and Meikle (1980) found both assertive and nonassertive persons achieved a better 'paralinguistic' rating (volume, intonation, fluency) in positive situations than in conflict ones and when responding to females than to males. These data are not very illuminating, yet common sense argues that fluency is important: hesitant, choppy speech is associated with anxiety (Linehan & Walker, 1983), which is presumed to be detrimental to effective assertion, and perhaps even incompatible with it (Wolpe, 1982).

Interestingly, despite the microanalyses of verbal response patterns, speech *rate* (Knapp, 1972) has not attracted the attention of researchers or clinicians. It, too, makes intuitive sense: nonanxious, assertive individuals would be expected to speak at an appropriately moderate rate, with reasonable fluency. Thus, the clinical guideline for speech fluency and rate is based only on unsystematic naturalistic observation, but, until data are collected, it will have to suffice.

Voice volume

The research on volume, unlike the previous paralinguistic elements, is fairly consistent and straightforward. Rose and Tryon (1979) found that the decibel level of the conflict assertion directly influenced judgements of the behavior. Verbalizations delivered at 76dB were consistently perceived as appropriately assertive, those at 68dB as marginally assertive, and those at 84dB as aggressive.[3] Appropriate volume is an important criterion of assertion (Romano & Bellack, 1980) and correlates strongly with evaluations of assertion by both trained (Bordewick & Bornstein, 1980; Kolotkin et al., 1984) and untrained (Romano & Bellack, 1980) observers. Assertive individuals speak louder than nonassertive ones (Eisler et al., 1973), particularly in conflict situations (Eisler et al., 1975). Only the Pitcher and Meikle (1980) study found the 'paralinguistic rating' (volume, fluency, intonation) to be unrelated to evaluations of assertive behavior, but that measure is difficult to interpret due to its combination nature. Therefore, we can confidently assert that a moderately loud volume is important for effective conflict assertion. Although the research has not clearly identified situational factors that influence the appropriateness of volume, it is obvious that loudness will vary somewhat depending on the particular context. However, very soft, low volume, even in private interactions, does not seem to be indicated by any of the data.

Voice intonation (inflection)

Intonation is considered by lay people to be one of the most important characteristics of effective assertion (Romano & Bellack, 1980), but, as with response duration, greater inflection is characteristic of both highly assertive and nonassertive individuals as compared to moderately assertive people (Heimberg et al., 1979). Inflection is therefore an important but not distinguishing feature of assertion. Intermediate levels of intonation are judged to be most appropriate (Rose & Tryon, 1979), a finding that is similar to the data for most of the previous paralinguistic components. Consequently, trainers emphasize the importance of an appropriate, moderate level of inflection.

Voice firmness (affect)

Judgements of assertion are strongly correlated with high levels of firmness (Bordewick & Bornstein, 1980; Kirschner & Galassi, 1983; Kolotkin et al., 1984), but firmness may not be a distinguishing feature of the response. Bourque and Ladouceur (1979) found assertive and nonassertive college students did not differ on this variable, while Kirschner and Galassi (1983) determined it was a more important criterion than content. Eisler, Miller, and Hersen (1973) found assertive psychiatric patients manifested greater affect than nonassertive ones. Firmness may also be affected by situational factors, at least in a patient population: conflict situations prompted greater affect than positive ones (Eisler et al., 1973). This is clearly an area needing additional research, but at present the meagre data indicate that the absence of firmness is likely to detract from the impact of the conflict assertion, and the development of an overall 'tone' should be a high training priority (Kirschner & Galassi, 1983).

Summary of paralinguistic qualities

The research is at best suggestive, and always tempered by the caution that situational variables must be considered when developing an appropriate response. Nevertheless, firmness, intermediate levels of volume and intonation, and moderate response latency and duration appear to characterize effective conflict assertion. Intuitively, a fluent response and a moderate speech rate make sense, but, as yet, neither has empirical support. Firmness, latency, and duration have demonstrated a particular sensitivity to situational factors: they are likely to increase in conflict situations as compared to positive ones, and when the assertion is directed toward a male as opposed to a female. The paralinguistic components, with the exception of fluency, have demonstrated a strong

35

relationship to judgements of effective assertive behavior; moderate levels, with the flexibility to adapt to varying environmental conditions, therefore appear to be the general goal.

Nonverbal behavioral components

Motoric behaviors convey a significant amount of information in an assertive interaction (McFall, Winnett, Bordewick, & Bornstein, 1982), as they do in interpersonal communication in general (Rozelle, Druckman, & Baxter, 1986). Assertion research has focused on eye contact, facial expression, gestures, and global 'body language', and, in general, there are sufficient data to permit a fairly thorough assessment of the contribution each makes toward effective conflict assertion.

Eye contact

Eye contact is an important feature of interpersonal communication in Western cultures (Kleinke, 1986). Not surprisingly, it contributes significantly to judgements of overall assertiveness (Kolotkin et al., 1984; St. Lawrence, 1982) and is identified by lay people as an important characteristic of conflict assertion (McFall et al., 1982; Romano & Bellack, 1980). The duration of eye contact is greater in conflict situations than in positive ones (Eisler et al., 1973). However, eye contact is not a clear distinguishing feature of assertion: skilled and unskilled individuals do not consistently differ in its duration (Bourque & Ladouceur, 1979; Heimberg et al., 1979). It is likely that the topography of eye contact, rather than simply the duration of it, will turn out to be a valid predictor of level of assertiveness. Eye contact must be emitted flexibly and perhaps somewhat intermittently, rather than in a fixed stare, especially since it is engaged in by the listener and *not* by the speaker in general social conversation between Caucasians (LaFrance & Mayo, 1976).

Facial expression

The general facial expression of the speaker contributes strongly to judgements of assertion (Romano & Bellack, 1980), as do specific mouth, eyebrow, and forehead cues (McFall et al., 1982). Uncontrolled fidgety mouth movements, wrinkled forehead, and animated, constantly moving eyebrows communicate unassertiveness. These cues convey more information when the speaker is male but are more influential in evaluating the degree of assertiveness when the speaker is female (McFall et al., 1982). Male and female observers in the McFall et al. study did not utilize these facial cues differentially, a finding at odds with that of Romano and Bellack (1980): '[M]ales and females differed substantially in the number, pattern and valence of the cues used...female judges seemed to be sensitive to and made use of more behavioral cues...' (p. 488). In particular, they observed that smiles, which in general have not been found to contribute greatly to perceptions of assertiveness (Kolotkin et al., 1984), strongly detract from women's – but not from men's – evaluations of female asserters.

These data indicate that facial expression is a critical nonverbal component of assertion, particularly for women. Females may be more astute than males at discriminating facial cues in speakers, but as asserters they emit these cues in more subtle ways that nevertheless strongly influence the perception of assertion. Males, therefore, may require particularly intensive training in attending to these cues and interpreting them, particularly when emitted by women. Females should recognize that other women may react negatively to smiles during an assertion, but that males seem unaffected by that response.

Gestures

Socially skilled individuals increase their use of gestures in conflict situations (Trower, 1980), and use their arms and hands differently than less skilled persons (McFall et al., 1982). Arm movements that are smooth and steady while speaking and inconspicuous while listening, and hands that are relatively still and not engaged in excessive manipulative activity, are the most significant nonverbal contributors to assertion by males (McFall et al., 1982). Such movements also moderate the judgement of assertion by females, especially when rated by males: physical gestures improve the evaluation while extraneous and restrained movements detract from the perception (Romano & Bellack, 1980). Furthermore, arm and hand movements may be most influential when the conflict situation involves opposite sexed participants (Rose & Tryon, 1979). Thus, it is clear that an appropriate behavioral repertoire of gestures will enhance the effectiveness of conflict assertions for both men and women.

Body language

General body posture contributes little to experts' ratings of overall assertion (Kolotkin et al., 1980), but it is an important variable for lay people (Romano & Bellack, 1980). Head, neck, shoulder, and torso positions that are upright, exhibit minimal extraneous movement, squarely face the other person, and involve purposive movement while speaking yet remain quiet while listening are associated with assertive behavior (McFall et al., 1982). Nonassertiveness is characterized by up-and-down nodding and side-to-side tilting of the head and neck, shoulders that are stooped, shrugging, or hunched, and torsos that are rotating, rocking, or squirming (McFall et al., 1982). Body language cues influence the perception of assertion emitted by males more than by females, but overall are less important than other nonverbal responses (McFall et al., 1982; Romano & Bellack, 1980). This is consistent with the general communication literature that finds body movements to be less important nonverbal cues than facial expressions, except for the detection of deception (Dittman, Parloff, & Boomer, 1965; Ekman & Frisen, 1969).

Finally, while meaningful posture shifts are appropriate (Trower, 1980), actually approaching the other person while asserting is judged by lay people to be aggressive (Rose & Tryon, 1979).

In summary, body language contributes modestly to perceptions of assertion, and appears to be more important for males. Some attention in training is warranted, especially since the behaviors themselves are generally discrete and easily acquired, providing a therapeutic opportunity through which to begin the shaping process designed to culminate in a fluid, flexible assertive response.

Summary of nonverbal responses

Eye contact, facial expression, gestures, and, to a lesser extent, body language all contribute to evaluations of conflict assertive behavior. Facial expression for female asserters and gestures for male asserters have emerged as particularly significant influences. Overall, steady but not rigid eye contact, a calm, sincere, serious facial expression, flexible use of arm and hand gestures, and a relaxed, involved body posture characterize behavior judged to be assertive. Body movements should be fluid and purposeful when speaking but quiet and inconspicuous when listening (McFall et al., 1982). Intuitively, these recommendations seem to be highly generalizable across conflict situations, but, admittedly, there is no research to confirm this speculation.

Process (interactive) skills

All of the previous overt skill components of assertion are emitted in an interactive sequence, but several responses are uniquely involved in the *process* of the ongoing conflict interaction. These include response timing, initiation and persistence, and stimulus control skills.

Response timing

Socially unskilled individuals fail to time their vocalizations and gestures adequately (Fischetti, Curran, & Wessberg, 1977; Peterson, Fischetti, Curran, & Arland, 1981) and respond inappropriately to situational cues (Fischetti, Peterson, Curran, Alkire, Perrewe, & Arland, 1984). Trower (1980), for example, found skilled persons not only spoke more than unskilled individuals, but did so at socially appropriate moments such as when the other person responded to verbalizations or engaged in long periods of silence, or when the situation invited an assertive response. In addition, skilled individuals engaged in greater eye contact when listening to the other person.

The AT literature, both research and applied, has not directly acknowledged the importance of skilled timing as has the more general field of social skill training. Nevertheless, the conflict assertion interaction is fundamentally composed of an ongoing exchange between two or more individuals, and the effectiveness of an assertive verbalization is likely to be directly related to the appropriateness with which it is introduced into the interaction. Trainees must learn to discriminate the verbal, nonverbal, and situational cues that indicate a response is – or is not – appropriate. However, frequently these stimuli will be insufficient to determine appropriateness, and other communication skills may be necessary, such as questioning, paraphrasing, reflecting, self-disclosing, explaining, or reinforcing (cf Hargie, 1986a). These additional skills may be necessary to assess the situation's appropriateness for an assertive response and will be discussed briefly in Chapter 9.

Initiation and persistence

The *decision* to emit an assertive response in a particular situation involves covert responses that will be discussed in detail in the next chapter. Once an individual decides that he or she desires to behave assertively, the initial verbalization should be the *minimal effective response*, which is the 'behavior that would ordinarily accomplish the client's goal with a minimum of effort and apparent negative emotion (and a very small likelihood of negative consequences)' (Rimm & Masters, 1979, p. 77). This is perhaps the most important general guideline to stress to clients who are beginning the process of improving their conflict resolution skills. In my experience, the novice asserter more often errs in the learning process by emitting an inappropriately strong response than by producing an inadequately weak attempt.

The minimal effective response (MER) is characterized by mild language, the absence of threats, moderate volume, firmness and affect, and limited use of gestures and body cues. For example, if someone cuts in front of you in a grocery line, the MER would be 'Excuse me, but I was in line ahead of you', accompanied by 'hyper-conversational' paralinguistic qualities (slightly increased firmness and volume, short latency and duration, good fluency), good eye contact, a 'serious' facial expression, few gestures, and the absence of nervous or extraneous body movements. The content of this assertion does not require inclusion of the subsequent elaborations since the interaction is one involving strangers who are not going to enter into a continuing relationship. Note also that this assertion falls into the category of a behavior change request, and the MER consists of the statement of the problem only, without the specific request to modify the offending behavior. It is, therefore, 'indirect' and 'mitigated' with respect to the rules governing ordinary conversation, and unlikely to be perceived as exceptionally challenging (cf Gervasio, 1987).

The MER in a more complicated situation, one that involves a continuing relationship, follows the same general principles. If your boss assigns too much work for you to complete in the allotted time, the initial refusal of this unreasonable request would involve calling the situation to her attention: 'Jane, you've just given me the Smith account but yesterday you also gave me the Jones account, and they are both due in two days. I know that each is complicated and can't be assigned to most of the people in the office, but I will not be able to complete them unless I work late, which I can't do this week due to prior commitments. Perhaps we can call Jones and ask for an extension.' The content of this MER eschews a direct 'no', since the unreasonable request is only implicitly stated through the work assignment. Nevertheless, noncompliance is clearly stated ('I can't do [it] this week') and appropriate subsequent elaborations (an explanation, an expression of understanding, and a proposal for a mutually acceptable compromise) are included. The paralinguistic and nonverbal components of this response should be characterized by relatively low intensity.

The MER will often resolve the problem in and of itself, avoiding the need to introduce statements that have a greater probability of prompting a negative reaction. It is important to bear in mind that many violations of an individual's rights are inadvertent, accidental, or nondeliberate. In such circumstances, a high intensity initial assertion is likely to be perceived as an overreaction and inappropriately aggressive. If the recipient replies accordingly, the asserter will experience negative consequences, which will then reinforce the already strong pre-existing beliefs that assertion entails risk and simultaneously punish any newly acquired (and therefore weakly learned) beliefs that are consistent with, and necessary for, appropriate assertive behavior. Thus, the MER is a critical concept for the generally overly enthusiastic novice.

However, the MER will at times prove to be inadequate. In such a case, the asserter must be able to *escalate* to a higher intensity response (Rimm & Masters, 1979). Escalation may involve modifications of all aspects of the MER. The paralinguistic components, particularly response duration and voice volume and firmness (affect), will increase or intensify. The use of nonverbal behaviors such as gestures and body language will expand. The content of the verbalization itself might specify aversive consequences, and if directed toward a person in a continuing relationship, might introduce further explanation, increased empathy, or additional potential compromises. The specific behavior change request may also be added if the statement of the problem alone fails to modify the offender's behavior. The training of persistence in general, and escalation in particular, is a critically important but often overlooked or deemphasized aspect of AT. As Rimm and Masters (1979) point out, some confidence in the ability to deal with a noncompliant or negative response to the MER is, for many clients, an essential prerequisite for the emission of the MER in the first place. Therefore, clients should be trained in the MER *and* escalation skills *prior* to real world experiments in assertion.

Persistence in noncontinuing relationships. Assertive behavior, whether the MER or an escalated response, requires that the focus of the problem be maintained. This is one reason why explanations, expressions of understanding, and apologies are not effective components of assertion in noncontinuing relationships. Such elaborations are not socially necessary (that is, they do not distinguish appropriate from inappropriate responses), yet they introduce extraneous material that can cause the focus to be shifted and perhaps lost. Several examples will illuminate this problem:

Situation: A salesman comes to your door selling a product you do not want.

Effective MER: 'No, thanks, I'm not interested.'

Ineffective MER: 'No, thanks, I'm not interested. I already have one (or: I don't need one).'

The first MER treats the salesman politely, but offers him little with which to continue the discussion. If he fails to respect your lack of interest, perhaps by inquiring why, the effective response (escalated) is to basically repeat the lack of interest: 'I'm sorry, I'm *simply* not interested' (in a firmer, louder voice, and with a very serious face!).

The ineffective MER increases the chances of a lengthy interaction, since you have permitted the salesman to get his 'foot in the door'. If you inform him that you already have a similar item, he may ask which one, and then go on to describe how his product is newer, more efficient, or otherwise superior. If you tell him you don't need one, he may describe the myriad of reasons why you really could use one. If you say it's too expensive, he is likely to point out the reasons why it is nevertheless good value as well as describing a credit plan. Salesmen, however, have no response for lack of interest. The salesman example provides a metaphor for assertion in noncontinuing relationships: the MER should not provide an open door into which a foot can be planted. A second example is presented to reinforce this recommendation.

Situation: A local cancer charity calls and asks if you will volunteer to make telephone calls to raise money for ill children. You do not want to do it.

Effective MER: 'No, I'm sorry, I can't help you out with that.' A second response, if necessary, would simply repeat the statement with slight escalation.

Ineffective MER: 'No, I'm sorry I can't help you out with that. I'm terribly busy right now (or: I don't like talking on the phone).' The requester can then say he is 'only' asking for a few calls that will take very little time, or ask when you will be less busy, or state that, if you would prefer, volunteers are also needed to staff a booth at the local shopping area. The requester might also remind you how important the cause is (who could not be concerned about ill children?). However, all of these issues are irrelevant if you do not wish to volunteer; you can choose the ways in which you express your concern for humanity. You have that right, and the requester in this situation is not entitled to an explanation or acquiescence.

When the MER fails, competent persistence requires escalation that still maintains the conflict focus and resists manipulations (Rakos & Schroeder, 1980). This is relatively easy in noncontinuing relationships.

Situation: A salesman who has just sold you a television tries also to sell you an extended warranty that you do not want.

MER: 'No, thanks, I'm not interested in the extended warranty.'

Salesman: 'Are you sure? It's a small investment to protect your much larger investment.'

Escalation 1: 'Yes, I'm sure, I'm not interested in it.' (Slight increase in firmness is appropriate; focus is maintained by ignoring the 'investment' issue.)

Salesman: 'You are buying a very good product, but a complicated electronic one. You know that problems can occur after the manufacturer's one-year warranty expires.'

Escalation 2: 'I am not interested in the extended warranty.' (Louder volume, greater firmness and intonation, perhaps a body cue such as side-to-side head movements; focus is maintained by ignoring the 'manufacturer's warranty' issue.)

Salesman: 'The extended warranty will mean you will not have to spend anything on this television in the next five years. I think that such peace of mind is worth the slight cost of the warranty. Haven't you ever had a TV go on the blink just when it's most inconvenient?'

Escalation 3: 'I told you I do not want the extended warranty. If you persist in trying to sell it to me, I will buy the TV from another store and also inform your supervisor of your behavior.' (Volume, affect, intonation increased slightly from previous response and aversive contingency specified; focus is maintained by ignoring the 'peace of mind' issue.)

It is certainly unlikely that a salesman would behave as obnoxiously as the one in the example. But extreme situations, though infrequent, do occur periodically, and the asserter must be prepared to handle them. The key to effective persistence is the maintenance of the focus. The focus, it must be stressed, concerns the other person's offending behavior (Rimm & Masters, 1979), and not his or her personality traits or the asserter's reasons or rights. Thus, name-calling or labeling behavior is counterproductive ('Are you deaf? I said no!' or 'You are obnoxious') as are explanations or defenses of your decision. The focus in noncontinuing relationships can be maintained best by restricting the basic content of any escalation to the repetition of the initial assertion.[4]

Persistence in continuing relationships. The ability to deal with difficult situations that arise in continuing relationships is, in a sense, much more important than skill in handling the relatively simple interactions with strangers. The investment is much greater in continuing relationships, and the overall value of the assertion is measured by both the outcome and the lasting integrity of the relationship. Therefore, the escalation responses must embed repetitions in diverse syntactic surface structures (Gervasio, 1987) and in elaborations (and perhaps elaborations of elaborations). Furthermore, when an individual begins to behave more assertively and less submissively, he or she fails to meet the expectations of others – and expectations that are not confirmed generally arouse one or more negative feelings (eg hurt, anger, rejection, depression, vengeance). Therefore, persistence by the novice asserter in ongoing relationships is even more problematic than for experienced asserters who have taught their social environment to expect self-enhancing behavior. Escalation must be very skillful to maintain the focus so that a desired immediate outcome is achieved while simultaneously addressing the factors that impact on the long-term health of the relationship. The following interaction exemplifies the complexities of the process.

Situation: Father expects his daughter to come for dinner every Sunday. Therefore, the situation requires the refusal of an unreasonable, but implicit, request.

MER: 'Dad, I won't be coming to dinner this Sunday. I've made plans to see some friends. I hope you won't be too disappointed, but we're going to a party. I'll see you next Sunday as usual.' (This MER includes explicit noncompliance and an explanation, attention to feelings, and a potential mutually acceptable compromise.)

Father: 'But we look forward to your visits so much. You know we don't get out very often any more, and your company is so important to us. Couldn't you meet your friends after dinner?' (Father is at this point responding with an appropriate assertion of his own that includes an explanation and a compromise.)

Escalation 1: 'Dad, if I come to dinner, I'll miss a lot of the party. I know how much you enjoy my visits, but this is an exception. It's a special party that I really want to attend. I know you and mother will miss me, but it's only one week.' (Repeated noncompliance, but further explanation and empathy are offered with a changed surface structure.)

Father: 'Go with your friends to your party then. We'll survive even if they are more important to you. I hope your kids care about you more than you care about us.'

Here we are dealing with one of the closest, most important continuing relationships, that of a child with a parent. The daughter is initiating assertive behavior, resulting in the father experiencing an unexpected loss of reinforcement and the feelings of hurt and anger that often accompany aversive consequences. Protecting the relationship and maintaining the focus in this situation generally requires: (1) increased empathic reflection of the underlying feelings; (2) repetition and possibly expansion of the explicit explanation; and (3) an expanded search for a mutually acceptable compromise, if conflicting rights are judged to be present. The maintenance of the focus will be enhanced if the asserter can address these verbalizations to the *existence* of the feelings rather than to the *content* of the feelings. However, this is often exceptionally difficult.

Escalation 2: 'Dad, I hear how angry and disappointed you are that I will not be coming for dinner this week. I know how important the family dinners are to you, but, as I said, I really want to go to this cocktail party. There will be a lot of new people there, and I've been feeling a bit isolated lately. I hope you understand my feelings. I am free Wednesday evening – I can stop by for a few hours after work instead of waiting until next Sunday. How does that sound?'

This escalated response repeats the noncompliance again, attends to the feelings the father is experiencing, expands the explanation, offers a new explicit compromise, and changes the surface structure, but does not lose the focus and become defensive by debating the extent of 'caring' for parents or the relative 'importance' of different relationships. Caring, if present, can be demonstrated through the compromise. Sometimes, however, the interaction will continue and the content of the feelings will have to be addressed more directly, resulting in an increased probability of losing the assertive focus.

Escalation 3: 'Dad, I really do understand how much you look forward to our Sunday dinners and the time we spend together. I enjoy the dinners tremendously too, but sometimes other important engagements occur on Sundays. I feel very close to you and mother, and care about you both very much. My missing dinner this week has nothing to do with how I feel about you. I am sad that you do not see this as I do. Anyway, as I said, I am free Wednesday evening, and I'd like to stop by then. Is that all right?'

Escalation in some continuing relationship contexts (such as the one in the above example) will primarily involve expanded content (and hence response duration), but may not necessarily include louder volume, greater firmness and inflection, or increased use of nonverbal cues. Other contexts, however, will require escalation of the paralinguistic and nonverbal components.

If the other person continues to experience negative feelings as a consequence of the assertion, and the relationship is a valued one, an assertion directed at the negative feelings may be necessary, either immediately or at a later time. This would probably involve a behavior change request of father as well as positive assertions expressing affection. Persistence should be conceptualized as the behaviors required to solve the problem as best as possible. As the interaction progresses, the issues may shift, and further escalation may be no longer appropriate or efficacious. A new, legitimate issue usually necessitates the emission of a new MER rather than endless escalation. In the example of the daughter and her parents, the issue at some point shifts from the particular Sunday dinner to the more general concern of flexibility in dinner arrangements.

MER: 'Dad, I want to talk to you about our phone conversation last week. You sounded pretty hurt and angry, and seemed to feel that if I cared about you I would always make the Sunday dinner. I would like to talk about that because I feel very differently about the situation.' (This MER includes an orienting verbalization and the conflict statement component of a behavior change request.)

Persistence increases the chances for a desired outcome but cannot guarantee it, since assertion is, by definition, risky. The car mechanic may not reduce unwarranted charges regardless of the extent of escalation. An assertion specifying a future contingency ('you will hear from my lawyer') will hardly be very satisfying. And though the desired outcome may be achieved in an ongoing relationship, the possibility of arousing negative feelings such as hurt, anger, or rejection introduces additional risks. Skillful employment of the covert components of assertion (see Chapter 4) is necessary to assess the situation accurately, avoid rationalizations that justify nonassertive behavior, and decide whether to assert. Furthermore, if the assertive option is selected, covert behaviors will be involved in determining the extent of escalation that is desirable given the nature of the relationship, the importance of the conflict at issue, and the realistic probability of the potential positive and negative outcomes. The acquisition of assertive skills increases the individual's behavioral freedom, and therefore provides him or her with the option of asserting. But no mandate exists to *always* assert oneself or continue the escalation sequence (Alberti & Emmons, 1970; Rakos & Schroeder, 1980).

Stimulus control skills

Antecedent and consequent stimulus control skills facilitate effective, socially acceptable assertion by altering the context in which the assertion is emitted. Antecedent stimulus control refers to the ability to arrange the environment prior to the assertion so that the possibility of a favourable outcome is maximized. These skills are generally assertive behaviors themselves: requests to move to a private room prior to a confrontation, requests for a delay before making a decision (which permits time to identify and rehearse appropriate responses), or inquiries to the other person regarding convenient times to set aside for the discussion of concerns. They may also involve self-management skills that inhibit assertion because the immediate context is judged to be inappropriate or counterproductive. Conflicts that are discussed at the right time (Alberti & Emmons, 1970; Lange & Jakubowski, 1976), in private, without time pressures, and with prior deliberation are more likely to be resolved with mutual satisfaction.

Consequent stimulus control refers to reinforcing the other person for listening to and/or complying with the assertion. The provision of contingent verbal reinforcement for desired behavior in response to an assertion is likely to encourage similar behavior in the future and may also minimize negative perceptions of the conflict interaction (Levin & Gross, 1984; St. Lawrence et al., 1985a).

Clinical implications and recommendations

One major theme has characterized the discussion of overt components: flexibility. I will try to summarize what has already been offered in the original discussion in such a manner that the training implications are salient.

1. The research clearly indicates that the empathic assertion combines the potency of an aggressive response with the social acceptability of a nonassertive response. It is, therefore, the assertive style most likely to maximize both the short-term impact on the other person and long-term health of the relationship. I recommend training clients to produce it primarily in relationships that are continuing ones, since those are the contexts in which long-term reinforcement is important. In interactions with strangers, I believe that the standard assertion is both efficacious and socially appropriate. Moreover, the standard assertion provides fewer opportunities for a shift of focus to irrelevant concerns or for the introduction of manipulative statements by the recipient. The research does not clearly indicate that the standard assertion avoids these problems, but since it is

perceived as positively as the empathic assertion in conflicts involving strangers (Heisler & McCormack, 1982), I believe that it is the proper response for most interactions involving noncontinuing relationships. As with each potential assertion, however, the individual must assess the situation and determine what is the desired response. Undoubtedly, there will be instances when the asserter will be more comfortable with a low level empathic assertion as the means for resolving a problem with a stranger.

The recommendation that empathic assertions be employed in continuing relationships is similarly flexible. I have distinguished continuing from non-continuing relationships, but in reality, continuing ones can be either *close* or *functional*. Close continuing relationships are ones that are valued and meaning-ful apart from any function that they may serve in the person's life. They may or may not involve positive affect; a relationship with a boss for whom you hold no love is nevertheless a close relationship. The value and meaning stem from the impact the person has on your life, an impact that must be assessed on a molar level instead of a molecular one. A functional relationship, on the other hand, will involve people with whom you negotiate particular daily living tasks. The importance of the relationship is assessed on a molecular level. Thus, a car mechanic whom you see every six months is in a continuing but functional relationship with you; he or she can easily be replaced by another service person. Your boss, however, cannot be replaced in the same sense, and is involved in a close relationship with you, however distasteful that may be.

The distinction between close and functional continuing relationships is important in the selection of the appropriate style of conflict assertion. Close relationships *always* demand the empathic assertion, but functional ones may or may not. An assertion to a new car mechanic probably should be a simple, standard one. However, after years and years of dealing with the same person, within a relationship that remains strictly on the business level, an empathic assertion may nevertheless be the most socially appropriate one for several reasons. First, through many years of service, the mechanic begins to acquire rights that he or she did not have at the beginning. At the very least, he earns the right to an explanation. Second, if you wish to continue to do business with him, explanation, understanding, and compromise may be necessary *and* appropriate.

An example from my own experience highlights the distinction between functional and close continuing relationships. My wife and I recently decided to purchase additional life insurance through a new agent. After a couple of months of meetings and information gathering, we made a decision to each purchase a certain amount of insurance from 'Acme', which was the company our agent recommended from among the dozen or so with whom he deals. However, at the last minute, we decided to reconsider, and I requested that the agent forward information from 'Ajax', a less expensive option. Finally, we decided (for reasons that were *not* terribly personal and hence theoretically *could* be shared) that this year only I would buy a policy from 'Ajax', my wife would purchase nothing, and next year we would both enroll with 'Acme' as originally intended for this year. I knew the agent would be disappointed on two counts: he has a much closer relationship with 'Acme' and he expected to make two sales. Nevertheless, I felt I certainly had the right to choose my insurance purchases, and, furthermore, I determined that he had no rights (other than to be treated respectfully) in the situation despite the time he had already invested in the sale. I decided that a standard assertion was not only appropriate, but also had the best chance of 'working'. I was worried that explanations and expressions of understanding (of his disappointment) would only permit him to get his 'foot in the door'. Therefore, I telephoned him and said the following:

'John, I wanted to get back to you on the life insurance (introductory orienting statement). My wife and I have decided that this year I will purchase the "Ajax" policy, but she will purchase no insurance this year. Next year, we will both buy the "Acme" policies we have been discussing.' He did not blink, an inference from his short response latency over the phone. He said 'Fine, I'll get the papers to you in the mail by the end of the week.' That was it – the end of the conversation. This assertion was probably a refusal of an (implicit) unreasonable request (though, conceivably, it could be viewed as an expression of an unpopular opinion). The 'next year' statement was not a negotiable compromise in the sense that it has been discussed in this chapter. Had the agent inquired about reasons for our decision, or tried to point out the disadvantages of our choice, I would have simply said: 'This is best for us now. Next year we intend to change.' I would not have offered additional explanation, expressed understanding of his disappointment, or agreed to 'think about it' as a compromise. But this was never necessary, for he understood that his rights in the situation were very limited and he had to respect our decision or risk losing us as clients. However, ten years from now, if he continues to sell us our insurance, I would deal with a similar situation with an empathic assertion. The main point of this discussion is, once again, that the overt components of assertion vary according to the situation. The guidelines I have offered are only starting points from which to develop the appropriate reply; they cannot encompass the situational variability without the notion of flexibility.

2. It is important to teach clients that the antecedent obligations discussed in Chapter 2 are critically important for assertions with all individuals, regardless of the nature of the relationship. In my assertion to my insurance agent, I first assessed the rights of all participants, developed an appropriate verbal response directed toward the issue and not the person, and determined the negative consequences he would experience as a result of my assertion were acceptable given the particular contextual parameters.

3. The paralinguistic and nonverbal components of the assertive response contribute significantly to the overall perception of assertiveness, and may do so independently of verbal content (Linehan & Walker, 1983). However, clients must be taught to utilize varying intensities that are appropriate to the particular

circumstances. Moderate levels seem to be the best guideline, but flexibility is a close second.

4. Assertion is emitted in the context of an ongoing interaction. Without adequate processing skills, such as response timing, initiation, persistence, and stimulus control, a client will have a sterile response in his or her behavioral repertoire: he or she will be unable to implement the response in an effective, appropriate manner. Rimm and Masters' (1979) point that escalated responses should be taught along with the MER, and prior to naturalistic experimentation, bears repeating. As they note, many clients will not even emit the MER unless they have confidence in their ability to handle negative reactions to the initial assertion. Furthermore, the client should be taught a variety of escalated responses: one can't predict with sufficient accuracy whether a recipient will react aggressively or exhibit feelings of rejection. I have seen many clinicians send a client home with instructions to 'try out' the response that was just trained. (Two training films for professionals actually model this intervention strategy.) Not only is the new response poorly learned and in need of much more rehearsal in a safe environment, but the client has, at best, only that one response to offer the recipient. Unless the initial response is completely effective, the 'experiment' will inevitably entail unnecessary stress and negative consequences for the novice asserter, and the behavior will not be reinforced nearly as much as it could have been had more extensive training been provided. The behavior may even be punished and thereby set therapy back unnecessarily. My general guideline here is: shape slowly, emphasize flexibility, train extensively, and experiment conservatively.

Chapter four

Conflict assertion: covert behavioral components

Over the past decade, cognitive skills have assumed an increasingly important role in the conceptualization of social skills (McFall, 1982; Meichenbaum et al., 1981; Morrison & Bellack, 1981; Trower, 1982). Ludwig and Lazarus (1972) were the first to suggest that irrational beliefs and poor discrimination of social behaviors were involved in the failure to perform assertively. Schwartz and Gottman's (1976) investigation of the role of positive and negative self-statements in the production of a conflict assertion was the ground-breaking empirical study of specific cognitive variables. Since then, dozens of studies have confirmed that the covert response components are essential elements of effective conflict assertion (Rakos, 1986; Stefanek & Eisler, 1983).

The cognitive components permit the individual to categorize and manipulate information, either automatically or consciously. As information-processing skills, they are crucial for the conscious self-direction of behavior when automatic responding is maladaptive or deficient (Kanfer & Schefft, 1988). In its simplest formulation, self-regulation involves three skills. First, behavior is *self-monitored*, which involves self-observation of overt and covert behaviors, the situations in which they are emitted, and the actual consequences they produce. Clients, through self-monitoring, learn the functional relationship between the environment and their responses, thereby gaining 'insight'. Next, self-monitored behavior is compared to a standard that articulates the criteria for a satisfactory level of performance. This *self-evaluation* provides feedback that prompts either *self-reinforcement or self-punishment* as well as the incorporation of improvements in the response so that it comes closer to the standard (Kanfer & Schefft, 1988).

Covert skills are involved in each stage of self-regulation. Accurate perceptual and discriminative abilities form the basis for veridical self-monitoring, to be discussed in greater detail later in this chapter and again when assessment strategies are addressed (Chapter 6). Self-reinforcement and self-punishment often involve private verbalizations that acknowledge competence or criticize inadequacy. The development of appropriate comparative standards is more complex, requiring the acquisition of a host of facilitative covert behaviors. In fact, socially skilled and unskilled individuals differ in the standards they employ to evaluate their behaviors. Skilled persons utilize objective criteria based on situational and interpersonal cues, which generate particular social roles, norms, and rules, as well as empirically based competency (self-efficacy) and outcome expectations. Unskilled persons, on the other hand, employ subjective standards that focus on idiosyncratic, nonempirical beliefs, perceptions, and expectations (Trower, 1982). For example, nonassertive individuals produce more assertive behavior after exposure to a severely passive model than to moderately or minimally submissive models, presumably because their subjective performance standards have been modified (Hung, Rosenthal, & Kelley, 1980).

The ability to utilize empirically based, objective criteria requires conceptual complexity (CC). Schroder, Driver, and Streufert (1967) suggested that CC encompasses the following sophisticated information processing skills: (1) the ability to make increasingly precise discriminations among situational cues, thereby allowing consideration of broader and more diverse viewpoints; (2) the increased reliance on internally but rationally developed standards for problem solving; and (3) the ability to integrate larger amounts of information and increase tolerance of conflict. The importance of CC for the emission of assertive behavior has been clearly demonstrated by Bruch (1981; Bruch, Heisler, & Conroy, 1981). Assertive individuals demonstrate greater CC than nonassertive persons, and further, high CC people, compared to low CC ones, manifest a better knowledge of assertive response content, superior oral delivery skills, and more effective use of facilitative cognitions (eg self-instructions). In addition, high CC individuals behave more assertively and emit elaborative statements to a significantly greater extent in conflicts involving continuing relationships, which make the greatest demand on cognitive skills. In such situations, asserters must be able to employ multiple perspectives and internal rational standards since greater flexibility as well as refined relationship-enhancing behaviors are necessary to produce a socially acceptable, effective response. Conceptual complexity is less important in interactions with strangers since social norms provide relatively straightforward behavioral guidelines.

Thus, cognitive abilities are crucial for the production of a sophisticated, rational, empirical analysis of the conflict situation. These capacities can be organized into seven basic skill categories: knowledge, self-statements (self-instructions), expectancies, philosophical beliefs, problem-solving skills, social perception skills, and self-monitoring skills.

Knowledge

It is probably erroneous to conceptualize knowledge *per se* as a covert skill; a more accurate representation would refer to the ability to utilize memories (covert stimuli) as prompts for the performance of technically appropriate overt responses. Knowledge is obviously a prerequisite for effective assertion, but, curiously, it may not be a distinguishing characteristic of assertive persons.

Recognition is one form of knowledge. Both nonassertive and assertive individuals can accurately categorize passive, assertive, and aggressive behavior (Alden & Cappe, 1981; Bordewick & Bornstein, 1980). Thus, the behavioral styles can be discriminated regardless of level of assertiveness. However, the extent to which nonassertive and assertive persons differ with respect to the recall knowledge of the actual content is currently unclear. Alden and Safran (1978), Schwartz and Gottman (1976), and Chiauzzi et al. (1982) found no differences in content knowledge or role play behavior as a function of level of assertiveness, suggesting that observed discrepancies in performance were due to other cognitive deficits. Later research by Vecsi (1984) obtained similar data: highly knowledgeable mothers of adolescent girls did not emit greater amounts of assertive behavior in a structured role play than did mothers with less knowledge. Wojnilower and Gross (1988) also failed to find a relationship between knowledge of assertion and social performance in learning disabled children, but did determine that knowledge was related to social perception skills. Bruch (1981) and Heimberg and Becker (1981), on the other hand, obtained data suggesting nonassertive individuals manifest deficits in recall knowledge and behavioral skill. The contradictory results mimic clinical observations that many candidates for AT clearly lack relevant cognitive knowledge, while others, perhaps due to the penetration of the self-help and popular media, possess adequate recall, yet are still unable to perform assertively.

Self-statements

Self-statements, often referred to as self-instructions or self-talk, are centrally involved in competent social functioning; in particular, negative self-statements appear to be critical elements that impede appropriate social responding (Meichenbaum et al., 1981). Negative self-statements are themselves behaviors, albeit private ones, and therefore part of the entire behavior chain. They function as either discriminative stimuli or reinforcing stimuli, depending on their placement in the chain, but, in either case, reduce the likelihood of the associated overt response. The research has primarily focused on self-statements as discriminative stimuli that set the occasion for the response by indicating a specific response in the particular situation is likely to produce a certain consequence (Martin & Pear, 1988). These self-statements are produced in response to the environmental context and *prior to* the emission of the overt behavior. Reinforcing self-statements, by contrast, occur *after* the overt response has been emitted, and function as would any reinforcer: if positive, they tend to increase the frequency of the behavior that produces them, and if negative, they tend to decrease the frequency of the behavior that produces them (Martin & Pear, 1988). As such, they provide the primary mechanism through which self-directed behavior is evaluated and either reinforced or punished.

Several examples of negative and positive self-statements will clarify their nature. A negative self-statement that functions as a discriminative stimulus might be the following, emitted in response to the environmental stimulus of an unreasonable request: 'He will feel hurt if I refuse' or 'I will get very anxious if I try to say no'. Positive alternatives of these statements might be: 'I have the right to refuse, even if he feels hurt by it' and 'I will be able to control my anxiety though diaphragmatic breathing'. Positive self-reinforcing statements follow the response and highlight the adaptive nature of the behavior: 'I did it! I said "no" appropriately and it worked. I feel good that I am in control of my life.' A negative self-reinforcing statement focuses on the maladaptive elements of the response: 'I stammered and barely said what I wanted to. He probably thinks I'm a jerk.' Even when the overt response has significant deficits, trainees must learn to identify and self-reinforce those aspects that are appropriate in order to facilitate the shaping and self-regulatory processes. Thus, the last negative self-statement would be replaced by: 'I said "no", and, even though it was far from perfect, he accepted it. That feels very good!'

Though the research is very scanty, some evidence suggests assertive and nonassertive individuals utilize self-reinforcement differently (Borgart, 1985), perhaps because nonassertive persons evidence greater reliance on internal, stable, and global attributions to explain interpersonal outcomes, compared to assertive individuals who emphasize external, transient, and specific attributions (Alden, 1984; Miglins, 1985). Another possibility may be that assertive and nonassertive persons differ in their use of appropriate standard setting (Borgart, 1985; Trower, 1982) upon which the self-evaluation of a response depends. Regardless of the mechanism, assertive persons are more willing to employ self-reinforcement, even when it is not justified: assertive individuals, in contrast to nonassertive ones, overestimate the competency of their response (Alden & Cappe, 1981) and accept (bogus) positive feedback as generally accurate (Alden, 1984). Thus, the performance of assertion may be more dependent on the frequency of self-reinforcement than on its veracity. However, for nonassertive persons learning to increase their use of self-reinforcement, accuracy will clearly form the basis through which negative self-statements will be reduced and positive ones increased. Through systematic training, subjective standards, such as an exceptionally incompetent model (Hung et al., 1980), eventually can be replaced by more appropriate ones. In fact, training in assertive criteria does improve self-evaluative accuracy somewhat (Barbaree & Davis, 1984; Muehlenhard & McFall, 1983), suggesting that improved use of self-reinforcement by novice asserters will likely depend on successful experience and consistent feedback from and modeling by the trainer.

The research, as mentioned above, has primarily investigated the importance of self-statements when they are functioning as discriminative stimuli. In this context, the utilization of positive and negative self-statements clearly distinguishes high from low assertive individuals. Assertive persons emit approximately twice as many positive as negative self-statements when confronted with social conflict, while nonassertive individuals emit approximately equal numbers of each (Borgart, 1985; Bruch, 1981; Heimberg, Chiauzzi, Becker, & Madrazo-Peterson, 1983; Pitcher & Meikle, 1980; Schwartz & Gottman, 1976). Guilt over assertion (Klass, 1981) and greater anxiety with suppressed performance (Safran, 1982) are also reflected in increased negative self-statements (Klass, 1981). Furthermore, the 'mix' of positive and negative self-statements is more important than the absolute frequency of each (Blankenberg & Heimberg, 1984). This finding is supported by Bruch (1981), who observed that assertive individuals often used negative self-statements as discriminative stimuli for the emission of positive, coping ones. Therefore, the presence of negative self-statements is a concern primarily in regard to the overall production and use of self-statements in general.

Finally, an observation by Wine merits discussion. She points out that a masculine perspective is presumed when self-statements associated with non-assertion are labeled as 'negative' or 'dysfunctional' (eg Schwartz & Gottman, 1976). Such self-verbalizations typically focus on negative self-image, fear of rejection, and the needs of others rather than the self (Pitcher & Meikle, 1980; Schwartz & Gottman, 1976). From a feminine standpoint, self-statements whose nature is conciliatory, affiliative, and nurturant are positive rather than negative. Wine's observation introduces additional clarity to the understanding of self-instructions: certain ones are *situationally ineffective or counterproductive*. In other contexts, the same self-verbalizations will be highly adaptive. Perhaps labeling self-instructions descriptively (rather than functionally) as *autonomous* and *affiliative* would explicitly acknowledge and eliminate some of the sexism underlying the construct (see Chapter 5), and clarify the values inherent in conflict assertion. From this perspective, conflict assertion is facilitated by autonomous self-instructions that do not address the long-term harmony of relationships.

In summary, the research indicates that autonomous self-statements are an important component of effective conflict assertion. Some studies have identified them as the critical components (eg Schwartz & Gottman, 1976), while others have observed them to be merely important, along with knowledge and overt performance skills (eg Bruch, 1981). In either case, they merit close analysis and assessment when examining the source of an individual's unassertiveness. Indeed, direct training in autonomous self-instruction, apart from any other intervention, has resulted in significant gains in assertiveness (Craighead, 1979; Glass, Gottman, & Schmurak, 1976; Twentyman, Pharr, & Connor, 1980).

Expectancies

An expectancy is a cognitive behavior that makes a specific prediction about performance in a particular situation. Three types of expectancies have been identified in the assertion literature (Chiauzzi & Heimberg, 1986). *Outcome expectancies* predict the probability that specific consequences will be produced by a particular response. Assertive and nonassertive individuals expect standard assertion, and to a lesser extent empathic assertion, to have greater negative long-term effects on a relationship than nonassertion (Zollo et al., 1985).

However, assertive individuals expect conflict assertion to produce more positive short-term consequences and fewer negative ones than do nonassertive persons (eg Eisler, Frederiksen, & Peterson, 1978; Fiedler & Beach, 1978).[1] Interestingly, these studies did not find differences between assertive and nonassertive persons in the generation of *possible* consequences, but rather, in the *probability* that those potential consequences will actually occur.

Furthermore, the possible outcomes are evaluated differently: assertive individuals perceive the potential positive consequences of assertion as more desirable and the potential negative ones as more undesirable (Blankenberg & Heimberg, 1984; Kuperminc & Heimberg, 1983). Nonassertive individuals, therefore, may 'rationalise' to reduce the perceived necessity for engaging in a conflict interaction. Not surprisingly, these differences in predicted probability and subjective importance of outcomes are manifested in overt performance: individuals with more negative expectations behave less assertively in refusal situations than persons with more positive expectations (Kaflowitz, 1986).

Self-efficacy expectancies refer to a person's belief that he or she can enact a particular desired behavior in a specific circumstance (Bandura, 1977a). Assertive individuals evidence much stronger self-efficacy in conflict situations than do nonassertive individuals (Chiauzzi & Heimberg, 1986). Efficacy expectancies are superior to outcome expectancies as predictors of subsequent assertive behavior (Lee, 1984), but not as accurate as other behavioral samples (Lee, 1983).

Finally, *situational efficacy expectancies*, which describe the confidence a person has in his or her ability to generate any response to deal successfully with a specific situation, are greater for assertive individuals, but only in those circumstances where the other person's behavior is judged to be highly unreasonable (Chiauzzi & Heimberg, 1986).

Thus, assertive persons approach conflict situations with an adaptive appraisal of the context, resulting in self-confidence in their ability to perform competently. AT addresses maladaptive expectancies through several strategies, including self-instruction training focusing on the production of realistic, autonomous self-statements (Meichenbaum, 1977) and graduated successful performance in the real-life or role-play situation (Bandura, 1977b).

Philosophical beliefs

Ellis (1962; Ellis & Grieger, 1977) proposed that maladaptive behavior is primarily due to strong irrational beliefs. He argues humans possess an innate tendency to engage in irrational thinking that is exploited by conditioning in Western society. Though there are limits to the extent of change possible by many individuals (Ellis, 1987), the dysfunctional beliefs can frequently be directly modified through verbal discourse and behavioral practice. Ellis (1962; 1970) identified twelve general irrational beliefs that may require such focused therapeutic intervention:

1. One must have complete approval from all significant people.
2. One must be thoroughly competent and achieving.
3. Undesired events or consequences are horrible and terrible.
4. People who behave in ways one does not like are bad and should be blamed.
5. Emotional misery is externally produced and unchangeable.
6. One should become upset about things that seem fearful.
7. It is easier to avoid dealing with life's difficulties than to attempt to resolve them.
8. The past is an unchangeable determinant of current and future behavior.
9. Life should be better than it is, and it is terrible if solutions to problems are not found quickly.
10. Inertia can produce happiness.
11. Order and certainty are necessary to feel comfortable, even if only through belief in a higher power or being.
12. One's self-evaluation is dependent upon achievements or approval from others.

Underlying all irrational thinking is a basic logical error: things, people, or events *should* be a certain way. Ellis argues that the use of 'should' elevates desires into demands, and prevents a rational analysis of the situation. Unmet demands lead to *upset*, which is not conducive to effective problem solving. If, on the other hand, unfulfilled desires are understood to be unfortunate events that one wished were otherwise ('it would be better if...' rather than 'it should not have happened'), the individual will exhibit *concern* rather than upset. Concern is seen as an appropriate emotion that facilitates the resolution of problems that can be solved and the acceptance of those that cannot. The specifics of Ellis's rational emotive therapy are beyond the scope of this book, but his system is well articulated in numerous writings (eg Ellis & Grieger, 1977). In addition, other writers modified his confrontative techniques while maintaining the presumed central role of irrational beliefs. This variant, called rational relabeling (Goldfried & Davison, 1976), emphasizes the modification of irrational beliefs through the use of the conventional facilitative relationship skills necessary for effective behavior therapy (O'Leary & Wilson, 1987).

Ellis's irrational ideas have become the foundation of some approaches to assertion training (eg Lange & Jakubowski, 1976) and social skill training (eg Trower, 1982). Rational relabeling, in particular, is commonly employed in AT, despite data suggesting, at best, a modest contribution to treatment outcome (Rakos, 1986; see Chapter 7). The popularity of rational relabeling no doubt stems partially from its intuitive appeal, but also from research that consistently finds nonassertive persons endorse more irrational ideas than do assertive individuals (Alden & Cappe, 1981; Alden & Safran, 1978; Lohr & Bonge, 1982; Lohr, Nix, Dunbar, & Mosesso, 1984). Furthermore, in conflict situations, nonassertive individuals entertain the possibility of many more negative 'overwhelming consequences' (irrational idea number 3 above, also known as 'cata-strophizing') than positive ones, while assertive persons consider similar fre-quencies of each. As with self-statements, the 'mix' of extreme outcome expectations seems more important than their intensity or frequency (Blanken-berg & Heimberg, 1984). Thus, rational alternatives to irrational beliefs seem likely to facilitate, or at least contribute to, the emission of assertive behavior in conflict situations.

Any particular nonassertive client may produce one or more of the twelve irrational ideas. In fact, research has failed to isolate any specific ones that distinguish assertive from nonassertive individuals. However, clinical work suggests the following are highly related to unassertiveness: demands for *perfection* by the self or others in important situations (#2); *blaming* self or other for human fallibility (#4); demands for universal *approval* from significant others (#1); defining personal rights and self-worth by external achievement or approval in subjectively important areas, and engaging in *self-denigration* when reinforce-ment is not forthcoming (#12); catastrophizing, or exaggerating the meaning of an undesired outcome (#3); and viewing *inaction* as preferable to deliberate intervention, believing that things will eventually work out without 'rocking the boat' (#7).

These irrational thoughts are generally produced only in response to subjec-tively important issues. The individual fails to recognize that events in the world occur without regard to the personal value ascribed to a particular situation. Thus, an individual may very rationally accept incompetence in a meaningless hobby (eg failure to perform well in a volleyball game), yet react with extraordinary emotion to an objectively similar event of subjective import (eg failure to get a desired role in a community play).

The typical nonassertive person might engage in the following thought process:

'I must assert myself without any mistakes or the assertion will fail (self-perfection), the other person will think I'm a jerk or will be hurt or angry (universal approval), and that would be terrible (catastrophizing). It would be my fault (self-blame) and confirm that I'm just no good (self-denigration). Things will be better if I let it pass and see what happens (inaction).' These belief statements may be prefaced by additional irrational ideas: 'I don't have the right to infringe or make demands on this other person' (self-denigration) and/or 'I should not even have to deal with this situation since the other person should not be acting this way' (other-perfection/other-blame).

Rational alternatives to the irrational beliefs described above can be directly taught through the application of behavioral principles in much the same way that overt skills would be conditioned (see Chapter 7). The initial step involves identifying the specific irrational thought(s) as it (they) are formulated by the client in response to a specific situation. Nonassertive people have often learned the irrational thoughts so well that they do not actually think them, but behave 'as if' they think them. After specification of the actual or implicit thought, the person is taught to challenge it and actively substitute a rational alternative. These alternatives must be practiced, first in safe, structured rehearsal and then in the actual situation. Finally, their utility must be evaluated (Goldfried & Davison, 1976). The general content of the rational alternatives would encompass the following (Ellis, 1962; Rakos, 1986; Rakos & Schroeder, 1980):

Imperfection and acceptance: 'I am human and the world is very complicated; therefore, I will make mistakes even when the situation is important to me and I very much want to behave competently. The importance of an issue does not change its objective status: there is no reason I *should* behave competently just because it is important that I do so, although *it would be nice* if I were able to behave competently. The other person is also human, lives in the same complex world, and will also make mistakes in situations that are important to me. There is no reason he or she *should* act in a desirable fashion, just because it is important to me, although *it would be nice* if he or she were able to do so.' (These thoughts avoid self- or other-blaming and accept the inevitable frailty and imperfection of the human condition.)

Rejection: 'There is no way I can always please everyone who is important to me, *even if I always place their needs first*, because the world is too complicated and its operation too capricious. *It would be nice* if I could, but I must recognize that there is no reason why I *should* please everyone.' (These beliefs accept the inevitability of some rejection or disapproval in the negotiation of interpersonal relationships.)

Noncatastrophizing: 'Negative outcomes *are* unfortunate, inconvenient, unpleasant, perhaps even bad – but they are not terrible, horrible, or awful. I will attempt constructive amelioration where possible, and adapt to the situation where change is not feasible. This must be my approach even when the undesired outcome involves a personally important issue, because the world does not know or care what is important to me. Things are as they should be, and demanding that they *should* be different ignores the complexity of the world, though *it would be nice* if they indeed were different.' (These thoughts clarify the nature of the world and promote a realistic understanding and acceptance of one's place in it.)

Action: 'Since the world is not oriented toward fulfilling my desires, active attempts to influence it are the only ways for me to increase the probability that my wishes will be achieved. Without action on my part, it is unlikely that events in the complex world will just happen to meet my desires.' (These cognitions accept personal responsibility for attempting change, though they do not demand that such attempts be successful.)

Self-worth: 'I am worthy, and have the same basic human rights as anyone else, regardless of how much or how little I or others have achieved. I have the basic right to assert myself, if I so choose, in an effort to influence the situation and maximize my rewards.' (These ideas accept one's basic, unconditional self-worth and human rights.)

I noted earlier that rational relabeling interventions do not appear, at present, to be essential components of AT. Though these procedures do increase assertive responding (Alden, Safran, & Weideman, 1978; Hatzenbuehler & Schroeder, 1982; Linehan, Goldfried, & Goldfried, 1979), they contribute minimally to an AT package consisting of behavioral skills training alone (Carmody, 1978; Hatzenbuehler & Schroeder, 1982; Hammen, Jacobs, Mayol, & Cochran, 1980; Linehan, Goldfried, & Goldfried, 1979; Tiegerman & Kassinove, 1977; Wolfe & Fodor, 1977). The irrational beliefs that characterize nonassertive individuals, and perhaps mediate nonassertive behavior, can clearly be altered through the modification of the behaviors on which they are based, as suggested by Bandura (1977b). Direct rational relabeling, however, may have greater utility in the promotion of generalization rather than in the initial acquisition of assertive behavior (Scott, Himadi, & Keane, 1983; see also Chapter 7).

Social perception skills

Argyle (1981) identified two distinct cognitive skills involved in interpersonal perception: accurate perception and empathic role taking. Accurate perception has been investigated in greater detail and the evidence, with one exception (Robinson & Calhoun, 1984), strongly suggests that nonassertive individuals are deficient in this skill. They are less sensitive to external cues (Trower, 1980), misjudge the amount of anger communicated by assertive and aggressive responses (Morrison & Bellack, 1981), and place exaggerated emphasis on the status of the other person and degree of social norm transgression when analyzing conflict situations (Rudy et al., 1982).

A realistic assessment of social and cultural conventions is essential for incorporating accurate, externally derived standards into a comprehensive analysis of the situation. Epstein (1980), for example, found compliance with, anger toward, and sympathy for an asserter making a request varied as a function of how reasonable the request was perceived to be and the extent of the sacrifice necessary to comply. In general, however, nonassertive persons perceive 'reasonableness', and therefore the legitimate rights of the other person and social transgressions, differently from assertive individuals. Nonassertive persons judge requests to be more reasonable (Blankenberg & Heimberg, 1984; Chiauzzi & Heimberg, 1986), especially ones that are consensually evaluated to be of low or moderate legitimacy.

Conflict situations of moderate legitimacy pose a particular challenge to accurate perception. Both assertive and nonassertive persons produce more thoughts in such circumstances, but fewer objective ones (Chiauzzi & Heimberg, 1983), and report a lessened intention to assert and weakened specific self-efficacy beliefs (Chiauzzi & Heimberg, 1986). Ambiguous situations present the individual with greater difficulty in determining the legitimate rights of all involved persons, and therefore require greater conceptual skills to assess situational considerations, make appropriate reasonableness determinations, and synthesize the resulting increase in positive and negative thoughts into adaptive, accurate discriminations.

The inaccurate assessment of situations, particularly those of questionable legitimacy and hence most appropriate for assertion, may be a major factor in the decision to behave nonassertively. Since the determination of the legitimate rights of all involved participants should precede the actual assertion, this skill must be a high training priority.

The second important perceptual skill is the ability to understand the viewpoint of the other person. This skill, termed role taking (Meichenbaum et al., 1981) or metaperception (Argyle, 1981), is involved in assertion in two ways. First, it is the basis of the antecedent obligation that determines the impact of potential negative consequences to the recipient of an assertion. Second, it is the foundation upon which the asserter will include an empathic statement (a subsequent obligation) in the assertion. The superior social reaction to the empathic assertion underscores the important contribution this skill makes to effective conflict resolution. The perceptual skill, however, does not involve the empathic content, but rather, discrimination of the cues that indicate an empathic response will facilitate the interaction. The only study to address this issue does so tangentially. Fischetti et al. (1984) found heterosocially skilled and unskilled individuals differed in their ability to recognize when a vocal or gestural response from them would help the speaker continue to talk. Facility with such social cue discrimination may explain why skilled and unskilled individuals differ in the timing or placement of vocalizations and gestures, but not in the frequency (Fischetti et al., 1977; Peterson et al., 1981).

Interpersonal problem-solving skills

Social competence requires effective, systematic problem-solving skills (Meichenbaum et al., 1981; Trower, 1982). Therefore, it is not surprising that they are deficient in a variety of clinical populations (Schroeder & Rakos, 1983). The problem-solving sequence involves problem recognition, problem definition and formulation, generation of potential response alternatives, decision making (assessment of alternatives in terms of likely consequences), and solution implementation and evaluation (D'Zurilla & Nezu, 1982). Chiauzzi and Heimberg (1986) investigated these abilities as they apply to assertion, and found that non-assertive individuals exhibited deficits in problem recognition and assessment (a social perception skill) and in their ability to select an appropriate response. No deficiencies were observed in the capacity to generate response alternatives, in terms of either number or quality. Robinson and Calhoun (1984) also failed to find any differences in the number of response alternatives generated as a function of level of assertiveness. They did obtain a situational effect, however: more complex and assertive alternatives were produced in response to an angry male as compared to a pleasant male. Finally, Deluty (1981b; 1985b) found assertive, aggressive, and submissive children generated equal numbers of response alternatives to conflict situations, but the assertive children's alternatives included assertive options to a proportionately greater extent.

More research on the relationship between problem-solving skills and assertion is needed, particularly when the construct is formulated as a sequence of overt and covert responses (Heimberg & Becker, 1981; Rakos, 1979; Robinson & Calhoun, 1984). Indeed, the antecedent obligations described in Chapter 2 are involved in problem definition and assessment (determining the rights of all involved persons and whether assertion is the preferred option) and generation of response alternatives (identifying the appropriate assertive content). The problem-solving sequence may be one modality through which the components comprising conceptual complexity (Bruch et al., 1981) can be operationalized and trained. However, therapist-generated alternatives, compared to client-generated ones, induce higher outcome expectancies (Arisohn, Bruch, & Heimberg, 1988), suggesting that, particularly in the early stages of problem-solving skill training, the clinician should assume an active role in prompting and then explicitly validating the most appropriate ones.

Self-monitoring skills

Self-monitoring, a basic behavioral assessment strategy (see Chapter 6), is also a component of social competence. Responsible assertion is based on an accurate perception that the situation appropriately calls for such action. In other words, an assertion situation must be distinguished from other social ones and acquire the properties of a discriminative stimulus. Discriminative stimuli can exert their power to guide behavior without conscious awareness, as the red and green traffic lights do for the experienced driver. However, social situations with numerous potential response alternatives are unlikely to gain automatic control over a response. Indeed, in AT, the emphasis on cognitively mediated, self-regulated responding is specifically intended to ensure the selection of the alternative that most fully satisfies the idiosyncrasies and nuances of the situation. Thus, for example, the antecedent obligations of an assertive response rely heavily on cognitive behaviors (Rakos, 1979).

However, before an individual will initiate an assertive response sequence with these covert behaviors, he or she must perceive the cues that suggest the situation *might* call for an assertive reply. The discriminative stimuli that prompt the covert antecedent obligations are, like all discriminative stimuli, learned cues. In the case of assertion, as for much behavior that is self-regulated (Kanfer & Schefft, 1988), these cues are contained in the person's own behavior. An individual must learn to attend to his or her own reactions, and discriminate those responses that indicate assertion should be considered.

These self-monitored discriminative stimuli can be behaviors, emotions, and/or cognitions (Rakos & Schroeder, 1980). Behavioral cues include coping strategies that are indirect, hostile, or avoidant, such as hinting at desires, employing phoney excuses and excessive apologies, and engaging in withdrawal, aggression, passive-aggression, and/or submission. Emotional cues include frustration, resentment, shame, guilt, anger, depression, and upset. Cognitive cues involve excessive ruminations about the situation and self-statements that blame and/or deprecate the self and others, rationalize the lack of importance of the issue in contention, and are generally excessively affiliative ('negative') and/or irrational.

When these behavioral, emotional, and cognitive reactions are produced in response to a social situation, they should serve as cues to initiate the antecedent obligations of assertion. In fact, these will usually be the only stimuli available for discriminating potential assertion situations. Trainees must, therefore, learn to attend very specifically and accurately to their own public and private behavior. Accurate self-monitoring of overt and covert responses is achieved by behavioral practice that (1) concretely and clearly specifies the behavior(s) and situation(s) to be observed, (2) initially limits the number of targets for observation to two or at most three, and (3) is reinforced by the trainer, the observer, and/or the information that is acquired (Ciminero, Nelson, & Lipinski, 1977). Behavioral practice in identifying the relevant cues is often accomplished through charting responses, thoughts, and feelings in social situations or through prose-style diaries (Watson & Tharp, 1988). Sometimes, however, purely cognitive self-monitoring may be sufficient or all the trainee is willing to do (see Chapter 6).

Clinical implications and recommendations

Experienced clinicians recognize that AT must teach the requisite covert skills upon which the overt assertive response is based. There is, however, significant disagreement concerning the modality through which the cognitive skills should be taught. Some, like Lange and Jakubowski (1976) and Trower (1982), argue that the strong relationship between these skills and assertion implies that direct cognitive restructuring procedures are indicated. Others, however, emphasize straightforward behavioral techniques, such as behavior rehearsal, modeling, and reinforcement (eg Rimm & Masters, 1979). This latter strategy is consistent with Bandura's (1977b) contention that the cognitive behaviors mediating the overt responses are most efficiently modified by first changing the overt behaviors on which the covert responses are based. In other words, if a nonassertive person emits low self-efficacy and affiliative self-statements (eg 'I will never assert myself well enough' and 'He will probably be mad at me if I assert myself'), Bandura argues that the best way to strengthen autonomous alternatives is to teach, prompt, and then reinforce the competent behavior, providing an empirical basis upon which to develop the facilitative self-statements and rational beliefs (eg 'I said what I wanted to fairly well'; 'He wasn't happy, but he wasn't angry, just disappointed'). Bandura (1977b) argues this is more effective that verbal persuasion or direct cognitive skill training, a position supported by the bulk of the research with respect to behavior therapy in general (O'Leary & Wilson, 1987) as well as to AT in particular (see Chapter 7).

Nevertheless, the vast majority of AT programs include a direct cognitive restructuring component (Rich & Schroeder, 1976). The central role that covert behaviors appear to play in the assertive response chain demands some attention in the initial stages of the training sequence. It is possible, at least for some clients, that early and partial modification of maladaptive cognitions may be a necessary precursor to effective behavioral intervention – sort of like getting a 'foot in the door' so that trainees seriously consider the legitimacy and appropriateness of the assertive option.

Clinicians who decide to train alternative cognitions directly should attend to the following issues.

1. It would be a mistake to assume that even high functioning clients have acquired the basic content of the assertive response (Bruch, 1981). Clinicians should assess this carefully (see Chapter 6) and not rely on verbal self-report of trainees.

2. The overall conceptual complexity of the client will determine many of the parameters of training. Clients who manifest modest complexity will require training that targets limited goals and programmes increased redundancy and practice. Thus, progress will be slower, as intensive training in the content of an effective assertion, appropriate paralinguistic skills, and autonomous self-statements (Bruch, 1981; Bruch et al., 1981) is implemented. These clients are also likely to have greater difficulty in discriminating the subtle nuances that guide behavior in social situations, and therefore to need extra training in social perception and problem-solving skills.

3. Nonassertive clients will probably have negative perceptions of conflict assertion (see Chapter 5) and must be taught that such behavior is a legitimate response option. Expanded knowledge of assertion may improve social perception skills (cf Wojnilower & Gross, 1988), but cognitive restructuring will be the primary intervention, since many of the inhibitions involve faulty (ie nonconsensual) interpretations of the situation. The reaction to an assertion is partly a function of the reasonableness of, and the amount of sacrifice involved in compliance to, the response. It is, therefore, quite appropriate to be sensitive to the limits and constraints imposed by social and cultural norms: highly unreasonable requests, and assertions that entail great sacrifice by the recipient, should prompt careful consideration of all response alternatives, including non-assertion (antecedent obligation 3) and compromise (subsequent obligation 4). However, both 'reasonableness' and 'sacrifice' are cognitively determined to a certain extent. Since nonassertive individuals perceive requests of low or moderate legitimacy to be relatively reasonable, they believe an assertion from them will infringe on the rights of the other person. Situations of moderate legitimacy are particularly ambiguous and problematic to interpret. The modification of inappropriate reasonableness determinations is likely to be hampered by the nonassertive individual's relatively low level of conceptual complexity, which will interfere with his or her ability to entertain new social perspectives.

Therefore, the initial training situation should involve a clear and unreasonable infringement of rights, lack subtle complexities, and have clear, highly probable positive consequences and few important negative ones. In selecting and structuring such situations, the data from Rudy et al. (1982) suggest attention to the status of the other person and the degree to which social norms are violated, since these variables appear to be important determinants of the nonassertive person's construal of the conflict situation. A simple refusal interaction with a stranger (see Chapter 5) appears to meet these criteria. Though cognitive restructuring will facilitate the behavioral response (initially in role playing), the major attitude changes will occur after the behavior has been successfully performed and contingently reinforced (cf Bandura, 1977b). When an assertion produces compliance without major upset, the novice asserter will recognize that his or her original interpretation of 'reasonableness' and/or 'sacrifice' was to some extent erroneous.

4. While autonomous and self-reinforcing self-statements and rational beliefs will facilitate the emission of assertive behaviors, the training of these skills may be difficult and in some cases unsuccessful, as some clients simply resist cognitive interventions (Ellis, 1987). Nevertheless, in my clinical experience, I have found four behavioral strategies particularly useful for prompting a tentative acceptance of the legitimacy of adaptive cognitions. First, the facilitative and rational alternatives should be introduced initially as abstract, intellectual propositions, rather than within the very personal and emotional context that they must ultimately enter. For example, clients can acknowledge that human perfection in an abstract sense is impossible and therefore an unreasonable goal. Acceptance of this perspective would not be likely to alter a client's belief that he or she nevertheless should have behaved differently (ie competently) in the situation under discussion. However, the assumption of an abstract and intellectualized rational belief is a first step in the *shaping* process that hopefully will culminate in personalized rational interpretations. Since most people produce rational beliefs in response to personally insignificant situations, this initial step is often quite easily accomplished.

Second, the clinician should begin cognitive restructuring with relatively unimportant situations, perhaps even nonsocial ones, that are nevertheless potent enough to produce some emotional reaction. The formal or informal employment of a *graded stimulus hierarchy* will permit the client to apply rudimentary autonomous and rational thoughts initially to situations that have few personally meaningful consequences and hence limited demands for 'shoulds'. The personalization of rational thoughts pertinent to coping with a minor irritation, such as forgetting to buy a needed grocery item, will almost certainly be accepted by the client: very few individuals will insist they should *never* forget a small item, and most will recognize their overreaction, inappropriate demands, and self-blame. A somewhat more important situation can then be selected as the next training target (eg forgetting to tell a coworker something that may lead to minor inconvenience). Attempts to apply rational restructuring in subjectively important situations without progressing through some sort of hierarchy inevitably will meet resistance. Third, the clinician should help the client identify maladaptive thoughts that occur early in the behavior chain comprising assertiveness. For example, many concerns involve repeated instances of the same undesired behavior. Such situations involve continuing relationships that do not necessarily require an assertion 'on the spot', since there will be numerous opportunities to address the issue. In fact, in such circumstances, I advocate that a client specifically select a 'good' time for the assertion. One way to do this is for the future asserter to approach the 'offender', and indicate there is an issue that needs to be discussed at a later time. Thus, for example, a wife might tell her husband in the morning that she wishes to discuss housework responsibilities that evening. For most people, the morning assertion will be less threatening than the evening one. Specific intervention to help the wife emit facilitative cognitions related to the morning assertion will probably be more effective than similar training devoted to the evening situation. However, the morning assertion is a form of precommitment (Watson & Tharp, 1988) and the wife probably will have to follow through with the evening assertion.

In essence, this strategy is designed to orient the behavior toward the desired goal at a point where resistance will be weaker: as the intervention approaches the specific target situation, the previously conditioned outcome expectancies, whether empirically based or fantasized, will exert increased control over behavior. In the case of a nonassertive person, these predicted consequences are likely to be negative and therefore prompt avoidance behavior. However, their weakened influence at early points in the chain provides the clinician with an opportunity for successful intervention. Of course, precommitment is commonly utilized in behavioral self-management programs (Watson & Tharp, 1988). It is much easier to tell a friend in the morning that you are going to work at home that evening, so 'please do not drop by', than it is to tell the friend as he is standing before you after a long day, 'I'd love to go out, but I must work now'. The precommitment principle may be harder to apply to assertiveness situations, but in the instances in which it is appropriate, it is potentially powerful. Of course, precommitment is predicated on the client having the skills in the behavioral repertoire necessary to cope with the later assertion. (If those skills have not been acquired, this strategy is akin to leading a sheep into a wolf's den!)

The fourth strategy for facilitating the acquisition of rational beliefs and autonomous and reinforcing self-statements is what I call the 'Best Friend' technique, which is probably a conceptual derivative of Kelly's (1955) fixed-role therapy, in which the client assumes the role of a competent fictitious person. When a client interprets a meaningful situation in maladaptive ways, I ask him(her) to pretend that his(her) best friend has just experienced the same situation and related it to the client. I then ask the client what his(her) response to the best friend would be. The interaction might go as follows:

Therapist: So let me see if I understand what happened to you yesterday. You came home after a lousy day at the office and greeted your wife. She immediately began berating you for leaving your dirty clothes on the dresser and for forgetting to pick up the groceries she requested. You lost your temper, screamed back at her, and now both of you are very angry – hardly speaking to each other. Is that about right?

Client: Yes. I was really stupid to lose my temper. I should have discussed the situation calmly and tried to resolve it maturely. Now I have a big mess. (Client is emitting numerous irrational thoughts: catastrophizing, self-denigration, self-blaming [perfection], perhaps universal approval, as well as the explicit use of 'should'.)

T: Well, you certainly didn't handle the situation the way you would have liked to. But I wonder if you are being fair to yourself. You are saying you *should* have handled it differently, that you were stupid, and that now you have a terrible mess on your hands. Let me ask you this: if your best friend came to you, and related the identical incident to you, would you say the following to him: 'Yes I agree with you. You are really dumb. How could you lose your temper that way? You should be more mature by this stage of your life. Your wife has a right to be furious with you, and you'll be lucky if she ever forgives you for this. You really have made a huge mess here!' Is that what you would say to your best friend?

C (often with a little smile curling around the lips): No, of course not.

T (also smiling a little in return): Well, then what would you tell your best friend?

C: I'd probably tell him it would have been better if he had handled the situation differently, but no one is perfect. I'd tell him that it's just a fight, and it will not ruin his marriage, that the important thing is to go back to his wife and tell her that he wants to talk to her about the argument. (This client has already learned 'rational relabeling' jargon; clients at an early stage of cognitive restructuring would say essentially the same thing in ordinary language.)

T: That's about what I thought you'd tell him. Now, for me, the puzzling thing is that you would think so rationally and constructively when it's your friend's dilemma, but not when it's yours.

C: I guess you're right.

T: You know, so many people treat their best friends a great deal better than they treat themselves. You'd berate yourself for doing the very thing that you'd accept if done by your best friend. I bet you'd be much more forgiving of your best friend if he forgot about a social arrangement than if you had done the same thing.

C: I probably would be. But, somehow it seems different when it happens to me.

T: I think I know the reason why. The only difference in the situations is that when an undesired event occurs to you, as opposed to your best friend, it is more important to you. But the event is still objectively the same. So interpreting it rationally in one case, but personally in the other, really makes no sense.

C: But it's hard to think rationally when I'm upset.

T: That is so very true. But next time you get upset about something, I want you to try an experiment. Stop and pretend that the upsetting incident happened to your best friend, and he has just told you about it. Then very specifically verbalize what you would tell him. Listen to what you are saying, and see if it also applies to your situation.

The 'best friend' technique is, in many cases, a very powerful way to demonstrate the fallacy in a client's reasoning. He or she is often powerfully struck by the employment of obviously different standards for judging behavior and people. But beyond the 'insight' that is acquired, the technique also provides a concrete means through which to impugn maladaptive cognitions and practice alternative constructive ones.

5. The clinician must very directly challenge the common misperceptions of nonassertive individuals that conflict assertion is dangerously risky. I summarize in a general way the large corpus of pertinent research and demonstrate how it is at odds with existing probability expectations. I acknowledge that the client is accurate in identifying the possible negative consequences, but stress he(she) has unjustifiably elevated the probability of those outcomes. I also introduce data indicating assertion is even less risky when it is empathic or in the context of other positive behaviors. The citation of empirical research to clients has been found to be highly effective in improving treatment outcome expectations (Kazdin & Krouse, 1983), and may function similarly in improving behavioral outcome expectations. The goal is to establish a realistic perspective: appropriate assertive behavior, which the client has not yet acquired, does entail some risk, but generally much less than is assumed.

The other expectancies, self-efficacy and situational efficacy, are generally low at the beginning of training, but will increase as intervention progresses. They should be assessed regularly, but higher confidence ratings will not emerge until the client has successfully enacted the desired response in behavior rehearsal (role playing). In some cases, increased efficacy beliefs will depend on performance in the natural environment; these clients will need greater structure and encouragement from the therapist to generalize their behavior from the training to the real-life context.

6. The covert skill components described in this chapter present a formidable training goal. Self-monitoring, social perception, problem solving, rational thinking, facilitative self-instruction, realistic expectancies, and knowledge must all become a part of the client's behavioral repertoire. It nevertheless would be a mistake, in my view, to commence AT with an exclusive focus on these components of assertion. First, there is simply too much to teach systematically within a reasonable period of time. Second, acquisition will be facilitated by real-life experience and assertion experiments that raise the covert issues for discussion and analysis. Third, most clients – even those resistant to cognitive modification – desire to improve their assertive abilities. They associate AT with

overt responses, behavior rehearsal, and feedback, and will be impatient and disappointed if the intervention focuses solely on cognitive processes, however germane they are in a theoretical and practical sense. AT clients want *action*! Therefore, even clinicians who utilize direct cognitive restructuring methods do so by integrating them within an active, experiential, and behavioral context.

Chapter five

The social validity of conflict assertion

The appropriateness of an assertion depends on the skill with which it is emitted and on the extent to which it adheres to the social and cultural norms of the environment in which it is produced. However, even a response meeting these standards may fail to produce the desired short-term outcome or result in the long-term growth of the relationship. These four criteria – technical proficiency, cultural appropriateness, short-term outcome, and overall net cost–benefit – were discussed in Chapter 2 as important evaluative measurements of the assertive response. In this chapter, I will examine the impact of the social and cultural context on these yardsticks by which assertion is measured. First, I will review the general social reaction to assertion, and then the influence of so-called 'moderator' variables on that reaction. Gender, race, level of assertiveness, response class, and situational influences have all been investigated to some extent. In addition, I will discuss cultural values and norms, despite a virtual absence of research on their relationship to the perception of assertion.

The social reaction to conflict assertion

General findings

This literature was reviewed in Chapter 3. Standard assertion is perceived to be more competent but less likeable than nonassertion. It is viewed as equally potent to, but more desirable than, aggression. Empathic assertion is judged to be more likeable than standard assertion and aggression, but of equal competency. It is perceived to be almost as desirable and likeable as nonassertion, but significantly more powerful.

Situational variables as well as response topography influence the social reaction to assertion: the evaluation is less positive when the assertion requires a significant sacrifice on the part of the recipient or is in response to a relatively reasonable request (Epstein, 1980; McCampbell & Ruback, 1985). Adults judge assertion to be most appropriate when directed toward strangers rather than toward friends or individuals with whom one is intimate (Linehan & Seifert,

1983), but undergraduates perceive it to be the preferred response option for resolving conflicts with friends and relatives (Heisler & McCormack, 1982).

The methodology utilized in the social perception research has been the focus of some criticism. A major concern has been that the subjects in the vast majority of these studies were university undergraduates who might be expected to have unique characteristics that limit the generalizability of the data they produce. However, their reactions prove to be fairly similar to adult nonstudent populations (Crawford, 1988), businesspeople (Mullinix & Galassi, 1981; Solomon et al., 1982), and general medical or psychiatric patients (Keane, Wedding, & Kelly, 1983), so this source of concern appears unwarranted.

Another methodological issue centers on the manner in which the different behavioral styles are presented to subjects. Typically, subjects are exposed to 4-8 vignettes depicting standard assertive, empathic assertive, aggressive, and/or nonassertive responses to 'common' conflict situations. The response class is frequently refusals of unreasonable requests, but sometimes behavior change requests or the expression of unpopular opinions. The vignettes are presented via typescript, audiotape, or videotape. These modes of presentation differ in their ability to include paralinguistic and nonverbal components of the response, and hence in their sense of 'reality'. Nevertheless, this variable does not seem to affect the social perception of conflict assertion (Rakos & Hrop, 1983), though increasing information may improve judgements of commendatory assertion and unassertive behavior (Cook & St. Lawrence, 1990). After exposure to the conflict vignette, subjects respond in role play and/or rate the asserter on paper-and-pencil measures designed to tap perceptions of appropriateness, competence, and likeability.

These studies demonstrate that conflict assertion, either empathic or standard, is judged by observers or role players to be socially appropriate and competent, though not always exceptionally likeable. However, the person whose reaction is most important is the real-life recipient, not an observer or role player. Though observers perceive assertion to be appropriate and desirable as an abstract concept, the natural social environment may react quite differently.

Gormally (1982) tested this possibility directly. Subjects who heard an audiotape of standard assertive and passive interactions involving a behavior change request rated the assertive style as more admirable, appropriate, and enjoyable to deal with. Subjects who were actively involved with an experimental confederate in an identical situation that they believed to be real *preferred* the passive responses, judging them to be more admirable, appropriate, and enjoyable. As Gormally noted, 'studies using objective raters have served to validate the commonly held notion that assertive behaviors will be viewed as more appropriate than nonassertive behaviors. What they fail to demonstrate is whether persons actually involved with an assertive person will respond more positively than to nonassertiveness' (p. 224). Thus assertion may be valued as an abstract concept but not as a concrete one. The implications of this finding will be discussed later in this chapter.

A third criticism concerns the nature of the majority of situations used to assess the reaction. Conflicts are typically impersonal, trivial, and therefore basically inconsequential (Gervasio & Crawford, 1989). Though situational importance is a variable that should be systematically investigated, the existing studies that did employ more complex conflicts obtained data consistent with the bulk of the research (e.g. Heisler & McCormack, 1982; Hrop & Rakos, 1985; Rakos & Hrop, 1983).

A fourth criticism concerns the degree to which conflict assertion may be perceived more positively if recipients experience it *and* nonconflict behaviors, as will frequently occur in the natural environment. In other words, all interactions except brief ones involving strangers provide a broader behavioral context in which to evaluate the asserter's response. Furthermore, the cumulative effects of observing a series of isolated conflict assertions may exacerbate this problem: subjects who witnessed four vignettes depicting standard assertion reacted more negatively than those who observed only two such situations (Wildman, 1986).

This methodological concern appears to be justified. Individuals who emit both standard assertion and commendatory assertions (such as requests or offers for help, receiving thanks, giving compliments) are viewed as more likeable and competent than persons who exhibit standard assertion alone (Levin & Gross, 1984; 1987; St. Lawrence et al., 1985a; Wildman, 1986). Preadolescent boys who observe both standard and commendatory assertion judge assertion more positively than nonassertion (Wojnilower & Gross, 1984). Conversational comments unrelated to the assertion also improve the perception of standard assertion (Lowe & Storm, 1986; Wildman, 1986), as does task-oriented interaction (Delamater & McNamara, 1985).

However, the moderating influence of commendatory assertions may be constrained by at least two factors. First, each of these studies used undergraduates as subjects, except for Wojnilower and Gross's. Although undergraduates may be similar to nonstudent adults in their perceptions of conflict assertion, their reactions to commendatory assertion may be different. For example, friendships and intimate relationships, which by their nature should include exposure to positive assertion, are seen by students as appropriate contexts for assertion (Heisler & McCormack, 1982; Lewis & Gallois, 1984), but less so by adults (Linehan & Siefert, 1983). Second, the reaction to an assertion within friendship also depends on the response class: the acceptability of refusals is comparable to behavior change requests but less than the expression of differing opinions (Lewis & Gallois, 1984).

The research, therefore, suggests the social reaction to conflict assertion can be enhanced, first, by the inclusion of empathic components, particularly in continuing relationships, and second, through the performance of 'contextual' behaviors, such as commendatory assertions and conversational comments. However, the nature (ie response class) of the assertion, particularly in the context of an ongoing relationship, may also influence the evaluation. Friends, for example, may be expected to assert their own opinions, even when the views are unpopular, but also to comply with requests, even those that are unreasonable, and to tolerate offensive behavior.

Gender

The rise of AT coincided with the stabilization of 'sexism' and feminism as legitimate social phenomena. As feminism matured in the seventies and eighties, it encompassed a greater diversity of viewpoints and strategies for achieving social equality. Despite (or perhaps because of) the masculine values inherent in conflict assertion, many feminist therapists embraced AT as a rational, scientific approach to combating the sexism to which women are subjected.

At the time the AT movement was just beginning, assertiveness was not considered by lay people or clinicians to be a characteristic of a 'healthy female' (Broverman, Broverman, Clarkson, Rosenkrantz, & Vogel, 1970), probably because such behavior is incongruous with the female sex-role stereotype (Broverman, Vogel, Broverman, Clarkson, & Rosenkrantz, 1972; Lao, Up-church, Corwin, & Grossnickle, 1975; Lohr & Nix, 1982). Masculine sex-role characteristics are attributed to asserters in conflict situations (Hess, Bridge-water, Bornstein, & Sweeney, 1980), masculinity and conflict assertion skills are significantly correlated (Nix, Lohr, & Mosesso, 1984), and 'androgynous' and 'masculine' women are more assertive than 'feminine' women (Rodriguez, Nietzel, & Berzins, 1980). Standard assertion is judged to be 'masculine', empathic assertion is viewed as 'masculine' or 'androgynous', and conversation is perceived as 'feminine' by *both* male and female observers (Wildman & Clementz, 1986). Thus, it is not surprising that females in the 1970s reported being less assertive than males (Hollandsworth & Wall, 1977), or that sexism was invoked to explain such differences. For example, Jakubowski-Spector (1973) suggested women inhibited assertive responding to avoid negative reactions associated with inappropriate normative behavior. In fact, the constraints of sex-role stereotypes may suppress assertion by females: Rodriguez et al. (1980) found instructions to increase assertive behaviors in role plays were effective with 'feminine' women. And early social validity research confirmed that males, but not females, indeed reacted negatively to assertion by females (Romano & Bellack, 1980).

Women, therefore, were quickly identified as appropriate consumers of the AT technology. Numerous self-help books were written specifically for women (eg Baer, 1976; Bloom, Coburn, & Pearlman, 1975; Butler, 1976; Osborn & Harris, 1975; Phelps & Austin, 1975, 1987; Taubman, 1976), and women, more than men, reported exposing themselves to such information (Schroeder & Rakos, 1978). Controlled studies found AT effective in enhancing the social skill and self-esteem of nonassertive women (eg Wolfe & Fodor, 1977; see Chapter 8). However, writers cautioned that since assertion was not a normative behavior for females, the possibility existed that female asserters will be subjected to a different, and more negative, social reaction than would male asserters (Kahn, 1981; MacDonald, 1982).

This apparently reasonable concern generated over 25 studies assessing the effect of sex of asserter and/or sex of judge on the evaluation of conflict assertion. Surprisingly, about half find no differences as a function of gender (eg Epstein, 1980; Gormally, 1982; Hull & Schroeder, 1979; Keane, St. Lawrence, Himadi, Graves, & Kelly, 1983; Kern, 1982a; Levin & Gross, 1987; Mullinix & Galassi, 1981; Solomon et al., 1982; St. Lawrence et al., 1985b; Woolfolk & Dever, 1979), while the other half find some differences (eg Crawford, 1988; Kelly et al., 1980; Lewis & Gallois, 1984; St. Lawrence et al., 1985a; Wildman & Clementz, 1986; Zollo et al., 1985). However, when gender effects are obtained, they are often part of complex interactions that are either difficult to interpret or limited in utility. Sometimes, the differences are in the unexpected direction (eg Schroeder et al., [1983] found that male asserters were devalued by *both* male and female judges!)

The existence of these contradictory and confusing findings led Schroeder et al. (1983) to suggest that gender effects on the social reaction to conflict assertion may reside in the sex-role orientation of the judge, rather than in his or her sex. Unfortunately, here too, the data are less than illuminating. Kern et al. (1985) found standard and empathic assertion by females was devalued by men *and* women who held traditional, conservative attitudes toward women's role in society, but not by those adhering to more liberal perspectives. However, Levin and Gross (1987) and St. Lawrence et al. (1985b) both failed to find any effect for sex-role orientation, and Wilson and Gallois (1985) found only a very weak one. These three studies reported that reactions to assertive behavior were primarily a function of response topography, though Wilson and Gallois also obtained a strong gender effect.

It is puzzling and counterintuitive that sex-role orientation is unrelated to the social reaction to conflict assertion by women. One possible explanation may be that assertion, and social competence in general, are based on models of behavior that stress active, constructive change (Wine, 1981). Every model has inherent values, and an examination of the ones germane to assertion proves enlightening.

[T]he metaphorical image that best captures the essence of the competence model is that of 'man against his environment' (masculine referents intended)...the rugged individualist actively shaping his environment – in the case of social competence, other people – to his own needs and purposes, a masculinized image closely associated with the growth of industrialized, technological society. The values conveyed by such a metaphor are antithetical, for example, to the Eastern philosophical or North American native peoples' values of living in harmony and communion with one's environment, and to the related female subcultural values of sensitivity to and concern for people and responsiveness to the needs of others.

(Wine, 1981, pp. 25–26).

Perhaps here is the reason why sex-role orientation does not predict response to assertion but attitude toward women does. While conflict assertion is not a stereotypically feminine behavior and is emitted relatively infrequently by females, the values it embodies are entirely consistent with a major portion of the ideology of most males, and, in particular, of 'masculine' males. Hence, such males may appreciate assertion by a female to an extent equal to that of an 'androgynous' male. A conservative male, however, is disturbed by the *change* in roles inherent in such behavior and reacts accordingly.[1]

This hypothesis could be experimentally tested. If the reaction by males to assertion by females is a function of masculine sex-role typing, then we would predict that masculine males would react to empathic assertions by women, which embody elements of the feminine sex role (compromise, empathy, understanding) within a proactive ideology, more positively than to the standard assertion that lacks these components. Unfortunately, no research has directly addressed this question. Alternatively, if the male reaction to females is in reality a concern with changed behavior, that is, change itself, then it should not matter whether the assertive style is standard or empathic, since either represents a divergence from the norm of passivity. This is exactly what Kern et al. (1985) found.

The clarification of the contradictory findings in regard to gender effects will require a great deal of additional research. At present, however, the data do not support a generalized and pervasive assumption that conflict assertion involves greater risks for women than for men (eg Gervasio & Crawford, 1989; Kahn, 1981; MacDonald, 1982). Nevertheless, a cautious advocacy of the assertive option to women is indicated for at least three reasons. First, the numerous gender-related interactions reported in the literature suggest there are *situations* in which the particulars will be arranged so that assertion is riskier for women than for men. Unfortunately, the research has been unable to identify any situational parameters consistently associated with increased risk, perhaps due to the focus on gender of observer and/or asserter that ignores other potentially influential factors. For example, only one study assessed the impact of assertion as a function of the *recipient's* gender. Zollo et al. (1985) found empathic assertion, but not standard assertion, was expected to produce more immediate positive consequences when the recipient was female, suggesting both men and women expect females to be more responsive than males to an assertion that includes elements of the presumed female sex-role stereotype.

The extent to which situational sex-typing variables influence the social reaction has also been poorly studied, although women appear to appreciate their importance. In the Zollo et al. study, female judges expected empathic assertion to produce greater immediate positive consequences as well as greater long-term negative consequences than did males. The authors interpret this to be congruent with female sex-role behaviors. Women may be more comfortable with the assertive style that includes typically feminine components, but they are also sensitive to societal restrictions that inhibit the expression of behavior still basically incongruent with sex roles. This concern is further illuminated by Linehan and Seifert (1983), who conducted the only study that systematically eliminated any sex-role involvement in the conflict situations. Under these circumstances, assertion by women was perceived slightly more positively than assertion by men, perhaps because, as the authors suggest, the expression of any emotion is more appropriate for females than for males. These researchers also found that assertion in such situations was more favorably evaluated when it occurred between opposite sexed individuals than when it occurred between participants of the same sex. It is clear, therefore, that each circumstance must be carefully assessed, and women must learn to attend to the relevant situational cues (eg gender of recipient, degree of sex typing) so that the risk is accurately predicted. Then the woman can make her decision whether to assert herself or whether to select another response option.

Another situational variable that requires further investigation is the effect of the social role in which the recipient operates, which may interact with, or perhaps determine, the attitude toward the role of women in society. Several studies suggest that in situations where pragmatism is important and general competence expected, and hence where one might expect an increased likelihood that nontraditional attitudes toward women will be manifested, conflict assertion by females is judged no differently than similar behavior by males. Adult businesspeople, both males and females, judge behavior change requests in work situations without regard to the gender of the asserter (Mullinix & Galassi, 1981). Corporate managers of both sexes value standard and empathic assertion by females as well as by males over self-effacing remarks in work-related conflicts (Solomon et al., 1982), and mock jurors respond equally well to assertive lawyer behavior by males and females and equally poorly to passive styles by both sexes (Sigal, Braden-Maguire, Hayden, & Mosley, 1985). Professional and situational role demands and stereotypes in these three studies appeared to be more potent than sex-role stereotypes in influencing the perception of assertive behavior. On the other hand, in situations where emotional considerations are primary, assertive females may be viewed more negatively. For example, an assertive female police officer who confronts a citizen on the street is judged more critically than a similarly acting assertive male officer (Sterling & Owen, 1982).

Therefore, the social context of the assertion may help predict the social response toward a women asserter. Professional role demands may select individuals with certain attitudes (eg modern corporate managers may be more 'liberal' than many other occupational subgroups) and some situational role demands (such as provided by the courtroom) may temporarily produce more 'liberal' attitudes in people who might ordinarily be quite conservative. Other situations (eg interacting with police officers) may exacerbate 'conservative' attitudes. However, it is quite possible that the effect of a situational role is limited to the relevant social context. The male corporate executive may be receptive to assertive behavior from his female subordinate but not from his wife, and the male reacting negatively to an assertive female police officer may be much more open to assertion from a female coworker. Thus, a fertile area for investigation is the effect of 'rational' and 'emotional' social contexts on the attitude toward women in general, and on the perception of their assertive behavior in particular.

A second reason for exercising caution when working with females is that the research has shown only that uninvolved raters evidence no consistent differences in their reactions to male and female asserters. Gormally's (1982) study found no sex differences when the judge was actively involved with a male versus a female confederate, but all of his subjects were female; therefore, the comparison of most interest, that of males actively involved with females versus males, was not possible. The results from studies such as Solomon et al. (1982) and Mullinix and Galassi (1981), which assessed the perceptions of corporate managers and businesspeople respectively, may have tapped only into their abstract value system, but not into their actual behavioral response. 'Most women coming for assertiveness training are in a work situation where they feel subservient to males. Such similar complaints are voiced by secretaries, managers in industry, and physicians that, if one were to listen to the content of tape sessions, it would be hard to distinguish a female secretary confronting her boss from a doctor confronting the ward administrator' (Fodor, 1980, p. 534). It is unlikely that these women are all excessively sensitive to, and inaccurate in their assessment of, the reactions of men. Thus, actual involvement may functionally alter a social context from a seemingly 'rational' one to an 'emotional' one.

Finally, the nature of the phenomenon under study may produce data having limited validity. Gergen (1973) observed that all contemporary social research is really an exercise in *social history* since the findings of the research impact, either immediately or after a delay, on the original phenomenon and change it so that the obtained data are no longer valid, ie they are now historical. Assertiveness provides a powerful example of this process, particularly with respect to women. There is no question that women were early avid consumers of popularized and professional AT materials and groups (Fodor, 1980; Schroeder & Rakos, 1978). The pervasive societal advocacy of assertiveness very likely modified their attitudes about assertion (MacDonald, 1982), but it also may have directly or indirectly affected the attitudes of males. Can we have confidence that results published in 1984, which means that the data were gathered in 1982 or earlier, are still meaningful today? There is no way to answer this except by further research, but, unfortunately, experimental replications in psychology are usually considered to be duplications rather than checks on the social historical process and are therefore rarely published (or even attempted).

Response classes

Several social validation studies have assessed the reaction to conflict assertion as a function of response class. Schroeder and his colleagues (Hull & Schroeder, 1979; Schroeder et al., 1983) determined that the expression of unpopular opinions was judged to require the greatest amount of assertiveness, with behavior change requests next, and refusals the least. Behavior change requests were perceived to be most socially acceptable, while the expression of unpopular opinions were seen to be least appropriate. Lewis and Gallois (1984), on the other hand, obtained essentially contradictory data. Behavior change requests consisting of the conflict statement only were judged to be most assertive and least socially desirable, while expressing unpopular opinions was perceived most favorably. In addition, as discussed earlier, they found the evaluation of assertive response classes was affected by situational variables. The verbalization of an unpopular opinion by a friend was more acceptable than such behavior by a stranger or a refusal by a friend. Refusals by strangers were judged more positively than refusals by friends or the conflict statement component of a behavior change request by strangers. Finally, Crawford (1988) found no differences in reactions to the expression of negative feelings, positive self-presentation, and the setting of limits. However, it appears that these three response categories were in reality all variations of behavior change requests, rather than representatives of distinct response classes.

The contradictory data obtained by Schroeder et al. (1983) and Lewis and Gallois (1984) may be due to methodological differences employed in the studies. For example, the differential reaction to behavior change requests may be partly a function of different response topographies (conflict statement plus specific request for change in Schroeder et al. versus conflict statement only in Lewis and Gallois). Thus, the specific request may add little to the potency of the response (cf Mullinix & Galassi, 1981), but be important (contrary to intuition, see Chapter 3) in improving its social perception. Additionally, level of acquaintance was specified quite clearly by Lewis and Gallois (either a 'good friend' or someone 'whom you don't know') while degree of familiarity was only implied by Schroeder et al. (a 'friend', a 'committee member'). It is also possible that cultural differences between the Australian subjects used by Lewis and Gallois and the American subjects in the Schroeder et al. study contribute to the divergent findings. Clearly, a great deal of additional research is necessary before we can specify with confidence the manner in which response class affects the perception of conflict assertion.

Level of assertiveness

AT assumes that socially competent persons prefer assertion as a conflict resolution strategy. Indeed, Frisch and Froberg (1987) found exactly this: individuals highly skilled in handling aggressive criticism judged assertive behaviors to be more likeable, effective, and appropriate than aggressive and nonassertive responses for dealing with hostile feedback. However, since non-assertive individuals expect assertion to result in more negative consequences (see Chapter 4), it would not be surprising if their perception of such behavior was less favorable. The bulk of the research tends to confirm this.

Kern (1982a; Kern et al., 1985) found nonassertive individuals rate compliant behavior in refusal situations as more likeable, desirable, and competent than either standard or empathic assertions, while assertive people produced opposite judgements. These results were partially replicated by Zollo et al. (1985), who found that empathic refusal, but not standard assertion or nonassertion, is judged more likeable by assertive individuals compared to nonassertive ones.

Behavior change requests are evaluated similarly. Assertive individuals tend to rate their appropriateness higher than passivity, while nonassertive people judge the behavioral styles similarly (Gormally, 1982). Behavior change requests are devalued by aggressive and submissive children, but not by assertive ones (Deluty, 1983). Thus, in research assessing reactions to the portrayal of only one response class, the data suggest that assertive and nonassertive individuals differ in their evaluation of assertion, including empathic assertion.

However, the negative perception by nonassertive people may be minimized by observing the asserter portray more than one response class. Alden and Cappe (1981) examined refusal, behavior change request, and expressing unpopular opinion situations and obtained similar evaluations of assertive and nonassertive behavioral styles from subjects high and low in assertiveness. Levin and Gross (1984), assessing reactions to refusals and commendatory (positive) assertions, also failed to find differing reactions as a function of subject level of asser-tiveness. They suggest that the greater social acceptability of the positive assertions may have moderated the nonassertive subjects' reactions. This possibility is supported by the results of Wojnilower and Gross (1984), who found nonassertive elementary school boys preferred nonassertion to standard and commendatory assertion, yet nevertheless rated the assertive response style positively. Thus, it is conceivable the unfavorable perception of assertion by nonassertive individuals is moderated by broader experience, even when the exposure involves additional conflict behavior. These persons, with their relatively low level of conceptual complexity, may require the concrete portrayal of response classes and situations that include those with increased social acceptability (cf Lewis & Gallois, 1984).

Overall, these data suggest that nonassertive trainees may enter AT with reservations, despite a desire to improve their social competency. Though they can clearly distinguish between assertion, aggression, and nonassertion (Alden & Safran, 1981; Bordewick & Bornstein, 1980), their perceptions of the legitimacy of assertion in the abstract are likely to be compromised by a relatively low level of conceptual complexity, inaccurate evaluations of the extent of rights infringe-ment, and adherence to numerous irrational beliefs (see Chapter 4). Furthermore, assertion to a nonassertive recipient may entail increased risk of a negative reaction. Thus, early performance success, cognitive restructuring, and attention to the antecedent and subsequent responsibilities will have to be priorities in training. In addition, the moderating influence of exposure to multiple response classes offers another intervention opportunity. These clinical issues are explored in greater depth at the end of this chapter.

Race

The American democratic values – individual activism, pragmatism, rationality, and relativism – that characterize both the modern *Weltanshauung* and AT are in reality the values of white, middle-class Americans (perhaps more accurately, of white, middle-class, American *males*, cf Wine, 1981). Thus, the specific behaviors and attitudes fostered by this ideology will not be consistent with the cultural assumptions of all societies or ethnic groups (Furnham, 1979; Rakos, 1986). Black writers in America, in particular, have questioned the appropriateness of applying general behavioral techniques without a thorough understanding of the African-American cultural perspectives (Mitchell-Jackson, 1982). A holistic view of the nature of humans, a group ethos that stresses kinship and shared responsibility, a concept of time that is elastic and associated with significant events, and a respect for elderly people that places them in revered positions are all central values that diverge from the mainstream of white America (Mitchell-Jackson, 1982).

Furthermore, the interpersonal behavior of blacks has been shaped by the discrimination that stained, and continues to stain, the bright portrayal of American society (Cheek, 1976; Minor, 1978). Blacks historically were prevented from expressing honest feelings and engaging in social discourse as equals to whites. The suppression of assertive expression of wants and desires ultimately resulted in their manifestation through aggressive and passive-aggressive behaviors, to which whites responded with apprehension and stereotyping. Blacks reacted to the entire situation with anxiety and low self-esteem that necessitated the development of alternative coping behaviors, including distinct communication and linguistic patterns (Caldwell-Colbert & Jenkins, 1982; Cheek, 1976; Minor, 1978). The discomfort of whites with black expressiveness, the African cultural value system, and the nonnormative coping behaviors all contribute to objections that question the appropriateness of AT for blacks.

These concerns are reinforced by findings demonstrating that the assessment, content, and perception of assertion are influenced by racial variables. Most fundamentally, the objective assessment of assertion may frequently be compromised by ingrained prejudice, as both trained (Turner, Beidel, Hersen, & Bellack, 1984) and untrained (Lethermon, Williamson, Moody, Granberry, Lemanek, & Bodiford, 1984; Lethermon, Williamson, Moody, & Wozniak, 1986) judges exhibit systematic racial bias in their ratings.

In studies that presumably eliminated such bias, differences in content are evident from childhood on: white youngsters perform more competently in role plays than their black counterparts (Williamson & McKenzie, 1988). As acculturation proceeds, the distinctions become more subtle: black and white undergraduates demonstrate equivalent knowledge of standard assertion (Lineberger & Calhoun, 1983) and perform similarly in role-play situations (Lineberger & Beezley, 1980), but blacks employ black English vernacular extensively when writing out assertive responses, and interracial assertions by both blacks and whites are more aggressive than intraracial ones (Lineberger & Calhoun, 1983). Ness, Donnan, and Jenkins (1983) obtained somewhat similar data: black psychiatric inpatients evidenced greater assertiveness to whites than to blacks, except for the critical criterion component of noncompliance to a clearly unreasonable request.

The impact of race on the perception of assertion has been the subject of a modest amount of investigation. Early interracial research on interpersonal behavior found that race did affect the evaluation of the actor (Feldman & Donohoe, 1978; Katz, Cohen, & Glass, 1975), suggesting that assertive behavior would be similarly influenced. In fact, the early assertion studies failed to demonstrate such differences. Kelly et al. (1982) found whites perceived standard assertion by blacks or whites similarly in terms of likeability and skilfullness. Furthermore, blacks evaluated standard assertion involving two blacks as more competent but less likeable than nonassertion (Keane et al., 1983), a finding consistent with the general social perception research. However, other research has found black judges, compared to whites, perceive black asserters to be more aggressive (Garrison & Jenkins, 1986) and judge assertive behavior by black women to be more aggressive and less assertive than identical behavior by white women (Henry & Piercy, 1984). Henry and Piercy also found that race of judge interacted with sex of judge and response class (refusal, behavior change request, expressing unpopular opinions) in affecting the evaluation of assertion. Dura and Beck (1986) found blacks rated standard assertive and aggressive behaviors of a white 'psychiatric patient' higher, and empathic-assertive behaviors lower, than did whites. Thus, the more recent research suggests there are some differences in the way blacks and whites react to conflict assertion. Blacks perceive assertive behavior by blacks as aggressive, or at least as more aggressive than similar behavior by whites. They seem to value aggressive and standard assertive behaviors more, and empathic assertions less, than do whites.

The major problem in this body of research is that the racial variables have not been completely investigated. In these studies, there are three participants: the observer (judge), the asserter, and the recipient of the assertion. It is likely that the social reaction to assertion is a function of the racial composition of all the participants. Hrop and Rakos (1985) investigated this possibility in a study comparing the reactions of black and white observers to standard and empathic assertion emitted in white–white, white–black, black–white, and black–black male dyads. White observers were influenced by race of asserter but not by race of recipient. They felt more intimidated by either style of assertion by a black than by a white. Furthermore, they evaluated the empathic assertion more positively than the standard assertion when the asserter was white but not when he was black. These data suggest that the elaboration components are appropriate training goals for whites asserting to whites, but that for blacks asserting *to* whites, training might deemphasize those elements in favor of awareness of, and additional strategies for decreasing, whites' discomfort with black assertiveness.

Blacks also had relatively negative perceptions of both types of assertion when performed by a white as compared to by a black. White asserters were judged to be more aggressive than black asserters emitting identical verbalizations and similar paralinguistic and nonverbal responses. In addition, blacks were also influenced by the race of both asserter and recipient. Blacks perceived empathic assertion by whites to blacks as less positive than standard assertion in the same context (consistent with Dura and Beck, 1986), but reversed their judgement for black-to-black interactions, in which the elaborative verbalizations significantly improved the perception of assertion. Therefore, different training goals for assertion *to* blacks may be indicated: standard assertion for white trainees and empathic assertion for black trainees.

Hrop and Rakos's (1985) results suggest that training goals should consider racial variables. Empathic assertions are preferred in *intraracial* conflicts while standard assertions are more desirable in *interracial* interactions. These data further underscore the discomfort each race experiences with assertion by a member of the other race, and are consistent with – indeed, may explain – the observation that interracial assertions involve more aggression than intraracial ones (Lineberger & Calhoun, 1983). The historically strained and distrustful relationship between blacks and whites appears to imbue the empathic assertion and its elaborative components with manipulative qualities. The direct, straightforward standard assertion minimizes the interaction and therefore the possibility of manipulation. It places the issue clearly and unambiguously in focus. However, it is more likely to be perceived as aggressive and in some circumstances indeed may be aggressive (Rakos, 1986).

Obviously, training recommendations based on race must be made cautiously. Gender variables have been incompletely investigated: blacks judge assertion by black females as more aggressive than assertion by white females (Henry & Piercy, 1984), but reverse their judgement for males (Hrop & Rakos, 1985). All of the studies used undergraduate students as subjects, except the Dura and Beck (1986) one, which utilized psychiatric hospital aides as well as undergraduates. Hrop and Rakos (1985) stress that, though their results were obtained from part-time, inner-city community college blacks in the US, there is no way to know whether they are representative of other black populations. Finally, all studies assessed 'objective' rather than in vivo reactions.

Subcultural values

Investigators have not yet directly assessed the reaction to assertion as a function of membership in a minority ethnic or religious group. There are simply no data to inform us whether Hispanics or born-again Christians, for example, perceive and react to assertion in a distinct manner. Nevertheless, familiarity with general cultural norms and values of such groups can help to predict the limitations imposed on expression in conflict situations. Many subcultures are more communitarian than American society, placing increased emphasis on the family and the group. Deference, subservience, and respect increase in importance when individualistic concerns are secondary, and may be prescribed by the age, status, or sex of the participants. Though cultural generalizations are hazardous and subject to numerous qualifications, the communitarian ethos can be found in diverse groups, including Koreans (Hong & Cooker, 1984), Japanese (Yanagida, 1979), Native American Indians (Mitchell-Jackson, 1982), Mexican-Americans (Grodner, 1977), Puerto Ricans (Comas-Diaz & Duncan, 1985) and African-Americans (Mitchell-Jackson, 1982). Sensitivity to normative values in the subculture as well as in the dominant culture increases in importance as greater numbers of minority individuals seek to improve their assertive skills (Hwang, 1977) or are identified as appropriate consumers of such intervention (Comas-Diaz & Duncan, 1985; Landau & Paulson, 1977). Specifically, trainers must prepare minority clients for assertion in their own subculture *and* in the mainstream culture, and, in the absence of data, predict the likely reaction from fundamental cultural guidelines.

Authority figures, and parents in particular, provide an excellent example of this deductive process. Respect for elders and parents is a particularly strong value in African-American (Mitchell-Jackson, 1982), Asian and Asian-American (Fukuyama & Greenfield, 1983; Hong & Cooker, 1984; Sue, Ino, & Sue, 1983), Puerto Rican (Comas-Diaz & Duncan, 1985), Mexican-American (Grodner, 1977; Mitchell-Jackson, 1982), and Native American (Mitchell-Jackson, 1982) cultures, to the extent that even empathic assertions to such persons are likely to be judged as highly inappropriate. This contrasts sharply with dominant American values, which encourage open expression to, and negotiated conflict resolution with, parents (eg Fodor, 1980). Even though the research has not been conducted, it is safe to assume that many, if not most, traditional parental figures in the minority cultures named above would react quite negatively to an assertion from an adult child. Therefore, such target goals are discouraged in a culturally adapted program for Native Americans (LaFramboise & Rowe, 1983) and considerably modified and softened in one for Puerto Ricans (Comas-Diaz & Duncan, 1985). Nevertheless, these same Native Americans and Puerto Ricans will be far more impactful in the dominant environment if they can confidently and effectively assert themselves to bosses, lawyers, etc, who are members of the majority culture. This is so even though Puerto Rican values, for example, stress deference toward another on the basis of social status (Comas-Diaz & Duncan, 1985). Puerto Ricans (and other minority clients) need to learn two sets of behavioral skills as well as the cognitive ability to discriminate the situations that are appropriate for each set (cf Wood & Mallinckrodt, 1990).

Cultural norms are also likely to affect gender variables. Puerto Rican (Comas-Diaz & Duncan, 1985) and Mexican-American (Grodner, 1977) value systems both emphasize the concept of 'machismo', or male dominance. The sexism that is inherent in mainstream (white) America is of a fundamentally different nature: more subtle and implicit, less role definitional, and ultimately more flexible and pragmatic. To be effective with Hispanic women, therefore, AT programs must teach assertive strategies that are consistent with this relatively intransigent cultural norm.[2] Thus, Comas-Diaz and Duncan (1985) encouraged Puerto Rican women to express their feelings openly and honestly with their husbands and communicate to them the difficulty they (the wives) will experience if conflicts and decisions are not discussed. Landau and Paulson (1977) emphasized positive assertions to husbands and refusals to others as initial assertion experiments. Later, the focus shifted to making requests of husbands, but refusals to them were still deemphasized. Both training programs were loosely evaluated, so definitive conclusions cannot be reached, but the participants seemed generally pleased with the results.

Asian cultures also expect females to exhibit deferential behavior. Thus, it is not surprising that Asian-American males are as assertive as Caucasian American males (Sue, Ino, & Sue, 1983) and that Korean males, but not females, benefited from a standard 'North American' AT program (Hong & Cooker, 1984). Modifications in AT that attended to the cultural conditioning of a Japanese-American woman, however, proved successful (Yanagida, 1979).

The reaction of religious individuals to assertion is likely to raise similar issues. The Eastern religions teach philosophies that are antithetical to the values promoted by AT (Wine, 1981). Korean society, for example, has been strongly influenced by Confucianism, resulting in a culture that 'has been structured with well-defined role expectations, patriarchal family structures, with authority and community flowing vertically from parent to child. "Filial piety" or respect for authority, parents, and ancestors, protecting the family name, and sacrificing personal wishes for the family or community have been seen as time-honored customs' (Hong & Cooker, 1984, p. 354). Judaism and Islam, especially in their orthodox sects, also prescribe strict behavioral norms and expectations, some of which are inconsistent with an assertive belief system, particularly in regard to the role of women. Christianity, which teaches self-sacrifice and the acceptance and forgiveness of transgressions and infringements, may also be seen by adherents as incompatible with a forthright assertive style. The dominance of Christianity in North America, where the major impetus for AT originated, led numerous writers to suggest interpretations of scripture that reconcile the values of devout Christianity with those of AT (Augsberger, 1979; Emmons & Richardson, 1981; Jones, 1984; Moy, 1980; Russell, 1983; Sanders & Malony, 1982). While the religious trainee may be able to adopt a new philosophical perspective incorporating both theistic and secular values, assertion by such a person within the religious subculture may entail significant short- and long-term risks. That is, religious recipients of a nonnormative assertion may react quite negatively, and such a possibility must be carefully considered during the process of AT.

Clinical implications and recommendations

The research reviewed in this chapter would seem to provide the clinician and the client with confidence that technically proficient and culturally consistent assertion will be perceived as appropriate social behavior. The data clearly contain some contradictions and ambiguities, yet the overall trend is clear, and clinicians should strive to convey this general sense to trainees as part of the cognitive restructuring process. This being said, numerous cautions also appear warranted and must be communicated to the trainee. At their most basic level, these caveats all concern the ability of the trainee to utilize sophisticated social perception and discrimination skills, since there seem to be particular situations in which assertion is indeed relatively risky in terms of immediate outcome and long-term cost–benefit considerations. A comprehensive functional analysis, which clarifies the potential risks as well as the anticipated benefits of an intervention should it prove to be successful, will identify such situations (see Chapter 6). The following points summarize the circumstances that require careful scrutiny.

1. The research strongly indicates that standard assertion is perceived as socially competent but somewhat unlikeable. However, in some contexts, such as business, it is appreciated and clearly preferred to self-effacing remarks (Solomon et al., 1982). The empathic assertion is even more positively evaluated: it is judged to be as competent as standard assertion and aggression, but more likeable, and as significantly more socially competent than nonassertion, yet of equivalent likeability. However, the social acceptability of conflict assertion may be compromised by the frequent display of such behavior (cf Wildman, 1986), suggesting reinforcement will not be maximized by the indiscriminate expression of feelings or desires.

Furthermore, the appreciation of these conflict skills may be of an intellectual nature, and the actual reception of an assertion may produce a distinctly less favorable judgement (Gormally, 1982). Thus, the risk of assertion may be somewhat greater than suggested by the bulk of the literature. On the other hand, aggression in the natural environment is even riskier. Christoff and Edelstein (1981) found the superior evaluation of assertion to be even greater in in vivo interactions than when objectively viewed. Similarly, McCampbell and Ruback (1985) found standard assertion with and without an apology to be equally effective to, and more likeable than, aggression in an in vivo situation. However, consistent with Gormally's results, both assertive variants were perceived to be somewhat unlikeable and unkind.

The clinical caveat is obvious here. Though we can be reasonably confident that an observer will agree assertion is more desirable than, and superior to, aggression and passivity, that individual may react very differently when the actual assertion is delivered to him or her. Unfortunately, none of the in vivo studies included an assessment of empathic assertion, either with strangers or, more importantly, with familiar persons. We simply do not know if involved recipients would judge the empathic assertion as acceptable, or at least as more acceptable than a standard assertion. Similarly, we do not know if broader experience with the asserter (conversation, compliments, etc) would moderate an involved recipient's perception of assertion, as it does with objective judges.

Nevertheless, based on the data that are available, thorough training in elaborative verbalizations, conversational and small-talk comments, and commendatory skills should precede assertion experiments in high-risk situations or important continuing relationships. Some writers (Delamater & McNamara, 1986; St. Lawrence et al., 1985a) even recommend that training begin with commendatory assertions so that the attractiveness of the asserter is enhanced. However, this strategy, which is also advocated as a way to facilitate group process (Lange & Jakubowski, 1976; Rimm & Masters, 1979), may have drawbacks with clients who are impatient to begin the process of conflict skill acquisition. Also, the selection of commendatory assertions as the initial target behaviors will be somewhat less compatible with the early cognitive re-structuring efforts, which typically focus on personal rights, the distinction between assertion and aggression, and social perception skills. It may be pre-ferable, therefore, to commence with simple conflict skills and then train com-mendatory abilities at the point when the client is ready to initiate real-life conflict resolution experiments.

2. The extent to which assertion by females is accepted as appropriate behavior by both males and females is a question that cannot be answered in a straightforward or definitive manner. Contradictory research findings, metho-dological inadequacies, insufficiently researched variables, and the social historical nature of the phenomenon all contribute to the obfuscation. Never-theless, the types of work and marital problems women present in AT suggest that stereotyped sex-role expectations are important factors, although, interestingly, the perception of assertion is not directly influenced by the sex-role orientation of the observer (and hence, presumably, the recipient) as it is commonly measured (Bem, 1974). Kern et al.'s (1985) results suggest that the focus should be on liberal versus conservative attitudes toward women's role in society, ie while many 'masculine' men will accept assertion from a women it seems likely that a 'conservative' man may not. Thus, clinicians should sensitize their female clients to the likely possibility that stereotypical sex typing will affect the reaction to assertion in subtle or indirect ways.

Specific clinical recommendations beyond this are only advanced tentatively, since the data simply do not coalesce into an unambiguous pattern. At the very least, the data do not directly contradict any of the following observations and suggestions.

a) Behaving assertively has historically been considered to be a masculine trait. Although we now know that assertive skills are learned behaviors and not traits, the association with masculinity remains (eg Hess et al., 1980; Nix et al., 1984; Rodriguez et al., 1980). Therefore, assertion will likely be viewed in some circumstances as at least somewhat unfeminine and therefore inappropriate and/or unacceptable.

b) Attitudes toward women and personal expression have changed in the past two decades to the point where many studies find assertion by males and females to be similarly valued. However, these studies generally tap intellectualized judgements of hypothetical situations rather than emotional reactions borne out of actual experience. Though self-report is often a good predictor of actual behavior (Bandura, 1977a), we frequently believe we know more about ourselves than we actually do (Nisbett & Wilson, 1977). Women trainees therefore must learn to acquire a comprehensive data base by which to judge the potential recipient of an assertion. Since previous behavior is the best predictor of behavior in a similar situation (Mischel, 1968), women must become astute observers of individuals in their natural environments. Additionally, they should try to acquire reliable information about others whose reactions have not been witnessed personally. Finally, a verbalization by another person that indicates he or she is receptive to a conflict assertion ideally would never be the sole basis for a decision, especially since a high percentage of these are at best indirect invitations to assert. A 'conservative' boss or husband is more likely to announce that he is 'open' to complaints or problems than to specifically request a direct confrontation when a conflict arises.

c) Since Kern et al.'s (1985) data stand alone, neither confirmed nor dis-confirmed, they must be interpreted cautiously. But caution here means pro-tection of females asserters. A woman should first determine whether the situation contains elements of sex-role stereotyping in it. If it does not, then the reaction to an assertion by her may be slightly more positive than if the assertion were emitted by a male, particularly when the assertion is directed toward a male (Linehan & Seifert, 1983). A situation characterized by sex-role typing requires careful evaluation of the potential recipient's attitude toward the role of women in society. If it is conservative, women must factor in the increased likelihood of a negative reaction to an assertion. A liberal perspective, on the other hand, increases the probability that an assertion will prompt a constructive response.

d) Female clients should be taught the skills necessary to analyze the professional and situational role demands experienced by the recipient. Such demands may be more influential than sex-role stereotypes and may select out, or moderate the reaction of, 'conservative' males and females. For example, situations in which pragmatism and rationality predominate may be much more receptive to female assertion than those guided by emotionality.

e) The generally superior evaluation of the empathic assertion suggests it will be a productive strategy for decreasing potential adverse reactions by male recipients. However, recall that Zollo et al. (1985) found that elaborative verbalizations enhanced the evaluation of assertion only when directed toward females. It is possible that when they are emitted to a male, such responses are judged to be manipulative. Females should engage in extensive behavior rehearsal to assure that the elaborative components are performed in a manner that is nonmanipulative and precludes misinterpretation, yet decreases the probability of a negative reaction.

f) As noted in Chapter 3, smiles by a woman emitting assertive behavior are judged negatively by females but do not appear to affect males (Romano & Bellack, 1980). This is probably because females are sex-role stereotyped as 'nurturant', and smiles are associated with such behavior. It would be tempting to suggest that women include smiles as 'precautionary softeners' when asserting to men, especially since smiles or their absence do not appear to be an important component of appropriate conflict assertion (Kolotkin et al., 1984). Such pragmatism has its risks, however. Smiles and other subtle nonverbal cues must be employed carefully, since there is great potential for misunderstanding, especially in heterosexual dyads. Many feminist trainers will be philosophically opposed to such a strategy, since it partially maintains the status quo rather than fundamentally altering power relationships. However, sometimes pragmatism will achieve much more than idealism, and this might be an efficacious means by which a woman can acquire important reinforcers. A 'precautionary softener', like a laxative, may facilitate movement. I do not advocate this strategy, but based on the research, only point out that it may 'work'.

I wrote this discussion of 'smiles' with some trepidation, lest I be branded sexist or worse. I was relieved, therefore, to find nonsexist female assertion trainers (Goldstein-Fodor & Epstein, 1983) who argued, on the basis of pragmatism, that traditional effective 'feminine wiles' (placating, stroking, smiling) be considered for inclusion in the overall assertion strategy for dealing with males. However, as discussed above, Zollo et al.'s (1985) data suggest that elaborative behaviors be used cautiously.

g) Women clearly must consider sex-role expectations when clarifying their goals and balancing the risks of assertion (Gambrill & Richey, 1986). However, since all assertion involves risk, women must determine how much, if any, *additional* risk an assertion from them, as opposed to a male, will entail. The recipient of an assertion by a woman may indeed mutter under his breath that she is a 'castrating bitch' and penalize her. But how does this same person react when his authority or freedom is challenged by a male? If he calls the man a 'goddamn bastard' and penalizes him, then he is simply a risky person for anyone to approach in an assertive manner.

h) While work situations are the stimuli that lead most women to seek AT, problems with mothers and with males in social and intimate relationships are also common (Fodor, 1980). These situations clearly call for an empathic assertion (Heisler & McCormack, 1982) and the utilization of all four of the subsequent obligations (explaining, expressing understanding, protecting rights, and seeking a mutually acceptable compromise). In Lewis and Gallois's (1984) study, female friends weakened the friendship more when they requested a behavior change than when they refused a request or expressed a different opinion. To the extent that these data can be generalized to other continuing relationships, they may provide some guidelines. It may be easier for women to begin to improve a close relationship by dealing with refusal situations (eg declining an offer of help) and opinion conflicts (eg expressing preferences) before introducing behavior change requests (eg telephone before dropping in to visit).

3. The social response to the different response classes, despite its ambiguities, has implications for the selection of the initial behaviors targeted for training. First, the common strategy of selecting refusals to strangers as the initial conflict target seems to be empirically indicated. Obviously, training must be individualized in accord with the expressed priorities, values, and behavioral competencies and deficits of the trainees: not all trainees will be unable to refuse an unreasonable request from a stranger, most do not rank such situations as important goals of training (Cooley, 1979; Lefevre & West, 1984), and in certain circumstances, refusals may be less culturally acceptable than other response classes (Janda & Rimm, 1977). Nevertheless, the refusal-to-stranger conflict minimizes contextual complexities, demands modest amounts of assertive behaviors, and is judged to be relatively socially acceptable. Thus, it provides an excellent medium through which AT can employ sound behavioral principles, including the assessment and *shaping* of the basic verbal and nonverbal components of conflict assertion. Empathic verbalizations, refinements in paralinguistic and nonverbal behaviors, flexibility, persistence, compromise, commendatory assertion, etc, can all be added as training progresses.

A second recommendation is also suggested by the data. It appears that expressing different or unpopular opinions to strangers is likely to be received negatively, and should be introduced in the training program after the client has already experienced success with other response classes and less risky situations. The ability to handle such interactions competently will be an important priority for many trainees (Cooley, 1979; Lefevre & West, 1984), but clinicians should resist pressure to focus on it until a basic assertive response repertoire, including positive as well as conflict skills, is developed and successfully performed.

4. The cognitive distortions that characterize the nonassertive individual's unfavorable interpretation of assertion necessitate that training begin with clearly unreasonable, simple situations (see Chapter 4). The refusal-to-stranger scenario usually meets these criteria, providing an additional reason to select it as the initial training goal: when complexities are minimized, the acquisition of a basic behavioral repertoire and accurate social perception skills (realistic assessments of situational cues relating to reasonableness, sacrifice, probable consequences, etc.,) will be facilitated. However, even in the early stages of training, the clinician should introduce and model other positive and negative response classes

to broaden the perspective of the trainee and thereby possibly moderate negative perceptions.

The novice asserter must also learn to discern the *recipient's* level of assertiveness, since the relatively negative evaluation of assertion by nonassertive individuals increases the likelihood of an adverse reaction by such persons. Sensitivity to this variable will improve a trainee's ability to anticipate likely consequences and select a desired response. Furthermore, one component of appropriate assertion according to the rights and obligations definition (Rakos, 1979) is to be cognizant of the potential negative consequences a recipient might experience (antecedent obligation 3). For nonassertive individuals, these are likely to include internally produced ones, such as self-statements of self-denigration, guilt, lack of worth, rejection, etc., as well as the more 'objective' ones, such as inconvenience. In addition, subsequent obligation 3 requires that the asserter protect the recipient's rights if he or she cannot, including the right to be treated in a respectful and dignified manner. If the nonassertive recipient cannot accept an appropriate assertion, and perceive the respect and dignity that is inherent in it, then it is the responsibility of the asserter to attempt to clarify the intent and ramifications of the assertion.

It is also possible that assertive individuals will react negatively to assertions directed at them, despite an abstract appreciation of the response style. Although there are no data addressing this possibility, my best guess is that truly assertive individuals can and will accept an appropriate assertion though they may have understandable and appropriately moderate negative reactions (eg disappointment). I would expect that it will be the aggressive person who will have greater difficulty accepting the assertion, since aggressive people, by definition, utilize social power to achieve their goals without regard for the other person. Unfortunately, as with assertive persons, no study has assessed the reaction of aggressive individuals to assertion. Nevertheless, we can predict that the denial of reinforcement may very well elicit a distinctly negative reaction (eg hostility, humiliation). Thus, the trainee must learn to distinguish assertive from aggressive individuals, since the social response may very well depend on that categorization. Assertion to aggressive individuals may still be appropriate and desirable, but the asserter must be aware of the possibility of increased risks so that a considered decision can be made between the available response alternatives.

5. Racial, ethnic, and cultural variables will also affect the social perception of conflict assertion, though research here is fairly scanty. As discussed earlier, Hrop and Rakos (1985) found important differences in the way whites and blacks in America perceive assertion. Both blacks and whites responded more positively to standard assertion in interracial conflicts, but preferred the empathic assertion when the interaction was between two individuals of their respective race. Thus, the training goals that emerge (empathic assertion for single-race dyads, standard assertion *and* strategies to reduce discomfort in mixed-race dyads) underscore the

importance of the *bicultural competence* model introduced by writers concerned with the impact of American Indian (LaFramboise & Rowe, 1983) and Asian-American (Fukuyama & Greenfield, 1983) cultural variables on AT.

Bicultural competency is established when a minority individual acquires two sets of responses, one that is adaptive in the subcultural environment and one that effectively influences the dominant white society. Interestingly, however, the data argue that the concept is more broadly applicable, in that many clients from majority cultures should be prepared for bi- or multicultural competency in a manner similar to members of minority groups. In America, where there is a significant black population in many areas of the country, whites need to know what interactive style is most appreciated by blacks if reinforcements by all parties are to be maximized. Majority clients, in other words, should acquire cultural competency for each subculture with which they frequently interact. Clearly, there are definite limits on the number of cultural competencies any particular individual can acquire. If, however, a Caucasian foreman in a plant or manager in an office has large numbers of black and Hispanic workers, it is obvious that her functioning will be increasingly effective as cultural competency with both groups is attained. The advantages of such skills will become increasingly evident as the citizens of the earth continue to expand their mobility, and people in all industrialized countries find their interactions with members of minority groups are more extensive and intensive.

For members of minority groups, bicultural competence is more than an efficiency strategy; it is probably one of survival. All cultural minorities, whether recent immigrants or long-standing ethnic communities, to some extent both resist *and* acquiesce to the pressures of assimilation (Kraut, 1982). Devout religious individuals are also subjected to conflicting pressures to a certain degree. The effective mediation of the struggle will result in the maximization of reinforcers in the minority and dominant communities only if the minority individual can, first, discriminate between situations in the two cultures, and, second, emit a broad range of behaviors including those that are only appropriate in one or the other context.

Clearly, the failure to consider relevant cultural, ethnic, and religious variables will result in a training program that is inappropriate to some extent – perhaps to a significant extent. I have discussed the minority groups that are present in the US because of my greater familiarity with them and because, as with the preponderance of the assertion research, most of the investigation has involved these groups. However, all industrialized nations have similar demographic considerations stemming from mistreatment of native peoples, historical and current immigration, and/or racial and ethnic discrimination. If AT is to be consistent with its democratic and egalitarian ideals of personal empowerment, it must respect, acknowledge, and conform to minority value systems while still maintaining a focus on effective functioning in the dominant system. Assertiveness trainers working with minority groups, or with clients who have extensive contact with minority groups, are ethically bound to thoroughly familiarize themselves with the relevant cultural variables and, moreover, to respect them, when training behavior intended for culturally defined situations[3] (American Psychological Association, 1990).

6. The data, despite all the ambiguities, suggest that the key element in producing a negative reaction to a conflict assertion is the asserter's failure to meet a stereotyped or normative expectation. Women who assert to a conservative man, friends who refuse requests, strangers who voice unpopular opinions, females who assert in machismo subcultures, and anyone who asserts in a close relationship without empathy are behaving incongruently with the expectations governing sex roles, friendships, casual relationships, Hispanic culture, and polite conversation, respectively. Similarly, interracial interactions, which are more generally characterized by distrust and social distance, meet expectations best when the simple and unambiguous standard assertion is employed to resolve conflict. This general guideline also suggests that the initiation of assertive behavior in a continuing relationship by a previously nonassertive individual will almost certainly engender a negative reaction, since the other person has learned to expect passivity and reinforcement.

Trainees, therefore, must learn to assess the degree to which assertion is a normative behavior in the specific intimate, social, cultural, or occupational context. If it is not, and assertion represents a distinct deviation from expectations, there is a greater likelihood that the social reaction will be more intense. The newly assertive person must be cognitively and behaviorally prepared to meet the challenge presented by these circumstances.

Assertiveness Training

ssment of assertion

The assessment of assertion provides an excellent example of the strengths and weaknesses of behavioral assessment in general. The hallmark of this approach is adherence to a model of behavior that emphasizes situation-specific skill competencies and deficits in lieu of generalized psychopathology and undesirable traits (O'Leary & Wilson, 1987; Wine, 1981). Behavior sampling in the three response modalities (verbal/cognitive, motoric, physiological/affective) is utilized to assess current functioning and its controlling variables. The tripartite assessment of 'anxiety', for example, involves the evaluation of (a) self-reports of subjective discomfort and anxiety-provoking cognitions; (b) anxious behaviors (eg avoidance, speech dysfluencies, immobility, compulsions); and (c) central nervous system indices (eg muscle tension) and autonomic responses of the sympathetic nervous system (eg increased pulse, blood pressure, skin conductance) (Lang, 1968). The fact that the three response modalities correlate poorly (Hodgson & Rachman, 1974; Lang, 1968, 1977; Rachman & Hodgson, 1974) increases the importance of conducting a broad and comprehensive assessment.

Unfortunately, situational and tripartite response specificities present formidable impediments to the evaluation of the adequacy of behavioral assessment strategies. The situations selected for sampling must correspond very closely to the naturalistic problem circumstances, since minimal generalization of responding is expected (Kazdin, 1979a). However, even when that is achieved, tripartite response specificity makes it extremely difficult to generate conclusive validity data. For example, the validation of a self-report scale by behavioral observation is hazardous since we would expect the correlation to be modest at best. Validation by another measure of the same response modality will produce a higher correlation, but much of that is due to the similarity in the assessment procedures ('method variance', Neale & Liebert, 1986).

Despite these inherent difficulties, some writers contend that behavioral assessments must meet the traditional psychometric criteria of reliability and validity against which all other diagnostic methods are measured (Cone, 1977). Researchers, as we shall see, responded to this plea, but the utility of the data they have generated is unclear. For example, given that assertiveness is situation specific, of what clinical value is it to know that a particular self-report instrument provides highly reliable summed (total) scores? Much more important to the behavioral assessor is the specific item-by-item test–retest reliability since the object of interest is assertive behavior in a particular situation rather than overall level of assertiveness. Nelson's (1983; Nelson, Hay, & Hay, 1977) argument that 'the use of psychometric criteria to select behavioral assessment techniques is generally antithetical to behavioral theory' (1983, p. 199), while a minority perspective, is one with which I have substantial agreement.

A comprehensive appreciation of behavioral assessment requires, as Nelson (1983) asserts, familiarity with conceptual issues as well as with the particular strategies and instruments. This chapter will first discuss the heuristic framework provided by the functional analysis, which identifies the types of data that need to be considered. Next, the major assessment techniques will be reviewed, and finally, clinical implications and recommendations will be offered.

The functional analysis

Behaviorists generally assume all responses, whether adaptive or maladaptive, serve to help the individual cope with his or her environment; it is in this sense that behavior is *functional*. The accurate determination of the relationship between behavior and environment necessitates that four elements be thoroughly investigated: the environmental context (including, but not limited to, the specific situation), the current organismic state of the person, the nature and character-istics of the targeted behavior, and the changes in the environment that the behavior produces (Kanfer & Phillips, 1970). The investigation of these elements constitutes the functional analysis.

The primary purpose of the functional analysis is the identification of the most appropriate treatment strategy (Nelson, 1983; Nelson & Hayes, 1979), rather than, for example, classification and formal diagnosis. To achieve this goal, the clinician must rearrange client-generated data such that the functional charac-teristics are salient (Kanfer & Schefft, 1988). The most comprehensive or-ganizational framework was developed by Kanfer and Saslow (1969); their guidelines do not describe a sequential process of information gathering, but, rather, the seven categories of data that must be assembled over the course of assessment:

1. Presenting problem analysis: specification and operationalization of the complaint into behavioral *excesses* and *deficits*; determination of quantitative characteristics of the problem behavior (frequency, intensity, duration); identification of behavioral *assets*. The behaviors that are assessed include overt (motoric) and covert (cognitive, physiological, affective) ones.

2. Situational analysis: identification of the (a) situations for which be-havioral competency is lacking and (b) consequences of the current maladaptive behavior. These discriminative and reinforcing stimuli are the variables that

maintain the behavior, though they are unlikely to be the ones that originally caused it (Kanfer, 1985). The positive and negative consequences of providing or refraining from offering intervention, information necessary for informed consent (see Chapter 9) as well as for treatment planning, are also evaluated.

3. Motivational analysis: clarification of the goals, values, and positive and negative reinforcers that are generally important to the client; estimation of the degree to which desired goals and reinforcers are actually attained.

4. Developmental analysis: assessment of the relevant biological, social, and behavioral changes that the client has previously experienced. This historical inquiry is limited to those areas that are posited to be involved in the presenting problem; it is not a complete social history of the client.

5. Self-regulation analysis: clarification of self-regulation skills and capacity for implementing systematic self-management strategies; assessment of variables (eg people, settings) that facilitate or inhibit the client's ability to engage in self-controlled behavior.

6. Social relationship analysis: identification of the extent and nature of social relationships and, in particular, of 'significant others'; determination of the impact of these relationships on the target problem and the degree to which they represent resources that can be utilized in the treatment regimen.

7. Broad environmental analysis: assessment of the sociocultural and physical environment to identify norms, expectations, and values, and their congruence with the client's current behavior and therapeutic goals. This analysis may identify resources that can promote therapeutic gain, but more typically will clarify the limitations within which therapeutic goals and techniques must be constrained.

Emerging research indicates that an eighth category is also essential: contextual analysis. First, 'behaviors exchanged by two persons can be influenced by events that do not include both of them' (Dumas, 1989, p. 235). For example, Dumas cites a variety of research demonstrating that past or current social support is associated with enhanced interpersonal effectiveness. Thus, two individuals with comparable behavioral competencies may react differently to similar conflict situations depending on the extent of social support they have experienced. Second, the matching law proposes that individuals behave so as to maximize reinforcement, and that the introduction of additional reinforcement will be most potent when the environment contains relatively few reinforcers (cf McDowell, 1982). Thus, while it is obvious that new reinforcers produced by assertion to a husband may have little impact if the response forfeits other reinforcers, the effect of new reinforcement will also be a function of the reinforcers the husband provides to his wife for other behavior *and* the total amount of reinforcement she acquires. Thus, assertion-related reinforcement will strengthen the response maximally when other concurrent reinforcement is limited, and may have little effect if accompanied by increases in other reinforcers. Third, seemingly unrelated responses may covary (Kazdin, 1982a) and be part of complex behavioral patterns controlled by powerful stimuli beyond the immediate situation (Dumas, 1989). Unfortunately, response covariation in regard to assertion has not yet been empirically addressed. However, when assertion fails to increase when it theoretically 'should', the reason may reside in this phenomenon.

A simplified example of a functional analysis is presented below. The numbers in parentheses place the information within the appropriate category described above.

Mary, age 30, enters therapy with the complaint of depression and marital dissatisfaction. She is attractive, bright, articulate, and college educated [1], and is a full-time homemaker. While she verbalizes contentment with this role, careful interviewing uncovers disappointment that she has not developed a career like most of her female friends and neighbors [3]. Mary minimizes the boredom she experiences at home [3], yet emphasizes the fact that she enjoys competitive, social, challenging situations [3]. Mary describes her husband as a good man and provider [8], but insecure and prone to verbal aggression when challenged [6]; she has learned that life is more pleasant, at least superficially, when she permits him to be in control [2]. His insecurity is manifested in a desire that Mary stay home with the children, thus reducing perceived competition from other men and breadwinners [2, 6]. Due to this, Mary has not discussed in the past several years the subject of her working [1, 4]. Instead of confronting her husband with her frustrations [1], she has begun to drink more than she desires [1].

Mary married her husband partly because she was pregnant [4], partly because at that time she was overweight and felt unattractive [4], and partly because she was infatuated with his apparent charm [4]. They never really discussed family role expectations, and her realization that she feels unfulfilled came slowly over the years through interaction with the working wives in her neighbourhood [4].

Mary is a competent woman who runs her household efficiently [5]. Her excessive use of alcohol is particularly disturbing since it is such a deviation from her usual self-restraint [5]. Mary lives in an upper-middle-class urban neighborhood of single homes, where the prevailing value system is a modern secular one (liberal, materialist) [7]. She has several close friends, but rarely visits them due to their work schedules [6, 8]. Consequently, she has few opportunities to socialize [3].

Mary's unhappiness is partly a function of her inability to assert herself to her husband, ie request behavior changes and verbalize different opinions [1]. She believes he will be furious with her and perhaps leave her if she firmly discusses her desire to belatedly pursue a career [1]. While these concerns seem exaggerated, he probably will have a difficult time accepting such assertions from his wife [2]. Therefore, if Mary asserts herself to him, the marital relationship will experience additional strain for at least some period of time [2]. Mary also fails to initiate social behavior with her working friends or to seek alternate outlets for socialization [1]. This absence of an important reinforcer [3] contributes to her low rate of adaptive behavior [2] and consequent feelings of 'depression' [2].

Several important characteristics of the functional analysis are highlighted in the above example. First, few clients initiate therapy with a clearly defined, circumscribed problem (Kanfer & Grimm, 1977). Instead, they usually verbalize global, nonspecific complaints, such as some combination of depression, tension, anxiety, meaninglessness, apathy, and anger. The behavioral assessment must initially convert the global to the specific (Mischel, 1986). This involves the identification of the concrete overt and covert behaviors involved in the production of the subjective distress. In Mary's case, excessive homemaker behaviors, avoidance responses with her husband, and maladaptive interpretation of certain events are readily specified. Next, the potential excessive and deficient *target behaviors* of intervention must be identified along with the conditions that maintain or control them. Mary's frustration, then, is a consequence of at least three target behaviors. Two overt skill deficits are present: Mary fails to emit socializing behaviors and assertive responses (behavior change requests and verbalizations of unpopular or differing opinions in conflict situations with her husband). She also manifests a covert behavioral excess of irrational thoughts and/or affiliative ('negative') self-statements, ie that her husband will reject and even leave her if she asserts. At this point in the assessment process, it is unclear whether the assertive response deficit is a function of inadequate knowledge, interfering excessive arousal and/or maladaptive cognitions, or actual behavioral incompetency (cf Bruch, 1981). It is possible that two or even three of the reasons are operating in Mary's case.

A second characteristic of the functional analysis is that it is an ongoing and evolving enterprise, one that never really ends throughout the course of intervention (Kanfer, 1985; O'Leary & Wilson, 1987). Target behaviors and controlling variables are constantly refined in light of new data. The initial targets are selected over other potential ones for a variety of reasons. Sometimes, the central behavior will be chosen because other problems are related to it. This is the direction in which Mary's case is moving. The excessive alcohol con-sumption was not identified as a target behavior since it was presumed to be primarily a function of the consequences produced by passivity. The ongoing assessment may eventually prove this interpretation wrong: Mary may in fact drink excessively for other reasons or may now be psychologically dependent on alcohol. On the other hand, there will be times when the central problem will not be the initial target. Occasionally, tangential but disruptive and/or pressing issues must be addressed prior to initiating a focus on the central problem. If Mary's excessive drinking is determined to impact negatively on her marriage and/or to be a maintaining cause of her limited social interaction, it may require remediation before the implementation of AT. Finally, some clients need to experience success early in therapy, and the clinician may choose to focus on a somewhat peripheral problem because it is changeable, instead of the clearly relevant, but difficult one (cf Kanfer, 1985). If this was indicated in Mary's case, the clinician might select assertion with her children or even a conceptually different problem such as, say, improved city driving skills.

The limited research suggests there is great variability among behavioral clinicians in the selection of initial target behaviors (Hay, Hay, Angle, & Nelson, 1979; Wilson & Evans, 1983). This is probably a consequence of the partially nonempirical clinical judgement process. Rather than attempting to find the theoretically 'correct' target behavior, Kanfer (1985) suggests that *utility* is the most important guideline for behavior therapists in the selection process: a target behavior must be identified that will help the client progress toward achieving his or her goals. In Mary's example, if her goals can be construed as greater independence, then improved driving skills and controlled drinking, as well as assertive and social behaviors, are all legitimate target behaviors.

A third hallmark of the behavioral assessment is the concentration on current functioning rather than on detailed historical analysis. Furthermore, the emphasis is on what the person *does* in a situation, not on what the person hypothetically *has* (eg psychopathology, unresolved infantile conflicts, excessive maladaptive traits) (O'Leary & Wilson, 1987). Original historical causes and hypothetical constructs are weak controlling variables compared to current environmental and organismic factors. Fourth, behavioral assessment seeks to identify strengths of the client as well as weaknesses. The focus on behavioral problems and assets, instead of hypothetical, generalized, internal 'pathological' states, provides a more balanced perspective on the client's functioning, and avoids exaggerating the extent of dysfunction, as is commonly done by traditional assessment (Langer & Abelson, 1974; Little & Schneidman, 1959).

Finally, the behavioral assessment conceptualizes the problem in a manner that permits ongoing evaluation of treatment effectiveness. The failure of behavior to change in desired directions suggests that the functional analysis was incomplete or erroneous. Thus, rather than ascribing failure to client 'resistance', the conditions that maintain resistant behavior are investigated (O'Leary & Wilson, 1987; see Chapter 9). Even after AT has progressed to what appears to be a sufficient degree, Mary may procrastinate in confronting her husband for any number of reasons that are as yet unidentified. The appropriate clinical response to ineffective therapy is to intensify assessment activities rather than to blame the client for being resistive. Perhaps the target behaviors are beyond her perceived capability, and further shaping is necessary. It is possible that a less demanding situation should be chosen at this point, and the graded stimulus hierarchy must be modified. Or, to generate one other possibility, Mary may be somewhat ambivalent about several of the changes she will experience if her attempts at assertion are successful. She may wonder how the children will react if she takes a job, how competent she will be in the unfamiliar work environment, or whether she will have time and energy for work, friends, and family. These doubts may then become target behaviors themselves, requiring operationalization and specification of their relationship to environmental events.

Sophisticated therapeutic relationship skills are required to conduct the ongoing behavioral assessment. The process involves astute attentional, questioning, paraphrasing, reflective, and empathic abilities (Ivey, 1988). The client must trust the therapist and feel that he or she is understood; without these elements, the clinician will be unable to acquire the information necessary to conceptualise systematically and ultimately redefine the client's difficulties (Kanfer & Schefft, 1988; O'Leary & Wilson, 1987).

Since the accuracy of the functional analysis depends on the quality of the data, assessment usually attempts to sample responses from as many of the three modalities as possible. The next section reviews the wide variety of measures specifically used to evaluate assertiveness deficits.

Behavioral assessment of assertion

Self-report strategies

The clinical interview

Behavior therapists, like most clinicians, employ the interview with virtually every client, though sometimes it must be with a parent or guardian (Swan & MacDonald, 1978). The interview serves the dual function of rapport building and assessment (Kanfer & Schefft, 1988; O'Leary & Wilson, 1987). Therefore, it must be flexible and supportive yet at times quite focused and directive. The goal of operationalizing global complaints and then identifying their particular controlling variables necessitates that the behavioral clinician ask more specific questions and investigate response sequences and individual cognitions more thoroughly than would a traditional clinician (Arkowitz, 1981). The interview also provides informal observational data on verbal and nonverbal social skills (Bellack, 1979a), such as social perception skills ('You look tired today, Doc'), social appropriateness (or lack thereof: 'are those insurance forms on your desk?'), ability to engage in small talk and humor, and avoidance behaviors (long digressions into nontargeted, nonproductive topic areas). Of course, the situational specificity of the interview must be recognized (Bellack, 1979a): these behavioral samples may not be representative of generalized responses.

Several structured interview frameworks are available to facilitate data acquisition. Arkowitz (1981) produced an interview guide that comprehensively investigates current and historical aspects of social functioning as well as other potentially related issues (see Figure 6.1). Galassi and Galassi (1977a) developed a grid to help structure the interview. The column headings are designated by the response classes of assertion, while the rows represent the client's significant others. The clinician inquires as to the specific behaviors required in each cell of the matrix (eg content of behavior change requests with spouse) and the perceived difficulty of enacting the response (eg on a scale of 1-100). Becker, Heimberg, and Bellack (1987) report that this procedure usually identifies problematic behaviors, situations, or combinations that permit the construction of relevant role plays for further assessment.

Figure 6.1 Interview guide for social inadequacy

I. *Physical description of the patient.* This includes dress and general appearance as well as any noteworthy physical features.

II. *Behavioral observation of the patient during the interview.* This includes a brief description of verbal and nonverbal behaviors, including how the patient relates to the interviewer.

III. *Patient's description of presenting problems and treatment goals in his or her own words.*

IV. *Operational definitions of problems and goals.* Operationalizing constructs is one of the hallmarks of behavioral interviewing. Terms reflecting traits, dispositions, and broad constructs are translated into behavioral referents.

V. *Major problems other than social inadequacy.* While there seems to be no consistent association between social inadequacy and other specific forms of psychopathology, it is often the case that socially inadequate patients do have diverse other problems. These may include depression, schizophrenia, alcoholism, sexual deviation, and sexual dysfunction.

VI. *Effects of the social dysfunction on the person's life functioning.* The major question here is the extent to which the social inadequacy may limit the patient in significant areas of their lives. For example, the social dysfunction may limit the patient in certain job opportunities. In my experience, severely inadequate patients seek out jobs which require little or no social contact (eg night watchman) in order to avoid dealing with difficult social situations.

VII. *Assessment of social functioning in specific areas.*
  A. Same-sex relationships
  B. Opposite-sex relationships
  C. Casual relationships
  D. Intimate relationships
  E. Ability to express positive feelings toward others
  F. Assertiveness and standing up for one's rights
  G. Interactions with 'authority' figures
  H. Interactions with family members
  I. Group situations
  J. Public speaking situations
  K. Initiating social interactions
  L. Maintaining and developing social interactions

VIII. *Estimates of social skill, social anxiety, and self-evaluations in each of the above areas.*

IX *Cognitions relating to social functioning.* This includes an emphasis on self-talk, irrational assumptions, unrealistic standards, and expectations regarding social encounters.

X. *Sexual knowledge, experiences, and fears.* Many socially inadequate patients have underlying fears relating to sexual failure, homosexual fears, or sexual ignorance. Interview assessment of the area of sexuality is often very significant for social inadequacy.

XI. *Current living situation with particular reference to potential social contacts.*

XII *Description of a typical day with particular reference to social contacts.*

XIII *Current employment and educational situation.*

XIV. *Family situation.* Is the patient married, divorced, or single? Is the patient living with family members?

XV. *Interests and pleasurable leisure activities.* These can often form the basis for a program of increasing social contacts.

XVI. *Obstacles to effective social functioning.* These may be any of a number of factors including an isolated living situation, aspects of physical appearance, or health restrictions which may limit social contact.

XVII. *History*
  A. Description of period of onset of social difficulties (or note if the difficulties have been chronic)
  B. Education
  C. Work history
  D. Family background
  E. Health background
  F. Description of period of 'best' social functioning
  G. Description of period of 'worst' social functioning

Reprinted with permission from: Arkowitz, H. (1981). Assessment of social skills. In M. Hersen & A. S. Bellack (Eds.) *Behavioral assessment* (2nd ed.) (pp. 296-327). Elmsford, NY: Pergamon.

The data generated by the interview can be categorized into five areas: behavioral deficits, behavioral excesses, inappropriate environmental stimulus control, inappropriate self-generated stimulus control, and problematic reinforcement contingencies (Kanfer & Grimm, 1977). These categories conform to the identification of target behaviors and their controlling conditions (steps 1 and 2) in the functional analysis of Kanfer and Saslow (1969). The resulting organization provides working hypotheses to be investigated by further assessment.

The limitations of the interview are currently unclear: despite its wide use and intuitive usefulness, it has not been thoroughly investigated (Haynes & Jensen, 1979). Interviewers do lose client data in their processing of the material (Hay et al., 1979) and arrive at varying conceptualizations of the target problems (Hay et al., 1979; Wilson & Evans, 1983). Self-report by clients may be reliable (Hay et al., 1979) but distorted (O'Banion & Arkowitz, 1977) and subject to demand characteristics (Schroeder & Rakos, 1983). Nevertheless, the interview remains the behavior therapist's most basic assessment strategy. It is even employed frequently with a client's significant others (Swan & MacDonald, 1978), in a effort to acquire data unavailable through alternative means or corroborate information previously obtained (Kazdin, 1979a).

Self-report scales

Verbal self-report of performance.[1] St. Lawrence (1987) assembled 28 self-report instruments employed in published research, and my own search uncovered an additional dozen or so. Most of these scales lack adequate psychometric support; their reliability and validity are currently unsubstantiated (St. Lawrence, 1987; Schroeder & Rakos, 1983). Beck and Heimberg (1983) provided a detailed description and critical analysis of several of the more commonly employed instruments. According to these authors, only the Conflict Resolution Inventory (CRI; McFall & Lillesand, 1971) and, to a lesser extent, the College Self-Expression Scale (CSES; Galassi, DeLo, Galassi, & Bastien, 1974) and Rathus Assertiveness Schedule (RAS; Rathus, 1973a) have accumulated adequate data to support their use. Instruments judged to lack a sufficient psychometric foundation include the Adult Self-Expression Scale (ASES; Gay, Hollandsworth, & Galassi, 1975), the Assertion Inventory (AI; Gambrill & Richey, 1975), and the Wolpe–Lazarus Assertiveness Schedule (WLAS; Wolpe & Lazarus, 1966).

The scales have been primarily normed and validated on US college student populations, with the exception of the Rathus, for which data with psychiatric patients (Rathus & Nevid, 1977) and young criminal offenders (Heimberg & Harrison, 1980) have been obtained, and, of course, the ASES. There are sporadic reports of psychometric data acquired in settings other than mainstream America. The CSES has been investigated in Israel (Kipper & Jaffe, 1976; 1978), Great Britain (Furnham & Henderson, 1981; Henderson & Furnham, 1983), and in the Mexican-American (Hall & Beil-Warner, 1978) and Native American (LaFramboise, 1983) subcultures. The RAS has been researched in Great Britain (Furnham & Henderson, 1981; Henderson & Furnham, 1983), Nigeria (Adejumo, 1981), and New Zealand (McCormick, 1982). Furnham (1979) assessed the WLAS in South Africa and the WLAS and AI in Great Britain (Furnham & Henderson, 1981; Henderson & Furnham, 1983). The AI has also been evaluated in Spain (Raich i Escursell & Vila i Vidal, 1985).

In addition, self-report measures have been developed for particular populations. The RAS has been modified for administration to adolescents (del Greco, Breitbach, Rumer, McCarthy, & Suissa, 1986a; McCullagh, 1982a; Vaal & McCullagh, 1977) and to individuals with low reading skills (McCormick, 1985; McCormick, Hahn, & Walkey, 1984). Scales have been developed specifically for male drug addicts (Callner & Ross, 1976), women at risk from sexual coercion (Muehlenhard, Julsonnet, Carlson, & Flarity-White, 1989), nurses (Michelson, Molcan, & Poorman, 1986), adolescents (Lee, Hallberg, Slemon, & Haase, 1985), and young adolescents (Connor, Dann, & Twentyman, 1982).

Several instruments have been developed for young children. The Children's Action Tendency Scale (CATS, Deluty, 1979) measures self-reports in conflict situations only. It has demonstrated significantly better concurrent validity for boys than for girls (Deluty, 1984), but is compromised by social desirability concerns (Deluty, 1984; Broad, Burke, Byford, & Sims, 1986). Three instruments assess children's responses to positive as well as conflict situations. Reardon, Hersen, Bellack, and Foley (1979) developed the Self-Report Assertiveness Test for Boys, but found it correlated poorly with role-play behavior. The Children's Assertiveness Inventory (CAI, Ollendick, 1983) identifies withdrawn children, and has proved useful in the comprehensive assessment of children's social interaction skills (Ollendick, 1981). However, it too correlates poorly with behavioral measures, particularly in conflict situations (Ollendick, Meador, & Villanis, 1986; Schneider, Ledingham, Poirier, Oliver, & Byrne, 1984). The Children's Assertive Behavior Scale (CABS; Michelson & Wood, 1982) evidenced preliminary validity (Michelson, Andrasik, Vucelic, & Coleman, 1981) that appears strongest for situations involving adults rather than peers (Hobbs & Walle, 1985). It distinguishes popular from unpopular boys (Waas & French, 1989) but fails to predict actual behavior (Shapiro, Lentz, & Sofman, 1985; Waas & French, 1989). Scanlon and Ollendick (1985) found a moderate relationship between the CABS, CAI, and CATS, but concluded the strength of the CATS and the CABS was in distinguishing assertive from aggressive behavior, while the CAI was superior in discriminating passive from assertive responding.

The general self-report scales are widely used in clinical work and research, and the instruments developed for specific populations are becoming increasingly common. However, despite their popularity, researchers repeatedly caution that important concerns have not been adequately resolved. First, reliable norms based on 'total scale scores' derived from summing all individual items are not available for many of the instruments (Beck & Heimberg, 1983; St. Lawrence, 1987). This, however, should not be considered a major limitation: if assertion is a situation-specific behavior (not a trait), and intervention requires identification of particular response deficits and problematic circumstances, then the extent to which accurate norms are clinically relevant is suspect (Bellack, 1979a; Schroeder & Rakos, 1983; St. Lawrence, 1987).

A second issue involves the content of and intercorrelations among the different scales. The various instruments do not sample the same behaviors and situations, though they all emphasize conflict assertion; not surprisingly, they are only modestly correlated with each other, particularly when common items are removed from the analysis (Furnham & Henderson, 1984). Thus convergent validity is suspect, despite occasional reports of acceptable intercorrelations (eg Beck & Heimberg, 1983; Kern & MacDonald, 1980; Swimmer & Ramanaiah, 1985).

Third, correlations between self-report and behavioral measures are also modest (Beck & Heimberg, 1983), thus limiting criterion validity. Self-reports of assertive behavior are minimally related to both role play (Frisch & Higgins,

1986; Rakos, Mayo, & Schroeder, 1982) and in vivo performance (Gorecki, Dickson, Anderson, & Jones, 1981; Higgins, Alonso, & Pendleton, 1979). The situational specificity of assertion and the different response modalities of self-report and overt performance increase the likelihood that modest correlations will be obtained. When situational variables are manipulated, higher correlations can be produced, consistent with behavioral theory. Thus, self-report is predictive of role-play performance when personal investment is high (Jenkins, Adams, & Rahaim, 1981) and when the situations are easy and role-play instructions ask subjects to respond 'normally' (Kolotkin & Wielkiewicz, 1984; see p. 109). Bellack, Hersen, and Turner (1979) obtained strong correlations between verbalizations of what one 'should' do in a situation and behavior in identical role play and in vivo interaction.

Finally, threats to the external validity of a scale may come from distortion by social desirability concerns (Kiecolt & McGrath, 1979) and the reactive effects of exposure to information about assertiveness (Schroeder & Rakos, 1978). These contaminations should be of concern to therapists since they affect the veracity of the self-report.

The perceived psychometric shortcomings of the existing scales have prompted the continual development of new instruments. Leah, Law, and Snyder (1979) developed the Difficulty in Assertiveness Scale, which assesses responding as a function of interpersonal contexts/partners and response classes. Though this might be expected to improve predictive ability, no validity data have been reported for this instrument. More recent offerings include the Assertiveness Self-Report Inventory (Herzberger, Chan, & Katz, 1984), the del Greco Assertive Behavior Inventory (DABI: del Greco, 1983), and the Personal Assertion Analysis (PAA: Hedlund & Lindquist, 1984). The DABI attempts to measure the assertive, aggressive, nonassertive, and passive-aggressive behaviors of persons residing in group-living situations, but again, very limited reliability and validity data have been obtained. The PAA is intended to distinguish between the passive, assertive, and aggressive behaviors of clients. The early data on this scale are encouraging, including its negative correlation with social desirability. Finally, German researchers have initially validated what is probably the only assertion inventory originally developed in a language other than English (Brandau, Skatsche, & Ruch, 1984; Skatsche, Brandau, & Ruch, 1982).

The psychometric limitations of the existing self-report inventories have not prevented their widespread use as one component of the data-gathering process. Clinicians either enthusiastically adopt the behavioral conceptualization that traditional psychometric validation is inappropriate for these measures (Nelson, 1983) and that the lack of concordance with actual behavior provides important information (Becker & Heimberg, 1988) or they use them because superior alternatives are unavailable. Specific recommendations for their use will be offered at the end of this chapter.

Cognitive knowledge of assertive content. Several instruments are available for the assessment of knowledge of assertive behavior. The Social Alternatives Test (Eisler, Fredericksen, & Peterson, 1978) assesses general knowledge of the content of assertive responding while the Assertive Knowledge Inventory (Schwartz & Gottman, 1976) and Written Assertiveness Knowledge Test (Bruch, 1988) evaluate knowledge pertaining to effective refusal responses. However, none of these instruments has accumulated significant reliability or validity data (Bruch, 1988; St. Lawrence, 1987). Measurements of the ability to discriminate assertive, aggressive, and nonassertive behaviors in general situations (Lange & Jakubowski, 1976) and in work settings (Warehime & Lowe, 1983) have been developed, but these too lack supporting data. For clinicians concerned with traditional psychometric validity, this is an unfortunate situation, obviously ripe for further research: '[a]lthough a logical first step in designing intervention is to assess the individual's current knowledge about the subject, until psychometric properties have been established for the knowledge tests their use cannot be recommended' (St. Lawrence, 1987, p. 159).

Verbal self-report of cognitions. The Assertiveness Self-Statement Test (ASST; Schwartz & Gottman, 1976) is widely used to assess self-verbalizations prompted by refusal situations in the college environment. Bruch, Haase, and Purcell (1984) determined that the ASST, constructed in terms of positive and negative self-statements, actually tapped four different factors: negative emotional consequences of conflict assertion, rational justification for assertion, morality and guilt, and personal inconvenience. A modified version of the ASST, the Assertion Self-Statement Test – Revised, was developed by Heimberg, Chiauzzi, Becker, and Madrazo-Peterson (1983) for use with diverse populations and response classes. It distinguishes assertive from nonassertive individuals, and psychiatric patients from college students and 'normal' adults. Recently, the Sexual Assertiveness Self-Statement Test has been developed to measure women's self-verbalizations when confronted with unwanted sexual advances (Muehlenhard et al., 1989). Finally, the Subjective Probability of Consequences Inventory (Fiedler & Beach, 1978), which evaluates expectancies about the likelihood of various consequences of compliance with, or refusal of, unreasonable requests, is capable of predicting effective assertive response formulation, as is the ASST (Bruch et al., 1984).

The Irrational Beliefs Test (IBT; Jones, 1969), a popular measure of irrational ideas, produces scores related to unassertiveness (Cash, 1984) and predictive of assertive behavior in role plays (Lohr, Nix, Dunbar, & Mosesso, 1984). The Irrational Beliefs Test (Alden & Safran, 1978) has been useful in identifying nonassertive individuals, but is still largely undeveloped and 'best used as an experimental instrument' (Alden, 1988). A general Cognition Scale of Assertiveness (Golden, 1981) discriminates high and low socially anxious individuals and reflects change after AT, but no data beyond an initial study are reported. Finally, the Irrational Beliefs About Assertion questionnaire (Craighead, 1979), a 24-item Likert-type scale, reflects improvement after participation in AT (Craighead,

1979) and is significantly correlated with other measures of assertion (Mizes, Morgan, & Buder, 1989).

Self-report of beliefs, thoughts, and self-statements is the most frequent modality of cognitive assessment, but a variety of other strategies have received some attention. For example, in postperformance videotape reconstruction (Chiauzzi & Heimberg, 1983), subjects verbalize their thoughts while viewing their videotaped role-play responses. This method is clearly more involved than a self-report inventory, and its public nature may cause it to be more sensitive to the social desirability concerns so often voiced by nonassertive people. It is not surprising, therefore, that reconstruction obtained results differing from those of self-report inventories (Chiauzzi & Heimberg, 1983). At this point, there are no cogent reasons to recommend this relatively cumbersome procedure in lieu of, say, the ASST. However, for those readers interested in pursuing alternative approaches to cognitive assessment, Merluzzi, Glass, and Genest (1981) will prove rewarding.

Self-monitoring

Behavior therapists utilize client-recorded naturalistic data in more than half their cases (Swan & MacDonald, 1978). The popularity of self-monitoring probably reflects an appreciation of its intermediate status between the total subjectivity of self-report and the objectivity of direct observation (Bellack, 1979a). Nevertheless, it is fundamentally a self-report procedure that has the usual problems with reliability and validity. In general, the accuracy of self-recorded data can be increased by engaging significant others to observe the behavior of interest and by making the procedure as simple as possible (Bellack, 1979a). Restricting the number of target behaviors, training the client in self-monitoring skills, and reinforcing appropriate self-monitoring can also improve the veracity of the data (Nelson, 1977).

However, self-monitored data may also be distorted by reactivity, in that behavioral changes often occur as a direct function of self-observation (Ciminero, Nelson, & Lipinski, 1977). Though these changes are generally in the desired direction (Nelson, 1977), they nevertheless pose a threat to the validity of the assessment data. It is then possible that an inefficient or erroneous treatment strategy will be developed on the basis of the reactive data.

Self-monitoring has been used extensively in studies investigating general heterosocial skills, but infrequently in those concerned with assertiveness (Schroeder & Rakos, 1983; St. Lawrence, 1987). Moon and Eisler (1983) had clients record 'anger' incidents throughout the course of AT, and could thereby demonstrate a significant reduction in such provocations. Rakos and Schroeder (1979) and Jacobs and Cochran (1982) asked trainees to record the details of naturalistic 'experiments' subsequent to the completion of an AT program. This use of self-monitoring, while not addressing itself to pre-intervention assessment, demonstrates the continuity of assessment throughout treatment; in these instances, the client-generated data helped determine the extent to which training benefits generalized to the natural environment.

Self-monitoring should be a component of every assertion assessment. Though there is no standardized method, the technique often generates a wealth of useful information, some of which is difficult or impossible to obtain by other means. However, clinicians must ensure client compliance, foster conditions that enhance accuracy, and control reactivity to some extent. The clinical implement-ation of self-monitoring will be addressed in detail later in this chapter.

Behavioral observation

Behavior sampling through observation of overt performance, virtually a defining characteristic of behavioral assessment (Kazdin, 1981), can be conducted in three settings varying in the degree of 'naturalness'. In vivo observations occur in the client's natural environment. Contrived situations contain the central natural stimulus elements, but are artificial in other ways. Role-play situations simulate natural stimuli in a completely artificial environ-ment. Each of these is discussed below.

In vivo observation. Direct observation in the environment of interest produces the most desired behavioral data (O'Leary & Wilson, 1987), but is often intrusive, reactive, and prohibitively time-consuming (Kazdin, 1981). The variable and private pattern of assertive responding escalates the cost further, and consequently this strategy has not been used frequently in the assessment of assertion (Bellack, 1979a). Inpatient settings offer a realistic potential for in vivo observation (eg King, Liberman, Roberts, & Bryan, 1977), but only when staff are adequately trained and then retrained to avoid 'observer drift' from predefined criteria (Kazdin, 1981, 1989).

The opportunities for in vivo observation in outpatient work are typically limited to client behavior during the interview (which constitutes a very specific setting) as well as behavior before and after the interview. As noted above, these data can prove quite valuable when conclusions are not inappropriately generalized. For example, a client's expression of displeasure with the therapist or failure to discuss a time conflict regarding the next session can be informative vignettes.

Contrived situations. A contrived situation is characterized by the inclusion of natural stimuli in a somewhat artificial setting. In assertion research, this is most often accomplished by engaging the individual in an interaction with an experimental confederate (Bellack, 1979a; Schroeder & Rakos, 1983; St. Lawrence, 1987). Clinically, however, confederates raise important ethical as well as practical issues. Therefore, in treatment, a contrived situation will involve the client and one or more significant other interacting in the clinician's office. For example, a married couple might be asked to discuss one of their perpetual

107

'problems' in the office, as the clinician observes. Or a mother might be asked to explain her reasoning about some issue to her children. The use of this strategy requires cooperative significant others and the identification of a real-life unsolved conflict. As with any direct observation procedure where the observer is readily identified, it is both intrusive and reactive (Kazdin, 1981). However, these may not be important issues, since habituation to the observer will occur over time. For example, if a conflict-ridden family discusses a 'hot' topic for more than a few minutes, it is likely that valid samples of behavior will emerge within a short period of time (cf O'Leary & Wilson, 1987). 'Good' or muted behavior cannot be maintained indefinitely if the issue is well chosen! On the other hand, this procedure would not be expected to identify problems or 'secrets' that are highly embarrassing, blatantly illegal, socially immoral, or contextually unacceptable/inappropriate.

Role-play assessment. The practical difficulties inherent to in vivo and contrived observations make role plays an attractive assessment alternative. A sample of the available instruments includes the Behavioral Role-Playing Assertion Test (McFall & Lillesand, 1971), which primarily assesses refusal responses; the Behavioral Assertiveness Test – Revised (Eisler et al., 1975), which measures positive and negative assertiveness in a variety of contexts; the Behavioral Assertiveness Test for Children (BAT – C: Bornstein, Bellack, & Hersen, 1977), an adaptation of the Eisler et al. test; the Children's Interpersonal Behavior Test (Van Hasselt, Hersen, & Bellack, 1981), a modified version of the BAT – C; the College Women's Assertion Sample (MacDonald, 1978), which assesses responses to rights-infringement situations encountered by college women; the Sexual Assertiveness Role-Play Test (Muehlenhard et al., 1989), a measure of noncompliance to sexual coercion; the Diabetes Assertiveness Test (Gross & Johnson, 1981), involving social situations experienced by pre-adolescent diabetics; and the Social Skills Test for Children (Williamson & McKenzie, 1988), which measures positive and conflict assertion skills. These tests vary greatly in the number of situations they sample (8-52) and in the amount of contextual background they supply for each vignette.

Role-play assessments are typically administered by first providing general instructions. The initial situation is then briefly described, and a protagonist delivers a verbal prompt to which the individual replies. For example:

Narrator: You have been on a queue at the grocery store for 15 minutes and are finally one person from the cashier. You still have several chores to do before you can go home and make dinner. A man approaches you with a basket of groceries about half the size of yours and says:

Protagonist: 'Would you mind if I cut in front of you? I don't have that much, and I am late for an important appointment.'

The formalized tests usually present the narrator on audiotape, while a live or taped confederate provides the prompt. These assessments are therefore structured and standardized. In clinical work, however, the therapist generally serves as both the narrator and the protagonist, and the scenes are developed in light of individualized hypotheses about the client's specific response deficits.

The role-play assessment is directly influenced by the manner in which the procedure is introduced. The most important variable appears to be the extent to which experimenter or therapist 'demand' for competent responding is conveyed by the instructions. Demand is lowest when clients are instructed to 'say what you normally would say in this situation'. A high demand is implicitly created by instructions that ask the individual to respond 'normally', but after receiving information on the content of assertive behavior. The highest demand is imposed with instructions to 'say what you think is best in this situation; stand up for your rights' (St. Lawrence, 1987). Performance is clearly superior when the instructions convey either of the high demands (Derry & Stone, 1979; Kolotkin & Wielkiewicz, 1984; Nietzel & Bernstein, 1976).

Role plays may also be affected by a variety of other contaminants, including specific response sets to fake 'good' or 'poor' (Kazdin, Esveldt-Dawson, & Matson, 1983), promizes of reinforcement for performing as competently as possible (Kazdin, Matson, & Esveldt-Dawson, 1981), information about the situation to be assessed (Frisch & Higgins, 1986), and specification of the particular response components to be measured (Kern, Miller, & Eggers, 1983). However, general information indicating the role play is designed to assess assertive skills exerts a minimal influence on responding (Frisch & Higgins, 1986; Higgins, Frisch, & Smith, 1983; Westefeld, Galassi, & Galassi, 1980).

Role-play performance is also a function of situational parameters. These include the difficulty of the situation (Kolotkin & Wielkiewicz, 1984), the sex of the protagonist (Eisler et al., 1975; Michelson, DiLorenzo, Calpin, & Ollendick, 1982), and the amount of personal investment in the situation (Jenkins et al., 1981). The context in which the entire role play is conducted may also be important. Kazdin, Esveldt-Dawson, and Matson (1982) found performance improved when the assessment followed the successful completion of a task that was materially and socially reinforced by the individual administering the subsequent role play.

Finally, the structure of the role-play assessment and the response requirements also influence responding. Live prompts, as opposed to taped ones, increase subjective anxiety (Galassi & Galassi, 1976) and physiological arousal (Kiecolt-Glaser & Greenberg, 1983). Multiple responses produce increased response duration (Galassi & Galassi, 1976) and arousal (Kiecolt-Glaser & Greenberg, 1983). Interestingly, Galassi and Galassi did not find that these variables altered assertive content.

The existence of instructional, situational, and structural variations increases the likelihood that role plays will demonstrate a limited correspondence to in vivo behavior. In addition, the brief interaction format may preclude accurate assessment of numerous interactive skills (Bellack, 1979a; 1983; Curran, 1978). Finally, the anxiety-arousing potential of role plays (Bellack, 1979a) may elicit

109

unusual responses. Therefore, it is not surprising that a minimal relationship between role play and in vivo responses is frequently obtained (Bellack, Hersen, & Turner, 1978, 1979; Burkhart, Green, & Harrison, 1979; Rakos et al., 1982). Furthermore, role-play performance is often superior (Frisch & Higgins, 1986; Gorecki et al., 1981; Higgins et al., 1979; Higgins et al., 1983), perhaps due to the lack of consequences attendant on it in comparison to those associated with in vivo interactions (Arkowitz, 1981). Role-play tests for assessing children's skill also have found limited evidence of criterion validity (Hobbs, Walle, & Hammersly, 1984; Ollendick, Hart, & Francis, 1985; Van Hasselt, Hersen, & Bellack, 1981).

On the other hand, several investigations suggest role play and in vivo behavior are comparable (Bornstein, Bellack, & Hersen, 1980; Helzel & Rice, 1985; Merluzzi & Biever, 1987; St. Lawrence, Kirksey, & Moore, 1983; Wessberg, Mariotto, Conger, Farrell, & Conger, 1979). The reconciliation of the contradictory findings is likely to be fostered by a variety of methodological and analytical modifications. The consistent demonstration of statistical validity, for example, may depend on more than simple correlations between isomorphic responses. Williamson, Moody, Granberry, Lethermon, and Blouin (1983) showed that multivariate statistics can identify significant relationships with criterion variables in situations where simple correlations prove inadequate. In addition, role-play responses may correspond better to global ('molar') assessments of assertive skills rather than to component ('molecular') skills such as specific verbal (content), paralinguistic, and nonverbal responses (McNamara & Blumer, 1982). In fact, several studies that found poor correspondence between specific in vivo and role-play responses did obtain reasonable correlations between 'molar' in vivo measures and 'molecular' and role-play responses (Bellack et al., 1979; Rakos et al., 1982).

The validity of role plays may also be greater for certain types of clients. Bellack (1979b), for example, has suggested that correspondence may be higher for skilled individuals. Consistent with this, Rakos et al. (1982) obtained correlations in the neighborhood of 0.70 for highly assertive males and Rakos and Schroeder (1979) found subjects who received comprehensive AT produced a correlation of 0.79 between self-monitored assertive behavior in continuing relationships and a role-play test one week later.

Finally, role-play validity may be enhanced by the employment of relevant, personalized content and by cognitive imagery preparation (Bellack, 1983). The use of personalized content has some empirical support. Chiauzzi, Heimberg, Becker, and Gansler (1985) found that multiple response role plays derived from the individual's past experience produced less skilled, but more valid, responses than the typical standardized multiple response format. Kern (1982b; Kern, Miller, & Eggers, 1983) reported that an extended role play replicating a previous in vivo interaction was clearly superior to both brief and extended role plays that were unrelated to the previous experience. Furthermore, 'specification' role plays, which instructed subjects to reproduce three randomly chosen behavioral components of a previously enacted in vivo interaction, produced the closest correspondence to the in vivo behavior and (unlike the general replication role play) did not foster greater behavioral competence. These data validate existing clinical practice: few therapists utilize standardized single response role plays (Becker et al., 1987), preferring instead multiple scenes that are personalized, often as replications or specifications.

Thus, a cautious employment of role-play assessments in the clinical context is warranted (see also Bellack, 1983). Carefully constructed scenarios can demonstrate convergent validity with self-report measures (though not with global self-ratings) and discriminant validity that is superior to self-reports (Kern & MacDonald, 1980; MacDonald & Tyson, 1984; see also Wessberg et al., 1979). However, role plays lacking replicative elements are likely to reflect behavioral skill potential rather than actual in vivo performance (Arkowitz, 1981; Kern et al., 1983). Even nonreplicative role plays introduced with 'low demand' instructions to act 'naturally' may still contain, as a function of the clinical context, a considerable demand for competence. Therefore, it is best to assume that nonreplicative and nonspecificative role plays assess behavioral capabilities rather than response probabilities. The role play then becomes an integral part of the multimodel assessment: adequate role-play performance in situations that are not replications, coupled with poor responding in reenactments and/or self-report of assertive deficits, suggests that the difficulty resides in excessive anxiety and cognitive distortion, rather than in overt skill deficits. Behavioral deficiencies are indicated through incompetent responding in nonreplicative role plays.

Physiological measures

The measurement of physiological functioning has had, to date, a very limited role in the assessment of assertive behavior. Assertion is a typical example of a clinical problem that does not lend itself well to such an evaluation in settings other than the laboratory. Thus, arousal is typically assessed via self-report data acquired through the interview, self-monitoring, and paper-and-pencil inventories.

Even laboratory investigations of physiological processes have been infrequent (Schroeder & Rakos, 1983). Autonomic responding is influenced by situational variables (Hersen et al., 1978) and bears little consistent relationship to overt social skill (Bellack, 1979a; St. Lawrence, 1987). These data could be interpreted to support the relative independence of the tripartite response system and, therefore, the importance of physiological assessment. Alternatively, the data could reflect a basic lack of utility of such measurement. Eisler (1976), for example, argued that physiological assessment is intrusive and may produce unrealistic responding. He also observed that 'some individuals may behave, to all outward appearances, in a highly socially skilled manner under conditions of high physiological arousal, while others may appear equally skilled under conditions of low or moderate arousal' (p. 386). Lehrer and Leiblum (1981) obtained some empirical support for this observation: assertive individuals initially manifested higher heart rates than nonassertive persons when observing filmed vignettes of assertive behavior. In addition, they found minimal relationships between behavioral, cognitive, and physiological indices of anxiety in assertion situations, thus supporting the tripartite response model.

On the other hand, some data suggest that individuals who report themselves to be unassertive have a generally elevated level of arousal (Kiecolt-Glaser & Greenberg, 1983; Lehrer & Leiblum, 1981) and that heart rate while asserting can be lowered through comprehensive AT (Twentyman, Gilbralter, & Inz, 1979). Bellack (1979a) argues that physiological data could be useful in distinguishing between performance deficits due to excessive arousal only versus those that are a function of both excessive arousal and overt response deficits. (In addition, of course, physiological measurement could also eliminate arousal as a controlling variable.) Furthermore, Bellack (1979a) suggests that intense arousal may require direct intervention (eg systematic desensitization) as an adjunct to AT. While this is theoretically true, the pragmatic obstacles to obtaining physiological measures and the failure of such data to demonstrate a consistent relationship to assertion renders this assessment approach cumbersome at best and unreliable at worst (St. Lawrence, 1987).

Clinical implications and recommendations

1. Every behavioral assessment involves a comprehensive functional analysis. Target responses (overt and covert), controlling variables, relevant background information, and personal and contextual resources and limitations must be identified and organized to clarify the relationship between behavior and environment. The primary goal is the identification of the optimal intervention given the client's needs, values, assets, and limitations. Assessment is continuous, serving to monitor progress and suggest modifications when desired changes are not forthcoming.

Many nonbehavioral clinicians, particularly 'eclectic' ones, utilize behavioral approaches in limited and specific ways. While an appreciation of empirically validated procedures of an unfamiliar theoretical orientation is commendable, the risk of implementing treatment that does not meet the ethical standard of competency increases, ie being a jack of all trades and a master of none. The standard for competency is not expertness (see Chapter 9), but, instead, technical proficiency, which, of course, still implies a certain level of conceptual facility. Behavioral intervention, despite its apparent logic and seeming simplicity, is no different from other approaches, yet it is not uncommon for practitioners to implement it with little or no understanding of the functional analysis. Such practice is bad practice.

2. The tripartite response system suggests that inappropriate behavior may be a function of interfering autonomic arousal (anxiety), maladaptive cognitions or

knowledge deficits, and/or overt skill deficits. The functional analysis must identify the relative contributions of each of these sources to the observed assertiveness deficit.

3. Self-report is a principal means of assessing assertion problems. The clinical interview, self-report scales, and self-monitoring should be utilized with each and every client.

a) The interview serves to build rapport as well as to acquire assessment data. Basic active listening skills (observing, attending, questioning, paraphrasing, reflecting feeling and meaning; Ivey, 1988) are required to achieve both purposes. The behavioral interview should be only as comprehensive as is necessary; it is initially limited to areas of presumed relevance to the presenting problem, and only gradually expanded when other data are required. Trainers can utilize the opportunity afforded by the interview to observe the client directly in situations that may be germane to social skill deficits. In addition, significant others may be interviewed when indicated and feasible.

b) Self-report scales should be primarily used as additions to the interview rather than as 'tests'. That is, a client's report of a response probability in a situation is only another *sample* of his or her behavior, not a *sign* of underlying traits or predispositions. Therefore, the clinician should analyze responses to a self-report inventory on an *item-by-item* basis, and use the information to prompt additional assessment (eg follow-up questioning in the interview, development of specific role-play situations, hypotheses regarding the extent to which maladaptive behavior has generalized). There is little utility in comparing a 'total score' to normative data to determine a client's relative standing in a given population. Specific situations must still be identified, and a generalized description of the client ('very nonassertive' or 'very assertive') can be generated quite easily by simply observing that many or most responses on a self-report measure are in the nonassertive (or assertive) direction. And a 'very assertive' person may still have specific situations that he or she cannot handle well. Since visual inspection of the item responses and subsequent corroboration can enlighten the clinician about the pervasiveness of the problem, there is no need to compare statistically the individual's relative ranking *vis-à-vis* others. In fact, such a practice may have deleterious consequences, in that the clinician may exaggerate the extent of dysfunction through unwarranted inference (ie test responses are a 'sign' of a 'trait of passivity' or of 'generalized lack of assertiveness'). Sign approaches to assessment are notorious for overestimating the degree of dysfunction (Little & Schneidman, 1959; Mischel, 1968), whereas 'sample' ones are relatively balanced (cf Langer & Abelson, 1974).

Since I recommend that responses on self-report inventories be used as behavior samples rather than as inferential signs, the external validity considerations are minimally important (Nelson, 1983). On the other hand, the scales should generate clinical hypotheses that can then be corroborated or disconfirmed. In this regard, the Assertion Inventory (AI; Gambrill & Richey, 1975)

113

emerges as a preferred instrument (see Figure 6.2). It contains a diverse sample of situations relevant to adults in the general and patient populations (as opposed to university students). The AI is unique in eliciting two responses to each situation: response probability and subjective discomfort. These scores correlate only moderately (Furnham & Henderson, 1984), suggesting the distinction is an important one for assessment (eg some assertive behavior may be emitted despite high discomfort). Furthermore, it contains a relatively high proportion of positive as well as conflict situations (Furnham & Henderson, 1984). A major drawback of the AI is its relatively high reading level (Andrasik et al., 1981); for individuals with limited reading skills, McCormick's (1985) simplified Rathus Assertiveness Schedule might be an attractive alternative. Finally, if refusal of unreasonable requests is clearly the only presenting issue, then the Conflict Resolution Inventory (McFall & Lillesand, 1971) might be appropriately administered. However, circumstances where all response classes save one can be confidently eliminated from assessment consideration will be extremely rare, and probably nonexistent, particularly when that response class is consistently reported by trainees to be of comparatively little concern (Cooley, 1979; Lefevre & West, 1984).

Self-report instruments for children have been developed relatively recently in comparison to those for adults. The Children's Assertiveness Inventory (Ollendick, 1979) currently appears to be the preferred instrument for distinguishing passivity from assertiveness, while either the Children's Action Tendency Scale (Deluty, 1979) or the Children's Assertive Behavior Scale (Michelson & Wood, 1982) are the choice for differentiating aggression from assertion. Thus, the referral complaint (nonassertion or aggression) should guide the selection of self-report scale when working with youngsters.

In regard to tests of assertive knowledge, St. Lawrence (1987) asserts that psychometric properties are necessary prior to advancing clinical recommendations. Again, if self-report is used as a sample of behavior, rather than as an overall measure of 'something', such concerns are of much less import. Therefore, the Assertive Knowledge Inventory (Schwartz & Gottman, 1976) may be a useful addition to the assessment process.

Finally, instruments that measure dysfunctional cognitions may also prove to be of value. The Assertiveness Self-Statement Test (Schwartz & Gottman, 1976) has demonstrated utility in identifying various types of negative and positive self-statements, but is limited to use with college students. The ASST–Revised (Heimberg, Chiauzzi, Becker, & Madrazo-Peterson, 1983) will be a better choice for general populations, but it is not widely available. The Irrational Beliefs Test (Jones, 1969), though developed to assess irrational beliefs in general, has proven adept at differentiating assertive from nonassertive individuals. Unfortunately, this test is somewhat longer and more involved (eg subscales) than might be desired. Though each instrument has drawbacks, clinicians are likely to find them useful for clarifying the role of inappropriate cognitions in the genesis of unassertive behavior.

Figure 6.2 The Assertion Inventory

Many people experience difficulty in handling interpersonal situations requiring them to assert themselves in some way, for example, turning down a request, asking a favor, giving someone a compliment, expressing disapproval or approval, etc. Please indicate your degree of discomfort or anxiety in the space provided *before* each situation listed below. Utilize the following scale to indicate degree of discomfort:

    1 = none
    2 = a little
    3 = a fair amount
    4 = much
    5 = very much

Then, go over the list a second time and indicate *after* each item the probability or likelihood of your displaying the behavior if actually presented with the situation.* For example, if you rarely apologize when you are at fault, you would mark a '4' after that item. Utilize the following scale to indicate response probability:

    1 = always do it
    2 = usually do it
    3 = do it about half the time
    4 = rarely do it
    5 = never do it

*NOTE: It is important to cover your discomfort ratings (located in front of the items) while indicating response probability. Otherwise, one rating may contaminate the other and a realistic assessment of your behavior is unlikely. To correct for this, place a piece of paper over your discomfort ratings while responding to the situations a second time for response probability.

Degree of Discomfort	*SITUATION*	*Response Probability*
————	1. Turn down a request to borrow your car	————
————	2. Compliment a friend	————
————	3. Ask a favor of someone	————
————	4. Resist sales pressure	————
————	5. Apologize when you are at fault	————

115

Degree of Discomfort	SITUATION	Response Probability
———	6. Turn down a request for a meeting or date . .	———
———	7. Admit fear and request consideration	———
———	8. Tell a person you are intimately involved with when he/she says or does something that bothers you	———
———	9. Ask for a raise	———
———	10. Admit ignorance in some areas	———
———	11. Turn down a request to borrow money	———
———	12. Ask personal questions	———
———	13. Turn off a talkative friend	———
———	14. Ask for a constructive criticism	———
———	15. Initiate a conversation with a stranger	———
———	16. Compliment a person you are romantically involved with or interested in	———
———	17. Request a meeting or a date with a person. .	———
———	18. Your initial request for a meeting is turned down and you ask the person again at a later time	———
———	19. Admit confusion about a point under discussion and ask for clarification	———
———	20. Apply for a job	———
———	21. Ask whether you have offended someone . .	———
———	22. Tell someone that you like them	———
———	23. Request expected service when such is not forthcoming, eg in a restaurant	———
———	24. Discuss openly with the person his/her criticism of your behavior	———
———	25. Return defective items, eg, store or restaurant	———
———	26. Express an opinion that differs from that of the person you are talking to	———
———	27. Resist sexual overtures when you are not interested	———
———	28. Tell the person when you feel he/she has done something that is unfair to you	———
———	29. Accept a date	———
———	30. Tell someone good news about yourself . . .	———

Degree of Discomfort	SITUATION	Response Probability
————	31. Resist pressure to drink	————
————	32. Resist a significant person's unfair demands	————
————	33. Quit a job	————
————	34. Resist pressure to use drugs	————
————	35. Discuss openly with a person his/her criticism of your work	————
————	36. Request the return of borrowed item	————
————	37. Receive compliments	————
————	38. Continue to converse with someone who disagrees with you	————
————	39. Tell a friend or someone with whom you work when he/she says or does something that bothers you	————
————	40. Ask a person who is annoying you in a public situation to stop	————

Lastly, please indicate the situations you would like to handle more assertively by placing a circle around the item number.

Reprinted with permission from: Gambrill, E. D. & Richey, C. A. (1975). An assertion inventory for use in assessment and research, *Behavior Therapy, 6,* 550-561.

c) Self-monitoring by nonassertive clients can provide a wealth of information.[2] Unfortunately, some clients will resist self-monitoring despite all efforts by the therapist (Mahoney, 1977); such behavior will often predict future noncompliance with other elements of the treatment regimen (Marlatt, 1985). For most clients, however, systematic self-monitoring will be an unfamiliar, or even novel, behavior that, like any response, will be strengthened through stimulus control and shaping procedures.

From this perspective, self-monitoring should be introduced with the clear and unambiguous specification of a limited number of target behaviors and/or situations. Since assertion is a deficient, infrequently performed skill, clients should be instructed to monitor their responses in *situations that they judge to be appropriate for an assertive response.* In this way, they record successful or partially successful assertions as well as the *alternative* behaviors emitted when they fail to perform assertively. If there is reason to believe the client will experience difficulty in complying with instructions or manifests pervasive skill deficits, the initial number of response classes and/or situations should be restricted.

The discrimination of situations requiring self-monitoring may be easy for some clients but difficult for others due to cognitive misinterpretation of relative rights, etc. Therefore, the clinician must clarify the characteristics that define an 'appropriate' situation, ie those in which one or more of the behavioral, cognitive, and/or affective cues discussed in Chapter 4 are present to a significant degree. Thus, clients begin to acquire a component of assertion through the assessment process.

The clinician should introduce several prompts to guide the actual self-monitoring (Mahoney, 1977). Explicit directions concerning what and how to self-monitor are critical. The 'what' involves the target behaviors and their antecedent and consequent stimuli and should include date, time, place, antecedent situation (people present, nature of conflict situation), antecedent thoughts and feelings, overt *molar* response (general description rather than specification of molecular components), consequent events (outcome of conflict, thoughts and feelings), ratings of discomfort/difficulty (1 = little, 10 = great) and degree of assertiveness (1 = little, 10 = great), and comments (open-ended). The 'how' refers to the recording mechanism, which typically will be either a prose-style diary or structured chart. Meichenbaum and Turk (1987) suggest that compliance will be greatest when the client chooses the modality most consistent with personal preferences.

Generally, most clients will select the structured format. For these persons, a second prompt involves the actual construction of the initial chart. This is essential: in my experience, simply describing the headings, and obtaining verbal acknowledgement from the client, is unlikely to result in useful data. Clients either forget certain aspects, or never 'get around' to constructing the chart. Therefore, the clinician should make the first chart with the client and have him or her inspect it and ask any questions. Clients who appear to have adequate self-management skills may be instructed to make additional charts as necessary, but other clients should be given photostatic copies for subsequent records.

After construction of the chart, it is advisable to engage in behavior rehearsal (Mahoney, 1977). I ask the client to recall a recent appropriate situation, and to enter it into the chart. We then discuss the entries, clarify any misunderstandings, and add absent data. This process provides the client with feedback and reinforcement for an early behavioral attempt (Mahoney, 1977). The completed entry is then left on the chart as an example to which the client can refer (see Figure 6.3).

Bellack (1979a) contends that reactive effects should pose little problem when the target behavior is a social skill deficit that presumably is not a part of the individual's behavioral repertoire. However, I have found that reactivity does occur when clients are asked to self-monitor situations appropriate for assertion. First, the degree of overt skill deficit demonstrated by clients ranges from extensive to moderate. Individuals with only modest deficits are primarily

Figure 6.3 Self-monitoring chart

Date	Time	Issue	Situation People/Place	Thoughts	Response	Outcome	Ratings* Assertion – Discomfort		Comments
3/15	9:10	Mark criticized my house-keeping; didn't acknowledge sick kids and hectic week.	Mark/Living room	If I disagree we're going to have another huge argument. He's so self-centered.	I said 'I know' and quickly changed the subject.	No argument but I'm angry at him, and very frustrated.	1	10	This is so typical of him – and me.

*Scales

1 = very nonassertive   10 = very assertive

1 = very comfortable   10 = very uncomfortable

inhibited by maladaptive cognitions and/or affective responses that can be self-modified to permit assertive responding under the specific conditions fostered by self-observation. Furthermore, persons with pervasive skill deficits can nonetheless *attempt* assertive behavior if the environmental conditions are favorable, as they are likely to be under self-monitoring instructions. Finally, the focus on target situations necessarily means that some behavior – either assertion or an alternative – will be monitored. The emission of the substitute undesired response (eg effusive apology, sarcastic comment) may then be *decreased* by reactivity. Thus, in my experience, clients who are monitoring assertive skills invariably report some increase in assertiveness or some alteration in the behaviors emitted in place of assertion.

Since the data are being collected for assessment purposes, and an accurate reflection of baseline performance is therefore critical, I provide an overview of the reactivity phenomenon that includes *anti-reactivity* instructions (Nelson, 1977). Basically, I ask clients to try to behave as they normally would and, if the conflict is either recurring or marginally important, to resist the temptation to change their behavior even though they are more aware of it and are in a program to do exactly that. I suggest that accurate baseline data will provide long-term benefits, in terms of the development of an efficacious training regimen, that will quickly outweigh the slight improvement afforded by reactivity.[3] This is particularly true since the reactive benefits frequently disappear over the course of several weeks if no other intervention is implemented (Haynes, 1978). Thus, clients are asked to resist reactivity as they collect baseline self-monitored data for one or two weeks and informed that, when intervention commences, the releasing of the reactive effect is likely to provide a rewarding impetus to the change process.

The interpretation of these data will be clearest when they are quantified through computation of a percentage: number of assertions divided by the number of situations deemed appropriate for assertion. Some clients prefer to decide subjectively whether they behaved sufficiently assertively to count a response as 'assertive', but I urge use of the 'degree of assertiveness' scale included in the chart; for example, a rating of 6 or above could be considered 'assertive'. An average percentage can be calculated on a weekly basis and graphed for rapid visual feedback. The clinician may prefer that two or more percentages be calculated when the situations or response classes are conceptually distinct. Thus, separate percentages may be calculated for conflict and positive assertions, refusals and behavior change requests, or spouse and coworker interactions. In addition, clients can compute daily and/or weekly average 'degree of assertiveness' and 'discomfort' scores. Some proficient self-monitors refine their data even further (eg percentage of highly, moderately, and minimally assertive responses).

The inclusion of cognitions and affective responses as antecedent and consequent events is intended to elucidate their functional relationship to the overt behavior. No causative relationship is implied; that is, an affiliative or irrational self-statement reliably preceding nonassertion should not be construed as the cause of it. The self-statement is simply part of the behavioral chain emitted in a particular situation (cf Baldwin & Baldwin, 1986; Martin & Pear, 1988). The situation prompts the negative self-statement that then prompts the nonassertive behavior. Since self-statements are covert responses, they may be identified as target behaviors to which intervention is directed. Their placement in the chart as 'antecedent' or 'subsequent' to the overt behavior should not obscure this possibility.

The self-recorded data should be carefully reviewed each session, with constructive feedback and positive reinforcement offered by the clinician. The process will be continued throughout intervention, providing the clinician with feedback concerning treatment efficacy and demonstrating to the client that behavior is changing in desirable ways. Such documented benefits will, of course, increase the self-efficacy beliefs of both the clinician and the client.

4. The impracticality of observing assertive behavior in in vivo and contrived situations leaves role plays as the primary means by which to acquire direct behavior samples. Role-play performance, as discussed above, can be influenced by numerous instructional and situational variables and hence appears to correspond to in vivo behavior only moderately. Furthermore, role-play responses correlate better with in vivo behavior appraised in global terms rather than in molecular response components. Despite these limitations, the role play contributes importantly to the assessment process. Perhaps its most powerful use is through reenactments of recent interactions experienced by the client. Replication role plays are obviously relevant to the client and usually fairly easy to generate, particularly when the focus is on a limited set of specified behavioral components (Kern, 1982b). In addition, to assess performance potential, the clinician should solicit 'likely' scenarios that, while also based in past experience, contain unique, novel, or otherwise 'nonreplicative' elements.

Both replicative and probable role plays are developed through careful inquiry as to the details of the situation and the actual or anticipated responses of the other person. When a comparison of behavior in the two role plays is the intent, their functional properties (ie difficulty levels, response requirements, situational considerations) should be comparable (Kolotkin, 1980). The instructions for a replication will ask the client to act as he or she did, ie 'naturally', while those for a probable conflict will direct the client to handle it 'assertively'.[4] Under these circumstances, the replication role play provides information on actual behavior, while the probable one assesses the competency of the assertive response repertoire (Kern, 1982b; Kern et al., 1983). The role plays may be tape-recorded for later scrutiny, but in actual clinical practice this rarely proves necessary.

Although all information from the various data sources must be integrated, the role-play performances will provide particularly important working hypotheses. Competent behavior in the probable role play, combined with deficient responding in the replication role play, suggests that the overt skill components have been learned but performance is inhibited by maladaptive cognitions, an unfavorable reinforcement history, and/or excessive arousal. On the other hand, consistently poor performance in probable role plays strongly indicates the presence of overt skill, and perhaps knowledge, deficits.

In my experience, both knowledge and skill inadequacies characterize the majority of nonassertive clients (cf Bruch, 1981). While some data reviewed in Chapter 4 suggest nonassertive individuals do not generally have knowledge deficits when assessed by paper-and-pencil tests, and some research discussed earlier in this chapter indicates such individuals can behave more competently on role-play tests when asked to do so, in actual clinical practice the assertive behavior produced in preintervention role-play assessment is simplistic, unrefined, stereotyped, and incredibly rigid. The knowledge to produce the response comes from rules rather than from experience (see Chapter 7) and the failure to emit such behavior regularly, not surprisingly, results in responses that are, at best, stilted, superficial facsimiles of the desired verbal, paralinguistic, and nonverbal components. Though these responses may score points in the outcome measures of research projects, they are clearly minimally functional in the natural environment. The following example of a 'probable' role play typifies this phenomenon:

Therapist: OK, John, let's role play a typical situation that is likely to arise at work. You say some of your coworkers constantly borrow things from you, such as calculators and instruction manuals, rather than finding their own. Let's role play one of these interactions. What do you think is most likely to arise in the next few weeks?

Client: Well, a major report is due in two weeks, and Bill will be on it. He may very well ask me to lend him my statistical tables. He never seems to have his handy. Just last week he borrowed them from Bob.

T: In what way would such a request cause problems for you?

C: Even when I am working on something that wouldn't seem to need the tables, I find that I frequently want to consult them. It's simply inconvenient when they are not readily accessible in my desk.

T: So you resent such a request because it unnecessarily hinders your work. (The therapist is beginning to teach the client to identify the self-produced cues indicating assertion may be appropriate.)

C: Right. If Bill took the time to be a little more organized, then he wouldn't need to ask me.

T: Well, feelings of resentment are often good cues that assertion may be indicated. Part of your resentment seems to stem from a feeling that Bill is unreasonably imposing on you. (The therapist is now assessing social perception skills.)

C: Well, people in the office do work together and share materials, but usually these are very specialized ones that are not distributed to everyone.

T: From your description, it does appear you have the right to expect that your statistical tables are reserved for your use only. In the context of your office,

Bill's request seems fairly unreasonable. So, this is a good situation for us to work with. Now, let's set the scene. Is it likely to be morning or afternoon? Where are you likely to be in the office?

C: It could be any time in the day. I'd be sitting at my desk and Bill will come over and just ask.

T: Does he sit down or talk to you while standing?

C: It depends. Sometimes he just runs in and out, sometimes he sits and chats first.

T: Well, for our role play, let's assume it's first thing in the morning and that he'll sit down. Now, what is he likely to say?

C: If he sits, first he'll talk about movies or the races. Then he'll laugh and say his tables are at home from another project he's working on, and ask to borrow mine.

T: OK, I think I have the idea. Now, for this role play, I want you to try to deal with Bill in an assertive manner. You don't want to lend him those tables, so I want you to do your best to refuse his request. I'll play Bill. Ready? (The therapist provides high demand instructions for this probable role play.)

C: I guess so.

T: OK. Let's begin... Hi, John. How are you this dreary morning?

C: OK. How are you?

T: I'm fine, thanks. I went to the movies last night, so I was up late. It was a great film. Have you ever seen 'Lawrence of Arabia'? It was spectacular.

C: Yes, I've seen it. It was very good.

T: But I got home late, and I didn't get well organized. I forgot to bring in my statistical tables, and I need them for the project we're working on. Could I borrow yours for a couple of hours while you work on the charts?

C: No, I feel very angry when you always ask to borrow my work materials (said excessively loudly, too rapidly, and with rigid eye contact and body posture).

Here the client tries to employ what he believes is appropriate assertion. The use of 'I language', the abrupt and unqualified refusal, the lack of explanation and expression of understanding, and the poor paralinguistic and nonverbal responses are commonly produced in such role plays. Clearly, this assertion is not an acceptable one by the definitions discussed in Chapter 2. The client's abstract knowledge about what to do bears little relationship to the knowledge required to enact the behavior in an adaptive manner.

The information provided by the clinical use of role-play assessments is invaluable and unlikely to lead to erroneous therapeutic decisions when conceptualized as behavior samples, obtained under certain circumstances, that may not necessarily represent actual behavior in identical in vivo situations. Appropriately constructed role plays will clarify the extent of the client's assertive skill repertoire and provide hypotheses concerning the primary sources of nonassertive behavior.

5. The reader may have noticed that I have not discussed formal assessment strategies to evaluate a client's social perception or problem-solving (response generation, selection, evaluation) skills. McFall (1982) describes several informal techniques to assess these covert components, but, at present, the judgement of their adequacy is accomplished primarily through the clinical interview.[5]

6. My 'package' for assessing nonassertive behavior of adults includes the following: detailed and ongoing clinical interview (occasionally including a significant other such as spouse, boss, friend, or coworker), continuous self-monitoring, the Assertion Inventory, a measure of cognitive behavior (eg The Assertiveness Self-Statement Test), and a series of replicative and probable role plays. I generally do not administer a measure of cognitive knowledge since such information can be obtained through careful interviewing.

For children, I rely on the interview to an even greater extent, particularly for the identification of maladaptive cognitions. I also interview as many significant others as possible (eg parents, siblings, teachers, peers). In addition, I utilize self-monitoring (adapted to the child's skill level), a series of replicative and probable role plays, and occasionally one of the three self-report scales (CATS, CABS, CAI) discussed earlier.

Assertive deficits will be only one of several possible target behaviors in many clinical contexts. In such circumstances, the assessment package must be broadened to clarify the relationship between assertion and the other problems and identify the target behavior(s) that should be the initial focus.

Finally, since the primary purpose of behavioral assessment is the development of an efficacious intervention strategy, the ultimate criterion by which the adequacy of the assessment is to be measured must be treatment effectiveness. Nelson (1983; Nelson & Hayes, 1979, 1981; Hayes, Nelson, & Jarrett, 1987) argues that this criterion ('treatment validity') is functional rather than structural: does the assessment procedure improve the quality of treatment? The functional approach obviates the need to demonstrate psychometric reliability and validity for the various instruments; indeed, the situational specificity of assessment makes such stability unlikely. Nelson (1983) contends low reliability and validity coefficients *confirm* the adequacy of behavioral strategies, rather than suggesting weakness, in that they exhibit sensitivity to environmental variables. In any event, the currently available assessment tools do not demonstrate adequate psychometric properties when judged by traditional criteria. The choice, then, is to utilize nonbehavioral strategies or to validate the behavioral ones against treatment effectiveness. Behavioral theory argues strongly for the latter option!

Chapter seven

Assertiveness training techniques and procedures

From its inception, assertiveness training was a multicomponent package built upon behavior rehearsal (Rimm & Masters, 1979), with modeling, coaching, feedback, and homework assignments as additional elements. Controlled studies consistently demonstrated this treatment was superior to various control groups (ie waiting list, attention-placebo)[1] and alternative interventions in improving assertive responding of passive and aggressive persons (Rimm & Masters, 1979). Though more limited, research also established AT as an effective way to teach various positive (commendatory) assertions (eg Geller, Wildman, Kelly, & Laughlin, 1980; Kelly, Frederiksen, Fitts, & Phillips, 1978; Nesbitt, 1981).

The empirical tradition of behavioral approaches, however, requires a deeper understanding of interventions, including those possessing experimental support. In particular, effective packages must be subjected to a *dismantling* research strategy to identify which components, or combinations, are responsible for the therapeutic gains. Furthermore, treatments also should be the focus of *constructive* research efforts that assess the impact of additional techniques (eg cognitive restructuring) beyond those included in the basic regimen (Kazdin & Wilson, 1978).

True to its behavioral heritage, AT has been the subject of vigorous dismantling and constructive investigations that have evaluated a score of specific techniques. Despite their diversity, each can be categorized into one of five basic operations (Rich & Schroeder, 1976): *response acquisition* strategies (instructions, overt and covert modeling, bibliotherapy), *response reproduction* procedures (overt and covert behavior rehearsal), *response refinement* techniques (shaping, coaching, self-evaluation, feedback, reinforcement), *cognitive restructuring* procedures (rational relabeling, self-instruction training, problem solving), and *response transfer* strategies (eg homework assignments, systematic naturalistic experimentation, self-instruction training, rational relabeling, self-monitoring, covert modeling and rehearsal, social perception skill training). This organizational scheme provides a useful framework through which the contributions of the various components can be reviewed and treatment implications generated.

Empirical assessment of AT techniques

A large percentage of the component research is methodologically flawed to some degree (cf Galassi et al., 1981). Mildly nonassertive subjects, reliance on self-report only as an outcome measure, truncated training packages, and inadequate control groups exemplify the types of problems that prevent the literature from pointing to unambiguous and definitive conclusions. In fact, the complexity of social science phenomena renders the 'unflawed' experiment highly improbable, though some research is so poorly constructed as to be virtually worthless. However, most studies rule out some interpretations, but not others. The data from a group of such studies with varying methodologies, each with its own flaws, is nevertheless highly suggestive if the convergent conclusions are not contradicted by methodologically superior research. This, then, is often the state of constructive and dismantling research, though frequently, it must be admitted, the lack of 'superior' contradictory data is due to the absence rather than the presence of methodologically improved experiments.

Response acquisition operations

Instructions

Information about the content of appropriate assertive responding is such a basic part of AT that it is rarely isolated as a technique in its own right. When this has been done, instructions enhanced assertive responding in psychiatric patients, both alone (Carmichael, 1976; Hersen, Eisler, Miller, Johnson, & Pinkston, 1973) and in combination with feedback (Eisler, Hersen, & Miller, 1974). Instructions, feedback, and modeling were superior to modeling alone in a single subject study (Edelstein & Eisler, 1976), and instructions and rehearsal were more effective than no treatment (McGuire & Thelen, 1983).

Instructions can be characterized as a deductive response acquisition modality: general rules are provided concerning appropriate behavior, from which the client must produce specific, adaptive responses (Marlatt, 1972). Rule-governed learning often produces new behaviors much more rapidly than shaping through direct experience (ie contingency-shaped learning, cf Skinner, 1974). Typically, responses guided by rules are unrefined, and acquire precision through experience with the extant contingencies. However, under certain circumstances, rules produce rigid responses that are insensitive to the actual reinforcement contingencies (Hayes, Brownstein, Haas, & Greenway, 1986; Hayes, Brownstein, Zettle, Rosenfarb, & Korn, 1986). For example, rules that are highly specific, establish arbitrary consequences, or promote limited contact with direct contingencies produce the least flexible responding (Hayes, Brownstein, Haas, & Greenway, 1986). Rigid rule-following is likely to prove maladaptive since behavior is not modified to be consistent with situational requirements. Thus, instructions should be presented as flexible guidelines rather than as absolute directives.

Modeling

Modeling, or observational learning, is a powerful means by which to acquire novel response patterns, disinhibit previously learned but unperformed behaviors, inhibit anxiety and avoidance responses, and facilitate socially appropriate learned behaviors (Bandura, 1977b). Since each of the four processes is involved with the remediation of assertive deficits, though to different extents with different clients, modeling has been viewed as one of the more powerful techniques in the AT package.

Despite the sound theoretical basis, the early investigations of symbolic (filmed) and live modeling produced contradictory data. Some researchers found it significantly contributed to treatment (Carmichael, 1976; Eisler, Hersen, & Miller, 1973; Hersen et al., 1973; Hersen, Kazdin, Bellack, & Turner, 1979) while others concluded it added little (McFall & Twentyman, 1973; Turner & Adams, 1977). More recently, Pentz and Kazdin (1982) demonstrated that modeling alone markedly improved the assertive behavior of passive and aggressive adolescents.

The conflicting results might be a function of methodological variables. The studies obtaining negative results used college students as subjects, while those producing positive effects employed psychiatric patients or adolescents. In fact, Eisler, Blanchard, Fitts, and Williams (1978) found modeling was essential for schizophrenics but superfluous for nonpsychotic patients, suggesting that certain clients (eg schizophrenic, adolescent) require more extensive response acquisition intervention (Fehrenbach & Thelen, 1981).

Another explanation for the discrepancy may reside in the type of assertive response that was trained. McFall and Twentyman taught refusal responses defined simply by saying 'no' and Turner and Adams (1977) trained simple refusal, behavior change request, and complimentary responses. In contrast, Pentz and Kazdin and the Hersen group targeted a more comprehensive response that incorporated components intended to convey social appropriateness. In a direct test of this possibility, McGuire and Thelen (1983) found modeling was superior to instructions plus rehearsal, and as effective as the full treatment of modeling, instructions, and rehearsal, for teaching comprehensive responses to college students. Furthermore, when the target behavior was a simple 'no', modeling alone, instructions plus rehearsal, and the full treatment were equally superior to a no treatment control. Voss, Arrick, and Rimm (1978) also found modeling enhanced AT only when the target behavior was complex. Since the vast majority of assertive responses of nonpsychotic trainees will fall into the 'complex' category, modeling is likely to prove to be a generally potent strategy.

Finally, modeling may differentially influence response components that are more subtle than verbal content, such as response duration, affect, and gestures (cf Eisler, Blanchard, Fitts, & Williams, 1978).

The impact of modeling will be determined by a variety of factors. Model reinforcement, multiple models, and therapist support and encouragement will enhance the effects (Bandura, 1977b). The topography of the model's behavior is an additional important factor: a 'coping' model who behaves hesitantly but persistently in overcoming obstacles is superior to a 'mastery' model who responds competently without any observable difficulty (Meichenbaum, 1972). Similarly, coping models who verbalize self-instructions that guide problem solving are more effective than 'silent' mastery models (Meichenbaum & Goodman, 1971). However, the only study to assess this variable as it relates to the acquisition of assertive skills obtained no differences as a function of model behavioral style (Schulman & Bailey, 1983).

Modeling also requires that the observer somehow code the modeled stimuli prior to performing the response (Bandura, 1977b). Decker (1984) compared three specific symbolic coding procedures and their effect on response reproduction and generalization. The *behavioral* learning point strategy, in which the key words of the model's verbal response and a description of each nonverbal behavior were presented to the observer, permitted greater response reproduction (ie imitation) than modeling with no learning point strategy, modeling with *summary* learning points (key words encompassing the model's behavior) or modeling with *rule-oriented* learning points (statement of the principles underlying the model's behavior). The opposite pattern was obtained for generalization. Both the summary label and rule-oriented learning points fostered greater generalization than modeling with behavioral learning points or modeling alone. Thus, in the early stages, when the basic responses are being acquired, a behavioral coding strategy is indicated. Later, when naturalistic experiments are occurring, the rule-oriented or summary label codes will be most appropriate. Furthermore, the clinician should ensure that appropriate learning points are salient to the client, since these coding strategies are more potent when formulated by the trainer than when developed spontaneously by the trainee (Decker, 1982).

The importance of coding strategies underscores the inductive process involved in modeling (Marlatt, 1972). Specific examples of appropriate behavior are provided, from which the individual must develop general guidelines that facilitate responding in diverse situations. Thus, AT provides response acquisition training through both deductive (instructions) and inductive (modeling) means.[2]

Covert modeling, in which the trainee imagines another person emitting an assertive response in a specified situation, is also a potent response acquisition procedure (Hersen et al., 1979; Kazdin, 1974, 1976a, 1979b, 1979c, 1980, 1982b; Kazdin & Mascitelli, 1982a; Pentz & Kazdin, 1982; Zielinski & Williams, 1979). Consistent with research on observational learning (Bandura, 1977b), outcome is enhanced by imagining multiple models and positive consequences for modeled assertion (vicarious reinforcement) (Kazdin, 1974, 1975, 1976a). The effects of imagining positive reinforcement for assertive responses or negative consequences for nonassertive ones appear similar (Maeda, 1985). Furthermore, 'reply training', in which the trainee visualizes noncompliance to an assertion followed by an effective response, is more beneficial than simply imagining immediate compliance (Nietzel, Martorano, & Melnick, 1977). This indirectly suggests that a coping covert model may be more effective than a mastery covert one.

Kazdin has studied several important facets of the covert modeling process. Client verbalization of the scenes does not enhance the efficacy of the technique (Kazdin, 1976b). Not surprisingly, trainees systematically introduce elaborations into the vignettes (Kazdin, 1975, 1976b), but such self-initiated expansion does not improve the outcome (Kazdin, 1976b). However, when trainees are instructed to elaborate the scenes, the efficacy of covert modeling is enhanced (Kazdin, 1979c, 1980). Finally, developing verbal codes of the modeled material significantly improves the impact of the covert modeling (Kazdin, 1979b), as does the addition of overt rehearsal and homework practice (Kazdin & Mascitelli, 1982a).

Overt and covert modeling appear to produce comparable gains in assertive responding (Hersen et al., 1979; Rosenthal & Reese, 1976). However, overt modeling plus rehearsal, while effective (Rathus, 1973b; Young, Rimm, & Kennedy, 1973), may be somewhat less beneficial than covert modeling plus rehearsal (Hersen et al., 1979). Since modeling and rehearsal are typical elements of an AT package, the suggestive evidence that the covert variant produces a modestly superior combination is worth noting.

Bibliotherapy, or the use of popular self-help materials, generally combines instructions and modeling through the provision of information and response exemplars. Despite their widespread use as adjuncts to psychotherapy (Starker, 1988), many clients fail to complete the materials or benefit from them, and some even experience negative side effects (Rosen, 1987). Unfortunately, none of the assertiveness self-help books have been empirically evaluated, though many are commonly assigned to trainees. (See Chapter 9 for bibliotherapy suggestions.)

Several audiotape programs are also available, but only Rakos and Schroeder's (1979; 1980) has been experimentally assessed. While the program produced impressive benefits, it included many techniques beyond the presentation of information via instructions and modeling, and therefore cannot be categorized as a response acquisition procedure only.

Response reproduction operations

Behavior rehearsal

Behavior rehearsal, the primary response reproduction procedure, provides independent benefits when the target behavior is simple and the trainee is not severely disturbed (Aiduk & Karoly, 1975; McFall & Twentyman, 1973; Voss et al., 1978), but not when the response is complex (Eisler, Hersen, & Miller, 1973; Hersen, Eisler, & Miller, 1974; Hersen et al., 1973; Rimm, Snyder, Depue, Haadstad, & Armstrong, 1976) or the individual is schizophrenic (Eisler,

Blanchard, Fitts, & Williams, 1978). When instructions are explicitly combined with rehearsal, the combination is effective in improving assertive functioning in simple and, at times, more complex situations (Kazdin, 1980, 1982b; Kazdin & Mascitelli, 1982a, 1982b; Thelen & Lasoski, 1980). In fact, Kazdin (1980; 1982b) found that instructions plus rehearsal were equivalent to covert modeling in therapeutic impact. However, the rehearsal procedure was enhanced when the client was encouraged to elaborate the scenes to make them closer to his or her own experience (Kazdin, 1980) and when covert modeling (Kazdin, 1982b), self-instructions (Kazdin & Mascitelli, 1982b), and homework practice (Kazdin & Mascitelli, 1982b) were added to the treatment package.

Twentyman et al. (1979) investigated several variations of behavior rehearsal and found the frequently utilized role reversal, in which the trainee assumes the role of the recipient while another enacts his or her role of the asserter, was less effective than traditional and exaggerated rehearsal. The exaggerated variant was most effective, along with a full treatment consisting of modeling, coaching, and traditional rehearsal. However, as Galassi et al. (1981) observe, the gains made by the exaggerated rehearsal group may reflect the trainees' response to demands to behave extremely assertively rather than actual improvement in behavioral competency.

Covert rehearsal is a second reproduction strategy. Undergradates benefited equally from overt rehearsal, covert rehearsal, and a combination of the two (McFall & Twentyman, 1973), but chronic psychiatric patients improved refusal skills more with the overt variant (Longin & Rooney, 1975). Markham (1985) determined covert rehearsal plus relaxation training (ie systematic desensitization) was equivalent to covert rehearsal with overt rehearsal and feedback. However, McFall and Lillesand (1971) reported a slight superiority for covert rehearsal compared to overt rehearsal plus audiotaped feedback. Since the covert rehearsal could not have feedback, this latter finding is difficult to interpret, especially in light of the generally negative effects of taped feedback (see p. 131).

Response refinement techniques

Contingent feedback

A small number of studies have investigated the effect of response contingent feedback (coaching, positive reinforcement, self-reinforcement) on the shaping of assertive responses. Coaching has been the more extensively investigated procedure. Thelen and Lasoski (1980), McFall and Twentyman (1973), Eisler, Hersen, and Miller (1974), and Turner and Adams (1977) all reported significant additive effects for coaching. Furthermore, trainees may be more effective coaches than the therapist, and may themselves benefit by providing the feedback (Flowers & Guerra, 1974). This latter finding is consistent with anecdotal and experimental observations that the act of helping in and of itself has a positive impact on the helper as well as the helpee (Rakos & Schroeder, 1976).

However, the data on coaching are not uniformly positive. Voss et al. (1978) concluded that this procedure did not enhance outcome, and in a study with dating-shy males, Christensen, Arkowitz, and Anderson (1975) found written feedback from the female after a date decreased subsequent dating performance. Clearly, under some circumstances, contingent feedback can be threatening and counterproductive. This may be part of the reason why client-coaches were more helpful than professional-coaches in the Flowers and Guerra (1974) study. On the other hand, researchers from four separate labs have confirmed the utility of coaching. Since behavioral principles suggest this type of feedback should contribute to response refinement, it is likely that the characteristics of the coach and the specific way coaching is implemented (eg the ratio of positive to critical comments) will determine its impact.

A second form of contingent feedback, positive reinforcement, has been the focus of only one study. Therapist praise not only failed to provide additive benefits, but also appeared to limit the extent of generalization (Young et al., 1973). On the other hand, reinforcement was associated with self-reports of improved assertion and consumer satisfaction. It is possible that the positive nature of praise improves subjective appraisals but, by failing to specify needed refinements, offers little guidance by which responding can be enhanced. Nevertheless, this limited effect would be valuable if not for the adverse impact on generalization. Rimm and Masters (1979), noting the use of social re-inforcement is strongly supported by the operant literature and clinical experience, speculate that reinforcement must be gradually faded to avoid negative effects on transfer. This hypothesis is consistent with the operant literature on programming generalization (Stokes & Baer, 1977; Stokes & Osnes, 1989); the training conditions should systematically approximate the natural environment. Since most natural situations do not produce immediate consistent reinforcement (ie a continuous reinforcement schedule), a theoretically plausible strategy here is to gradually shift to an increasingly thin variable ratio schedule of reinforcement.[3]

Finally, self-evaluation, a critical component of self-regulated behavior (Kanfer & Schefft, 1988), has also been the subject of only one study, in which it did not provide benefits beyond those associated with behavior rehearsal alone (Aiduk & Karoly, 1975). Although additional research is obviously indicated, the negative result is not unexpected. Self-evaluation, which involves careful self-observation and contingent self-reinforcement or punishment, is likely to prompt trainees to focus on inadequate or otherwise negative aspects of their response. This technique, therefore, should be used only with extensive guidance by the clinician.

Observation of performance

Audiotaped and videotaped playback of behavior rehearsals also offers response feedback. McFall and Marston (1970) reported a very minimal benefit from audiotape feedback, but all subsequent studies failed to find evidence for *any* contribution, regardless of whether the feedback was audiotape (Melnick & Stocker, 1977) or videotape (Aiduk & Karoly, 1975; Brown, 1980; Gormally, Hill, Otis, & Rainey, 1975; Scherer & Freedberg, 1976; Thelen & Lasoski, 1980). While neither audio- nor videotaped feedback prevents the acquisition of assertive behavior (McCullagh, 1982b), the inadvertent emphasis on inadequate and inappropriate behaviors is counterproductive, particularly in the initial stages of training. The client, in other words, may be overwhelmed by the negative facets of his or her response. This possibility is supported by research showing individuals who experienced AT without videotape feedback, unlike those who received the feedback, perceived themselves to be more competent and satisfied than control subjects, despite the fact that trainees in both AT groups improved their assertive skills comparably (Brown, 1980). Indeed, a technique sometimes described as 'self-confrontation' (Thelen & Lasoski, 1980) can hardly be expected to produce uniform positive change irrespective of individual behavioral and cognitive competencies.

Perhaps taped feedback will have greater utility if employed later in therapy, at a point when responding is already fairly refined. Under such circumstances, trainees would have fewer inadequacies to process and could attend to subtle response components. Furthermore, the increased self-esteem and self-efficacy beliefs that are consistent consequences of the earlier behavioral improvement would naturally facilitate the constructive use of the taped feedback.

Cognitive restructuring

Self-instruction training

The direct modification of maladaptive, affiliative, and nonreinforcing self-statements produces improvement in assertive responding (Carmichael, 1976; Carmody, 1978; Craighead, 1979; Derry & Stone, 1979; Kaplan, 1982; Safran, Alden, & Davidson, 1980; Thorpe, 1975; Twentyman, Pharr, & Connor, 1980; Valerio & Stone, 1982). Furthermore, self-instruction training provides incremental benefits to an instruction and rehearsal treatment (Jacobs & Cochran, 1982; Kazdin & Mascitelli, 1982b), though not to a more comprehensive behavioral AT package consisting of modeling, rehearsal, coaching, and homework (Kaplan, 1982; Valerio & Stone, 1982).

The Jacobs and Cochran study is particularly interesting since it utilized personally relevant situations and response classes in the training, and employed self-monitoring of naturalistic encounters as the outcome measure. Individuals who were exposed to the cognitive as well as the behavioral training reported greater verbal and nonverbal assertiveness, less initial and concurrent anxiety, and more satisfaction than persons receiving only behavioral AT. Cognitive-behavioral treatment also resulted in assertion in a greater percentage of appropriate situations at a 6-week follow-up. These data may reflect actual anxiety reduction and behavioral improvement or a constructive modification in the self-perception and self-evaluation processes so important in setting the occasion for future attempts at assertion. Alternatively, the self-monitored data may simply reflect intrinsic demand characteristics engendered by the emphasis placed in the cognitive training on control over the thinking process. The authors correctly point out the interpretation of the results is clouded by the lack of objective performance data, but this study, as well as several others, suggests that self-instruction training may prove most valuable in the maintenance and generalization of training gains (see p. 137).

Rational relabeling procedures

Cognitive restructuring that employs rational-emotive therapy (Ellis, 1962) or rational relabeling (Goldfried & Davison, 1976) is effective in enhancing assertive behavior, but not superior to a behavioral skills intervention (Alden, Safran, & Weideman, 1978; Carmody, 1978; Hatzenbuehler & Schroeder, 1982; Linehan, Goldfried, & Goldfried, 1979; Tiegerman & Kassinove, 1977). Furthermore, the efficacy of combined treatments is essentially comparable to skills-only interventions (Hatzenbuehler & Schroeder, 1982; Hammen, Jacobs, Mayol, & Cochran, 1980; Hammond & Oei, 1982; Linehan, Goldfried, & Goldfried, 1979; Tiegerman & Kassinove, 1977; Wolfe & Fodor, 1977), though the former may result in poorer performance of overt components (Hammond & Oei, 1982; Hatzenbuehler & Schroeder, 1982). The time and focus demanded by the rational relabeling component, which is at the expense of further overt skill practice, may entail a cost that is not balanced by other immediate behavioral or cognitive improvements. However, as with self-instruction training, some research suggests that rational relabeling may contribute to the maintenance and transfer of training (see p. 137).

Other cognitive interventions

Twentyman et al. (1980) assessed the impact of a component of problem solving, the generation of alternative responses, and determined it was as effective as self-instruction training and a social skills-covert modeling package. Meehan and Goldkopf (1982) found attitudinal restructuring that focused on assertive rights and sex-role stereotyping did not provide immediate added benefits to a behavioral treatment for women; however, at follow-up, it was associated with increased self-reported assertiveness.

Client characteristics and cognitive restructuring

It is possible that cognitive restructuring interventions will prove most valuable with clients whose assertive deficits are associated with certain cognitive characteristics. The matching of clients to treatments is consistent with current psychotherapy outcome research that attempts to identify which therapy is most effective with which client under which circumstances (Paul, 1969).

Hammen et al. (1980) compared skills training to skills plus rational relabeling

133

with clients who exhibited either high or low levels of dysfunctional attitudes. They found the two treatments had comparable effects, with both producing greater changes in clients who had low levels of cognitive dysfunction. Thus, the extent of inappropriate cognitions does not appear to be related to differential treatment efficacy, but rather, to treatment effectiveness in general.

The influence of knowledge of assertive behavior was investigated by Valerio and Stone (1982). Presumably, nonassertive individuals who have significant knowledge are inhibited from performing assertively by inappropriate covert responses and therefore should benefit more from a cognitive intervention. However, Valerio and Stone failed to find any differences in the impact of behavioral, self-statement, and combined treatments as a function of knowledge.

High social anxiety and faulty self-appraisal may be a function of skill deficits or of maladaptive cognitions. It is therefore difficult to predict whether such clients should be expected to benefit more from a cognitive or a behavioral intervention. Elder, Edelstein, and Fremouw (1981) addressed this issue and found self-instruction training with highly socially anxious persons produced significant improvement, particularly in self-reports of interpersonal anxiety and discomfort. However, such training had a negligible impact on individuals with low levels of social anxiety while behavioral procedures were equally effective for persons with high or low anxiety. Safran et al. (1980) also found behavioral treatments produced equivalent gains in high and low anxious persons but, contrary to Elder et al. (1981), observed that self-instruction training was effective only with individuals with low anxiety. Though these data are inconsistent in regard to the specificity of self-instructions, they strongly indicate the skills approach is a broader one whose efficacy is less dependent upon client characteristics.

Conceptual sophistication is another potentially important moderator variable. Stoppard and Henri (1987) assessed the response of high and low conceptual clients to interventions that were either high (behavioral) or low (cognitive restructuring) in structure. Individuals low in conceptual level benefited more from the behavioral than the cognitive treatment, but clients high in conceptual abilities gained equally from the two training procedures. Again, the behavioral approach, unlike the cognitive treatment, demonstrates a generally robust impact that is unrelated to client characteristics. However, when structure is extreme and inflexible, client characteristics may emerge as important. Schwartz and Higgins (1979) found that the response to an automated AT procedure was superior for clients who had an external as opposed to internal locus of control.

Thus, it appears that the effects of behavioral skills training are relatively independent of the cognitive characteristics of trainees. Once again, indirect support is gathered for Bandura's (1977b) contention that the most efficacious way to modify the cognitions that may mediate behavior is to alter the behaviors on which the cognitions are based, rather than to attempt to modify them directly (also see Latimer & Sweet, 1984). Furthermore, the modest influence of cognitive restructuring is particularly interesting since most of the researchers appeared to have strong biases in favor of the cognitive intervention (Galassi et al., 1984).

Response transfer

Generalization of responding can be measured in terms of transfer across situations at one point in time or in terms of maintenance within a situation over a period of time (cf Scott et al., 1983). The facilitation of generalization requires the implementation of specific procedures that are planned from the onset of treatment (Kanfer & Schefft, 1988; Stokes & Baer, 1977). In Kanfer and Schefft's (1988) view, the basic strategies involve the (a) use of learning principles to prompt stimulus and response generalization,[4] (b) training of new behaviors in natural settings or in analogs and replications of these settings, (c) inclusion of the client's social system in training, and (d) use of self-regulation and verbal mediation to transcend specific circumstances and behaviors. Stokes and Osnes (1989) provided a similar breakdown of the critical processes: (a) exploit current functional contingencies (contact and if necessary recruit natural reinforcers, modify maladaptive consequences, reinforce occurrences of generalization); (b) train diversity (use sufficient stimulus and response exemplars, make antecedents and consequences less discriminable); and (c) incorporate functional mediators (utilize common salient physical and social stimuli and self-mediated physical, verbal, and covert stimuli). The AT package incorporates a variety of techniques to effect these transfer priciples.

Stimulus generalization in AT is prompted by varying the stimulus situations in training, employing a range of stimuli similar to naturalistic ones, and replicating different settings and cues in behavior rehearsal. The use of a graded stimulus hierarchy, which systematically introduces increasingly difficult environmental variables, is often critical to the success of the process. Response generalization is facilitated by increasing the breadth of target behaviors, requiring overlearning of a variety of behaviors included in a response class, training variants of target behaviors that are adaptive in a range of situations, and instilling flexibility by modeling and rehearsing effective response alternatives that vary in terms of specific content and structure.

Both types of generalization are involved in training individuals to respond to the 'general case' (Kazdin, 1989). In this procedure, the clinician first identifies the specific stimulus situations in which the newly developed behavior is to be emitted. Next, several of the most salient characteristics that are likely to vary in each of the target situations are delineated. These might include the physical setting (eg in the supervisor's office vs in the trainee's), the amount of structure (eg during a formal meal in a restaurant vs lunch in the office), the number of people present, etc. The third step requires the definition of the range of acceptable response variations for use in the contexts identified in the previous step. Finally, training experiences that sample the domain of the stimulus and response variations are arranged. In addition to 'general cases' concerning specific response classes, this strategy should be employed in training clients to escalate responses and request time prior to formulating a response.

The transfer of new behaviors to the natural environment is also facilitated in AT by the frequent use of homework assignments involving self-monitoring, analysis of potential conflict situations, observation of others, and actual assertion. In vivo experiments will facilitate transfer only if they are successful – either by producing a positive outcome or prompting a positive self-evaluation of response quality. Actual positive reinforcement for assertion is preferable, since it is the goal and, as such, is likely to initiate a 'behavioral trap' (Stokes & Baer, 1977), the maintenance of newly developed responses that are 'trapped' into the system of reinforcers available in the person's environment. However, since positive reinforcement cannot be ensured, self-reinforcement for behavior achieving a criterion standard will also be critically important. The probability that a response will produce either natural or self-reinforcers will be greatly increased when in vivo experiences are programmed to be consistent with the current behavioral competency of the individual. Homework assignments, like in-session training experiences, must also be placed on a graded hierarchy.

Significant others are rarely directly involved in AT. However, trainees are sometimes asked to practice at home with, say, a spouse, or to request supportive prompting and encouragement from such a person.

Self-regulation and verbal mediation involve the self-generation of cues and behaviors that influence the external and internal (body) environment. Self-produced cues, instructions, and behaviors reduce the individual's reliance on external environmental stimuli and permit him or her to cope with situational variants not specifically targeted in training (Kanfer & Schefft, 1988).

The generalization and maintenance of newly acquired assertion skills has been an enduring concern of AT researchers. Some AT packages have been successful to at least some degree (Eisler, Hersen, & Miller, 1974; Foy, Eisler, & Pinkston, 1975; Frederiksen, Jenkins, Foy, & Eisler, 1976; Galassi, Kostka, & Galassi, 1975; Longin & Rooney, 1975; McFall & Twentyman, 1973; Piccinin, McCarrey, & Chislett, 1985; St. Lawrence, Hughes, Goff, & Palmer, 1984) while others have failed (Kirschner, 1976; McFall & Lillesand, 1971; McFall & Marston, 1970; Young et al., 1973).[5] In an effort to develop procedures that would consistently result in the desired long-term and transfer effects, researchers began to investigate more systematically the contributions of individual components and ancillary techniques.

Homework

Homework experimentation, commonly utilized in both behavioral (Shelton & Levy, 1981) and nonbehavioral (Goldfried, 1980) interventions, is an integral component of AT, yet only three studies have assessed its direct impact on improved long-term functioning. Kazdin and Mascitelli (1982a, 1982b) determined that homework contributed significantly to maintenance and generalization of assertive gains by trainees from the community. Falloon, Lindley, McDonald, and Marks (1977) found that homework produced marked benefits for psychiatric outpatients who completed the assignments. Unfortunately, only half of the subjects complied with instructions, underscoring the need to employ specific behavioral programming to facilitate adherence (cf Shelton & Levy, 1981).

Becker et al. (1987) describe the clinical use of homework in AT. They assign tasks only when the targeted skill has achieved a minimal level of proficiency and appropriate situations are likely to be encountered. The development of each homework assignment is a collaborative venture, as the therapist and client first discuss the specific situation, desired responses, interactive factors, and probable consequences, and then construct a written response guide for future reference. The homework experience will be reviewed at the next session, with the clinician determining response adequacy and additional training requirements. As treatment progresses satisfactorily, homework assignments become less structured, the written response guides less detailed, and the focus shifts from molecular response components (eg eye contact, voice volume) to improved social perception and discrimination skills.

Booster sessions

Periodic booster sessions frequently have been employed to promote maintenance in behavioral self-management programs (eg weight control). Unfortunately, such meetings often fail to improve the durability of gains (Sternberg, 1985). Riedel, Fenwick, and Jillings (1986) investigated this strategy with AT, and found results consistent with work on other target problems. Booster sessions did not differentially maintain gains in assertion, though they did have some effect on self-reported depression ratings. A 'booster program', consisting of newsletters and phone calls, also failed to improve long-term maintenance (Rose, Roessle, & Solomon, 1980). While these studies constitute an inadequate basis from which to generalise, the fact that booster sessions have not consistently proved to be an effective strategy for a variety of problems suggests this technique is not particularly potent, despite common sense notions.

Cognitive restructuring

A direct focus on maladapative self-statements has promoted generalization in some studies (Derry & Stone, 1979; Twentyman, et al., 1980) but not in others (Craighead, 1979; Kazdin & Mascitelli, 1982b; Thorpe, 1975). Similarly, in some investigations, rational relabeling has been associated with improved maintenance (Hammond & Oei, 1982) and transfer of training (Carmody, 1978), while in others it contributes little beyond skill training (Linehan, Goldfried, & Goldfried, 1979). In addition, Meehan and Goldkopf (1982) reported greater maintenance through a focus on rights and sex-role stereotypes.

Jacobs and Cochran (1982) speculated that performance in novel role plays, the common measure of generalization, may not be a sufficiently sensitive criterion. The stimuli are standardized and hence minimally relevant, high demand instructions are communicated either implicitly or explicitly, and no actual risks are associated with different responses. These researchers reasoned that both behavioral and cognitive-behavioral interventions teach adequate performance skills, and that therefore, under typical role-play conditions, comparable responding is likely to be prompted regardless of variations in training. 'Only when pressed with situations that are most personally frightening, and when faced with dealing with people whose responses have serious consequences for one's life, perhaps is there the necessity to draw on the skills learned through cognitive restructuring' (pp. 75–76). Jacobs and Cochran, therefore, had subjects self-monitor actual encounters in the natural environment. With this outcome measure, in essence a *de facto* test of generalization, cognitive-behavioral intervention proved superior to behavioral training alone. Rakos and Schroeder (1979) also obtained skilled, self-monitored in vivo behavior with a cognitive-behavioral training package, though they did not have a comparison group lacking the cognitive component. Thus, there is suggestive evidence that cognitive restructuring may teach clients the skills necessary to emit learned competencies in the natural environment.

At this point, it is difficult to arrive at a consensus concerning the impact of cognitive restructuring on maintenance and generalization. The contradictory findings may reflect a weak intervention, unidentified moderator variables, or methodological problems (ie weak tests of generalization, subject attrition at follow-up, self-report measures only at follow-up). However, no study has reported relatively poorer long-term and transfer effects as a function of cognitive procedures. Therefore, at the very least, the use of such techniques seems unlikely to impede maintenance and generalization.

Covert modeling

Kazdin's work strongly suggests that covert modeling produces generalization to novel role-play situations as well as maintenance of self-reported gains at 4–6-month follow-ups (Hersen et al., 1979; Kazdin, 1974, 1975, 1976a, 1976b, 1979b, 1979c, 1980, 1982; Kazdin & Mascitelli, 1982a). The effects were increased by multiple models, model reinforcement, summary verbal coding of modeled stimuli, imagery elaboration, overt rehearsal, and homework. Nietzel et al. (1977) also obtained generalization effects with covert modeling, particularly when reply training to initial noncompliance with the assertion was also imagined. However, these researchers failed to find generalization at 4-month follow-up.

Observational learning coding strategies

Decker (1984) found that rule-oriented and summary label coding strategies facilitated generalization of gains, while a behavioral one was most beneficial during the initial response acquisition process. These results are intuitively sensible. The more specific behavioral strategy, by focusing on coding response sequences, should promote rapid behavioral reproduction. However, maintenance and generalization are based on response utility, not response reproduction: a behavior must be functional in the natural environment. Since few natural circumstances will mimic the training situation exactly, a response acquisition procedure that codes behaviors according to general principles or summaries, rather than by specific components, is more likely to facilitate both transfer and maintenance.

Covert rehearsal

Two studies evaluated the potential of covert rehearsal, in combination with another procedure, to promote transfer. Twentyman et al. (1980) found covert rehearsal with modeling equal to self-instruction training and superior to generation of response alternatives. Markham (1985) theorized that excessive anxiety may impede the transfer of treatment gains. However, systematic desensitization (a variant of covert rehearsal) produced generalization and maintenance comparable to, but not better than, that induced by a behavioral package consisting of covert rehearsal and overt rehearsal with feedback. Since neither study assessed covert rehearsal alone, its contribution to transfer effects remains unclear.

Problem solving

The technique of problem solving (D'Zurilla & Goldfried, 1971) may also facilitate generalization since it teaches clients to develop new solutions to novel circumstances or situations in which old solutions are no longer adequate. The basic process involves: (a) definition of the problem; (b) brainstorming or generation of alternative responses (identification of all potential solutions regardless of feasibility or appropriateness); (c) selection of the optimal potential solution (which may involve combinations of individual solutions generated in brainstorming); (d) implementation of the selected solution; and (e) evaluation of the solution. If the outcome is judged to be unsatisfactory, the individual is taught to return to the problem-solving sequence at the point where the process failed (Goldfried & Davison, 1976). The wrong problem may have been formulated, inadequate alternatives may have been generated, an inappropriate or ineffective solution may have been selected, and/or the solution may have been implemented poorly. The potential of problem solving is suggested by the observation that highly assertive individuals possess this skill in a more sophisticated manner than nonassertive persons. However, the generation of alternative responses appears to be a relatively weak generalization intervention (Twentyman et al., 1980). It remains to be seen whether the full problem-solving sequence is more potent.

Social perception skills

Generalization and maintenance are likely to be facilitated by sophisticated social perception skills, such as the ability to discriminate situations appropriate for assertion and then conduct cost–benefit risk analyses for those situations. In general, there are few formal, specific discrimination training strategies; instructions (rules) and contingent feedback are the typical means by which this skill is acquired. Written exercises that attempt to quantify 'appropriateness' are included in some programs (eg Rakos & Schroeder, 1980), but these are not yet empirically validated. Risk analyses – the assessment of the potential gains from an assertion in a specific situation in comparison to the different risks of varying probability and aversiveness – are taught similarly: rules and contingent feedback. Rakos and Schroeder (1980) also developed an exercise that quantifies costs versus benefits, but this too has not been experimentally verified. Therefore, at this point in time, this is an area holding great promise for both researchers and clinicians. In the absence of research, clinicians might be encouraged to experiment with various mechanisms to teach these social perception skills. Perhaps the researchers will take the cue from them!

Self-regulation training

An integral component of self-regulation is self-observation. Continuous self-monitoring, by providing a discriminative stimulus (ie prompt) to emit assertive behavior and by producing data that can then be used to shape and reinforce responding, constitutes a potentially powerful intervention. In fact, since self-monitoring by definition occurs in the natural environment, the technique is, in actuality, concerned with transfer effects. Unfortunately, AT research has only minimally and inconclusively investigated self-monitoring; two studies (Jacobs & Cochran, 1982; Rakos & Schroeder, 1979) found it was associated with competent in vivo experimentation, and two suggested it directly produces generalization and maintenance (Kelly, 1983; Warrenfeltz-Rodney, 1981). However, research from other areas involving self-management, such as weight reduction, consistently supports the importance of continuous self-monitoring on the durability and broadening of gains (Craighead, 1985).

Comprehensive self-management training that goes beyond self-monitoring may also facilitate transfer (cf Van Hasselt, Hersen, & Milliones, 1978). For example, Rakos and Schroeder (1979; 1980) obtained strong generalization effects with a self-administered program that included instruction in basic self-management skills to help clients complete the regimen independently. An interesting feature of the program was the utilization of self-mediated physical stimuli (Stokes & Osnes, 1989) in the form of detachable index cards containing client-generated assertive rights and obligations, rational thoughts, self-instructions to control anxiety, likely assertion situations, and response guidelines. Client reports of frequent reference to the cards in the natural environment suggest this strategy merits systematic investigation. Perhaps the strongest data supporting the inclusion of self-regulation training were provided by Schefft and Kanfer (1987), who assessed the impact of AT within a process model of therapy that included specific self-management instruction. Their process model includes seven phases: (1) role structuring and creation of a therapeutic alliance; (2) developing a commitment to change; (3) conducting a behavioral analysis; (4) negotiating treatment objectives; (5) executing treatment and maintaining motivation; (6) monitoring and evaluating progress; and (7) programming generalization and maintenance and preparing for termination (cf Kanfer & Grimm, 1980). Group AT conducted within this sequential framework resulted in greater immediate gains and superior maintenance and generalization than AT presented in a typical group format (ie Lange & Jakubowski, 1976) emphasizing initial assessment and treatment execution only. This training approach, while obviously requiring additional research, highlights the emphasis of this book: AT is a complex clinical intervention that will demonstrate its maximum impact when the trainer possesses competent therapeutic skills.

Clinical implications and recommendations

An overview of the research suggests the five basic AT operations can be incorporated within AT in diverse ways. The structure, content, and selection of specific procedures can vary. In addition, AT can be an isolated intervention or one that is a part of, or adjunctive to, broader treatment. Finally, the AT model, which is educative rather than 'curative', can be introduced within a therapeutic or nontherapeutic framework. These issues will be addressed in the following discussion.

1. The AT training package should be constructed from the following procedures: instructions, bibliotherapy, overt and covert modeling, behavior rehearsal, covert rehearsal, coaching, verbal reinforcement, self-instruction training, rational relabeling, problem-solving training, homework assignments, social perception skill training, self-management training, and continuous self-monitoring. Each of these has an empirical or theoretical basis for inclusion, and none has any real basis for exclusion. Self-evaluation and audiotaped and videotaped feedback, however, are likely to prove beneficial only in the advanced stages of training.

A few points about each of the different techniques are worth highlighting. Instructions are clearly justified in terms of the AT research and our general knowledge of rule-governed behavior. Rules are powerful regulators of behavior, but their potential to foster rigidity can constrain adaptability (and hence generalization and maintenance). Therefore, it is essential to present instructions as empirically derived guides that must be flexibly adapted to individual preferences and situational requirements. Bibliotherapy, despite the lack of empirical investigation, provides the clinician with an adjunctive instructional modality that can increase treatment efficiency and help bridge the time between sessions. Numerous self-help books, many focusing on specific settings or populations, are available at a variety of reading levels (Heimberg, Andrasik, Blankenberg, & Edlund, 1983; see Chapter 9).

Modeling is most useful for the acquisition of complex responses that involve significant potential social consequences and for the refinement of subtle paralinguistic components. In addition, it may be essential for improving the performance of poorly functioning individuals (eg psychiatric patients). Efficacy will be enhanced when a coding system for processing the modeled stimuli is developed. However, the complexity of these stimuli should not exceed the trainee's symbolic processing capabilities (cf Schroeder & Black, 1985). For example, Pentz and Kazdin (1982) found adolescents gained significantly in self-efficacy only when training stimuli belonging to a single conceptual class (eg teachers), but not multiple stimulus classes (eg teachers, parents, peers), were used. The relatively socially inexperienced adolescents may have been forced by the multiple stimuli to engage in excessive coding processes and stimulus generalization before the target response was firmly acquired.

Covert modeling is a powerful response acquisition and transfer technique. It is as efficacious as overt modeling, and may produce a superior combination with behavior rehearsal. Covert modeling has a significant pragmatic advantage since its stimuli do not rely on others or prior preparation (eg films). Multiple models, model reinforcement, and coping models are easily employed. Elaboration of the scenes can be prompted, thereby making them more relevant to the trainee.

However, the utility of covert modeling in clinical application may be constrained by three factors. First, the technique requires some skill at visual imagery. Since Kazdin (1975; 1976b) found subjects generally adhered to imagery instructions, deviating in the direction of expanded imagery, it is likely that most trainees could participate in this technique. The few who simply lack such covert imagery skills could be exposed to guided imagery practice or provided with alternative intervention. Second, covert modeling, in actuality, is more a *response discrimination* procedure than a response acquisition one, since it requires preexisting knowledge of the content of an appropriate response in a particular situation. Clients who have acquired the requisite knowledge, but are unassertive due to cognitive factors or excessive anxiety, could readily profit from the technique. However, for knowledge-deficient clients, covert modeling will require prior cognitive response acquisition training (instructions, overt modeling, bibliotherapy). Finally, some data suggest covert modeling is less preferred, and produces fewer positive expectations of improvement, than an 'active' treatment package consisting of instructions, overt modeling, rehearsal, and coaching (Zielinski & Williams, 1979). This phenomenon may be of little importance when the covert modeling is only one component of a multifaceted treatment package. All three factors (imagery skill, prerequisite knowledge, lack of overt structure) suggest that covert modeling is unlikely to be highly effective with severely disturbed clients. All studies demonstrating its efficacy used nonpsychiatric subjects, and, furthermore, the relatively similar procedure of covert rehearsal is inferior to overt rehearsal with chronic psychiatric patients (Longin & Rooney, 1975).

The impact of modeling is likely to increase when the clinician assumes an active role. The direct introduction of appropriate learning point strategies (Decker, 1982; 1984) and instructions to elaborate scenes presented in covert modeling (Kazdin, 1979b; 1980) produce better outcomes than reliance on client initiation.

Behavior rehearsal is clearly necessary for effective training. Responses acquired cognitively (through instructions, books, and/or modeling) require behavioral performance for refinement and reinforcement (Bandura, 1977b). The AT literature clearly indicates behavior rehearsal is a necessary, though often not a sufficient, condition of training. Overt and covert rehearsal appear comparable for individuals without severe psychological disturbance, but the overt variant, as noted above, is more efficacious with chronic psychiatric patients (Longin & Rooney, 1975). Role reversal may not be a particularly powerful variant (Twentyman et al., 1979), perhaps because it does not actually engage the trainee in rehearsal of assertion. However, role reversal offers the trainee an opportunity to, first, observe a model perform a personally relevant assertion and, second, experience the response from the perspective of the recipient, which is likely to teach empathic social perception skills (Argyle, 1981; Meichenbaum et al., 1981). Exaggerated rehearsal produces impressive behavior changes (Twentyman et al., 1979), but this procedure cannot be recommended. The changes may be due to demand characteristics (Galassi et al., 1981), but even more importantly, the training of exceptionally intense responses is likely to increase the frequency of an already common error of the novice asserter, that of producing an inappropriately escalated, and hence aggressive, response.

Response refinement procedures such as coaching, verbal reinforcement, self-evaluation, and taped feedback appear to have less effect than predicted by theory. Coaching has the strongest support, but even here, two studies question its utility. As a group, the way these procedures are implemented may very well determine their effect: they must be experienced by the trainee as constructive yet predominantly positive. A useful clinical guideline, for which I could not locate documentation in the general operant literature, is to program three positive reinforcements for each negative or critical comment; a lower ratio is likely to be perceived by the recipient as aversive.

Therefore, coaching should highlight the positive aspects of the response, regardless of its objective adequacy. Only one, or at most two, facets should receive critical commentary, and then only in the context of significant positive feedback. Shaping principles should be employed in the process: initially, the most basic elements receive the feedback, and only when behavior is at the next level of functioning is feedback directed toward increasingly subtle facets. For example, an initial role play by a highly skill-deficient person may result in a few unintelligible mumbles, poor eye contact, and no objective impact. The feedback should be something like this: 'John, that was a fine first attempt. I know how difficult it is for you to confront someone. Even so, you *tried* to express yourself, you looked in Mary's general direction, and you made a little gesture with your right hand. However, there are several things you could do to improve your response. One thing would be to try to speak louder; it was very hard to hear what you were saying. Ready to try it?'

The clinician should resist the temptation, especially in the early stages of training, to add additional constructive feedback, no matter how apparently innocuous it may seem. Thus, the following should be reserved for the second role play, after voice volume has increased: 'While you looked in Mary's direction, I'd like you to try this time to look at her mouth – not her eyes, just her mouth. Looking at her mouth is less threatening and she won't know you are not making direct eye contact.'

The trainer is responsible for ensuring that feedback is predominantly positive. In the above example, the trainer did not withhold his own feedback and ask the client how he 'felt about the response' since it was too inadequate to expect feelings of even partial satisfaction. Later, when responding is further along the shaping continuum, such a preliminary query prompting self-evaluation is appropriate and desired. Similarly, when the response is clearly deficient, other group members are likely to provide predominantly negative feedback, particularly in the initial role plays. After all, since they are also struggling with the difficult task of improving assertion, the demands to appear competent are increased while those to discern positive features are diminished. In these circumstances, the advantages of group feedback (involvement, and superiority over therapist comments along with benefits for the coach [cf Flowers & Guerra, 1974]) are negated, and the therapist should assume that responsibility, thereby modeling appropriate coaching behavior (cf Kelly, 1985). The therapist would then structure another rehearsal, which hopefully will be somewhat improved and more accessible to positive feedback from the group. However, at all times, the clinician must protect the trainee by breaking in when the group is not sufficiently positive.

Verbal reinforcement, as noted earlier, should be faded gradually over the course of training. Initially, every component of every response that achieves the criterion for a particular stage of shaping should be singled out for social praise, since response acquisition is facilitated by contingent reinforcement presented on a continuous schedule. Later, when responding is both close to the desired terminal response *and* stable, praise should be slowly reduced and irregularly offered. This will more closely approximate conditions in the natural environment (where praise is unpredictably sporadic) and facilitate generalization and maintenance (Stokes & Baer, 1977).

Clients should be taught to self-evaluate their responses, since such feedback is an essential element of self-regulation. However, training in self-evaluation must explicitly convey to clients that their response must be judged against the current standard established in the context of shaping, and not against an ideal or terminal criterion. Failure to do this will inevitably result in a comparison that produces punishing consequences.

Taped feedback has consistently produced limited gains, possibly due to the predominance of inadequate behavior in the early stages of training. Currently, there are few compelling reasons to recommend this technique, but it would be interesting to know whether taped feedback introduced toward the end of training, when behavior is closer to the terminal criterion, facilitates the final refinement of the response. This is a nice, manageable thesis or dissertation topic!

Cognitive restructuring, primarily self-instruction training and rational re-labeling, appears to provide limited additive benefits and, in two studies, rational relabeling actually impaired outcome somewhat. Furthermore, unlike skills packages, benefits may be restricted to clients with certain types of cognitive dysfunctions. Despite the discouraging data, virtually all current AT programs include some form of direct cognitive modification. Clients seem to respond positively to these techniques, which provide readily accessible, concrete ways to alter maladaptive thinking. Perhaps cognitive restructuring will acquire empirical validation with modifications in the research methodology (cf Jacobs & Cochran, 1982). Thus, though the evidence does not support Trower's (1982) contention that cognitive methods should be placed at the centre of social skills training, it is too early to conclude that they should be deemphasized.

AT must program specific generalization and maintenance strategies into the basic training paradigm (Van Hasselt et al., 1978). Homework assignments, covert modeling, coding of overt and covert modeled stimuli, self-monitoring, and self-regulation training show the greatest potential for facilitating these effects. Self-instruction training and rational relabeling may also promote transfer, but the data are conflictual. Problem solving and social perception skill training are theoretically suggestive but require systematic investigation. Booster sessions, while intuitively appealing, do not appear to offer much.

The actual implementation of AT is beyond the scope of this book. Excellent resources for clinical procedures include Alberti and Emmons (1986a), Fodor (1980), Lange and Jakubowski (1976), and Masters, Burish, Hollon, and Rimm (1987). Numerous case examples and client–therapist transcripts are provided by Fodor (1980), and Lange and Jakubowski (1976) include specific instructions, content, sequencing suggestions, and participant exercises, from which written handouts and introductory and advanced role plays can be developed. In addition, the creative utilization of nontraditional strategies – ones not found in the manuals – may prove beneficial. For example, Carlisle and Donald (1985) used art exercises to help trainees practice newly acquired skills; Hamm and Brodt (1982) utilized a game (GUTS: Growing Up Through Selectivity) to teach assertive skills to juvenile delinquents; and Jordan, Davis, Kahn, and Sinnott (1980) found sharing 'eidetic' imagery of assertion attempts within AT produced gains in assertiveness and self-acceptance.

2. AT can be conducted successfully either individually or in groups (Rimm & Masters, 1979). In fact, the two modalities produce equivalent improvement (Linehan, Walker, Bronheim, Haynes, & Yevzeroff, 1979). Nevertheless, the group format introduces a unique social process that may provide increased opportunities to acquire, refine, and generalize new assertive skills (Kelly, 1985). Among these are (a) increased numbers of stimulus persons for behavior rehearsal, modeling, and generalization training; (b) numerous sources of feedback, reinforcement, encouragement, and alternative response generation; and (c) consensual confrontation and support. Furthermore, trainees in a group

setting experience the impact of assertive and aggressive responses as recipients in behavior rehearsal, observe the remediation of a broad range of specific problems, and employ assertive behavior within the normal group process (ie speak up, compliment, reinforce, confront) (Fodor, 1980). Finally, the wide range of nonassertive behavior displayed by group members, particularly the exceptionally inadequate responses, may provide new referents by which some participants can re-evaluate performance standards and their own abilities (Hung et al., 1980). Because of these advantages, most AT manuals presume a group approach, usually with 6 to 12 participants (Alberti & Emmons, 1986a; Lange & Jakubowski, 1976).

The group format requires that the trainer develop criteria by which to admit participants. An initial decision concerns the extent to which the group members should evidence homogeneity in terms of a central characteristic. For example, Kelly contends that potential participants should share a comparable baseline level of social skill:

> [i]f group members vary too widely from one another in the types of social situations they find troublesome, if they vary greatly in initial skill level, if some are expected to acquire new skills much more quickly than others, it becomes difficult to achieve good group pacing, to tailor training to meet the members' individual needs, and to ensure that the more proficient group members do not become bored while slower ones are trying to master key skills.
>
> (Kelly, 1985, p. 94).

Thus, many groups are composed of basically well-functioning persons without severe and/or pervasive behavioral problems other than nonassertion. On the other hand, the group could be formed with individuals who have similar general complaints that are functionally related to assertion deficits, such as depression, low self-esteem, or sexual inhibition. Alternatively, groups can be organized around themes such as women's issues, couples, particular social situations, or work conflicts (Fodor, 1980; Lange & Jakubowski, 1976).

Individuals who exhibit widely generalized nonassertive or aggressive behavior are not ideal candidates for a general group (Emmons & Alberti, 1983; Lange & Jakubowski, 1976). These persons are likely to be frustrated by the focus on specific situations and, consequently, to disrupt the group process (Lange & Jakubowski, 1976). They may profit more from a homogeneous group composed of persons with similar problems, perhaps with simultaneous individual therapy (Fodor, 1980).

Lange and Jakubowski (1976) suggest potential group members should be motivated to change, willing to expend effort, able to self-disclose, somewhat comfortable in group settings, appreciative of group processes, and realistic in their expectations. They should be able to acknowledge their anger directly, and view the leader realistically – not as an omnipotent figure to be rebelled against or blindly followed. Furthermore, they should not be significantly manipulative, paranoid, schizoid, or psychopathic. In addition, Lange and Jakubowski observe that single-sex groups often develop greater cohesion and self-disclosure, but the outcomes of single-sex and mixed-sex groups are comparable (Brummage & Willis, 1974). Finally, since many conflicts are related somewhat to age (work, parents, children, etc.), group members are most likely to be fully involved when they are roughly at comparable stages of life.

Individual AT offers the trainee an opportunity for much more intensive work, since he or she is the sole focus of intervention. The absence of the facilitative group conditions places the onus on the therapist as the medium through which change will occur (Fodor, 1980). The therapist must provide support and encouragement, assume the roles of significant other, model, and coach, and utilize the natural therapeutic interactions with the client as real-life behavior samples. More so than in group work, the therapeutic relationship provides the foundation on which individual AT is implemented.

Individual AT is rarely as efficient as the group variant and demands greater clinical expertise. Most clients have a hierarchy of problems (Kanfer & Schefft, 1988; Kazdin, 1982a), but in group (and research) settings, the external structure firmly limits the introduction of issues other than assertion. Individual clinical work lacks these predefined constraints and actually provides a setting that encourages wide-ranging self-disclosure. As a consequence, it is common for concerns and issues to emerge that may be, at best, tangentially related to assertiveness problems, even with clients who are basically functioning adequately and/or who verbalize assertion as their primary dysfunction. These other problems may be evident from the outset, but more typically are raised after some improvement in assertive skills has been experienced. Such emergence of secondary and tertiary concerns, and the introduction of additional techniques to remediate them, is a common phenomenon in behavior therapy that reflects a problem hierarchy rather than symptom substitution (Kazdin, 1982a). In general, these other concerns are appropriate therapeutic foci that should not be ignored and often cannot be put off until later. Depending on the content and timing of the new problems, AT may be delayed, abandoned temporarily, or integrated with other treatment. Furthermore, individual AT with severely maladjusted clients is invariably interrupted by a series of endless 'crises'. The instability of such clients diverts attention from the stated goals of therapy and prevents systematic intervention; in fact, the instability itself often must become the primary focus of treatment.

Thus, formal individual AT with most clients is usually difficult or impossible to maintain for the typical 16–20 hours, and progress in improving assertion is slow. In fact, I have not treated a client in individual AT, including those who specifically contacted me for AT, without a divergence into problem areas beyond assertion.

3. An important structural parameter of AT is the continuum defined by the

amount of predetermined process and content. Groups, in particular, vary widely on this dimension. Exercises and session themes can be pre-selected (Lange & Jakubowski, 1976) and didactic instruction and experiential involvement can be combined in a variety of ways. Piccinin et al. (1985) found a highly structured didactic format and a less formal, more participative and individualized arrangement produced comparable gains. Schulman and Bailey (1983), on the other hand, found a highly structured and sequenced procedure produced greater gains than a less elaborate program that presented less information. Despite these findings, most group participants expect a significant experiential component, and didactic material will be received best when it is presented in short segments that are interspersed with behavioral exercises (cf Fodor, 1980; Lange & Jakubowski, 1976). Besides the therapeutic value attendant on meeting participants' expectations (O'Leary & Wilson, 1987), the inclusion of early experiential exercises establishes the foundation for much of the didactic material and, in so doing, provides a context for incorporation of the new knowledge. For example, a short presentation (eg 15 minutes) on the distinctions between assertion, aggression, and nonassertion is appropriate and necessary, but the subtle aspects of the distinguishing characteristics can be better highlighted through detailed analyses of actual in-session behavior rehearsals.

Individual AT is generally characterized by a less predefined structure than the group variant. The individualized focus, reduced audience for didactic material, absence of formal (group) exercises, and almost inevitable introduction of other (non-assertion) concerns all contribute to a relatively flexible and informal training regimen.

A second structural variable concerns the amount and scheduling of training. AT workshops may be scheduled for as few as 2 hours. Generally, AT groups span 6 to 10 sessions of $1^1/2$ or 2 hours each. Individual AT is usually open-ended and intertwined in ongoing therapy. The amount of training is particularly relevant to the short workshop format. Fodor (1980) anecdotally observes that well-focused, theme-oriented ones can still prove valuable to the participants. However, studies that manipulate the amount of training, not surprisingly, obtain greater benefits as contact time is increased. Bander, Russell, and Weiskott (1978) found no effect from two hours of training, significant changes after eight hours' intervention, and proportional gains from 4- and 6-hour training packages. Similarly, Michelson and Wood (1980a) observed that 8 hours of group sessions were less effective than 16 hours.

Clinically, 8 hours would seem to be a minimum amount for group AT. There is simply too much didactic information to present, and too many essential behavior rehearsal–modeling–feedback sequences to facilitate, for training to be any more truncated. A more ideal amount of time appears to be in the 12- to 16-hour range. The spacing of the sessions does not appear to affect outcome: groups that meet for intensive massed practice, traditional distributed practice, or a combination regimen do equally well (Berah, 1981).

Individual AT is typically open-ended, and the trainer should expect that the introduction of additional problems will extend treatment beyond the time frame of a typical group. Clients who request individual AT are likely to be engaged in treatment for 20 or more (50-minute) sessions. The probable time frame should be thoroughly discussed when obtaining informed consent, without necessarily prompting the disclosure of the additional concerns.

4. AT can be the only intervention, an adjunctive treatment to ongoing therapy, or an integral component of comprehensive therapy. Independent AT groups and workshops typically solicit basically well-adjusted individuals, screen out candidates who are inappropriate, and conduct a focused, self-contained intervention. Adjunctive AT is most typically conducted in institutions such as hospitals and mental health centers; participants with diverse and perhaps extensive psychological dysfunctions are solicited for an AT group from various wards, programs, therapists, or health providers. The AT is conducted simultaneously with the primary prescribed treatment regimen, and, after training is completed, further therapeutic gains are the responsibility of the original service provider. AT is a component of comprehensive, multifaceted therapy when it is one of several techniques implemented by the primary therapist. As discussed above, this arrangement is likely to dilute the intensity and efficiency of the AT due to consideration of multiple issues. An empirically validated self-administered AT program (eg Rakos & Schroeder, 1980) can be utilized as a cost-effective adjunct to ongoing general therapy or as the component AT intervention within a multifaceted treatment program.

AT groups that function independently of, or as adjuncts to, other therapy are often conducted by trainers who, though they may have significant background in AT, lack extensive clinical skill. This is unfortunate, because clinical expertise in group dynamics (Lange & Jakubowski, 1976) and in general therapeutic processes (Schefft & Kanfer, 1987) will be helpful in working with all clients, including those who are basically well adjusted. For example, independent group AT with nonassertive, mildly dysfunctional participants was significantly enhanced by attention to clinical issues such as the therapeutic relationship, maintaining motivation, goal clarity, continuous assessment, and programming generalization (Schefft & Kanfer, 1987). Similarly, the inclusion of relationship-facilitating interchanges within a structured AT program led to a reduction in discomfort associated with assertion (Chiappone, McCarrey, Piccinin, & Schmidtgoessling, 1981). Ford (1978) found nonassertive trainees' perception of the therapist and therapeutic relationship was an effective predictor of both dropping out, and the outcome, of training. Furthermore, important clinical issues that are addressed through the therapeutic relationship, such as the development of goal clarity (Flowers, 1978) and the resolution of value conflicts (Montgomery & Heimberg, 1978), will facilitate improved assertive abilities. Finally, competency in general behavioral principles will permit the trainer to utilize additional strategies as necessary to shape improved behavioral performance. The use of a graded stimulus hierarchy ensures that clients are focusing on issues commensurate with their current skill level and hence likely to result in a positive, reinforced experience (Rimm & Masters, 1979). Contingency contracting can be utilized to improve attendence, participation in session exercises, and completion of extra-therapy self-monitoring and experimentation (Rose, 1977, 1978; St. Lawrence, 1981). Token reinforcement (Paulson, 1975), relaxation training (Rakos & Schroeder, 1979; 1980), and hypnosis (Smith, 1985) provide additional examples of the utilization of sophisticated behavior change techniques within AT.

Chapter eight

Target populations

The bulk of the research reviewed in the previous chapters assessed the effectiveness of AT with psychiatric patients or basically well-adjusted, though nonassertive, individuals. A small number of studies dealt with persons from various subcultures. In actuality, AT has been successfully conducted with clients of such diversity that it would be only a slight exaggeration to proclaim it to be universally applicable. Trainees have varied in demographic variables (gender, age, race, ethnicity, physical and mental impairments), geographic location (much of the First World and parts of the Second and Third Worlds), and behavioral characteristics (diverse clinical dysfunctions, nonnormative life-styles). The widespread application of AT is no doubt related to the perception of AT as a panacea for all personal woes, though we cannot, of course, determine whether its popularity is a cause or result of the perception!

This chapter will survey the efficacy of AT with various 'special' populations. The extraordinary range of clients for whom AT has been successful will prevent an exhaustive examination. Instead, I will select groups that have been researched beyond a token study or two or are potentially important though currently neglected.[1] In a deviation from past chapters, extensive clinical implications will be generated only for selected populations – depressed persons, psychiatric patients, and women – and will immediately follow the general topical presentation. For the other groups, clinical issues will be integrated within the review of the data.

Behavioral problems and styles

Aggressive behavior

The conceptualization of assertion as the midpoint on the continuum between nonassertion and aggression clearly implies AT is appropriate for hostile individuals. Nevertheless, the vast majority of investigations have focused on passive persons. The disparity may be due to several factors: (a) nonassertive subjects are more easily recruited for research, perhaps because there are more of them and/or the greater social acceptability of passive behavior increases the private and then public acknowledgement of interpersonal difficulties; (b) researchers no doubt prefer to work with passive individuals; and (c) by definition, nonassertive persons will have greater difficulty refusing participation in a research study.

The research that has been conducted with aggressive individuals supports the single continuum conceptualization. AT promoted anger management (Moon & Eisler, 1983; Rahaim, Lefebvre, & Jenkins, 1980; Rimm, Hill, Brown, & Stuart, 1974), reduced abusive and assaultive rages (Foy et al., 1975) and verbal outbursts (Frederiksen, Jenkins, Foy, & Eisler, 1976; Matson & Stephens, 1978), modified hostile comments, negative verbalizations, and/or verbal and physical aggression of adolescent psychiatric patients (Bornstein, Bellack, & Hersen, 1980; Elder, Edelstein, & Narrick, 1979; Feindler, Ecton, Kingsley, & Dubey, 1986), and improved the functioning of aggressive adolescents (Dong, Hallberg, & Hassard, 1979; Huey & Rank, 1984; Pentz, 1980; Pentz & Kazdin, 1982). AT also contributed to the successful treatment of genital exposure (Langevin et al., 1979) and harming obsessions (Emmelkamp & van der Heyden, 1980) presumably related to unexpressed anger and aggressive feelings. Furthermore, AT has been an integral component of comprehensive treatment for abusive husbands (Saunders, 1984) and mothers (Scott, Baer, Christoff, & Kelly, 1984). Only Fehrenbach and Thelen (1981) and Galassi and Galassi (1978b) obtained marginal effects in attempts to improve anger control.

A fair amount of attention has been devoted to AT with violent criminal offenders or others who have become formally involved with the legal system. AT reduced verbal and physical aggression by a female prisoner (Calabrese & Hawkins, 1988) and improved the interpersonal functioning of delinquents (Thelen, Fry, Dollinger, & Paul, 1976), the assertive skills of male prisoners (Gilmour, McCormick, & de Ruiter, 1981), and the social and sexual approach skills of sexual offenders (Keltner, Scharf, & Schell, 1978). AT programs in correctional institutions may also improve the climate of the facility (Novotny & Enomoto, 1976). Beidleman (1981) reviewed the literature on AT in correctional settings and concluded that, while the results were generally positive, serious methodological flaws rendered the conclusions suggestive at best. Given the difficulty of conducting well-controlled studies in such settings, it may be a while until more definitive data are generated.

The logical assumption that individuals who commit violent acts fall toward the aggressive end of the aforementioned continuum is not clearly supported by the data. While Kirchner, Kennedy, and Draguns (1979) found male convicts were indeed more aggressive than demographically similar male vocational trainees, other data suggest that both aggressive behavior and assertive skills of general prison inmates and sexual offenders are less than (Keltner et al., 1978; Keltner, Marshall, & Marshall, 1981), or equal to (Segal & Marshall, 1985), those of controls.

One explanation for these conflicting data may be that the aggression anchoring one of the ends of the continuum has been construed too broadly.

Rimm and Masters (1979) contend two distinctions in the aggression literature have important implications for AT. The first is between *instrumental* and *drive-mediated* aggression (Feshbach, 1970). Instrumental aggression is highly goal directed toward the acquisition of tangible external reinforcement. Anger, if it is involved, is not the primary motivator, and may in fact interfere with goal attainment. Instrumental aggression may cause injury in pursuit of the goal, but injury is not the intent of the act. Drive-mediated aggression, in contrast, is characterized by anger and high levels of emotion; its goal may very well be injury rather than attainment of an external reinforcer. Rimm and Masters point out AT is best suited for modifying drive-mediated aggression, since the acquisition of alternative responses may increase the probability of resolving the anger-provoking situation. Assertion, however, is not intended to produce the reinforcements that maintain instrumental aggression and hence is unlikely to be a functionally acceptable alternative.

Rimm and Masters also distinguish between *overcontrolled* and *under-controlled* aggression (Megargee, 1966). The former is emitted by persons who have learned to inhibit expressions of anger, often to the point where it is uncontrollable, and a violent outburst is probable. The latter style is characteristic of individuals who have been conditioned to express anger in a variety of situations, even those containing minimal provocation. These persons emit verbal and physical aggression repeatedly, with little sign of guilt or regret. Rimm and Masters contend that the overcontrolled person, with feelings of guilt and penitence and a desire to change, is a far superior candidate for therapy, including AT, than is the undercontrolled individual, who typically has a long history of social and subcultural reinforcement for aggressive behavior as well as a minimal motivation to change that is completely derived from external demands.

Several studies with incarcerated individuals support Rimm and Masters' speculations. Quinsey, Maguire, and Varney (1983) found murderers with overcontrolled hostility were significantly less assertive and aggressive than undercontrolled murderers, other inmates, and unemployed persons from the local community. Henderson (1983) obtained similar results with persons in prison for committing violent crimes: overcontrolled inmates self-reported less conflict assertion and aggression than undercontrolled prisoners. Thus, aggressive behavior that is functionally related to the inability to cope with aversive situations rather than to the acquisition of potent external reinforcement may anchor the extreme end of the nonassertion–assertion–aggression continuum. Overcontrolled and drive-mediated aggressors lack socially appropriate conflict resolution and anger management skills for which AT is a viable treatment, while undercontrolled and instrumental aggressors possess acceptable assertive responses that are infrequently emitted due to extant reinforcement contingencies (ie other operant behaviors, such as aggression, produce reinforcers of greater quality and quantity). Though AT may be implemented with these persons (see Rimm and Masters for an example), two cautions are worth noting. First, since many of these individuals are members of distinct subcultures, it is critical that the therapist be culturally knowledgeable. Second, persons who exhibit undercontrolled or instrumental aggression should be considered for a homogeneous group (Rimm & Masters, 1979), since their generalized aggressive behavior is likely to intimidate other group members, particularly the timid ones. Obviously, the facilitator of such a group must be experienced, stable, firm, and supportive, and should clearly delineate the rules prior to the initiation of treatment, eg no physical violence or threats of violence.

Substance abuse

Researchers in the substance abuse field have speculated that excessive consumption of psychoactive chemicals may be functionally related to assertive skill deficits in some cases (eg Doyle, 1982; Orosz, 1982). Though an unambiguous functional relationship is difficult to demonstrate, numerous studies suggest assertion is a significant problem for some alcoholics and drug abusers.

Twentyman et al. (1982) found that alcoholics manifested significant assertive skill deficits when compared to nonclinical individuals. Hamilton and Maisto (1979) reported that alcoholics experienced greater discomfort than non-alcoholics when dealing with conflict situations, particularly those involving familiar persons. Individual differences exist among alcoholics: those who possess poor conflict assertion skills evidence more clinical dysfunction than alcoholics with adequate skill levels (Sturgis, Calhoun, & Best, 1979). Furthermore, as with assertion in general, the emission of competent behavior by alcoholics is partially determined by situational variables such as sex of the recipient and the general social context (Zielinski, 1978).

Additional data indicate that excessive alcohol consumption is directly related to the adequacy of the assertive behavior repertoire. Miller and Eisler (1977) obtained a correlation of -0.63 between the drinking behavior of alcoholics and their conflict assertion skill levels. Furthermore, alcoholics, but not social drinkers, increase their alcohol consumption following exposure to interpersonal stress (Miller, Hersen, Eisler, & Hilsman, 1974). These data converge with those of Marlatt, who found that interpersonal conflict and social pressure are two of the three primary precipitants associated with relapse by persons attempting to control excessive drinking, smoking, gambling, drug use, and eating behaviors, accounting for 16 and 20 per cent of the relapses, respectively (Marlatt & Gordon, 1985).

Alcoholics have responded well to AT: improvements have been demonstrated in social skills (Adinolfi, McCourt, & Geoghegan, 1976; Foy, Massey, Duer, Ross, & Wooten, 1979; Hirsch, von Rosenberg, Phelen, & Dudley, 1978; Materi, 1977; Scherer & Freedberg, 1976), assertion and control of drinking (Chaney, O'Leary, & Marlatt, 1978; Ferrell & Galassi, 1981; Foy, Miller, Eisler, & O'Toole, 1976; Nelson & Howell, 1982–83), and work performance (Freedberg & Johnston, 1981). However, programs that fail to deal adequately with assertion-related discomfort and social pressures to drink will probably experience high relapse rates (Rist & Watzl, 1983).

Considerably less research has focused on drug abusers, but the pattern is similar to that of problem drinkers. Heroin addicts exhibit fewer assertion abilities and more social anxiety than nonaddicts (Lindquist, Lindsay, & White, 1979), and college students who experimented with marijuana and hashish but ceased using them were more assertive than both current users and 'drug virgins' (Horan, D'Amico, & Williams, 1975). AT has improved the conflict resolution skills of drug abusers (Callner & Ross, 1978) and has been a principal component of behavioral treatment packages (Kumaraiah, 1979; Lesser, 1976).

Perhaps the most exciting application of AT in this area is the potential for prevention of abusive consumption. 'Resistance skills training' programs developed for undergraduates (Williams, Hadden, & Marcavage, 1983) and junior high school students (Dupont & Jason, 1984; Graham, Rohrbach, Hansen, Flay, & Johnson, 1989; Horan & Williams, 1982) have shown significant promise in decreasing students' desire for, and ingestion of, drugs. Efficacy will be enhanced by a focus on specific 'substance refusal skills', since deficits in those responses, rather than inadequate general skills, are associated with tobacco, alcohol and marijuana use by youngsters (Wills, Baker, & Botvin, 1989). The effectiveness of AT in this context may be related to the social validity of assertion, which is viewed by adolescents as the preferred means to refuse drug or alcohol offers and to help a friend cease substance use (Englander-Golden, Elconin, & Satir (1986).

AT has been applied to other excessive consummatory responses, but the data are too sparse to generate conclusions. AT improved the refusal skills of obese persons needing to deal with social pressures to eat (Hautzinger, 1979), but was ineffective in preventing the onset of smoking behavior by adolescents (del Greco, Breitbach, Rumer, McCarthy, & Suissa, 1986b).

Depression

Lewinsohn (1975) theorized that there is a direct link between depression and inadequate social skills that fail to maximize reinforcement and minimize punishment. In fact, depressed persons do emit greater numbers of dysfunctional and/or aversive social behaviors than nondepressed persons (Becker et al., 1987). Assertion deficits, in particular, appear to contribute importantly to dysphoric behavior. Depressed individuals, compared to nondepressed persons, are less assertive (Barbaree & Davis, 1984) and experience higher levels of assertion-related discomfort (Youngren & Lewinsohn, 1980). Furthermore, correlational studies consistently demonstrate a negative relationship between assertive skills and depression (Langone, 1979; Lea & Paquin, 1981; Pachman & Foy, 1978; Olinger, Shaw, & Kuiper, 1987; Sanchez & Lewinsohn, 1980). Sanchez and Lewinsohn, for example, found a correlation of -0.5 between assertiveness and depression in 12 depressed outpatients over a 12-week period. Interestingly, they noted 'that the rate of emitted assertive behavior may indeed be better able to predict subsequent level of depression than level of depression can predict subsequent rate of assertive behavior' (p. 120), suggesting that AT may be an important component of treatment for depression.

Experimental evaluations of AT with depressed persons have generally produced positive results (Dobia & McMurray, 1985; Hayman & Cope, 1980; Rehm, Fuchs, Roth, Kornbluth, & Romano, 1979; Sanchez, Lewinsohn, & Larson, 1980; Zeiss, Lewinsohn, & Munoz, 1979). Even 'post-partum depression' has been alleviated by AT (Phillips, 1986). However, AT alone may not produce maximum improvement with dysphoric individuals. Though Zeiss et al. (1979) found skills training to be equally effective to interventions focusing on cognitions and pleasant events in ameliorating depression, Rehm et al. (1979) found AT improved assertive skills more but depression less than a self-control training program.

Clinical implications and recommendations: depression

Becker et al. (1987) thoroughly but concisely discuss the application of social skills training to depressed persons. In addition to providing clear suggestions for skill acquisition, refinement, maintenance, and generalization, they delineate the types of clinical problems likely to be experienced when implementing a goal-directed, focused intervention with this population.[2] Essentially, they observe that impediments to positive change will be encountered with depressed clients who:

   i) refuse to accept the functional relationship between inadequate social skills and depressed mood, which will likely result in noncompliance with treatment;

   ii) refuse to allow the clinican to control the pace and strategy of intervention;

   iii) refuse to attempt homework assignments;

   iv) adhere to inflexible, dysfunctional cognitions;

   v) adopt a passive role in treatment;

   vi) lack direct links to a supportive social environment.

On the other hand, Becker et al. (1987) specifically note that clients who 'have interpersonal difficulties in the areas of positive or negative assertion are likely to benefit' from social skills training (p. 82). Thus, in their experience, the assertion deficits of depressed individuals are among the social skill difficulties most responsive to treatment.

In addition, Becker et al. (1987) highlight other concerns that arise when working with depressed clients. Overpractice, prompting, and fading are seen as essential for the replacement of well-learned but maladaptive behaviors and cognitions. Treatment may be constrained by the clinician's dependence on the client as the sole source of information (a problem that is, of course, not unique to working with depressed individuals) and by the client's variable mood states, which may require periodic shifts to supportive, empathic intervention instead of direct skill training. Suicidal ideation and intent must be closely monitored in all depressed persons, and appropriate additional intervention arranged when necessary. Finally, as discussed in earlier chapters of this book, successful skill acquisition does not guarantee that the outcome will be completely desirable for the client. Enhanced competency may present the client with new situations for which he or she is unprepared, and may result in undesired or noncompliant responses from significant others in the social environment. This situation may be particularly problematic for depressed persons, with their restricted behavioral repertoire, limited acquisition of general reinforcement, and strongly conditioned dysfunctional cognitions.

Anxiety disorders

Wolpe's (1982) contention that anxiety and assertion are incompatible responses received strong support in a correlational study by Pachman and Foy (1978). Thus, it is interesting that the research shows only limited specific benefits from AT with such problems. Two studies with agoraphobics arrived at essentially identical conclusions: exposure in vivo improved approach behavior to phobic stimuli more than AT, which was more effective in increasing assertive responding (Emmelkamp, Van der Hout, & de Vries, 1983; Thorpe, Freedman, & Lazar, 1985). Similarly, AT improved assertion but did not decrease social anxiety in persons experiencing both problems (Marshall, Keltner, & Marshall, 1981). However, success with AT in the treatment of contaminating obsessions and checking compulsions (Emmelkamp, 1981), fear of scrutiny (Lande, 1980), facial tics in children (Mansdorf, 1986), chronic fingernail biting by adolescents (Christmann & Sommer, 1976), public speaking anxiety by college students (Hoffmann, von Kalkstein, & Volger, 1978), and stuttering by young adults (Schloss, Espin, Smith, & Suffolk, 1987) has been reported. In addition, Haimo and Blitman (1985) found that AT as an adjunct to an agoraphobia treatment program significantly increased the women's masculinity scores on a sex-role concept measure.

Clearly, the inverse relationship between anxiety and assertion does not imply AT is always an appropriate treatment strategy for anxiety problems. Anxiety-based disorders are complicated syndromes that maintain a significant functional independence from assertive skill level. For example, though bulimic binge–purge episodes are widely believed to be precipitated by the aversive emotional consequences of nonassertion, leading to the routine inclusion of AT in treatment, there is little evidence to suggest the dysfunctional eating patterns are in fact related to assertion skill deficits (Mizes, 1989). And though maladaptive assertion-related cognitions are characteristic of bulimics, they appear to be much less important than cognitive distortions concerned with dieting standards, weight, and body image (Mizes, 1989). Thus, unless excessive anxiety is a direct consequence of inadequate social performance, interventions specifically designed to promote appropriate approach behavior to the noxious or otherwise problematic stimuli should be selected. The behavioral literature is replete with empirically validated treatments for these cases (cf O'Leary & Wilson, 1987).

Marital interaction

Distressed couples frequently manifest inadequate communication skills, including those involved in conflict and commendatory assertion (Jacobson, 1982). Indeed, marital adjustment appears to be related to assertion of spouse-specific concerns (Nisonoff, 1977; O'Leary & Curley, 1986; Rosenbaum & O'Leary, 1981) and effective responses in conflict situations involving trans-gressions of rights (Smolen, Spiegel, Bakker-Rabdau, Bakker, & Martin, 1985). In particular, the ability to express disagreement and anger, the ability of wives to initiate a conflict discussion and behave noncompliantly, and the ability of husbands to engage in conflict with their wives without defensive, stubborn, or withdrawal responses is strongly correlated with long-term marital satisfaction (Gottman & Krokoff, 1989). Thus, it is not surprising that AT has improved marital relationships in a variety of ways, including improved satisfaction (Powell, 1978), increased communication clarity (Epstein, DeGiovanni, & Jayne-Lazarus, 1978) and higher levels of trust and intimacy (Gordon & Waldo, 1984). These effects have been achieved in conjoint training sessions (Epstein et al., 1978) as well as when only one member of the dyad participated in therapy (Eisler, Miller, & Hersen, 1974; Gordon & Waldo, 1984).

AT directed at marital (or other intimate) relationships raises an issue not encountered in quite the same manner with most other applications. The goal of increased expressiveness is explicitly directed toward one other person – the spouse or significant other. Depending on this other person's response to the trainee's change in assertive competence, assertion may entail generally greater or lesser risks than training directed toward a more dispersed application. Assessment must clarify both the extent to which nonassertion is functional in the relationship and the potential for the recipient spouse to accept or tolerate changes that may be perceived as challenging in a variety of ways. For example, O'Leary, Curley, Rosenbaum, and Clarke (1985) discuss the cautions that are necessary when working with abused wives. These women do not exhibit generalized nonassertion (Rosenbaum & O'Leary, 1981), nor are they more unassertive than women in stressed but nonabusive marriages (Morrison, Van Hasselt, & Bellack, 1987; O'Leary & Curley, 1984). Rather, they are unassertive with their abusing spouses, who themselves are likely to exhibit assertive deficits (Morrison et al., 1987). However, since the wife's passivity is a functional coping behavior, producing important negative reinforcers (ie avoidance or reduction of abuse) that are unlikely to be acquired through alternative behaviors, it is generally unwise to attempt to increase the frequency of assertion to the abusing spouse. If an AT treatment focus is judged to be necessary or desirable, it should be offered to an abused wife only after extensive clarification of the distinction between assertion and aggression, practice in assertion to other individuals, and discussion that has clearly identified the risks and alternative interventions (see Chapter 9). However, O'Leary et al. (1985) recommend that AT for abused wives usually is most appropriate when, as part of a comprehensive treatment, it focuses on nonmarital concerns. AT in this context is likely to improve the battered woman's self-esteem, perceptions of control, and fear of leaving the abusive relationship (Jansen & Meyers-Abell, 1980). AT may also be appropriate – and effective – for women already residing in battered women's shelters as a means to help them permanently leave the abusive situation (Meyers-Abell & Jansen, 1980).

Severely disturbed behavior

Inpatient schizophrenics constituted the subjects for many of the early AT component studies (eg Hersen et al., 1973; 1974). Over the years, research consistently demonstrated that AT improves the interpersonal functioning of psychiatric patients (Fiedler, Orenstein, Chiles, Fritz, & Breitt, 1979; Finch & Wallace, 1977; Goldsmith & McFall, 1975; Longin & Rooney, 1975; Monti et al., 1979; Monti, Curran, Corriveau, DeLancey, & Hagerman, 1980; Williams, Turner, Watts, Bellack, & Hersen, 1977). Furthermore, Monti and his colleagues report significant generalization and maintenance effects (Monti, Corriveau, & Curran, 1982). Thus, recent literature reviews of social skill and assertiveness training programs conclude these interventions produce clinically significant, durable, and generalizable gains (eg Donahoe & Driesenga, 1988).

This favorable evaluation of social skill training with schizophrenics is reinforced by meta-analytic data quantifying the change reported by 27 studies (Benton & Schroeder, in press): significant gains, comparable to those obtained for other 'effective' treatments, were achieved for behavioral skill, self-rated assertiveness, generalization and maintenance, and hospital discharge rate. Relapse rate decreased moderately, but there was little impact on broader symptomatology and functioning. Interestingly, outcome was unaffected by numerous 'moderator' variables, including sex, chronicity, setting (in- or outpatient), number of training techniques, training format, or hours of training.

These data are encouraging, since inadequate and unusual social behaviors are distinguishing characteristics of schizophrenia (see *Diagnostic and Statistical Manual* of the American Psychiatric Association, 1987). Distinct patterns of social interaction are observed even by schizophrenics who are 'in remission' or who are responding positively to pharmacological treatment (St. Lawrence, 1986). Nevertheless, AT should be implemented with psychotic persons only when a thorough functional analysis indicates it is warranted (Morrison & Bellack, 1984). In particular, while overt skill deficits are likely to be present, a significant emphasis must be placed on the perceptual and information-processing components of social skill (Morrison & Bellack, 1984), which may produce the greatest impediments to successful interpersonal functioning in this population (Morrison, 1988). For example, psychiatric patients are particularly poor at decoding the messages contained in the nonverbal behavior of others (Fingeret, Monti, & Paxson, 1985). In fact, intensive problem-solving training and other strategies designed to ameliorate various cognitive deficits have yielded promising initial results, including reduced relapse rates (Liberman, Neuchterlein, & Wallace, 1982; Wallace, 1982).

Clinical implications and recommendations: severely disturbed individuals

It is almost unnecessary to note the therapeutic challenges presented by the complexity, pervasiveness, and chronicity of psychotic disorders. Thorough therapist training in the AT protocol is indicated, even for experienced clinicians (Monti et al., 1982). The establishment of the minimal goals necessary to place the individual in a less restrictive setting is preferred to the articulation of optimal goals, which are probably unrealistic (Paul, 1981).

AT will almost certainly be an adjunctive or partial treatment with severely disturbed clients, who require comprehensive multimodal therapy. The therapist must be well acquainted with the theoretical and clinical issues that are likely to impact upon treatment efficacy; in other words, AT cannot be conducted with schizophrenics in a theoretical vacuum, as it is with some other disorders. Morrison (1988) notes, for example, that (a) the social skills of these clients are related more to deficit or negative behaviors (eg avolition, anhedonia) than to positive ones (eg hallucinations, delusions), (b) affect recognition and information processing directly influence social responding, and (c) the chronic yet episodic nature of schizophrenia may have important implications for social skills assessment and training. Thus, Liberman et al. (1982) contend the following factors must be incorporated into any social skills training program for schizophrenics:

1) Family: dysfunctional communication patterns and excessive emotional expression and overinvolvement.

2) Social and community factors: identification of the actual stimuli that present critical difficulties in interpersonal adjustment for each client; these factors are often different from the situations targeted in training.

3) Assessment: integration of social skills training within broader treatment (eg drug), and the determination of when and for how long to intervene.

4) Motivational deficits: therapists must be prepared to develop a long-term, trusting, open relationship with the schizophrenic that will span at least several months but more likely years; such a relationship will be formed only if the therapist accompanies the client into the community for both therapeutic and nontherapeutic (ie pleasure) purposes. The efficacy of other motivational techniques such as contingent positive (eg money) and negative (eg social criticism) reinforcement depends on the quality of the therapeutic alliance.

5) Cognitive deficits: training in problem solving and social perception skills,[3] though exceptionally important for these clients, must not be too demanding. Sound behavioral shaping principles, clear prompts and instructions, ample learning opportunities, and a supportive, sensitive, competent therapist who can prevent client withdrawal due to understimulation or symptom exacerbation due to overstimulation (cf Wing, 1978) become particularly important.

6) Pragmatism: coping behaviors beyond assertion, such as avoidance and

escape, as alternatives to managing stress and overstimulation; thus, terminating politely and rudely, ignoring criticism, and coming back later should be taught as alternatives to the more traditional AT targets of compromising, persisting, refusing, explaining, and empathizing.

Finally, Liberman, DeRisi, and Mueser's (1989) concise, specific, yet comprehensive therapist manual is an outstanding clinical resource for conducting social skill training with psychiatric patients.

Unconventional lifestyles

Homosexuals, as a group, do not appear to evidence assertion deficits. In Argentina, male homosexuals and heterosexuals demonstrated equivalent levels of self-reported skill, while female homosexuals self-reported greater assertion than their heterosexual counterparts (Granero, 1984). However, homosexuals whose goal is to deal with, and change, an oppressive social structure (cf Davison, 1976; 1978) may require a skill level more advanced than that necessary for adaptive functioning by a heterosexual. While AT appears to offer promise for improving homosexual functioning (Duehn & Mayadas, 1976; McKinlay, Kelly, & Patterson, 1978; Russell & Winkler, 1977; St. Lawrence, Bradlyn, & Kelly, 1983), research has completely neglected these clients in the past decade, perhaps as a reflection of the Western turn toward conservatism and conventionality.

Populations defined demographically

Women

AT for women is inherently political, stemming from its early association with the women's movement of the late sixties and early seventies (Goldstein-Fodor & Epstein, 1983). The promotion of AT as a means to female 'liberation' encouraged women to become avid consumers of self-help and formal programs. This investment in self-empowerment, at least in regard to therapist-facilitated training, may pay significant dividends: the research confirms that such interventions can significantly enhance the conflict assertive skills of females in university settings (eg Berah, 1981; Craighead, 1979; Gulanick & Howard, 1979; Rathus, 1973b; Thelen & Lasoski, 1980; Young et al., 1973), women in outpatient counseling (Wolfe & Fodor, 1977), and women volunteers from the general community (Linehan, Goldfried, & Goldfried, 1979; Linehan, Walker, Bronheim, Haynes, & Yevzeroff, 1979; Meehan & Goldkopf, 1982; Stoppard & Henri, 1987). AT has been employed successfully with community women in Australia (Smith, 1985) and the Netherlands (Rijken & deWildt, 1978) and with high school and college females in Japan (Maeda, 1985). Wolfe and Fodor (1975) and Kincaid (1978) describe the observed and reported benefits that accrued to the numerous women who participated in their clinical AT groups. Finally, AT with women has been frequently combined with 'consciousness raising' (Lange & Jakubowski, 1976), producing a treatment that provides even greater benefits (Meehan & Goldkopf, 1982).

AT has also been applied to specific problems primarily or uniquely experienced by women. Sexually unassertive women increased their expressions of needs and desires (Hammond & Oei, 1982), a result that appears to provide benefits to men (Sirkin & Mosher, 1985) as well as to women. AT and 'personal defense training' produced important changes in women's perceptions of their rights (particularly refusal ones) and ability to identify circumstances in which their rights were violated (Kidder, Boell, & Moyer, 1983). Three sessions of AT, focusing on physical defenses, sexual rights, and verbal noncompliance, significantly improved women's resistance to unwanted sexual advances (Muehlenhard et al., 1989). Finally, female rape victims reduced their fear, anxiety, and depression and increased their self-esteem, self-concept, and assertion skills in six sessions of cognitive-behavioral AT (Resick, Jordan, Girelli, Hutter, & Marhoefer-Dvorak, 1988).

Nevertheless, a significant portion of female trainees fail to improve or maintain and generalize their gains in the natural environment (Goldstein-Fodor & Epstein, 1983).[4] Several writers suggest this may be due to a more negative reaction from others, particularly males, to assertion initiated by women than by men (Goldstein-Fodor & Epstein, 1983; MacDonald, 1982), but the extensive literature reviewed in Chapter 5 indicates that differential consequences as a function of gender are not a pervasive and consistent phenomenon. While it is undoubtedly true that assertion by women entails enhanced risk in certain (currently unspecified) situations, this variable, at best, seems to be only a partial explanation for the treatment failures with females. Other possibilities, such as resistance to change in stereotyped sex roles by both men and women (proposed in Chapter 5) or the strongly conditioned beliefs and values incorporated by women into their self-concept as a consequence of a sex-typed socialization process, merit careful exploration.

Reviews of AT with women invariably do focus on the societal sex-role stereotyping and sexual discrimination presumed to underlie female nonassertion (Kahn, 1981; Linehan, 1984; Linehan & Egan, 1979; MacDonald, 1982; Muehlenhard, 1983; Goldstein-Fodor & Epstein, 1983). Sexism is manifested in complex ways that defy simple elucidation and resolution. For instance, sexism is so engrained in the fabric of Western culture that the possession of socially defined physical attractiveness may facilitate the emission of assertive behaviors by women (Jackson & Huston, 1975). Or, to take a second example, despite possessing a myriad of social competencies that allow their needs for relatedness and equality to be met in same-sexed friendships, women do not experience similar satisfactions in intimate heterosexual relationships (Worell, 1988). Since virtually all clinicians who conduct AT are likely to have female trainees, the authors cited above should be consulted so that a full appreciation of the social discriminations encountered by women can be acquired.

Clinical implications and recommendations: women

1. Same-sexed groups (including leaders) often result in greater self-disclosure and intimacy than mixed-sex groups (Lange & Jakubowski, 1976). In addition, groups composed only of females provide opportunities to relate social and political factors directly to the problems experienced by women (Gottlieb, Burden, McCormick, & Nicarthy, 1983). Therefore, when women's issues are targeted as the focus of AT (even without consciousness raising), Lange and Jakubowski suggest that males be excluded from participation. However, Goldstein-Fodor and Epstein (1983) speculate that a female group fails to 'give women the opportunity to test out their new assertive behaviors in areas where men are present during training and [allows women] to persist in their own definition of what is important for them to work on' (p. 154). Alberti and Emmons (1986a) also find increased training opportunities in mixed-sex groups.

Heterosexually composed groups also provide men with a direct opportunity to increase their awareness of, and then challenge and change, sexist attitudes and behaviors. For example, men need to learn to accept the expression of anger by women (Kahn, 1984) and to interact with them on the basis of behavior rather than attire (Hess & Bornstein, 1979).

2. Commendatory assertion is frequently neglected in AT groups of all kinds. Not surprisingly, the evidence suggests that women, compared to men, emit more positive assertions, are more polite and supportive, use emotional language more frequently, and laugh more in mixed-sex dyads (Muehlenhard, 1983). The deemphasis on commendatory assertion may particularly hinder the growth of women through missed opportunities to capitalize on existing strengths. Thus, numerous writers advocate an explicit focus on positive emotional expressiveness (Kahn, 1981) and 'traditional' feminine behaviors such as placating, stroking, and smiling (Goldstein-Fodor & Epstein, 1983; to be employed cautiously – see Chapter 5). In addition to improving interpersonal efficacy, an emphasis on commendatory assertion would enhance the validity of stereotypical feminine behaviors and values, countering their devaluation by society, assertiveness trainers, and the women's movement (Goldstein-Fodor & Epstein, 1983).

3. While the assertive abilities of women are strongly associated with long-term marital satisfaction (Gottman & Krokoff, 1989), the amount of change a woman will demonstrate after AT is likely to be directly related to the reaction of her 'significant other'.[5] Goldstein-Fodor and Epstein (1983) and Kahn (1981) contend the active involvement of the man is essential for the development of effective assertion by the woman. With conjoint participation, the failure of the man to appreciate assertion might be avoided, predictions of his response to assertion may be improved, and power struggles can be defused. Most basically, the social power inequities embedded within the marital relationship (cf

Jacobson, 1989) could be directly addressed. Conjoint participation may also provide benefits for the man: Powell (1978) found training that included empathic listening increased husbands' marital satisfaction.

4. AT trainers must recognize that certain situations pose an increased risk for women that may contraindicate AT or suggest more modest goals and/or additional interventions. Abused wives, as previously discussed, may receive severe negative consequences for assertion (Goldstein-Fodor & Epstein, 1983; O'Leary et al., 1985). Women who are economically dependent upon their husbands may be inhibited from asserting themselves without comprehensive skill and cognitive training (Goldstein-Fodor & Epstein, 1983). Victims of sexual harassment in the workplace can lose their jobs, even when assertion is appropriately confined within company grievance procedures.

5. Because of sexism, AT with women will probably require more intensive intervention than training with men. Women are victimized by sex-role stereotyping in at least two ways: they are subjected to overt social and vocational discrimination and, as a consequence, internalize specific societal expectations. Thus, women must deal with social oppression *as well as* ambivalence in abandoning the traditional wife and mother roles (Kahn, 1981).

This combination of external and internal pressure is likely to present women with specific, complex issues that require intensive 'working through'. In the realm of internalized sex-role expectations, for example, many women appear to base their moral reasoning on the concepts of attachment and relationships, which are different than, but not inferior to, the male values of autonomy and competition (Gilligan, 1982).[6] AT should not simply impose the masculine orientation on women trainees (Gervasio & Crawford, 1989), but, rather, must engineer a conciliation between 'gender' sources of behavioral guidance. A second issue likely to arise is anger. Women – as members of a subordinate group – are taught that the expression of anger is permissible only under very limited circumstances, such as in the defense of their children. Consequently, women may perceive its expression in other situations as a threat to their relationships, and hence identity (Miller, 1983). Some data do suggest that women express anger less frequently than men (Doyle & Biaggio, 1981) and receive sanctions when its expression is sex-role incongruent (Kahn, 1984). For many women, the acceptance of anger and its appropriate expression as legitimate phenomena will require a fundamental change in basic beliefs. This contention is supported by data that, unfortunately, are from the early 1970s. Female students (Hartsook, Olch, & deWolf, 1976) and professionals (Brockway, 1976) who requested AT were found to exhibit excessive anxiety and irrational thoughts (eg exaggerated desire for approval) rather than overt behavioral deficits. It is the fundamental conditioned beliefs relating to *ideal* self-concept that are likely to require intensive intervention – more so than superficially similar beliefs that might relate to a man's *actual* self-concept. Women, but also trainers, must therefore have realistic expectations concerning the length of training necessary to effect meaningful life changes (Goldstein-Fodor & Epstein, 1983).

The social discrimination experienced by women is also likely to necessitate more intensive training. MacDonald (1982) suggested females are subjected to more rights-infringement situations than are males. She reviews literature that indicates parents prefer male offspring (and therefore value males more than females), and that males receive preferential treatment throughout the socialization process, from childhood through adulthood.[7] Thus, women are valued less than men in an objective sense. However, cultures adhering to notions of traditional democratic 'rights' assert that both sexes have equivalent rights. Since women have equal theoretical rights, but fewer actual ones, they will be faced with a greater number of abstractly appropriate assertion situations. This prediction is consistent with data indicating that men treat women differently than they treat other men: they are more likely to ask women to change undesired behavior and less likely to offer a spontaneous favor to men (Eisler et al., 1975; Deaux, 1971; Unger, Raymond, & Levine, 1974). And in her own research, MacDonald found that women are confronted with over 50 per cent more situations appropriate for assertion than are men. Thus, even ignoring potential qualitative differences in the difficulty of the assertion-relevant situations faced by each sex, which given the existing sexism are likely to further increase the obstacles to effective female expression, the sheer number of additional situations with which women must contend suggests that training for them will generally require more intensive intervention.

6. Clinicians working with nonassertive women must be cognizant of the infiltration of unintended sexism within psychotherapy in general (Hare-Mustin, 1983) and AT theory and practice in particular, with its masculine definition of social adaptation (Gervasio & Crawford, 1989; Kahn, 1981; MacDonald, 1982; Wine, 1981). Wine, as noted earlier, argues that Schwartz and Gottman's (1976) classic study characterized 'positive' and 'negative' self-statements in terms of a value orientation rather than a functional distinction: positive self-statements exemplify a self-centered pursuit of independent goal acquisition, while negative ones relate to sensitivity, altruism, and nurturance. She contends such value differences do not imply that one set is better or worse, or more or less functional, than the other. In fact, the study's main finding – that assertive and nonassertive individuals differed primarily in self-statement content rather than behavioral skill – is seen by her to confirm an interpretation that stresses values instead of one that emphasizes adaptiveness.

Goldstein-Fodor and Epstein (1983) likewise challenge Schwartz and Gottman's interpretation that most negative self-statements overestimate the likelihood of negative consequences, and suggest, in many instances, they are accurate representations of an oppressive social environment.

7. The situations selected for AT should be personally meaningful to the trainee.

While this recommendation appears obvious, data collected by Cooley (1979) in the US and Lefevre and West (1984) with English-speaking Canadians indicate that packaged AT programs often focus on issues of low priority to trainees. Both studies, for example, demonstrated that refusal situations, interactions with sales- and service-persons, and accepting and giving compliments were judged to be less important than increased competency in dealing with aggressive verbalizations and high-status professionals, expressing opinions and negative feelings, social conversations, and job interviews and work-related interactions. These studies are particularly relevant to AT with women since the subject samples in both studies were predominantly female (80 per cent in Cooley and 76 per cent in Lefevre and West) and, hence, support Goldstein-Fodor and Epstein's (1983) contention that AT groups frequently fail to focus on the current real-life issues faced by women and therefore fail to prepare them adequately for new social roles.

Medical patients

Van Dijk (1977) hypothesized that many of the physical complaints experienced by clients may be a function of unexpressed emotions and suggested AT was the treatment of choice in such cases. Modest support for this proposal can be found in several studies. Williams and Stout (1985) reported that highly assertive individuals experienced fewer health problems than persons with assertion deficits, while Heiser and Gannon (1984) demonstrated psychosomatic symptomatology was consistently associated with the indirect expression of anger (though it was not inversely related to the direct expression of hostility).

Two studies investigated the relationship between assertiveness and hypertension. Keane et al. (1982) found both hypertensive and normotensive medical patients responded less assertively than nonpatients. Thus, while Keane et al. failed to differentially identify assertive skill deficits in hypertensives, they did provide additional data suggesting such behavioral incompetency is related to chronic illness. Morrison, Bellack, and Manuck (1985) examined hypertensives more closely. They divided these patients into groups experiencing large or small increases in pulse pressure during interpersonal conflict. The minimal-change patients performed unassertively compared to normotensives and hypertensives who manifested large changes. In contrast, the large-change hypertensives demonstrated inappropriately excessive assertion, ie aggression. Thus, the behavior of both groups of hypertensives was socially dysfunctional. Unfortunately, no research has evaluated the utility of implementing AT with either type of hypertensive patient.

The handful of studies that do assess AT's impact on medical problems are not encouraging. AT was ineffective in ameliorating migraine headaches (Gainer, 1978) and contributed minimally to the treatment of chronic low-back pain; instead, relaxation training and social reinforcement of increased activity were identified as the effective component interventions (Sanders, 1983). Bhargava (1983) employed relaxation training and AT in the successful treatment of severe tension headaches. In light of the well-documented effects of relaxation training alone on tension headaches (cf O'Leary & Wilson, 1987), as well as the Sanders (1983) study on low-back pain, there is little reason to be sanguine that the AT contributed to the observed improvement. A similar conclusion seems warranted for a package that combined anxiety management and AT in the effective treatment of duodenal ulcers (Brooks & Richardson, 1980). Finally, in a study with implications for the prevention of medical problems, AT failed to produce changes in the Type A (coronary-prone) behavior of university faculty (Thurman, 1985a, 1985b).

The situation with physical symptoms is, at present, similar to that of anxiety disorders; there is little reason to utilize AT procedures with such problems except, perhaps, when they can be directly linked to a failure to assert. Clearly, there is a pressing need for research of the type conducted by Sanders (1983) to assess the contribution, if any, of AT to the remediation of a wide variety of stress-related physical complaints. Until those studies are completed, clinicians are advised to utilize those interventions that have already garnered empirical support (cf O'Leary & Wilson, 1987).

Recently, researchers working with chronic illness patients suggested assertive skills may facilitate compliance with medical treatment (Meichenbaum & Turk, 1987). In particular, diabetes in pre-adolescents (Gross & Johnson, 1981) and adults (Ary, Toobert, Wilson, & Glasgow, 1986) has been the focus of interest. Ary et al. (1986), for example, found refusal skills were critical for resisting temptations that violated the prescribed treatment regimen, and behavior change requests (for alternative menu items) were necessary when dining in restaurants. Since treatment adherence essentially involves self-regulation in resisting powerful proximate stimuli, AT may prove quite useful in working with chronically ill patients, as it has with other self-management problems (eg substance abuse).

The elderly

The application of AT with the elderly is in its infancy, but is highlighted here to stimulate further work with this population. Corby (1975) discussed the utilization of AT with nursing-home staff and relatives of the aged as a means to encourage greater assertion by the elderly. Edinberg, Karoly, and Gleser (1977) and Ruben (1984) attempted to refine assessment procedures for this group. Finally, Doty (1987) developed a communication and assertion skills workbook for persons who are involved with the care of elderly persons. Clearly, much additional research is necessary before meaningful conclusions can be generated regarding AT with the aged.

Children and adolescents

Appropriate assertive skill appears to be an important contributor to adaptive social functioning of children (Deluty, 1981c; Van Hasselt, Hersen, & Bellack, 1984), and may represent a critical developmental accomplishment (Michelson & Wood, 1980b), although the relationship of *nonassertion* to general adjustment remains unclear (Hops & Greenwood, 1988). AT has been successfully implemented with children specifically identified as nonassertive (Bornstein, Bellack, & Hersen, 1977; Dopfner, Schluter, & Rey, 1981) as well as with samples of children who spanned the range of assertiveness (Michelson & Wood, 1980a; Rotheram, Armstrong, & Booraem, 1982; Vogrin & Kassinove, 1979). Rotheram et al.'s results are particularly interesting since they suggest the efficacy of AT as a primary prevention intervention. Students who received AT demonstrated improved school behavior, increased popularity, and better academic achievement (including higher grade point averages at a one-year follow-up). AT has also been used with children experiencing stress-related problems: it eliminated facial tics that were functionally related to nonassertion in conflict situations (Mansdorf, 1986) and, as a component of treatment, improved children's attitudes and beliefs about their parents' divorce (Roseby & Deutsch, 1985).

AT with adolescents has been shown to have a variety of beneficial effects, though individual differences such as verbal aptitude skills and anxiety may influence the outcome (Pentz, 1981). Increased assertiveness (Kirkland, Thelen, & Miller, 1982; McCullagh, 1982b; Pentz & Kazdin, 1982), self-esteem (Stake, DeVille, & Pennell, 1983; Waksman, 1984a, 1984b), and self-efficacy (Pentz & Kazdin, 1982), and decreased aggressiveness (Huey & Rank, 1984; Pentz & Kazdin, 1982) and anxiety (Wehr & Kaufman, 1987) are among the gains reported in the literature. AT has also been utilized to teach coping skills to adolescent diabetics (Johnson, Gross, & Wildman, 1982), improve the adjustment of incarcerated delinquents (Ollendick & Hersen, 1979), and remediate school refusal and social withdrawal (Yamasaki, 1985). As noted earlier, AT is a promising approach to the prevention of adolescent drug and alcohol consumption (Dupont & Jason, 1984; Graham et al., 1989; Horan & Williams, 1982), but has not demonstrated similar potency in regard to tobacco use (del Greco et al., 1986b).

Impaired and handicapped persons

Physically handicapped individuals have been the focus of several investigations. Joiner, Lovett, and Hague (1982) found disabled applicants for vocational rehabilitation services were less assertive than non-handicapped persons, but Gambrill, Florian, and Splaver (1986) determined that disabled undergraduates evidenced higher levels of assertion and less discomfort than 'normal' students. However, high discomfort and low assertion were directly related to feelings of loneliness and lack of control over social life. Clearly, the development of appropriate assertive skills is an important goal for many physically handicapped persons.

Thus, it is encouraging that AT increased the verbal assertion skills of spinal-cord-injured clients (Dunn, Van Horn, & Herman, 1981) and severely disabled individuals in rehabilitation center (Grimes, 1980) and university (Mishel, 1978; Starke 1987) settings. Participation in AT has also improved perceived assertiveness, acceptance of disability, self-concept, and social discomfort in individuals confined to wheelchairs (Glueckauf, Horley, Poushinsky, & Vogel, 1984; Morgan & Leung, 1980).

Visually impaired persons are another potential target group. Harrell and Strauss (1986) observed many such individuals are either nonassertive or aggressive due to learned helplessness (Seligman, 1975).[8] Assertive skills, by improving communication, are proposed to enhance feelings of control. Ryan (1976) suggested visually handicapped persons require help in accepting the concept of leisure, and proposed that AT can be an important tool in communicating that ethic to others. While no research has studied perceptions of control and leisure in relation to assertive skills of visually handicapped individuals, Van Hasselt, Kazdin, and Hersen (1985) determined that AT could provide traditional gains for such persons. They found stereotyped nonverbal behaviors (eg body rocking, head swaying, hand flapping) and maladaptive paralinguistic responses (eg long latency, excessive speech dysfluency) characterized the social interactions of blind adolescents. AT, consisting of modeling, instructions, behavior rehearsal, feedback, and manual guidance, significantly enhanced the assertive skills of the visually impaired females. Obviously, AT with the visually handicapped will be most effective when the clinician is highly sensitive to the physical limitations of these clients. Ruben (1983) discussed methodological adaptations necessary for implementing AT with blind persons, suggesting that additional auditory and gestural manipulations be included. Other specific training suggestions for AT with this population are offered by Harrell and Strauss (1986) and Ryan (1976).

Hearing impaired persons experience even greater social and emotional problems than do the visually impaired (Matson & Ollendick, 1988), yet have been the focus of even less attention than the few articles devoted to the latter group. Nevertheless, three investigations suggest this population has been unjustifiably neglected. The first study found hearing impaired children were less assertive than nonhandicapped cohorts (Macklin & Matson, 1985). The second study (Lemanek, Williamson, Gresham, & Jensen, 1986) used AT procedures (behavior rehearsal, feedback, instructions, modeling, shaping, social reinforcement) to increase the frequency of communication, open-ended questions, smiles, eye contact, and gestures in four socially withdrawn, significantly hearing impaired individuals (ages 11–18). Marked improvements in the target behaviors were noted regardless of the child's primary mechanism of communication (sign language or oral speech). A third study employed AT with deaf adolescents and found the gains generalized to a classroom setting (Martin-Laval, 1983).

Mentally handicapped (retarded) individuals may also be appropriate consumers of AT (Bregman, 1985). Kirkland and Caughlin-Carver (1982) demonstrated improvement, generalization, and maintenance of refusal skills in individuals with IQs ranging from 43–75. Bregman (1984) taught a similar population to assert more effectively, but failed to improve their ability to discriminate between nonassertive, assertive, and aggressive responses. Other researchers have also documented a positive response to AT by educable (Bates, 1980; Bornstein, Bach, McFall, Friman, & Lyons, 1980; Fleming & Fleming, 1982; Ryba & Brown, 1979; Turner, Hersen, & Bellack, 1979) and even severely (Senatore, Matson, & Kazdin, 1982; Wortmann & Paluck, 1979) retarded persons. Modifications in the traditional AT package may be necessary for maximizing the gains of these individuals. For example, Senatore et al. (1982) found 'active rehearsal' (detailed scene reenactment, overt rehearsal, prompts, props, and solitary practice) produced a more potent treatment package with instructions, modeling, performance feedback, and social reinforcement than did simple role playing. Bregman (1985) discusses the specific variables that appear important for working with this population (eg increased focus, reinforcement, and group process time) and provides an AT outline.

Social roles

AT has been utilized to improve the performance of individuals functioning in various socially defined roles. In business, managers (Shaw & Rutledge, 1976) and women (Brockway, 1976; Pilla, 1977) have appeared to improve their assertive skills through AT, though only Brockway conducted a controlled study. In addition, job performance self-esteem of working women increased after participation in AT (Stake & Pearlman, 1980).

Programs have been developed for job applicants (McGovern, Tinsley, Liss-Levinson, Laventure, & Britton, 1975), and controlled research with disadvantaged interviewees, such as stutterers (Schloss et al., 1987) and welfare-rehabilitation clients (Arnold & Parrott, 1978), suggests AT significantly improves skilled behavior. For years, this application was based only on common sense. However, recent data by Phillips and Bruch (1988) indicate that AT directed at shy job applicants may be particularly indicated. They found socially withdrawn young adults were more undecided about their career, engaged in fewer information-seeking behaviors, and performed fewer assertive interview behaviors than their more outgoing colleagues. Shy men also expected assertion in an interview to result in relatively unfavorable consequences. Unfortunately, there are no data to confirm the intuitive assumption that such a response style before, during, or after the interview improves the applicant's chances of being hired. In fact, Cianni-Surridge and Horan (1983) found that employers reacted negatively to certain assertive job-seeking behaviors performed before or after the actual interview, despite the fact that most belong to positive response classes. Furthermore, the reaction to several of the behaviors was related to the size of the prospective employer. Thus, a cautious approach to the training of job-seeking skills is warranted, particularly those not directly involved in the actual interview.

Workers in the mental health field have been identified as appropriate consumers of AT. Nurses, a high-priority group due to their historical, sex-typed subordination to doctors, have improved their skills after participation in AT (McIntyre, Jeffrey, & McIntyre, 1984). Assertiveness in nurses is particularly important since it is related to a role conception that is professional rather than bureaucratic or service-oriented (Kinney, 1985). AT programs have been designed to increase the assumption of the professional role (Numerof, 1978), but they appear primarily to improve assertiveness without altering role conception (Dunham & Brower, 1984). However, leading AT groups (Gordon & Goble, 1986) or participating in AT with residents and interns (Bair & Greenspan, 1986) may be more promising mechanisms for stimulating role reconceptualization.

Resident assistants in college dorms are more effective when they possess assertive skills (Shelton & Mathis, 1976) and, therefore, have been targeted for AT (Layne, Layne, & Schoch, 1977). Paraprofessional helpers (Flowers & Goldman, 1976) and counselor trainees (Jansen & Litwack, 1979) have also benefited from AT.

Finally, participation in AT has been advocated as a means to improve the interpersonal effectiveness of high school coaches (Miller, 1982) and the self-esteem and influence of parents (Clifford, 1987). These programs raise interesting possibilities, but their value must await experimental investigation.

Chapter nine

Clinical issues in assertiveness training

This chapter will survey selected problems and phenomena associated with the implementation of AT procedures. First, I will identify the factors that most frequently present obstacles to effective intervention. Next, a discussion of positive assertion will be offered, in an effort to broaden the focus and scope of traditional AT. The third section will review the ethical issues involved in AT, with particular attention devoted to informed consent. The chapter will conclude with a review of intervention resources available for use by the clinician.

Limitations to change

Therapist variables

Inadequate assessment

The behavioral assessment is the foundation upon which the success of any behavioral intervention rests, and AT is no exception. Each candidate for AT must be thoroughly assessed to ensure he or she manifests assertive performance deficits that either limit social adaptation or directly result in other problems (eg marital discord, anxiety). The clinician must then determine whether AT should be the primary intervention, a component of comprehensive treatment, or delayed until other problems have been addressed. The functional analysis must also identify the constraints on treatment presented by client and environmental characteristics; failure to do so will increase the probability that the client will resist treatment (see p. 174).

Furthermore, trainers conducting groups must assess individual candidates in terms of their appropriateness for inclusion in the planned group. As noted earlier, homogeneous groups may be essential for effectiveness in some cases. Interpersonal skill level, extent of general dysfunction, type of inappropriate non-assertive behavior (passivity vs aggressiveness), age, and, according to some writers, gender, have all been identified as important variables (Alberti & Emmons, 1986a; Emmons & Alberti, 1983; Kelly, 1985; Lange & Jakubowski, 1976). In addition, the group process will be facilitated by homogeneity in the degree of acculturation to the mainstream societal values that permeate the training philosophy.

Inadequate intervention

The AT procedures themselves must meet the needs and competencies of the trainees. Emmons and Alberti (1983) point out that many trainers implement 'canned procedures' that fail to capitalize on the opportunities afforded by AT. They note, for example, that some clients may require more extensive visual and auditory stimuli while others may respond best to didactic and demonstration methods. Other media through which assertiveness might be efficaciously taught include art exercises, games, and imagery sharing (see Chapter 7). Some extremely timid clients may perceive behavior rehearsal as highly threatening, and may respond more positively to training initiated with introductory exercises focusing on greetings, compliments, positive self-statements, and small talk (Lange & Jakubowski, 1976; Rimm & Masters, 1979). Sophisticated behavioral techniques that are not typically part of the package may prove immensely helpful in some cases; these include relaxation training, hypnosis, contingency contracting, and token economies. The clinician conducting AT, in other words, must be as creative and flexible as any good behavior therapist, indeed, as any good therapist!

Reliance on canned packages may also lead to the selection of minimally relevant behaviors and situations. While there are good reasons to initiate AT with a focus on refusal situations (see Chapter 5), it is obvious that the emphasis must soon shift to issues holding a higher priority for most trainees. Typically, these include dealing with aggressive behavior, being assertive with supervisors and high-status professionals, expressing negative feelings to people in close relationships, expressing unpopular or differing opinions, and requesting behavior changes from service people. In addition, several positive assertions are also highly prioritized: initiating or participating in social conversations, behaving assertively in job interviews, asking for help or making requests of others, and, to a lesser extent, expressing positive feelings and talking positively about personal accomplishments (Cooley, 1979; Lefevre & West, 1984).

Finally, canned procedures may be insufficiently intense to effect desired change. An 8-session group may be adequate for college undergraduates, but too short for women coping with sexism (Goldstein-Fodor & Epstein, 1983), schizophrenics who are severely skill deficient (cf Wallace, 1982),[1] or mentally handicapped individuals (Bregman, 1985).

Goldstein-Fodor and Epstein (1983) offer the intriguing suggestion that progress in AT may be impeded by the competent, independent role model that the clinician almost invariably presents to trainees. Such a 'mastery' model may create psychological distance between the trainees and therapist and miss the opportunity to teach clients that 'behaving assertively' is often difficult even for individuals who possess sophisticated interpersonal competencies. AT facilitators, therefore, should consistently share with trainees their own struggles with

173

assertiveness. However, though a coping therapist model may enhance impact (O'Leary & Wilson, 1987), self-disclosures must be concise, offered with discretion, and intended for the benefit of trainees, or the therapist will be focusing on him or herself (ie 'working out personal problems').

Inadequate training

Accurate assessment and effective intervention are obviously based on the knowledge and competence of the practitioner. Minimal standards of formal training, proposed in a statement of 'Ethical Principles' for AT (cf Alberti & Emmons, 1986b), explicitly emphasize thorough education in behavioral principles, AT research and intervention procedures, and, for trainers working with clinical populations, the characteristics of relevant psychological dysfunctions. In addition, trainers must be familiar with the sociopolitical and structural determinants of social dysfunction (Gervasio & Crawford, 1989) and subcultural variables that influence individual behavior. As a graduate student remarked to me upon reading a comprehensive chapter on AT (Rakos, 1986), 'I didn't realize there was so much involved in AT'. My reply was something like 'Wait until you read my book!'

Client variables

Baseline behavioral repertoire

Candidates for AT may be characterized by a variety of behavioral excesses and deficits, some of which militate against successful, or at least efficient, participation in treatment. The following are among the more common impediments:

Noncompliance. Behavior therapists conceptualize the common phenomenon of 'resistance' as noncompliant behavior rather than as an internal motivational state produced by intrapsychic dynamics (O'Leary & Wilson, 1987). From this perspective, the key to understanding and eliminating noncompliance is to conduct a thorough functional analysis of the resistant behavior, with the presumption that the initial assessment failed to isolate all the relevant variables. Frequently, noncompliant behavior is maintained by negative reinforcement – for example, a woman may resist asserting herself to her boss because a deserved promotion might entail responsibilities for which she feels unprepared; continued passivity allows her to avoid the new, and to her, noxious duties. Positive reinforcement may also maintain noncompliance; the husband of the woman deserving the promotion may express a great deal of sympathy for her predicament and take a second job to supplement their income, both of which would be discontinued if her pay rise was forthcoming. Sometimes the agreed-upon homework assignment is beyond the client's perceived capabilities; in this case shaping has probably proceeded too rapidly. An inadequate assessment may have identified an irrelevant problem situation or failed to clarify cultural variables that impede assertion; an example of the latter might occur if our woman lived in a male-dominated cultural milieu and resisted asserting to men due to a concern for their, and her husband's, reaction. Each of these is theoretically remedied by a more accurate assessment: intervention can be developed to help the woman increase her work skills (or evaluation of them), assertive responses designed to produce similar or alternative positive reinforcers can be taught, shaping can return to an earlier level, the correct problem can be targeted, or the cultural issues can be addressed through cognitive restructuring and training in bicultural competencies.

Resistant behavior in AT is often a function of the assertion deficits themselves; for example, clients may fear presumed negative consequences, confuse assertion with aggression, or discount their right to express themselves. These misunderstandings of assertion, particularly when they are independent of severe psychological dysfunction and pervasive skill deficits, are appropriate foci of AT, and do not necessarily hinder therapeutic progress.

Finally, a negative client reaction to a specific AT technique is not uncommon: imagery procedures, videotaped feedback, behavior rehearsal, rational relabeling, and homework arouse the greatest resistance. An unpalatable technique should never be imposed on the trainee; this will only foster new, and perhaps more creative, ways to resist. Rather, the source of the client's discomfort must be explored and intervention altered so that it is consistent with client desires. The research does not suggest that all techniques are necessary for improvement; on the contrary, components are often as effective as packages. Therefore, an obvious strategy would be to omit, or provide a substitute for, an offensive technique. Sometimes, a simple procedural modification will suffice. For example, a high-demand role-play exercise might be enthusiastically embraced by self-reliant (internal locus of control) trainees, but fairly dependent (external locus of control) ones may well prefer to observe a model first (Kipper, 1988). Similarly, trainees who resist the philosophical underpinnings of rational relabeling may respond positively to a presentation that emphasizes rational thinking as a 'possibly helpful perspective in some situations' rather than as a fundamental alteration in the way events are cognitively interpreted.

The isolation of the determinants of noncompliant behavior will not, of course, guarantee client cooperation. Clients who are generally unmotivated, for whatever reasons, are unlikely to make many changes in any therapy. Some clients, though motivated, are unable to make the commitment to work on change, perhaps due to current environmental circumstances, but often due to ambivalence about the ramifications of change per se. While techniques exist to enhance a client's commitment to change (Kanfer & Schefft, 1988), such an effort in AT is facilitated only when treatment is conducted individually. However, even when individual training is contemplated, clinicians should consider postponing AT with ambivalent persons until the other issues have been resolved.

175

Behavioral excesses and deficits. Certain skill deficits will seriously impede a client's ability to profit from AT. Personal disorganization, lack of self-control, depressed responding, and pervasive social incompetence are particularly troublesome – not only because individuals with such characteristics are likely to have numerous difficulties, but also because these deficits will hamper involvement in, and compliance with, treatment. Disorganized people and those lacking in self-control miss part or all of many sessions, and have difficulty 'doing' the homework, even when it is clearly within their capability. They fail to 'do' the assignment in the same way they fail to complete the many other important, though 'little', tasks that make daily life function smoothly. Depressed persons often avoid full involvement in AT during the session and may resist pressure to increase participation, yet, paradoxically, will only respond to externally introduced structure. Clients with severe interpersonal deficits also present challenges. Besides the difficulty involved in teaching complex empathic assertions to people who can barely interact in everyday social situations, the assertions, if learned, will be perceived less positively by the social environment due to the lack of complementary nonconflictual skills, such as commendatory assertions and conversational abilities (see Chapter 5). Thus, these clients require additional social skill training, preferably prior to AT, to place the assertive behaviors in an appropriate social context.

Finally, severe cognitive skill deficits involving facilitative self-statements and rational beliefs can limit training benefits. Commonly, nonassertive clients will be pessimistic that AT can help them acquire desired responses (low self-efficacy) and impact constructively on their social environment (low outcome expectations, ie learned helplessness). Since client expectation of treatment potency is an important contributor to outcome (Kanfer & Schefft, 1988; O'Leary & Wilson, 1987), the therapist must induce positive alternatives. Kazdin and Krouse (1983) demonstrated that this can be facilitated by (1) describing treatment as based on scientific research, tested with clients, novel and improved, and designed to increase self-control and coping abilities; (2) providing case exemplars that concretely highlight the benefits of treatment; and (3) emphasizing, in technical jargon, that treatment will comprehensively address affect, cognition, and behavior. Fortunately, these strategies lend themselves well to AT, and should be particularly effective with the many nonassertive clients possessing low conceptual complexity.

Occasionally, the nature of the cognitive deficits will contraindicate AT. Garcia and Lubetkin (1986) report a case in which these deficits resulted in extreme feelings of worthlessness that prevented the client from accepting assertion as a legitimate option for her. After extensive, general cognitive restructuring, AT was successfully implemented, leading Garcia and Lubetkin to hypothesize that trainees will benefit from AT only if they possess a minimal, albeit low, level of self-acceptance.

Problematic behavioral excesses include overt aggression and covert responses like anxiety, cognitive rigidity, and unrealistic expectations. Aggressive persons, particularly those whose behavior is motivated by aversive situations that produce unexpressed anger (see Chapter 8), can benefit from AT, but progress is often slow and tedious. Unlike the passive person who is discovering a new world of enhanced control, many aggressive persons will experience a diminution in immediate impact. Furthermore, while the previously passive person may have to deal with a recipient's transient negative feelings (eg hurt, anger), the formerly aggressive person must contend with enduring negative social reactions that developed in response to his or her earlier coercive interactive style. Thus, consistent performance of conflict assertion will be impeded by a decrease in immediate reinforcement *and* the failure of others to reinforce new behavior. The ex-aggressor gets less of what he or she wants and people still dislike, and avoid, him or her. Furthermore, positive assertions will be constrained by enduring anger toward and distrust of others, both of which will initially increase as conflict assertion produces variable immediate reinforcement. Clearly, the therapist will have to provide a great deal of support and encouragement throughout treatment, until newly acquired assertive skills slowly produce their own reinforcers. Alternatively, a 'fresh start' is sometimes possible (eg a job transfer to a new division in the company), but even here, a reputation often hangs like an albatross around the neck.

Excessive anxiety is commonly experienced by nonassertive persons (Garcia & Lubetkin, 1986; Montgomery & Heimberg, 1978). Anxiety related to issues beyond assertiveness may require direct treatment prior to AT (Emmons & Alberti, 1983; Alberti & Emmons, 1986b), but in most cases arousal can be effectively controlled by a slower pace in AT that intensifies behavioral experimentation and cognitive restructuring and allows for direct instruction in anxiety-control techniques such as relaxation training, stress inoculation training (Meichenbaum, 1985), and diaphragmatic breathing (Girdano & Everly, 1986). Of course, variable pacing and individualized interventions are very difficult to engineer in group formats, suggesting that these clients be treated through individual AT.

Cognitive rigidity can seriously undermine the efficacy of AT. Some clients will challenge the basic premise of 'behavior in one's own interest', adhere to absolutistic value systems, or insist rational thinking is simply a rationalization for the acceptance of failure and mediocrity. When beliefs are inflexible and closed to examination, progress with any therapy will be slow, perhaps not even measurable. A heterogeneous group that presents alternative perspectives with some sense of social consensus is indicated for these clients, as individual therapy will probably be perceived to be offering 'psychobabble' in the wind. Alternatively, these clients might be referred to therapists who either share their convictions or have more 'face validity'. For instance, a very religious client with an absolutistic moral belief system should be urged to visit an appropriate pastoral counselor. Interestingly, when faced with such a recommendation, many inflexible clients verbalize an increased openness to self-exploration.

Unrealistic expectations that AT will be a panacea for all troubles and unhappiness constitute another problematic behavioral excess. An unassertive man, in a miserable marriage with a dominating woman, will not achieve marital happiness through greater assertiveness, and if that is his goal, he will be sorely disappointed. However, if his goal is to cope with the marriage until the children are grown, and assertiveness skills can help achieve that, then AT may be a viable treatment. Similarly, improved conflict skills may help an employee with poor interpersonal abilities cope with coworkers who take advantage of him, but alone, without other social competencies, assertion is unlikely to improve his general relationship with them. The informed consent process will provide the therapist with an early opportunity to challenge excessive expectations and instil more realistic ones (see p. 184).

Environmental constraints

The individual's natural environment may fail to prompt and/or reinforce assertive behavior, and, in some cases, may actually punish its emission. However, since most individuals assume roles in several natural contexts, the values and norms of each relevant one must be assessed independently so that behavioral goals can be tailored to maximize reinforcement.

Since the potency of reinforcers varies among individuals, 'maximization of reinforcement' can only be clarified through reference to the client's values. However, the situation is complicated since the values of the therapist must inevitably influence the selection of goals (Corey, Corey, & Callanan, 1988), resulting in the very real possibility that different notions of a 'best outcome' will be articulated. Such conflicts will be most problematic when the therapist assumes a social activism stance while the client desires only pragmatic improvements that do not fundamentally alter existing power structures. In such cases, the clinician should ensure that the trainee understands (1) inequities in power and resource allocation have sociopolitical as well as personal environmental determinants, (2) nonassertion is a socially conditioned adaptation to one or both sources, and does not reflect a personal illness or defect, and (3) AT can be directed toward either or both the sociological or personal constraints on behavior, but the informed choice is the client's. While some will be motivated to challenge illegitimate social forces, the majority will not wish to risk assertion in contexts that discourage or punish it, or resist change. The clinician with a social activist orientation will respect the desires of these clients only through full awareness and self-disclosure of personal values and an open exploration of all potential treatment goals.

Even clients who choose to focus on small, perhaps superficial, modifications in their immediate environment must balance the risks, and the possibility of adverse reactions should not be underestimated. Abused spouses, as discussed earlier, may receive additional beatings as a consequence of asserting. However, most negative social reactions are much more subtle than those of the spouse abuser; more typically, an asserter is confronted with verbal aggression, passive-aggression, withdrawal, avoidance, and/or negative emotions. While the research suggests the adverse consequences of assertion are exaggerated by nonassertive persons, the trainer must recognize those data represent average responses, and some appraisals of nonsupportive contexts are highly accurate. In such circumstances, the practitioner might suggest alternative therapy (eg exploration of the reasons for staying in an unhappy situation, conjoint therapy) or an alternative AT focus (eg assertion with friends rather than spouse).

A useful framework for working with clients who choose to deal with immediate (rather than structural) environmental impediments is *multicontextual competence*, a generalization of the bicultural competence strategy suggested for minority individuals adapting behavior to dominant and ethnic norms. First, the supportive and nonsupportive environments must be differentiated. Second, assertive skills intended for use in the supportive environment are trained. Finally, modifications of, or alternatives to, assertive responses are trained for employment in the nonsupportive milieu.

However, another caveat is necessary: even environments perceived to be supportive may nevertheless discourage assertion. Rotheram (1984) observed that interpersonal networks, such as families and small groups, develop communication rules whose implicit assumptions provide order and predictability to relationships. The introduction of assertive behaviors may disrupt familiar patterns and force a readjustment of the rules, or, more likely, prompt opposition to change – that is, punish assertiveness. Thus, a family network guided by the rule 'avoid confrontation' or 'parental control is not to be questioned' will be markedly disrupted by one member's emission of conflict assertive behavior. Similarly, families guided by 'emotional restraint' will experience great difficulty with positive expressions such as affection and compliments. Since few families will enter therapy as a unit, the client must be prepared to recognize and confront these network disruptions and their probable consequences.

Positive assertion

The four positive response classes include initiating and maintaining interactions, admitting personal shortcomings, and the two 'commendatory' categories of giving and receiving compliments and expressing positive emotions (Schroeder et al., 1983). Reiterating research findings by Cooley (1979) and Lefevre and West (1984), starting and participating in conversations, expressing opinions in group settings, and asking for help are very high priorities of trainees. An assertive style in job interviews, expressing positive feelings, and talking affirmatively about personal achievements are moderately important, while giving and receiving compliments are judged to be less pressing issues. Thus, comprehensive AT that meets the needs of participants must include attention to deficient positive skills. Furthermore, even when these behaviors are not a high priority, their acquisition and performance should not be ignored, since conflict responses are received better when associated with positive assertions.

In contrast to the hundreds of studies focusing on the assessment and acquisition of conflict skills, only a handful of investigations have attended to the complementary procedures involved in the development of positive assertion. The only published self-report scale, the Behavioral Test of Tenderness Expression (Warren & Gilner, 1978), appears to evidence acceptable reliability and validity, but has not been subjected to investigation beyond the initial study. The two commendatory response classes, positive expressiveness and giving and receiving compliments, have been successfully taught through conventional AT procedures to a psychiatric patient (Kelly et al., 1978), a mentally retarded adolescent (Geller et al., 1980), unexpressive females in intimate relationships (Dubinsky, 1980), a gay male (St. Lawrence, Bradlyn, & Kelly, 1983), and unassertive male college students (Nesbitt, 1981). Obviously, the verbal content and several paralinguistic and nonverbal components of these assertions will differ from conflict ones. In particular, response duration is longer, affect is softer, facial expression is warmer and includes smiles, and gestures and body posture are more open. Positive assertions, however, retain some characteristics of the conflict variants, including brief latency, moderate volume, and direct eye contact (Geller et al., 1980; Kelly, 1982; Kelly et al., 1978).

Admitting personal shortcomings is difficult for many people, perhaps because such behavior places the asserter in a subordinate position and arouses fears of looking foolish or somehow inadequate. Unfortunately, this response class has been ignored by assertion researchers except for two studies. Wallston, Wallston, DeVellis, McLendon, and Percy (1978) facilitated question-asking behavior by nonassertive women through modeling and direct instruction. The total number of questions increased as a function of instructions, while a decrease in latency required the combination treatment. Knapczyk (1989) improved questioning abilities of young, mildly handicapped students through modeling, rehearsal, and feedback.

Other behaviors that acknowledge personal limitations include direct requests for help and certain self-disclosures. The latter has been extensively studied, though not in the context of positive assertion. Self-disclosure belongs to this response class when the content expresses a weakness, failure, or problem of the speaker. The verbal content includes a personal self-reference pronoun (I, my, mine) and describes, in terms of past, present, and/or future facts and feelings, either a personal experience or reaction to the experience of another (Hargie, 1986b).

The utility of AT with the final positive response class, the initiation and maintenance of interactions, is implied by a descriptive study of assertiveness in group discussions (Kimble, Yoshikawa, & Zehr, 1981). In particular, the results suggest the importance of the skill of conversation-initiation by women in mixed-sex groups. The experimental groups consisted of two males and two females; the first woman to speak was judged to be equivalent to the males in verbal and paralinguistic assertiveness, while the woman who spoke second was significantly less verbally assertive than the other woman in both structured and unstructured discussions, and less paralinguistically assertive than the other three participants in structured conversations. Interestingly, in same-sexed groups, verbal assertiveness of the first and last (fourth) speaking woman were similar, but the first speaking male was significantly more assertive than the male who spoke fourth. These data are consistent with those summarized by Worell (1988; see Chapter 8), which suggest women's needs for intimacy and equality are met in same-sexed, but not mixed-sex, relationships. Furthermore, the results high-light the dominance of competitive values in males and interdependent ones in females, in that hierarchical power relationships were established only when men were involved.

Kimble et al. (1981) observe that other research (eg Piliavin & Martin, 1978) has also found that a female is much more likely to be the least involved participant in four-person mixed-sex groups, and suggest '[t]he sexual identity of the participants in mixed groups seems to elicit certain role expectations and the fulfillment of those roles' (p. 1053). In fact, a significant body of research indicates women, though performing competently in same-sex interactions, participate less than men in small, mixed-sex, task-oriented group discussions, even when relevant knowledge and professional status are equivalent (cf Lewittes & Bem, 1983). Thus, in positive assertion situations that involve 'dom-inance', as in conflict situations, 'it appears to be the presence of men per se – rather than any lack of substantive knowledge or conceptual skill – that depresses women's participation in the context of mixed-sex interaction' (Lewittes & Bem, 1983, p. 582).

Since the variables that hinder women's involvement in discussions are similar to those impeding conflict assertion, AT may offer a powerful remedial strategy. Indeed, AT that incorporated material clarifying the relationship of low participation to the role of women in society increased conversational comments by females and improved their self-perceptions (Lewittes & Bem, 1983). Specifically, the women learned how to initiate and sustain a discussion, speak frequently, interrupt monopolizing verbalizations of others, and resist in-appropriate interruptions of their own comments. Moreover, the increase in 'dominance' by the trained women was not associated with negative side effects; on the contrary, the other male and female discussants felt these women maintained behavior intended to keep group interactions cordial and friendly, increased substantive contributions as well as total involvement, and enhanced their likeability. The authors note these results must be interpreted cautiously, since they were obtained in noncompetitive interactions among individuals of equal status. Even so, the data suggest an important role for AT in the develop-ment of conversational skills.

The ability to initiate interactions is likely to be important in other contexts besides small group discussions. Many unstructured social conversations, such as introducing oneself or chatting at a cocktail party, require that someone take the lead and begin talking. Superficial self-disclosure ('Hello, I'm John. I work in the chemical division') is a basic (Hargie, 1986b), but insufficient, discourse initiator, since it can only be used once with any particular person. Of much greater value is Schroeder and Black's (1985) 'general stimulus–response strategy' that can be applied to any specific situation. Clients are taught in AT to continuously identify topics for discussion through observation of their social environment and own internal reactions and then to verbalize those observations. This model is an outstanding example of the transfer strategy of 'training for the general case' (Kazdin, 1989).

Once a discussion has commenced, general conversational skills must be available to maintain the interaction. Unfortunately, many nonassertive individuals lack these additional abilities as well and require 'small talk' training. The clinician must first determine whether the client possesses sufficient background information to form the content of small talk; in my experience, this general knowledge is often lacking ('I can't think of anything to say' or 'I have nothing to add' are frequent complaints). Though small talk is rarely critically evaluated (Rimm & Masters, 1979), participation that is on-topic and more diverse than a string of questions will require familiarity with appropriate content. Knowledge deficits can be remedied through homework assignments to read the daily paper carefully, including editorials and opinion columnists, and/or one of the general news magazines. Over a period of several weeks, most clients acquire a broad, though superficial, acquaintance with political events, international news, the arts and social scenes, sports, etc, which provides an adequate basis upon which to maintain one of those meaningless, aversive conversations that we all lampoon, but which, nevertheless, often constitute a necessary component of social competence.

After some content is acquired, the clinician can begin training the para-linguistic, nonverbal, and process skills that will facilitate the conversation and perhaps help develop a continuing relationship. These include good eye contact; fluent speech; appropriate affect, intonation, gestures, body posture, and facial expression; increased response duration and frequency; on-topic skills (eg responsivity to partner's talk about her- or himself, open-ended questions to elicit information or invite elaboration, paraphrasing, reflecting feelings, and summarization to communicate understanding); appropriate self-disclosure to share information and establish commonalities; and reinforcing or compli-mentary expressions (Kelly, 1982; Faraone & Hurtig, 1985; Hargie, 1986a; Ivey, 1988; Schroeder & Black, 1985). The diverse conversation skills necessary to make the specific assertive response of initiating social interactions functionally useful, and hence generalizable, once again highlights the need for clinically astute trainers who can provide comprehensive treatment. (See, for example, St. Lawrence, Bradlyn, & Kelly's [1983] work with a socially withdrawn gay male.)

The positive skills, like the conflict ones, also require training in social perception and discrimination abilities, such as timing and quantity. Trainees must learn at which points in an interactive sequence a positive assertion is facilitative; clearly, under most circumstances, the verbalization is expected to follow completion of the other person's statement. However, some positive assertions will be prompted by nonverbal behavior and the situation. Initiating an interaction, almost by definition, requires discrimination of nonverbal and contextual cues. In established relationships, skilled timing could be exhibited by providing a pertinent compliment to an individual who is observing himself in a mirror wearing new clothes, expressing support to a person who is sitting alone after receiving a negative evaluation of some sort, or sharing a relevant self-disclosure with a person who is upset over the unintended impact of her actions.

The quantity of positive assertion is also critical. Compliments and expressions of positive feelings that are too frequent, long, or effusive are likely to be devalued by the recipient. Self-disclosures that are too detailed, frequent, or intimate for the context will be judged to be inappropriate (Hargie, 1986b). Incessant questions and requests for help will quickly be perceived as aversive intrusions, as will interactions initiated indiscriminately. As with conflict assertions, novice trainees, eager to experiment with newly acquired positive skills, are more likely to err through excess than minimalism. Moderation, appropriate to the context, is always the goal of AT. Furthermore, as with conflict skills, each situation offers the choice, not the mandate, to positively assert. Commendatory expressions, self-disclosures, and initiations might quite appropriately be withheld if the recipient will be uncomfortable with such expressions. Similarly, reasonable requests for help may place an excessive burden on the other person, and might therefore be delayed or abandoned. Obviously, legitimate reasons to inhibit positive assertion do not include ones derived from irrational or unrealistic interpretations of the situation (eg 'he will think I'm foolish if I ask that' or 'she will think I am too emotional if I say that').

Males, in particular, may have great difficulty distinguishing between reality and their cognitive distortions of it. It is here that sexism, perpetuated by males, is likely to come home to roost, despite the increasing popularity of androgyny as a style for men as well as for women. Some men will still undoubtedly need extensive cognitive restructuring and then behavior rehearsal before they will feel comfortable verbalizing self-disclosures, compliments, requests for help, and expressions of affection. Performance of these skills can be further encouraged by a review of the generally favorable data on the social acceptability of positive assertion by males. Neither males nor females devalue men when they express commendatory assertions (Levin & Gross, 1987; St. Lawrence et al., 1985a; Wildman, 1986), and such responses by boys are not perceived negatively by school-age boys (Wojnilower & Gross, 1984). Conversational behaviors by men are not negatively evaluated by either males or females (Wildman & Clementz, 1986) and may even enhance perceptions of kindness when associated with conflict assertion (Wildman, 1986).

However, some positive assertions by males – such as admitting personal shortcomings – may entail increased risk: males concluding a speech with an appeal based on helplessness rather than expertise were judged less likeable, qualified, and competent (Falbo, Hazen, & Linimon, 1982), and men who exhibited distress in small group discussions were repeatedly attacked (Kahn, 1984). Unfortunately, since these studies were not conceptualized in terms of assertion, it is unclear whether the adverse reaction is related to the nature of the response class (e.g. masculine sex-role incongruity) or to appeals and distress expressed in a nonassertive manner.

In addition, cultural variables are likely to influence judgements of positive assertion by males. It is quite possible, for example, that in the Hispanic subcultures, dominated by the 'machismo' ethic, such behavior will be devalued or arouse discomfort in the recipient. If this is the case, training in bicultural competence may be necessary. Members of Asian cultures, which emphasize emotional restraint, may also require such intervention. Until these hypotheses are systematically explored, training must be guided by the individual's subjective interpretation of his or her situation, anecdotal evidence, theoretical propositions, and, in groups, the feedback from members.[2]

Finally, some males may be reluctant to express positive emotions simply because those stereotyped feminine behaviors are personally devalued. In fact, the high priority trainees place on these skills may primarily reflect the experiences of women, since the research subjects were 75–80 per cent female (Cooley, 1979; Lefevre & West, 1984; unfortunately, neither study analyzed the data by sex). Thus, three reasons emerge for emphasizing positive assertions within AT: clinically, they are often high-priority concerns; empirically, they provide a moderating context for the social evaluation of conflict assertion; and socially, they are inappropriately devalued in the sex-role socialization process. AT can contribute to progressive social change by bestowing on 'feminine' assertive behaviors the same esteem accorded to the 'masculine' conflict skills (Goldstein-Fodor & Epstein, 1983).

Ethical issues

Assertiveness trainers identify with a wide variety of professions, most of which advance a set of ethical principles to establish standards believed necessary for, first, the protection of client rights, and, second, professional self-regulation to ensure insulation from outside interference (Bray, Shepherd, & Hays, 1985). Although the specific principles vary, several tenets consistently emerge; thus, in this section, the generalized propositions derived from the *process* of helping, rather than discipline or theoretical orientation, will be reviewed.

Informed consent

In the United States, the helping professional is both ethically *and* legally mandated to obtain fully informed consent before commencing treatment, except in emergency situations. Thus, the clinician's expert judgement that an intervention is in the best interests of the client does not supersede the client's or legal guardian's right to prevent the imposition of any particular intervention. Compared to much of the rest of the world, individual rights are a foundation of the *Weltanshauung* of Americans, often to the detriment (in my view) of social needs. Thus, this ethical dilemma may be of greater practical significance to clinicians in the US than elsewhere. On the other hand, while the deification of individual rights in the US may at times be individually and socially counter-productive, sensitivity to them is good clinical practice, even in other social-political climates.

Informed consent in the US includes three elements: (1) the individual giving consent has the *legal capacity* to do so, ie has achieved the minimum legal age and has not been legally judged incompetent to manage his or her personal affairs; (2) the information conveyed to the client is *understood* by him or her; and (3) the consent is *not coerced* (Bray et al., 1985). The first criterion, while an unambiguous legal definition of competence, nevertheless may be at odds with ethical practice. For example, should an exceptionally mature adolescent be unable to consent to treatment without parental approval, the current situation in the US for all but a handful of crisis situations (eg abortion counseling)? Or should consent be considered to be informed when the client, though not adjudicated as incompetent, nevertheless is clearly, by psychological criteria, able to comprehend the information and/or its implications only superficially?

Understandable information, the second criterion of informed consent, must clarify the (1) therapist's qualifications, training, experience, and theoretical orientation; (2) proposed treatment plan, including fees, time frame, goals, and techniques; (3) anticipated benefits and possible risks of participating in the treatment plan; (4) predicted risks if treatment is not implemented; (5) thera-peutic and nontherapeutic alternatives to the treatment; and (6) client rights and responsibilities in treatment (Corey et al., 1988).

Comprehension can only be achieved by adapting language and conceptual complexity to client capabilities. Furthermore, the information must contain sufficient detail to form the basis for an informed decision. Though it is not possible to present exhaustive information that delineates every conceivable risk, benefit, and alternative, therapists are legally and ethically enjoined to achieve a standard of comprehensiveness that is considered acceptable within the profession. Thus, a clinician should inform a client about to enter individual AT that the time frame is likely to be considerably greater than the 8 sessions so typical of group formats, probably in the range of 16–20 sessions, and perhaps even more if other problems are introduced into therapy. With this information, most clients would not be surprised or upset if therapy required 30–40 sessions. Similarly, a careful description of the AT procedures, particularly behavior rehearsal, cognitive restructuring, and homework assignments, will foster appropriate client expectations. On the other hand, a failure to describe potential negative social reactions to conflict assertion is likely to be viewed as un-professional, and perhaps even negligent in some instances (eg with abused wives). Furthermore, trainers must not overstate the possible treatment benefits ('you will be in complete control of your life'),[3] magnify the risks of declining treatment ('you will become even more depressed unless you learn these skills'), or downplay the potential benefits of alternative intervention ('self-help groups and your minister cannot effectively deal with your type of problem').

Finally, the client's rights and responsibilities must be clarified. For example, many clients will not be aware they are expected to participate actively in therapy, engage in homework assignments, and take certain risks. Additionally, most clients expect the clinician to treat all communications as confidential, and are unaware of the limitations to this right. In the US, for example, therapists are not bound to maintain confidentiality in crisis situations, and are specifically enjoined to break it when (a) the client is judged to pose a grave danger to him- or herself or to others or (b) there is even the *suspicion* of child abuse (Corey et al., 1988). Failure to inform clients of these limits will undoubtedly disrupt the therapeutic relationship if, in the course of AT, an aggressive person verbalizes homicidal thoughts or self-discloses current incestuous behavior, each of which requires that confidentiality be immediately abrogated. Further legal, and hence ethical, ambiguities surround confidentiality in terms of treatment of children, spouses, families, and groups (see p. 187).

Finally, clients generally have the right to refuse or drop out of treatment, though under some circumstances therapy may be imposed by a court of law. Such cases clearly violate the third element of informed consent, ie agreement is voluntary or at least noncoerced. But, is the reluctant assent by a child, or the feeble acquiescence by a prison inmate or hospitalized mental patient lacking attractive alternatives, an acceptable basis from which to conclude consent is truly voluntary? The noncoerced nature of consent can be particularly ambiguous when shy, timid trainees – the bulk of the AT clientele – are pressured by significant others into requesting treatment. The trainer must exert special care with such clients, extensively discuss the reasons for initiating therapy, and determine whether AT, at this point in time and under the existing circumstances, is the appropriate intervention choice.

The provision of informed consent is best thought of as a *process* rather than as a discrete event. The bulk of the information may be communicated in an oral and/or written package, and a form perhaps signed by the client, but the process must be interactive and continuing rather than unilateral and static. The clinician should explain complicated issues in several ways, prompt questions, encourage the expression of reservations regarding treatment, and request reformulations of specific points in the client's own words. Only through such interactions can the therapist be confident the client truly *understands* that to which he or she is consenting; certainly a closed question ('do you understand what I have said?'), no matter how sincere, is an inadequate prompt for most clients. Furthermore, the therapist is obligated continually to update the client with newly identified relevant information pertaining to treatment. For instance, the therapist may discover, in the middle of individual AT, that a local hospital is forming social skill groups. The availability of this alternative form of therapy should be brought to the client's attention if the therapist has reason to believe it would be of interest. Another common occurrence is the emergence of previously unforeseen risks to which the client should be alerted. The therapist, for example, may receive a call from a husband complaining about his wife's newly independent behavior, while the wife believes he is fully supportive of her personal growth.[4]

Confidentiality

All therapy presupposes that a significant degree of confidentiality will be maintained regarding material disclosed within the sessions. As noted in the discussion on informed consent, however, there are circumstances under which this right will be appropriately breached. In addition, treatment of children and more than one client in a session pose further problems. Clinicians may not be able to guarantee confidentiality to children, since parents have the legal right to oversee treatment (Corey et al., 1988). Because of this, I will not treat a child unless the parents agree that confidentiality will be respected. Therapeutic progress is then shared with the parents in general terms, and specifics are communicated only with the approval of the child (or preferably, *by* the child), unless the issue poses a significant danger.

Confidentiality in groups is also ambiguous. Though the trainer will no doubt stress the importance of each group member adhering to a strict rule that all disclosures remain within the group, there is little that can be done truly to ensure that such confidentiality is maintained. Because of this, many US courts do not recognize group communications as *privileged*[5] (Corey et al., 1988), a status that prohibits their disclosure in legal proceedings under all but a few specific circumstances. Thus, group members should be aware that their self-disclosures may ultimately go beyond the group, and, in some cases, may even be used against them in the future (eg child custody cases, divorce proceedings). The nature of short, one- or two-session workshops, which typically enrol numerous participants, exacerbates this problem, and these trainees should be cautioned against introducing sensitive issues.

Trainer qualifications

Lange and Jakubowski (1976) and Alberti and Emmons (1986a) distinguish between assertiveness *training* for the personal growth of well-adjusted individuals and assertiveness *therapy* for clinically dysfunctional persons. This distinction, without explicit labels or unique terms, has been raised repeatedly in this book. Obviously, clients with clinical problems will introduce phenomena of greater diversity and complexity. The ethical imperative for trainers is to recognize the bounds of their competency and to utilize referrals as indicated by the situation.

Trainers should also be highly competent in the modality through which they deliver AT; individual, conjoint (couples), family, and group approaches all demand particular competencies that do not necessarily generalize well. A therapist most familiar with individual or group AT, for example, is unlikely to be well acquainted with the concepts of systems theory necessary to conduct efficacious family therapy.

Welfare of the client

The trainer is responsible for ensuring intervention is (1) in the best interests of the client and (2) implemented in a manner that respects the dignity and rights of the client. The best interest of the client may be clouded by missing information, ambivalent motivations, situational complexities, or, as noted earlier, the values of the therapist. Respect for the client is conveyed in several ways. First, each client should be held in unconditional positive regard (Rogers, 1959), regardless of demographic characteristics, personal lifestyle, or clinical dysfunction. If the therapist simply cannot fully accept the basic worth of certain types of people (eg race or ethnicity), lifestyles (eg homosexual), or problems (eg child abuse, sexual violence), then he or she must refer such individuals to others. Second, therapeutic communications should be open and honest, and include explanations of both what is being implemented and why (Lange & Jakubowski, 1976). Provocative and excessively manipulative interventions, such as paradoxical ones, even if directed toward a worthy goal, raise particularly troublesome ethical issues (ie do the ends justify the means?; see Corey et al., 1988, for a discussion). Third, confrontations should have a specific therapeutic purpose for the client, and not be primarily an exercise in therapist self-aggrandizement. Fourth, and perhaps most basically, both behavior therapy (Woolfolk & Richardson, 1984) and AT (Emmons & Alberti, 1983) are derived from, and openly subscribe to, the tenets of classical humanism – the belief in all humans as equal and equally deserving. Trainers must convey to clients the perspective that they are, to a large extent, products of their social and material environment. Blaming the victim (Ryan, 1971), either by the therapist or the client him- or herself, is anathema to the humanist philosophy. On the other hand, trainers must introduce this perspective with sensitivity, since most trainees are likely to believe in the 'just world hypothesis'[6] (Lerner, 1970) and therefore resist a rigid and dogmatic presentation of environmental determinism.

Training resources

Trainer manuals

Lange and Jakubowski's (1976) original effort remains, by far, the best practical guide for the general implementation of group AT. A minimal, though sufficient, amount of theory and research is integrated into the material concerned with the concrete operationalization of AT; charts, client 'tests', and over 20 experiential exercises are included. Another valuable source is the short manual produced by Alberti and Emmons (1986a), an expansion of the 'trainer' section of earlier editions of *Your Perfect Right* (1970). The 118-page book is basically a compilation of their extensive direct and vicarious experience with AT in numerous applied contexts; theory, research, and systematic content of AT are left to others. Nevertheless Alberti and Emmons offer numerous suggestions that will facilitate individual or group AT, making the manual a nice supplement to Lange and Jakubowski's more detailed presentation. Fodor (1980) and Masters et al. (1987) offer additional useful clinical suggestions.

Professional guidebooks from a more broadly based social skills training perspective are also available (Eisler & Frederiksen, 1980; Kelly, 1982). Manuals for particular populations include Becker et al. (1987; depression), Liberman et al. (1989; psychiatric patients), Matson and Ollendick (1988; children), Waksman and Messmer (1979; adolescents), and Cheek (1976; African-Americans).

Self-help books

Commercial books and materials are likely to remain both popular and untested. Clinicians, at the very least, should be thoroughly familiar with any product used as bibliotherapy. *Your Perfect Right* (Alberti & Emmons, 1986b), now in its fifth edition and considerably expanded, remains a solid introductory vehicle for clients presenting assertive deficits. Jakubowski and Lange (1978) is similarly strong; both books present assertion as a desirable skill likely to enhance one's quality of life when used judiciously, rather than as a panacea for all ills. Other general books adhering to this basic perspective include Alberti and Emmons (1975), Bower and Bower (1976), Galassi and Galassi (1977b), Gambrill and Richey (1976), and Kelly and Winship (1979). As with the field in general, conflict skills are the primary focus, though positive skills are addressed in Galassi and Galassi (1977b) and Jakubowski and Lange (1978). Less recommended due to their extravagant claims for AT are Smith (1975) and Fensterheim and Baer (1975).

Numerous popular books, as noted earlier, have been written specifically for women (Baer, 1976; Bloom et al., 1975; Butler, 1976; Osborn & Harris, 1975; Phelps & Austin, 1975, 1987; Taubman, 1976). These authors all have an obvious and admitted 'cause' to promote: the self-actualization, if not 'liberation', of women through the use of conflict assertion skills in diverse settings. Thus, these books actually combine consciousness raising with AT, a strategy advocated by some trainers (eg Lange & Jakubowski, 1976) and supported by some data (Meehan & Goldkopf, 1982).

Finally, many self-help books are directed at specific populations besides women. Zuker (1983) has produced a useful book for managers in the work environment, while Palmer and Shondeck creatively present assertiveness concepts in ways appropriate for children (1977a: ages 5–9; 1977b: ages 8 and over). Supervisors (Drury, 1984) and parents (Canter & Canter, 1988) have also been the targets of recent books.

Audiotapes

Alberti (1986) developed a 3-cassette self-help program, accompanied by a 40-page manual, that focuses on general conflict skill acquisition, while Guerra,

Cotler, and Cotler (1976) offered a similar set of 4 tapes. Rakos and Schroeder (1980) included extensive behavior rehearsal, modeling, and feedback opportunities in a 4-cassette program that includes a 56-page workbook and 6 detachable index cards. These tapes are intended for use as an adjunct to therapist-administered treatment that does not necessarily focus primarily on assertion difficulties. However, research suggests that clients with general behavioral assets (such as college students) can profitably utilize the program through independent self-administration (Rakos & Schroeder, 1979).[7] The tapes focus on the acquisition of refusal abilities appropriate for conflicts with strangers and significant others, and hence emphasize discriminative and risk assessment skills as well as assertive obligations intended to strengthen relationships (see Chapter 3).

Films

Two films, *Actualization Through Assertion* (Liberman, 1976) and *Responsible Assertion* (Lange & Jakubowski, 1978), demonstrate AT procedures and processes to clinicians. They complement each other well: the Liberman film demonstrates a behavioral package applied to clinically dysfunctional clients, while Lange and Jakubowski model cognitive-behavioral AT with graduate and undergraduate students. Finally, *What Could I Say?* (Lange, 1979) presents numerous vignettes in which rights are violated and a conflict assertive response is probably appropriate. This film is useful in groups and classes, as it can be stopped after each vignette, permitting discussion of rights and their infringement and the generation and critique of alternative response possibilities.

Games

Two commercially available board games may have utility in some circumstances. 'The Assertion Game' (Berg, no date), intended for work with dysfunctional school-age children, assesses and encourages appropriate conflict skills. It focuses on verbal content and facilitative self-statements. 'Assert With Love' (Childswork/Childsplay, no date) employs role playing between a 'problem solver' and a 'problem maker' and feedback forms designed to provide reinforcement. It is directed toward teenagers, adults, and families.

Notes

Chapter 1 Assertive behavior in societal context

1. I am tempted to add a fifth element – that of sexism. Modern industrial society shapes 'masculine' behaviors (competition, aggression, mobility, etc.) at the expense of 'feminine' ones (cooperation, nurturance, succorance). The AT movement was prompted by behavioral definitions of social competence whose criteria were derived from male perspectives of social potency – that is, survival in conflict situations (cf Wine, 1981). There was no perceived urgency for the acquisition of positive assertive skills such as initiating conversations, providing compliments, and expressing caring. Such behaviors are considered 'feminine' and are found to be deficient in males (Pitcher and Meikle, 1980). The emphasis in AT on conflict assertion, rather than on positive assertion, clearly reflects the dominance of male values in the social construction of reality (cf Hare-Mustin & Maracek, 1988).
2. However, Alberti & Emmons (1986b) have largely retained their early activist stance.
3. A notable omission from this list is the United Kingdom, where a general social skills training model (Argyle, 1981) is more popular than AT.

Chapter 2 Conceptualizing assertive behavior

1. Assertive responses are hypothesized to be learned through the same basic mechanisms, primarily operant conditioning and observational learning (cf Deluty, 1981a), that account for the acquisition of other skills. Unfortunately, the socialization processes that result in assertive deficits have not been the subject of systematic investigation. Two retrospective, correlational studies suggest there is a modest relationship between adult children's perceptions of parental assertiveness and the adult children's self-reported assertiveness (Moss, 1985; Plax, Kearney, & Beatty, 1985). An intergenerational study obtained significant correlations between self-reported assertiveness of parents and children (Powell, 1985).
2. Schroeder and Rakos (1983) provide a detailed discussion and critique of Trower's (1982) and McFall's (1982) models of social skills.
3. An exception to this general finding was obtained by LaFramboise (1983), who found that American Indians scored similarly to established norms on an assertiveness self-report measure.
4. Recently, for example, Arrindell and Van der Ende (1985; Arrindell, Sanderman, Van der Molen, Van der Ende, and Mersch, 1988) employed confirmatory factor analysis rather than the more typical exploratory procedure and identified four response classes: display of negative feelings (behavior change requests, refusals, expression of unpopular opinions), expression of personal limitations (admissions of ignorance,

requests for help), initiation of assertion (expression of opinions and feelings), and verbalization of positive affect (praising others, giving and receiving compliments). These response classes were consistently obtained from a variety of clinical and nonclinical populations.

5. Hollandsworth's own research confirms that the 'threat' criterion is conceptually inadequate. He found statements with verbal disparagements were judged to be aggressive, but the one specifying a threat was evaluated as assertive (Hollandsworth, 1985). Nevertheless, threats must be employed cautiously and appropriately. When included in initial assertions, they are perceived to be hostile and inappropriate (Mullinix & Galassi, 1981).

6. The subsequent obligations are intended to function as relationship-enhancing behaviors, and are in this sense pragmatic (Rakos, 1979). They improve the social reaction to conflict assertion (see Chapters 3 and 5) and therefore increase the net benefits and social validity of the response. While they can be emitted as part of an assertion to a stranger with whom you expect to have no further contact, I believe they are unnecessary (there is no relationship to maintain) and potentially problematic (they extend the conflictual interaction and expand the content that is open for discussion). Furthermore, in the infrequent instances when legitimate rights of strangers conflict, the nature of the situation will usually prohibit a search for a mutually acceptable compromise. You and a stranger, reaching the last subway seat at precisely the same moment, are unlikely to agree to share the seat or to alternate standing with sitting. It is far more likely that one or both commuters – even if assertively competent – will decide that the issue is not worth pursuing or to relinquish any claims to the seat for other reasons (eg negative consequences to the other person [antecedent obligation 3]). Heisler and McCormack (1982) provided some empirical support for this recommendation. They found that an empathic statement improved the reaction to assertion when the recipient was a familiar person, but had little effect when he or she was unfamiliar.

Chapter 3 Conflict assertion: overt behavioral components

1. Also Cook & St Lawrence (1990), Epstein (1980), Gormally (1982), Keane, St. Lawrence, Himadi, Graves, & Kelly (1983), Keane, Wedding, & Kelly (1983), Kelly, Kern, Kirkley, Patterson, & Keane (1980), Kelly, St. Lawrence, Bradlyn, Himadi, Graves, & Keane (1982), Kern (1982a), St. Lawrence, Hansen, Cutts, Tisdelle, & Irish (1985a), Woolfolk & Dever (1979), and Zollo, Heimberg, & Becker (1985).

2. Also Heisler & McCormack (1982), Kern (1982a), Kern et al. (1985), Solomon et al. (1982), Wildman & Clementz (1986), Woolfolk & Dever (1979), and Zollo et al. (1985). Only Mullinix and Galassi (1981), assessing behavior change requests in the work environment, failed to obtain benefits with the addition of an empathic statement to standard assertion.

3. For comparison, common sounds have the following decibel levels (Gabe, 1989): normal conversation (60), vacuum cleaner (70), hair dryer (80), lawn mower (90), and subway train (100). Though the empirically determined decibel level (76) of assertive speech may seem a bit excessive for some situations, confidence in the data may be derived by comparing the level judged to be 'marginally assertive' (68dB) with that of normal conversation (60dB).

4. Though repetition violates the postulates of normal conversation (Gervasio, 1987), situations involving escalation in noncontinuity relationships will rarely be conventional social interactions. Hence, repetition will be appropriate.

Chapter 4 Conflict assertion: covert behavioral components

1. Also, Arisohn, Bruch, & Heimberg (1988), Blankenberg & Heimberg (1984), Borgart (1985), Chiauzzi & Heimberg (1986), Kuperminc & Heimberg (1983), Robinson & Calhoun (1984), and Zollo et al. (1985).

Chapter 5 The social validity of conflict assertion

1. By this reasoning, 'masculine' females ought to value assertion by females. Since such an effect has not been obtained, the variables affecting female judges cannot be the same as those hypothesized here for males. On the other hand, 'conservative' females devalue both standard assertion and empathic assertion by females (Kern et al., 1985), so *change* in sex-role behaviors may be an issue for them as well as for 'conservative' males.
2. The extent to which a behavior therapist should assume the role of a social activist and train clients to fundamentally change their immediate and extended social environment has been fiercely debated in the literature. Davison (1976; 1978), for example, argued that it is an ethical responsibility of the therapist to teach clients the skills necessary to challenge and modify social inequities since extant social pressures and discriminations prevent the clients from identifying what they truly desire. Others (eg Halleck, 1976; Sturgis and Adams, 1976) disagreed, asserting that such an approach by the therapist is arrogant and unethical, since it is unlikely to be in the best interests of that particular client, regardless of how beneficial it may ultimately prove to future clients or society in general.
3. Pedersen (1985) and Sue (1981) are excellent sources for multicultural intervention with minority clients in the US. Behavior modification with African-Americans is extensively examined by Turner and Jones (1982).

Chapter 6 Assessment of assertion

1. The present discussion is restricted to instruments that focus solely on assertion. Numerous scales include assertion as one of several social skills of interest (eg Goldsmith & McFall, 1975; Levenson & Gottman, 1978).
2. The clinical application of self-monitoring has been extensively discussed by Mahoney (1977) and Watson and Tharp (1988) and the interested reader will find both sources well worth reading; the present discussion, however, will be more narrowly focused to issues germane to the self-monitoring of assertion.
3. I may provide several simple examples of the impact of reactivity on assessment and intervention. If, for example, a client 'forces' himself to assert to his wife in a situation in which he would normally withdraw, assessment may fail to identify this type of interaction as particularly problematic. Furthermore, the 'unnatural' assertion may modify behavior in other circumstances. He may now fail to assert himself to his wife in a relatively easy situation for any number of reasons related to the earlier assertion (wife's reaction, emotional fatigue, not wanting to 'bother' her again, avoidance of a second conflict). I also offer examples from different target behaviors, such as eating and smoking. If a client refrains from eating at a habitual time (eg upon arriving home from work) due to self-monitoring, he or she will be hungrier at dinner-time, and will be likely to consume more and/or different food than usual. Self-monitoring will then point to dinner-time as the problem, rather than the after-work snack.
4. Clients can also engage in a replication of the replication role play under high-demand 'assertive' instructions as a means to compare actual behavior to behavioral potential.

However, the effects of the previous experience and the first replication may influence responding. Though empirical data are lacking, it seems possible that some clients may have learned the contents of an appropriate response for *that* situation only (eg through reflection and self-analysis or post-performance discussion with others). The probable role play, by presenting a nonexperienced, nonrehearsed situation may provide a better assessment of behavioral potential.

5. The social problem-solving literature is burgeoning, and new assessment instruments are constantly being introduced, primarily for children. The Open Middle Interview (Polifka, Weissberg, Gesten, de Apodaca, & Picoli, 1981), for example, appears to be quite promising (cf Waas & French, 1989).

Chapter 7   Assertiveness training techniques and procedures

1. Behavioral interventions, to demonstrate benefits superior to those obtained simply as a function of participating in treatment, are generally compared to an *attention-placebo* control group containing 'generic' therapy factors. These variables include: (a) participation in therapy and focusing on a problem; (b) attention from a therapist; and (c) amount of treatment. Furthermore, a fourth generic variable, expectations of improvement, must be controlled through the careful construction of a placebo treatment that is as credible as the behavioral intervention (Kazdin & Wilson, 1978). Thus, for example, Rakos and Schroeder (1979) compared their self-administered AT program to a self-administered relaxation training program. The programs were judged to be equally credible by both assertive and unassertive individuals, probably due to the rationales provided for each, ie nonassertion as a function of skill deficits (AT) or of excessive anxiety (relaxation). Furthermore, the two interventions were equated in terms of length of treatment, amount of therapist contact, and amount of home practice.

2. However, Bruch (1978) points out that models who verbalize problem-solving instructions and coping self-statements (eg Meichenbaum & Goodman, 1971) are modeling rules as well as behavioral exemplars: observers 'learn "how to" generate strategies and response alternatives, and not just "what is" an appropriate response' (p. 66). Observational learning with such models is, therefore, deductive as well as inductive.

3. In a *variable ratio schedule*, reinforcement is contingent upon the performance of an *average* number of desired responses. A VR-3 schedule delivers reinforcement, on the average, after 3 acceptable responses have been emitted, e.g. reinforcement after responses 1, 2, 5, and 12 (12 responses/4 reinforcements = 3). In contrast, a *fixed ratio schedule* delivers reinforcement each time the required number of responses is emitted. Thus, an FR-3 schedule would present the reinforcer after responses 3, 6, 9, and 12. A *continuous schedule*, in which each and every response is reinforced, is in reality an FR-1 schedule. Operant research has consistently demonstrated that intermittent reinforcement schedules produce superior maintenance of responding than continuous schedules. This *partial reinforcement effect* is particularly evident with VR schedules and with moderately high ratios (cf Klein, 1987; Rachlin, 1970).

4. Stimulus generalization occurs when the target response is emitted in the presence of a stimulus that differs from the one used in training. The effect is greatest when the training and new stimuli are similar; the more they differ, the less generalization is observed (cf Klein, 1987; Martin & Pear, 1988). In AT, a man might be trained assert to a female boss. This response may generalize to a similar stimulus (eg a female coworker) but not to one that, for him, is very different on important dimensions (eg his wife).

Response generalization occurs when a response similiar to the target one is emitted in the presence of the training stimulus. If the response variation is not great, and the central functional element of the response is retained, the variant will produce reinforcement and be strengthened (cf Martin & Pear, 1988). For example, a client may develop an effective response to her boss in behavior rehearsal, and then, when role playing it again, modify the specific verbalizations. However, the message remains the same.

5. Not surprisingly, generalization between conflict positive response classes is unlikely (Kelly et al., 1978; Talbert, Lawrence, & Nelson, 1980).

Chapter 8   Target populations

1. Assertion in the context of racial or cultural variables was examined extensively in earlier chapters, and will not be reviewed in the present discussion.

2. General clinical obstacles are discussed in detail in Chapter 9.

3. For example, Wallace (1982) developed approximately 200 interpersonal scenes representing hospital, community, friendship, and family settings. Role plays are followed by a series of questions pertaining to perceptual and processing abilities (eg what are the people talking about? what is the best solution?). Inadequate responses are then specifically remediated.

4. However, this concern must be placed in a proper context. At present, there are no data indicating that the failure rate for females is greater than for males. In fact, clinicians observe that AT, despite the impressive research, does not provide benefits to all participants (Emmons & Alberti, 1983).

5. Assertive abilities are correlated with, but do not necessarily cause, marital satisfaction. Rewarding marriages may develop conditions that facilitate assertive expression, or marital happiness and spousal assertion both may be a function of something else (eg generalized cooperative and problem-solving behaviors of both partners).

6. Recent research suggests this dichotomy is an oversimplification, as the two orientations are not invariably gender-related (Friedman, Robinson, & Friedman, 1987). Furthermore, some feminist writers object to the whole notion of Gilligan's 'different voice'. Hare-Mustin and Maracek (1989) contend that such a maximization of differences is an arbitrary social construction no different from previous ones used to justify the subordination of women. Mednick (1989) argues that the dichotomy blames the victim and 'places the burden of change *entirely* on the person...[and avoids] an examination of cultural, socioeconomic, structural, or contemporaneous situational factors that may affect behavior' (p. 1120). In fact, she suggests that 'individuals' level of autonomy or relatedness may depend more on their position in the social hierarchy than on gender' (p. 1120).

   My discussion assumes, first, any observed gender differences in values are sociopolitically determined rather than innate inclinations, and, second, great diversity in values exists within each sex. However, I disagree with Mednick's contention that a focus on individuals, rather than social structures, must inevitably result in reactionary ideologies that maintain the status quo, even when individual gender differences are attributed to social conditioning processes. A woman can be taught to assertively change her social as well as personal world, though in clinical contexts the former will generally be exceptionally difficult and the latter a greater personal priority. (The same, by the way, may be said of other oppressed groups.) The clinician's values will, and should, influence treatment goals, but those goals must respect the desires and 'best interests' of the client (see Chapter 9).

7. Indirect data bearing on this issue are provided by Rotheram and Armstrong (1980),

who found assertion-related discomfort was greater for female high-school students than for their male counterparts. Interestingly, but not surprisingly, self-reported assertion *decreased* for girls over grade levels while it *increased* for boys.

8. However, not all visually handicapped persons evidence assertion deficits, at least in role plays. Ammerman, Van Hasselt, Hersen, and Moore (1989) found that even severely impaired youngsters performed similarly to nonhandicapped adolescents. As the authors note, conclusions must be tempered since (a) their subjects may have been higher functioning, in that they were mainstreamed in public schools and came from intact families, (b) the role-play assessment may not be sensitive to actual (as opposed to potential) performance, and (c) the positive and negative assertion situations did not assess the response class of initiating interactions and the outcome measures did not include 'process' ones such as timing.

Chapter 9   Clinical issues in assertiveness training

1. Though Benton and Schroeder's (1989) meta-analysis suggests few additional benefits from longer training, they did not evaluate the impact of extended intervention with *severely* dysfunctional schizophrenics.

2. Consensual validation or disconfirmation of an anticipated negative reaction to positive assertion by males provides an additional reason to those articulated in Chapter 8 for forming groups composed of both males and females.

3. Efforts to increase treatment expectations (cf Kazdin & Krouse, 1983) may inadvertently promote an overly enthusiastic and unjustified description of treatment potency. The empirical and clinical foundations of AT are sufficiently secure to improve client expectations of gains without employing exaggeration.

4. The husband, of course, should be informed *before he divulges his information* that he is not the client and, therefore, his communication will be shared with his wife.

5. In actuality, communications made in the presence of *a third party* are viewed as nonprivileged by most US courts. This presents a legal and ethical dilemma for marital, family, and group therapies (Corey et al., 1988).

6. People generally adhere to a conception of justice in which personal responsibility for distress must be assumed: 'they want to believe in a world where people get what they deserve... [and] deserve what they get' (Lerner, 1970, p. 207). Events that can be attributed to personal characteristics increase the appearance of order and predictability in the world, and seemingly 'protect' people from the unfortunate but capricious occurrences that befall others (Lerner, 1970).

7. This is the only experimentally validated AT audiotape or self-help book; unfortunately, even here, only one study has been conducted. One noncommercial AT film has been researched, but the study found it had little impact, even though the dependent measures relied totally on self-report (Kwiterovich & Horan, 1977).

References

Adejumo, D. (1981). Sex differences in assertiveness among university students in Nigeria. *Journal of Social Psychology, 113*, 139-140.

Adinolfi, A. A., McCourt, W. F., & Geoghegan, S. (1976). Group assertiveness training for alcoholics. *Journal of Studies in Alcohol, 37*, 311-320.

Aiduk, R. & Karoly, P. (1975). Self-regulation techniques in the modification of non-assertive behavior. *Psychological Reports, 36*, 895-905.

Alberti, R. E. (1977). Comments on 'Differentiating assertion from aggression: Some behavioral guidelines'. *Behavior Therapy, 8*, 353-354.

Alberti, R. E. (1986). *Making yourself heard: A guide to assertive relationships*. New York: BMA Audio Cassettes.

Alberti, R. E. & Emmons, M. L. (1970). *Your perfect right: A guide to assertive behavior*. San Luis Obispo, CA: Impact.

Alberti, R. E. & Emmons, M. L. (1975). *Stand up, speak out, talk back*. New York: Pocket Books.

Alberti, R. E. & Emmons, M. L. (1986a). *The professional edition of 'Your Perfect Right': A manual for assertiveness trainers*. San Luis Obispo, CA: Impact.

Alberti, R. E. & Emmons, M. L. (1986b). *Your perfect right: A guide for assertive living* (5th edn). San Luis Obispo, CA: Impact.

Alden, L. (1984). An attributional analysis of assertiveness. *Cognitive Therapy and Research, 8*, 607-618.

Alden, L. (1988). Irrational Beliefs Inventory. In M. Hersen & A. S. Bellack (Eds.) *Dictionary of behavioral assessment techniques*. New York: Pergamon Press.

Alden, L. & Cappe, R. (1981). Non-assertiveness: Skill deficit or selective self-evaluation? *Behavior Therapy, 12*, 107-115.

Alden, L. & Safran, J. (1978). Irrational beliefs and non-assertive behavior. *Cognitive Therapy and Research, 2*, 357-364.

Alden, L., Safran, J., & Weideman, R. (1978). A comparison of cognitive and skills training strategies in the treatment of unassertive clients. *Behavior Therapy, 9*, 843-846.

American Psychiatric Association (1987). *Diagnostic and statistical manual of mental disorders* (3rd edn, revised), Washington, DC: American Psychiatric Association.

American Psychological Association (1990). *Ethical standards of psychologists* (rev. edn). Washington, DC: American Psychological Association.

Ammerman, R. T., Van Hasselt, V. B., Hersen, M., & Moore, L. E. (1989). Assessment of social skills in visually impaired adolescents and their parents. *Behavioral Assessment, 11*, 327-351.

Andrasik, F., Heimberg, R. G., Edlund, S. R., & Blankenberg, R. (1981). Assessing the readability levels of self-report assertion inventories. *Journal of Consulting and Clinical Psychology, 49,* 142-144.

Argyle, M. (1981). The contribution of social interaction research to social skill training. In J. D. Wine & M. D. Smye (Eds.) *Social competence.* New York: Guilford Press.

Argyle, M., Furnham, A., & Graham, J. (1981). *Social situations.* Cambridge: Cambridge University Press.

Argyle, M., Graham, J., Campbell, A., & White, P. (1979). The rules of different situations. *New Zealand Psychologist, 8,* 13-22.

Arisohn, B., Bruch, M. A., & Heimberg, R. G. (1988). Influence of assessment methods on self-efficacy and outcome expectancy ratings of assertive behavior. *Journal of Counseling Psychology, 35,* 336-341.

Arkowitz, H. (1981). Assessment of social skills. In M. Hersen & A. S. Bellack (Eds.) *Behavioral assessment: A practical handbook* (2nd edn). New York: Pergamon Press.

Arnold, B. R. & Parrott, R. (1978). Job interviewing: Stress management and interpersonal-skills training for welfare-rehabilitation clients. *Rehabilitation Counseling Bulletin, 22,* 44-52.

Arrindell, W. A., Sanderman, R., Van der Molen, H., Van der Ende, J., & Mersch, P. (1988). The structure of assertiveness: A confirmatory approach. *Behaviour Research and Therapy, 26,* 337-339.

Arrindell, W. A. & Van der Ende, J. (1985). Cross-sample invariance of the structure of self-reported distress and difficulty in assertiveness. *Advances in Behavioural Research and Therapy, 7,* 205-243.

Ary, D. V., Toobert, D., Wilson, W., & Glasgow, R. E. (1986). Patient perspective on factors contributing to nonadherence to diabetes regimen. *Diabetes Care, 9,* 168-172.

Augsberger, D. (1979). *Anger and assertiveness in pastoral care.* Philadelphia: Fortress Press.

Baer, J. (1976). *How to be an assertive (not aggressive) woman in life, in love, and on the job.* New York: Signet.

Bair, J. P. & Greenspan, B. K. (1986). TEAMS: Teamwork training for interns, residents, and nurses. *Hospital and Community Psychiatry, 37,* 633-635.

Baldwin, J. D. & Baldwin, J. I. (1986). *Behavior principles in everyday life* (2nd edn). Englewood Cliffs, NJ: Prentice-Hall.

Bander, R. S., Russell, R. K., & Weiskott, G. N. (1978). Effects of varying amounts of assertiveness training on level of assertiveness and anxiety reduction in women. *Psychological Reports, 43,* 144-146.

Bandura, A. (1977a). Self-efficacy: Toward a unifying theory of behavior change. *Psychology Review, 84,* 191-215.

Bandura, A. (1977b). *Social learning theory.* Englewood Cliffs, NJ: Prentice-Hall.

Barbaree, H. E. & Davis, R. B. (1984). Assertive behavior, self-expectations, and self-evaluations in mildly depressed university women. *Cognitive Therapy and Research, 8,* 153-171.

Bates, P. (1980). The effectiveness of interpersonal skills training on the social skill acquisition of moderately and mildly retarded adults. *Journal of Applied Behavior Analysis, 13,* 237-248.

Beck, J. G. & Heimberg, R. G. (1983). Self-report assessment of assertive behavior: A critical analysis. *Behavior Modification, 7,* 451-487.

Becker, R. E. & Heimberg, R. G. (1988). Assessment of social skills. In A. S. Bellack & M. Hersen (Eds.) *Behavioral assessment: A practical handbook* (3rd edn). New York: Pergamon Press.

Becker, R. E., Heimberg, R. G., & Bellack, A. S. (1987). *Social skill training treatment for depression.* New York: Pergamon Press.

Beidleman, W. B. (1981). Group assertive training in correctional settings: A review and methodological critique. *Journal of Offender Counseling, Services and Rehabilitation, 6*, 69-87.

Bellack, A. S. (1979a). Behavioral assessment of social skills. In A. S. Bellack & M. Hersen (Eds.) *Research and practice social skills training.* New York: Plenum Press.

Bellack, A. S. (1979b). A critical appraisal of strategies for assessing social skill. *Behavioral Assessment, 1*, 157-176.

Bellack, A. S. (1983). Recurrent problems in the behavioral assessment of social skill. *Behaviour Research and Therapy, 21*, 29-41.

Bellack, A. S., Hersen, M., & Turner, S. M. (1978). Role playing tests for assessing social skills: Are they valid? *Behavior Therapy, 9*, 448-461.

Bellack, A. S., Hersen, M., & Turner, S. M. (1979). Relationship of role playing and knowledge of appropriate assertive behavior to assertion in the natural environment. *Journal of Consulting and Clinical Psychology, 47*, 570-578.

Bem, S. L. (1974). The measurement of psychological androgyny. *Journal of Consulting and Clinical Psychology, 42*, 155-162.

Benton, M. K. & Schroeder, H. E. (in press). Social skill training with schizophrenics: A meta-analytic evaluation. *Journal of Consulting and Clinical Psychology.*

Berah, E. F. (1981). Influence of scheduling variations on the effectiveness of a group assertion-training program for women. *Journal of Counseling Psychology, 28*, 265-268.

Berg, B. (n. d.). *The assertion game.* Philadelphia: Center for Applied Psychology.

Bhargava, S. C. (1983). Progressive muscular relaxation and assertive training in a case of tension headache. *Indian Journal of Clinical Psychology, 10*, 23-25.

Blankenberg, R. W. & Heimberg, R. G. (1984, November). Assertive refusal, perceived consequences, and reasonableness of request. Paper presented at the annual convention of the Association for Advancement of Behavior Therapy, Philadelphia.

Bloom, L. Z., Coburn, K., & Pearlman, J. (1975). *The new assertive woman.* New York: Dell.

Boice, R. (1982). An ethological perspective on social skills research. In J. P. Curran & P. M. Monti (Eds.) *Social skill training: A practical handbook for assessment and treatment.* New York: Guilford Press.

Boisvert, J. M., Beaudry, M., & Bittar, J. (1985). Assertiveness training and human communication processes. *Journal of Contemporary Psychotherapy, 15*, 58-73.

Bordewick, M. C. & Bornstein, P. H. (1980). Examination of multiple cognitive response dimensions among differentially assertive individuals. *Behavior Therapy, 11*, 440-448.

Borgart, E. J. (1985). Cognitive processes and nonassertiveness. *Zeitschrift fur Klinische Psychologie, 14*, 185-199.

Bornstein, P. H., Bach, P. J., McFall, M. E., Friman, P. C., & Lyons, P. D. (1980). Application of a social skills training program in the modification of interpersonal deficits among retarded adults: A replication. *Journal of Applied Behavior Analysis, 13*, 171-176.

Bornstein, M. R., Bellack, A. S., & Hersen, M. (1977). Social skills training for unassertive children: A multiple baseline analysis. *Journal of Applied Behavior Analysis, 10*, 183-195.

Bornstein, M. R., Bellack, A. S., & Hersen, M. (1980). Social skills training for highly aggressive children: Treatment in an inpatient setting. *Behavior Modification, 4*, 173-186.

Bourque, P. & Ladouceur, R. (1979). Self-report and behavioral measures in the assessment of assertive behavior. *Journal of Behavior Therapy and Experimental Psychiatry, 10*, 287-292.

Bower, S. A. & Bower, G. H. (1976). *Asserting yourself: A practical guide for positive change*. Reading, MA: Addison-Wesley.

Brandau, H., Skatsche, R., & Ruch, W. (1984). The predictive validity and behavioral relevance of a multidemensional test battery for the assessment of 'assertiveness'. *Zeitschrift fur Klinische Psychologie/Forschung und Praxis*, 13, 77-87.

Bray, J. H., Shepherd, J. N., & Hays, J. R. (1985). Legal and ethical issues in informed consent to psychotherapy. *The American Journal of Family Therapy*, *13*, 50-60.

Bregman, S. (1984). Assertiveness training for mentally retarded adults. *Mental Retardation*, *22*, 12-16.

Bregman, S. (1985). Assertiveness training for mentally retarded adults. *Psychiatric Aspects of Mental Retardation Reviews*, *4*, 43-48.

Broad, J., Burke, J., Byford, S. R., & Sims, P. (1986). Clinical application of the Children's Action Tendency Scale. *Psychological Reports*, *59*, 71-74.

Brockway, B. (1976). Assertive training for professional women. *Social Work*, *21*, 498-505.

Brooks, G. R. & Richardson, F. C. (1980). Emotional skills training: A treatment program for duodenal ulcer. *Behavior Therapy*, *11*, 198-207.

Broverman, I. K., Broverman, D. M., Clarkson, F. E., Rosenkrantz, P. S., & Vogel, S. R. (1970). Sex-role stereotypes and clinical judgments of mental health. *Journal of Consulting and Clinical Psychology*, *34*, 1-7.

Broverman, I. K., Vogel, S. R., Broverman, D. M., Clarkson, F. E., & Rosenkrantz, P. S. (1972). Sex-role stereotypes: A current appraisal. *Journal of Social Issues*, *28*, 59-78.

Brown, S. D. (1980). Videotape feedback: Effects on assertive performance and subjects' perceived competence and satisfaction. *Psychological Reports*, *47*, 455-461.

Bruch, M. A. (1978). Cognitive modeling: There's more than meets the eye. *Cognitive Therapy and Research*, *1*, 65-67.

Bruch, M. A. (1981). A task analysis of assertive behavior revisited: Application and extension. *Behavior Therapy*, *12*, 217-230.

Bruch, M. A. (1988). Written Assertiveness Knowledge Test. In M. Hersen & A. S. Bellack (Eds.) *Dictionary of behavioral assessment*. New York: Pergamon Press.

Bruch, M. A., Haase, R. F., & Purcell, M. J. (1984). Content dimensions of self-statements in assertive situations: A factor analysis of two measures. *Cognitive Therapy & Research*, *8*, 173-186.

Bruch, M. A., Heisler, B. D., & Conroy, C. G. (1981). Effects of conceptual complexity on assertive behavior. *Journal of Counseling Psychology*, *28*, 377-385.

Brummage, M. E. & Willis, M. H. (1974). How three variables influence the outcome of group assertive training. Paper presented at the convention of the American Personnel and Guidance Association. New Orleans, April.

Burkhart, B. H., Green, S. B., & Harrison, W. H. (1979). Measurement of assertive behavior: Construct and predictive validity of self-report, role-playing and in vivo measures. *Journal of Clinical Psychology*, *35*, 376-383.

Butler, P. E. (1976). *Self-assertion for women*. San Francisco: Canfield Press.

Calabrese, D. N. & Hawkins, R. P. (1988). Job-related social skill training with female prisoners. *Behavior Modification*, *12*, 3-33.

Caldwell-Colbert, A. T. & Jenkins, J. O. (1982). Modification of interpersonal behavior. In S. M. Turner & R. T. Jones (Eds.) *Behavior modification in black populations: Psychosocial issues and empirical findings* (pp. 171-208). New York: Plenum.

Callner, D. A. & Ross, S. M. (1976). The reliability and validity of three measures of assertion in a drug addict population. *Behavior Therapy*, *7*, 559-567.

Callner, D. A. & Ross, S. M. (1978). The assessment and training of assertive skills with drug addicts: A preliminary study. *International Journal of the Addictions*, *13*, 227-239.

Canter, L. & Canter, M. (1988). *Assertive discipline for parents* (rev. edn). New York: Harper & Row.

Carlisle, J. S. & Donald, K. M. (1985). The use of art exercises in assertiveness training. *Journal of Counseling & Development, 64,* 149-150.

Carmichael, S. R. (1976). The use of self-instruction in an assertion training program with chronic, institutionalized patients. *Newsletter for Research in Mental Health and Behavioral Sciences, 18,* 20-22.

Carmody, T. P. (1978). Rational-emotive, self-instructional and behavioral assertion training: Facilitating maintenance. *Cognitive Therapy and Research, 2,* 241-253.

Cash, T. F. (1984). The irrational beliefs test: Its relationship with cognitive-behavioral traits and depression. *Journal of Clinical Psychology, 40,* 1399-1405.

Chaney, E. F., O'Leary, M. R., & Marlatt, G. A. (1978). Skill training with alcoholics. *Journal of Consulting and Clinical Psychology, 46,* 1092-1104.

Cheek, D. A. (1976). *Assertive black...puzzled white.* San Louis Obispo, CA: Impact.

Chiappone, D., McCarrey, M., Piccinin, S., & Schmidtgoessling, N. (1981). Relationship of client-perceived facilitative conditions on outcome of behaviorally oriented assertive training. *Psychological Reports, 49,* 251-256.

Chiauzzi, E. & Heimberg, R. G. (1983). The effects of subjects' level of assertiveness, sex, and legitimacy of request on assertion-relevant cognitions: An analysis by post performance videotape reconstruction. *Cognitive Therapy and Research, 7,* 555-564.

Chiauzzi, E. & Heimberg, R. G. (1986). Legitimacy of request and social problem-solving: A study of assertive and non-assertive subjects. *Behavior Modification, 10,* 3-18.

Chiauzzi, E. J., Heimberg, R. G., Becker, R. E., & Gansler, D. (1985). Personalized versus standard role plays in the assessment of depressed patients' social skill. *Journal of Psychopathology and Behavioral Assessment, 7,* 121-133.

Chiauzzi, E. J., Heimberg, R. G., & Doty, D. (1982). Task analysis of assertive behavior revisited: The role of situational variation in female college students. *Behavioral Counseling Quarterly, 2,* 42-50.

Childswork/Childsplay (n. d.). *Assert with love.* Philadelphia: Center for Applied Psychology.

Christensen, A., Arkowitz, H., & Anderson, J. (1975). Practice dating as a treatment for college dating inhibition. *Behaviour Research and Therapy, 13,* 321-331.

Christmann, F. & Sommer, G. (1976). Behavior therapy of fingernail biting: Assertive training and self-control. *Praxis der Kinderpsychologie und Kinderpsychiatrie, 25,* 139-146.

Christoff, K. A. & Edelstein, B. A. (1981). Functional aspects of assertive and aggressive behavior: Laboratory and in vivo observations. Paper presented at the annual meeting of the Association for Advancement of Behavior Therapy, Toronto, November.

Christoff, K. A. & Kelly, J. A. (1985). A behavioral approach to social skills training. In L. L. L'Abate & M. A. Milan (Eds.) *Handbook of social skills training and research.* New York: Wiley.

Cianni-Surridge, M. & Horan, J. J. (1983). On the wisdom of assertive job-seeking behavior. *Journal of Counseling Psychology, 30,* 209-214.

Ciminero, A. R., Nelson, R. O., & Lipinski, D. (1977). Self-monitoring procedures. In A. R. Ciminero, K. S. Calhoun, & H. E. Adams (Eds.) *Handbook of behavioral assessment.* New York: Wiley.

Clifford, T. (1987). Assertiveness training for parents. *Journal of Counseling and Development, 65,* 552-554.

Comas-Diaz, L. (1985). Cognitive and behavioral group therapy with Puerto Rican women: A comparison of content themes. *Hispanic Journal of Behavioral Sciences, 7,* 273-283.

Comas-Diaz, L. & Duncan, J. W. (1985). The cultural context: A factor in assertiveness training with mainland Puerto Rican women. *Psychology of Women Quarterly, 9,* 463-476.

Cone, J. D. (1977). The relevance of reliability and validity for behavioral assessment. *Behavior Therapy, 8,* 411-425.

Connor, J. M., Dann, L. N., & Twentyman, C. T. (1982). A self-report measure of assertiveness in young adolescents. *Journal of Clinical Psychology, 38,* 101-106.

Cook, D. J. & St. Lawrence, J. S. (1990). Variations in presentational format: Effect on interpersonal evaluations of assertive and unassertive behavior. *Behavior Modification, 14,* 21-36.

Cooley, M. L. (1979). Interests of assertiveness trainees. *Journal of Counseling Psychology, 26,* 173-175.

Corby, N. (1975). Assertion training with aged populations. *Counseling Psychologist, 5,* 69-74.

Corey, G., Corey, M. S., & Callanan, P. (1988). *Issues and ethics in the helping professions* (3rd edn). Pacific Grove, CA: Brooks/Cole.

Craighead, L. W. (1979). Self-instructional training for assertive-refusal behavior. *Behavior Therapy, 10,* 529-542.

Craighead, L. W. (1985). A problem-solving approach to the treatment of obesity. In M. Hersen & A. S. Bellack (Eds.) *Handbook of clinical behavior therapy with adults.* New York: Plenum.

Crawford, M. (1988). Gender, age, and the social evaluation of assertion. *Behavior Modification, 12,* 549-564.

Curran, J. P. (1978). Comments on Bellack, Hersen, and Turner's paper on the validity of role play test. *Behavior Therapy, 9,* 462-468.

Curran, J. P. (1979). Social skills: Methodological issues and future directions. In A. S. Bellack & M. Hersen (Eds.) *Research and practice in social skills training.* New York: Plenum.

Davison, G. C. (1976). Homosexuality: The ethical challenge. *Journal of Consulting and Clinical Psychology, 44,* 157-162.

Davison, G. C. (1978). Not can but ought: The treatment of homosexuality. *Journal of Consulting and Clinical Psychology, 46,* 170-172.

Deaux, K. (1971). Honking at the intersection: A replication and extension. *Journal of Social Psychology, 84,* 159-160.

Decker, P. J. (1982). The enhancement of behavior modeling training of supervisory skills by the inclusion of retention processes. *Personnel Psychology, 35,* 323-332.

Decker, P. J. (1984). Effects of different symbolic coding stimuli in behavior modeling training. *Personnel Psychology, 37,* 711-720.

Delamater, R. J. & McNamara, J. R. (1985). Perceptions of assertiveness by high- and low-assertive female college students. *Journal of Psychology, 119,* 581-586.

Delamater, R. J. & McNamara, J. R. (1986). The social impact of assertiveness: Research findings and clinical implications. *Behavior Modification, 10,* 139–158.

del Greco, L. (1983). The del Greco Assertive Behavior Inventory. *Journal of Behavioral Assessment, 5,* 49-63.

del Greco, L., Breitbach, L., Rumer, S., McCarthy, R. H., & Suissa, S. (1986a). Further examination of the reliability of the Modified Rathus Assertiveness Schedule. *Adolescence, 21,* 483-485.

del Greco, L. D., Breitbach, L., Rumer, S., McCarthy, R. H., & Suissa, S. (1986b). Four-year results of a youth smoking prevention program using assertiveness training. *Adolescence, 21,* 631-640.

Deluty, R. H. (1979). Children's Action Tendency Scale: A self-report measure of aggressiveness, assertiveness, and submissiveness in children. *Journal of Consulting and*

Clinical Psychology, 47, 1061-1071.

Deluty, R. H. (1981a). Assertiveness in children: Some research considerations. *Journal of Clinical Child Psychology, 10*, 149-155.

Deluty, R. H. (1981b). Alternative-thinking, ability of aggressive, assertive, and submissive children. *Cognitive Therapy and Research, 5*, 309-312.

Deluty, R. H. (1981c). Adaptiveness of aggressive, assertive, and submissive behavior for children. *Journal of Clinical Child Psychology, 10*, 155-158.

Deluty, R. H. (1983). Children's evaluations of aggressive, assertive, and submissive responses. *Journal of Child Psychology, 12*, 124-129.

Deluty, R. H. (1984). Behavioral validation of Children's Action Tendency Scale. *Journal of Behavioral Assessment, 6*, 115-130.

Deluty, R. H. (1985a). Consistency of assertive, aggressive, and submissive behavior for children. *Journal of Personality and Social Psychology, 49*, 1054-1065.

Deluty, R. H. (1985b). Cognitive mediation of aggressive, assertive, and submissive behavior in children. *International Journal of Behavior Development, 8*, 355-369.

Derry, P. A. & Stone, G. L. (1979). Effects of cognitive adjunct treatments on assertiveness. *Cognitive Therapy and Research, 3*, 213-221.

Dewey, J. (1957). *Reconstruction in philosophy.* Boston: Beacon Press.

Dittman, A. T. (1972). *Interpersonal messages of emotion.* New York: Springer.

Dittman, A. T., Parloff, M. B., & Boomer, D. S. (1965). Facial and bodily expression: A study of receptivity of emotional cues. *Psychiatry, 28*, 239-244.

Dobia, B. & McMurray, N. E. (1985). Applicability of learned helplessness to depressed women undergoing assertiveness training. *Australian Journal of Psychology, 37*, 71-80.

Donahoe, C. P. & Driesenga, S. A. (1988). A review of social skills training with chronic mental patients. In M. Hersen & P. M. Miller (Eds.) *Progress in behavior modification, vol. 23.* Newbury Park, CA: Sage.

Dong, Y. L., Hallberg, E. T., & Hassard, J. H. (1979). Effects of assertion training on aggressive behavior of adolescents. *Journal of Counseling Psychology, 26*, 459-461.

Dopfner, M., Schluter, S., & Rey, E. (1981). Evaluation of a social skills training program for unassertive children aged 9 to 12: A treatment comparison. *Zeitschrift für Kinder und Jugend Psychiatrie, 9*, 233-252.

Doty, L. (1987). *Communication and assertion skills for older persons.* Washington: Hemisphere Publishing.

Doyle, K. M. (1982). Assertiveness training for the drug dependent woman. *N.I.D.A.-Treatment Research Monograph Series: Treatment Services for Drug Dependent Women, 2*, 213-246.

Doyle, M. A. & Biaggio, M. L. (1981). Expression of anger as a function of assertiveness and sex. *Journal of Clinical Psychology, 37*, 154-157.

Drury, S. S. (1984). *Assertive supervision: Building involved teamwork.* Champaign, IL: Research Press.

Dubinsky, I. H. (1980). Positive feeling expression: Generalization in the intimate dyad. *Dissertation Abstracts International, 40*, 5401-B.

Duehn, W. D. & Mayadas, N. S. (1976). The use of stimulus/modeling videotapes in assertive training for homosexuals. *Journal of Homosexuality, 1*, 373-381.

Dumas, J. E. (1989). Let's not forget the context in behavioral assessment. *Behavioral Assessment, 11*, 231-248.

Dunham, R. G. & Brower, H. T. (1984). The effects of assertiveness training on the nontraditional role assumption of geriatric nurse practitioners. *Sex Roles, 11*, 911-921.

Dunn, M., Van Horn, E., & Herman, S. H. (1981). Social skills and spinal cord injury: A comparison of three training procedures. *Behavior Therapy, 12*, 153-164.

Dupont, P. J. & Jason, L. A. (1984). Assertiveness training in a preventive drug education program. *Journal of Drug Education, 14*, 369-378.

Dura, J. R. & Beck, S. (1986). Psychiatric aides' perceptions of a patient's assertive behaviors. *Behavior Modification, 10*, 301-314.

D'Zurilla, T. J. & Goldfried, M. R. (1971). Problem-solving and behavior modification. *Journal of Abnormal Psychology, 78*, 107-126.

D'Zurilla, T. J. & Nezu, A. (1982). Social problem solving in adults. In P. Kendall (Ed.) *Advances in Cognitive-Behavioral Research and Therapy (Vol. 1)*. New York: Academic Press.

Edelstein, B. A. & Eisler, R. M. (1976). Effects of modeling and modeling with instructions and feedback on the behavioral components of social skills. *Behavior Therapy, 7*, 382-389.

Edinberg, M. A., Karoly, P., & Gleser, G. C. (1977). Assessing assertion in the elderly: An application of the behavior analytic model of competence. *Journal of Clinical Psychology, 33*, 869-874.

Eisler, R. M. (1976). The behavioral assessment of social skills. In M. Hersen & A. S. Bellack (Eds.) *Behavioral assessment: A practical handbook*. New York: Pergamon.

Eisler, R. M., Blanchard, E. B., Fitts, H., & Williams, J. G. (1978). Social skill training with and without modeling for schizophrenic and non-psychotic hospitalized psychiatric patients. *Behavior Modification, 2*, 147-172.

Eisler, R. M. & Frederiksen, L. W. (1980). *Perfecting social skills*. New York: Plenum.

Eisler, R. M., Frederiksen, L. W., & Peterson, G. L. (1978). The relationship of cognitive variables to the expression of assertiveness. *Behavior Therapy, 9*, 419-427.

Eisler, R. M., Hersen, M., & Miller, P. M. (1973). Effects of modeling on components of assertive behavior. *Journal of Behavior Therapy and Experimental Psychiatry, 4*, 1-6.

Eisler, R. M., Hersen, M., & Miller, P. M. (1974). Shaping components of assertive behavior with instructions and feedback. *American Journal of Psychiatry, 131*, 1344-1347.

Eisler, R. M., Hersen, M., Miller, P. M., & Blanchard, E. B. (1975). Situational determinants of assertive behavior. *Journal of Consulting and Clinical Psychology, 43*, 330-340.

Eisler, R. M., Miller, P. M., & Hersen, M. (1973). Components of assertive behavior. *Journal of Clinical Psychology, 29*, 295-299.

Eisler, R. M., Miller, P. M., & Hersen, M. (1974). Effects of assertive training on marital interaction. *Archives of General Psychiatry, 30*, 643-649.

Ekman, P. & Frisen, W. (1969). Nonverbal leakage and clues to deception. *Psychiatry, 32*, 88-106.

Elder, J. P., Edelstein, B. A., & Fremouw, W. J. (1981). Client by treatment interactions in response acquisition and cognitive restructuring approaches. *Cognitive Therapy and Research, 5*, 203-210.

Elder, J. P., Edelstein, B. A., & Narrick, M. M. (1979). Adolescent psychiatric patients: Modifying aggressive behavior with social skills training. *Behavior Modification, 3*, 161-178.

Elkins, G. R., Osborne, S., & Saltzberg, L. (1983). An investigation of adult perceptions of 'assertiveness'. *Psychology: A Quarterly Journal of Human Behavior, 20*, 34-37.

Ellis, A. (1962). *Reason and emotion in psychotherapy*. New York: Lyle Stuart.

Ellis, A. (1970). *The essence of rational psychotherapy: A comprehensive approach to treatment*. New York: Institute for Rational Living.

Ellis, A. (1987). The impossibility of achieving consistently good mental health. *American Psychologist, 42*, 364-375.

Ellis, A. & Grieger, R. (1977). *Handbook of rational-emotive therapy*. New York: Springer.

Emmelkamp, P. M. G. (1981). Recent developments in the behavioral treatment of obsessive-compulsive disorders. In J. C. Goulougouris (Ed.) *Learning theory approaches to psychiatry.* New York: Wiley.

Emmelkamp, P. M. G. & van der Heyden, H. (1980). Treatment of harming obsessions. *Behavioural Analysis and Modification, 4,* 28-35.

Emmelkamp, P. M., Van der Hout. A., & de Vries, K. (1983). Assertive training for agoraphobics. *Behaviour Research and Therapy, 21,* 63-68.

Emmons, M. L. & Alberti, R. E. (1983). Failure: Winning at the losing game in assertiveness training. In E. B. Foa & P. M. G. Emmelkamp (Eds.) *Failures in behavior therapy.* New York: Wiley.

Emmons, M. & Richardson, D. (1981). *The assertive Christian.* Minneapolis: Winston Press.

Englander-Golden, P., Elconin. J., & Satir, V. (1986). Assertive/leveling communication and empathy in adolescent drug abuse prevention. *Journal of Primary Prevention, 6,* 231-243.

Epstein, N. (1980). The social consequences of assertion, aggression, passive aggression and submission: Situational and dispositional determinants. *Behavior Therapy, 11,* 662-669.

Epstein, N., DeGiovanni, I. S., & Jayne-Lazarus, C. (1978). Assertion training for couples. *Journal of Behavior Therapy and Experimental Psychiatry, 9,* 149-155.

Falbo, T., Hazen, M. D., & Linimon, D. (1982). The costs of selecting power bases or messages associated with the opposite sex. *Sex Roles, 8,* 147-157.

Falloon, I. R., Lindley, P., McDonald, R., & Marks, I. M. (1977). Social skills training of out-patient groups: A controlled study of rehearsal and homework. *British Journal of Psychiatry, 131,* 599-609.

Faraone, S. V. & Hurtig, R. R. (1985). An examination of social skill, verbal productivity, and Gottman's model of interaction using observational methods and sequential analyses. *Behavioral Assessment, 7,* 349-366.

Fehrenbach, P. A. & Thelen, M. H. (1981). Assertive-skills training for inappropriately aggressive college males: Effects on assertive and aggressive behavior. *Journal of Behavior Therapy and Experimental Psychiatry, 12,* 213-217.

Feindler, E. L., Ecton, R. B., Kingsley, D., & Dubey, D. R. (1986). Group anger-control training for institutionalized psychiatric male adolescents. *Behavior Therapy, 17,* 109-123.

Feldman, R. S. & Donohoe, L. F. (1978). Non-verbal communication of affect in interracial dyads. *Journal of Educational Psychology, 70,* 979-987.

Fensterheim, H., & Baer, J. (1975). *Don't say yes when you want to say no: How assertiveness training can change your life.* New York: David McKay.

Ferjencik, J. (1979). Cognitive approach to modifying non-assertive behavior. *Psychologia a Patopsychologia Dietata, 14,* 37-43.

Ferrell, W. L. & Galassi, J. P. (1981). Assertion training and human relations training in the treatment of chronic alcoholics. *International Journal of the Addictions, 16,* 959-968.

Feshbach, S. (1970). Aggression. In P. H. Mussen (Ed.) *Carmichael's manual of child psychology (Vol. 2).* New York: Wiley.

Fiedler, D. & Beach, L. R. (1978). On the decision to be assertive. *Journal of Consulting and Clinical Psychology, 46,* 537-546.

Fiedler, P., Orenstein, H., Chiles, J., Fritz, G., & Breitt, S. (1979). Effects of assertive training on hospitalized adolescents and young adults. *Adolescence, 14,* 523-528.

Finch, B. E. & Wallace, C. J. (1977). Successful interpersonal skills training with schizophrenic inpatients. *Journal of Consulting and Clinical Psychology, 45,* 885-890.

Fingeret, A. L., Monti, P. M., & Paxson, M. A. (1985). Social perception, social performance, and self-perception: A study with psychiatric and nonpsychiatric groups. *Behavior Modification, 9*, 345-356.

Fischetti, M., Curran, J. P., & Wessberg, H. W. (1977). Sense of timing: A skill deficit in heterosexual-socially anxious males. *Behavior Modification, 1*, 179-194.

Fischetti, M., Peterson, J. L., Curran, J. P., Alkire, M., Perrewe, P., & Arland, S. (1984). Social cue discrimination versus motor skill: A missing distinction in social skill assessment. *Behavioral Assessment, 6*, 27-32.

Fleming, E. R. & Fleming, D. C. (1982). Social skill training for educable mentally retarded children. *Education and Training of the Mentally Retarded, 17*, 44-50.

Flowers, J. V. (1978). Goal clarity as a component of assertive behavior and a result of assertion training. *Journal of Clinical Psychology, 34*, 744-747.

Flowers, J. V. & Goldman, R. D. (1976). Assertion training for mental health paraprofessionals. *Journal of Counseling Psychology, 23*, 147-150.

Flowers, J. V. & Guerra, J. (1974). The use of client coaching in assertion training with large groups. *Community Mental Health Journal, 10*, 414-417.

Fodor, I. G. (1980). The treatment of communication problems with assertiveness training. In A. Goldstein & E. B. Foa (Eds.) *Handbook of behavioral interventions: A clinical guide*. New York: Wiley.

Ford, J. O. (1978). Therapeutic relationship in behavior therapy: An empirical analysis. *Journal of Consulting and Clinical Psychology, 46*, 1302-1314.

Foy, D. W., Eisler, R. M., & Pinkston, S. (1975). Modeled assertion in a case of explosive rages. *Journal of Behavior Therapy and Experimental Psychiatry, 6*, 135-137.

Foy, D. W., Massey, F. H., Duer, J. D., Ross, J. M., & Wooten, L. S. (1979). Social skills training to improve alcoholics' vocational interpersonal competency. *Journal of Counseling Psychology, 26*, 128-132.

Foy, D. W., Miller, P. M., Eisler, R. M., & O'Toole, D. H. (1976). Social-skills training to teach alcoholics to refuse drinks effectively. *Journal of Studies on Alcohol, 37*, 1340-1345.

Frederiksen, L. W., Jenkins, J. O., Foy, D. W., & Eisler, R. M. (1976). Social skills training to modify abusive verbal outbursts in adults. *Journal of Applied Behavior Analysis, 9*, 117-125.

Freedberg. E. J. & Johnston, W. E. (1981). Effects of assertion training within the context of a multi-modal alcoholism treatment program for employed alcoholics. *Psychological Reports, 48*, 379-386.

Friedman, W. J., Robinson, A. B., & Friedman, B. L. (1987). Sex differences in moral judgements? *Psychology of Women Quarterly, 11*, 37-46.

Frisch, M. B. & Froberg, W. (1987). Social validation of assertion strategies for handling aggressive criticism: Evidence for consistency across situations. *Behavior Therapy, 18*, 181-191.

Frisch, M. B. & Higgins, R. L. (1986). Instructional demand effects and the correspondence among role-play, self-report, and naturalistic measures of social skill. *Behavioral Assessment, 8*, 221-236.

Fukuyama, M. A. & Greenfield, T. K. (1983). Dimensions of assertiveness in an Asian-American student population. *Journal of Counseling Psychology, 30*, 429-432.

Furnham, A. (1979). Assertiveness in three cultures: Multidimensionality and cultural differences. *Journal of Clinical Psychology, 35*, 522-527.

Furnham, A. & Henderson, M. (1981). Sex differences in self reported assertiveness. *British Journal of Clinical Psychology, 20*, 227-238.

Furnham, A. & Henderson, M. (1984). Assessing assertiveness: A content and correlational analysis of five assertiveness inventories. *Behavioral Assessment, 6*, 79-88.

Gabe, C. (1989). Today's noisy world is hurting our ears. *Cleveland Plain Dealer*, July 18, pp. 9B-10B.

Gainer, J. C. (1978). Temperature discrimination training in the biofeedback treatment of migraine headache. *Journal of Behavior Therapy and Experimental Psychiatry, 9*, 185-187.

Galassi, J. P. & Galassi, M. D. (1977a). Assessment procedures for assertive behavior. In R. E. Alberti (Ed.) *Assertiveness: Innovations, applications, issues*. San Luis Obispo, CA: Impact.

Galassi, J. P., DeLo, J. S., Galassi, M. D., & Bastien, S. (1974). The college self-expression scale: A measure of assertiveness. *Behavior Therapy, 5*, 165-171.

Galassi, J. P., Galassi, M. D., & Fulkerson, K. (1984). Assertion training in theory and practice: An update. In C. M. Franks (Ed.) *New developments in behavior therapy: From research to clinical application*. New York: Haworth Press.

Galassi, J. P., Galassi, M. D., & Vedder, M. J. (1981). Perspectives on assertion as a social skills model. In J. Wine & M. Smye (Eds.) *Social competence*. New York: Guilford Press.

Galassi, M. D. & Galassi, J. P. (1976). The effects of role playing variations on the assessment of assertive behavior. *Behavior Therapy, 7*, 343-347.

Galassi, M. D. & Galassi, J. P. (1977b). *Assert yourself: How to be your own person*. New York: Human Sciences.

Galassi, M. D. & Galassi, J. P. (1978a). Assertion: A critical review. *Psychotherapy: Theory, Research and Practice, 15*, 16-29.

Galassi, M. D. & Galassi, J. P. (1978b). Modifying assertive and aggressive behavior through assertion training. *Journal of College Student Personnel, 19*, 453-456.

Galassi, J. P., Kostka, M. P., & Galassi, M. D. (1975). Assertive training: A one year follow-up. *Journal of Counseling Psychology, 22*, 451-452.

Gambrill, E. D., Florian, V., & Splaver, G. (1986). Assertion, loneliness, and perceived control among students with & without physical disabilities. *Rehabilitation Counseling Bulletin, 30*, 4-12.

Gambrill, E. D. & Richey, C. A. (1975). An assertion inventory for use in assessment and research. *Behavior Therapy, 6*, 550-561.

Gambrill, E. D. & Richey, C. A. (1976). *It's up to you: The development of assertive social skills*. Millbrae, CA: Les Femmes.

Gambrill, E. D. & Richey, C. A. (1986). Criteria used to define and evaluate socially competent behavior among women. *Psychology of Women Quarterly, 10*, 183-196.

Garcia, L. & Lubetkin, B. S. (1986). Clinical issues in assertiveness training with shy clients. *Psychotherapy, 23*, 434-438.

Garrison, S. & Jenkins, J. O. (1986). Differing perceptions of black assertiveness as a function of race. *Journal of Multicultural Counseling and Development, 14*, 157-166.

Gay, M. L., Hollandsworth, J. G., & Galassi, J. P. (1975). An assertiveness inventory for adults. *Journal of Counseling Psychology, 22*, 340-344.

Geller, M. I., Wildman, H. E., Kelly, J. A., & Laughlin, C. S. (1980). Teaching assertive and commendatory social skills to an interpersonally-deficient retarded adolescent. *Journal of Clinical Child Psychology, 9*, 17-21.

Gergen, K. J. (1973). Social psychology as history. *Journal of Personality and Social Psychology, 26*, 309-320.

Gervasio, A. H. (1987). Assertiveness techniques as speech acts. *Clinical Psychology Review, 7*, 105-119.

Gervasio, A. H. (1988). Linguistic analysis of an assertiveness training film. *Psychotherapy, 25*, 294-304.

Gervasio, A. H. & Crawford, M. (1989). Social evaluations of assertiveness: A critique and speech act reformulation. *Psychology of Women Quarterly, 13*, 1-25.

Gervasio, A. H., Pepinsky, H. B., & Schwebel, A. I. (1983). Stylistic complexity and verb usage in assertive and passive speech. *Journal of Counseling Psychology, 30*, 546-556.

Gilligan, C. (1982). *In a different voice.* Cambridge, MA: Harvard University Press.

Gilmour, D. R., McCormick, I. A., & de Ruiter, C. A. (1981). Group assertion training for adult male offenders: Internal validity. *Behavior Therapy, 12*, 274-279.

Girdano, D. A. & Everly, G. S. (1986). *Controlling stress and tension: A holistic approach* (2nd edn). Englewood Cliffs, NJ: Prentice-Hall.

Glass, C. R., Gottman, J. M., & Schmurak, S. H. (1976). Response acquisition and cognitive self-statement modification approaches to dating skills training. *Journal of Counseling Psychology, 23*, 520-526.

Glueckhauf, R. L., Horley, J., Poushinsky, M. F., & Vogel, R. (1984). Assertiveness training for disabled individuals in wheelchairs: Preliminary findings. *International Journal of Rehabilitation Research, 7*, 441-443.

Goffman, E. (1956). *The presentation of self in everyday life.* Edinburgh: Edinburgh University Press.

Golden, M. (1981). A measure of cognition within the context of assertion. *Journal of Clinical Psychology, 37*, 253-262.

Goldfried, M. R. (1980). Toward the delineation of therapeutic change principles. *American Psychologist, 35*, 991-999.

Goldfried, M. R. & Davison, G. C. (1976). *Clinical behavior therapy.* New York: Holt, Rinehart, & Winston.

Goldsmith, J. B. & McFall, R. M. (1975). Development and evaluation of an interpersonal skill-training program for psychiatric patients. *Journal of Abnormal Psychology, 84*, 51-58.

Goldstein-Fodor, I. & Epstein, R. C. (1983). Assertiveness training for women: Where are we failing? In E. B. Foa & P. M. G. Emmelkamp (Eds.) *Failures in behavior therapy* (pp. 137-158). New York: Wiley.

Gordon, S. & Waldo, M. (1984). The effects of assertiveness training on couples' relationships. *American Journal of Family Therapy, 12*, 73-77.

Gordon, V. B. & Goble, L. K. (1986). Creative accommodation: Role satisfaction for psychiatric staff nurses. *Issues in Mental Health Nursing, 8*, 25-35.

Gorecki, P. R., Dickson, A. L., Anderson, H. N., & Jones, G. E. (1981). Relationship between contrived in vivo and role play assertive behavior. *Journal of Clinical Psychology, 37*, 104-107.

Gormally, J. (1982). Evaluation of assertiveness: Effects of gender, rater involvement and level of assertiveness. *Behavior Therapy, 13*, 219-225.

Gormally, J., Hill, C. E., Otis, M., & Rainey, L. (1975). A microtraining approach to assertion training. *Journal of Counseling Psychology, 22*, 299-303.

Gottlieb, N., Burden, D., McCormick, R., & Nicarthy, G. (1983). The distinctive attributes of feminist groups. *Social Work with Groups, 6*, 81-93.

Gottman, J. M. & Krokoff, L. J. (1989). Marital interaction and satisfaction: A longitudinal view. *Journal of Consulting and Clinical Psychology, 57*, 47-52.

Graham, J., Argyle, M., & Furnham, A. (1980). The goal structure of situations. *European Journal of Social Psychology, 10*, 345-366.

Graham, J. W., Rohrbach, L. A., Hansen, W. B., Flay B. R., & Johnson, C. A. (1989). Convergent and discriminant validity for assessment of skill in resisting a role play alcohol offer. *Behavioral Assessment, 11*, 353-379.

Granero, M. (1984). Differences between homosexuals and heterosexuals (males and females) in fears, assertiveness and autosufficiency. *Revista Latinoamericana de Psicologia, 16*, 39-52.

Grice, H. P. (1975). Logic and conversation. In P. Cole & J. L. Morgan (Eds.) *Syntax and semantics, Vol. 3: Speech Acts* (pp. 41-58). New York: Semina Press.

Grimes, J. W. (1980). The effects of assertion training on severely disabled student/clients. *Journal of Applied Rehabilitation Counseling, 11*, 36-39.

Grodner, B. S. (1977). Assertiveness and anxiety: A cross-cultural and socioeconomic perspective. In R. E. Alberti (Ed.) *Assertiveness: Innovations, applications, issues.* San Luis Obispo, CA: Impact.

Gross, A. M. & Johnson, W. G. (1981). Diabetes assertiveness test: A measure of social coping skills in pre-adolescent diabetics. *The Diabetes Educator, 7*, 26-27.

Guerra, J. J., Cotler, S. B., & Cotler, S. M. (1976). *Assertion training series: An audio-cassette program.* Champaign, IL: Research Press.

Gulanick, N. A. & Howard, G. S. (1979). Evaluation of a group program designed to increase androgyny in feminine women. *Sex Roles, 5*, 811-827.

Habermas, J. (1973). *Theory and practice.* Boston: Beacon Press.

Haimo, S. & Blitman, F. (1985). The effects of assertive training on sex role concept in female agoraphobics. *Women and Therapy, 4*, 53-61.

Hall, J. R. & Beil-Warner, D. (1978). Assertiveness of male Anglo and Mexican-American college students. *Journal of Social Psychology, 105*, 175-178.

Halleck, S. L. (1976). Another response to 'Homosexuality: The ethical challenge'. *Journal of Consulting and Clinical Psychology, 44*, 167-170.

Hamilton, F. & Maisto, S. A. (1979). Assertive behavior and perceived discomfort of alcoholics in assertion-required situations. *Journal of Consulting and Clinical Psychology, 47*, 196-197.

Hamm, B. H. & Brodt, D. (1982). GUTS: Teaching assertiveness skills by simulation and gaming. *Nursing Research, 31*, 246-247.

Hammen, C. L., Jacobs, M., Mayol, A., & Cochran, S. D. (1980). Dysfunctional cognitions and the effectiveness of skills and cognitive behavioral assertion training. *Journal of Consulting and Clinical Psychology, 48*, 685-695.

Hammond, P. D. & Oei, T. P. (1982). Social skills training and cognitive restructuring with sexual unassertiveness in women. *Journal of Sex and Marital Therapy, 8*, 297-304.

Hare-Mustin, R. T. (1983). An appraisal of the relationship between women and psychotherapy: 80 years after the case of Dora. *American Psychologist, 38*, 593-601.

Hare-Mustin, R. T. & Maracek, J. (1988). The meaning of difference: Gender theory, postmodernism, and psychology. *American Psychologist, 43*, 455-464.

Hargie, O. (Ed.) (1986a). *Handbook of communication skills.* London: Croom Helm.

Hargie, O. (1986b). The skill of self-disclosure. In O. Hargie (Ed.) *A handbook of communication skills.* London: Croom Helm.

Harrell, R. L. & Strauss, F. A. (1986). Approaches to increasing assertive behavior and communication skills in blind and visually impaired persons. *Journal of Visual Impairment and Blindness, 80*, 794-798.

Hartsook, J. E., Olch, D. R. & deWolf, V. A. (1976). Personality characteristics of women's assertiveness training group participants. *Journal of Counseling Psychology, 23*, 322-326.

Hassan, R. (1973). Code, register and social dialect. In B. Bernstein (Ed.) *Class, codes and control (Vol. 2)* (pp. 253-292). London: Routledge & Kegan Paul.

Hatzenbuehler, L. & Schroeder, H. E. (1982). Assertiveness training with out-patients: The effectiveness of skill and cognitive procedures. *Behavioral Psychotherapy, 10*, 234-252.

Hautzinger, M. (1979). Assertive training procedure in the treatment of obesity. *The Behavior Therapist, 2*, 23-24.

Hay, W. M., Hay, L. R., Angle, H. V., & Nelson, R. O. (1979). The reliability of problem identification in the behavioral interview. *Behavioural Assessment, 1*, 107-118.

Hayes, S. C. (1988). Contextualism and the next wave of behavioral psychology. *Behavior Analysis, 23,* 7-22.

Hayes, S. C., Brownstein, A. J., Haas, J. R., & Greenway, D. E. (1986). Instructions, multiple schedules, and extinction: distinguishing rule-governed from schedule-controlled behavior. *Journal of the Experimental Analysis of Behavior, 46,* 137-147.

Hayes, S. C., Brownstein, A. J., Zettle, R. D., Rosenfarb, I., & Korn, Z. (1986). Rule-governed behavior and sensitivity to changing consequences of responding. *Journal of the Experimental Analysis of Behavior, 45,* 237-256.

Hayes, S. C., Hayes, L. J., & Reese, H. W. (1988). Finding the philosophical core: A review of Stephen Pepper's *World Hypotheses. Journal of the Experimental Analysis of Behavior, 50,* 97-111.

Hayes, S. C., Nelson, R. O., & Jarrett, R. B. (1987). The treatment utility of assessment: A functional approach to evaluating assessment quality. *American Psychologist, 42,* 963-974.

Hayman, P. M. & Cope, C. S. (1980). Effects of assertion training on depression. *Journal of Clinical Psychology, 36,* 534-543.

Haynes, S. N. (1978). *Principles of behavioral assessment.* New York: Gardner Press.

Haynes, S. N. & Jensen, B. (1979). The interview as a behavioral assessment instrument. *Behavioral Assessment, 1,* 97-105.

Hedlund, B. L. & Lindquist, C. U. (1984). The development of an inventory for distinguishing among passive, aggressive, and assertive behavior. *Behavioral Assessment, 6,* 379-390.

Heimberg, R. G., Andrasik, F., Blankenberg, R., & Edlund, S. R. (1983). A readability analysis of commercially available self-help books for assertiveness. *Behavioral Counseling and Community Intervention, 3,* 198-204.

Heimberg, R. G. & Becker, R. E. (1981). Cognitive and behavioral models of assertive behavior: Review, analysis and integration. *Clinical Psychology Review, 1,* 353-373.

Heimberg, R. G., Chiauzzi, E. J., Becker, R. E., & Madrazo-Peterson, R. (1983). Cognitive mediation of assertive behavior: An analysis of the self-statement patterns of college students, psychiatric patients, and normal adults. *Cognitive Therapy and Research, 7,* 455-464.

Heimberg, R. G. & Etkin, D. (1983). Response quality and outcome effectiveness as factor in students' and counselors' judgements of assertiveness. *British Journal of Cognitive Psychotherapy, 1,* 59-68.

Heimberg, R. G. & Harrison, D. F. (1980). Use of the Rathus Assertiveness Schedule with offenders: A question of questions. *Behavior Therapy, 11,* 278-281.

Heimberg, R., Harrison, D. F., Goldberg, L. S., DesMarais, S., & Blue, S. (1979). The relationship of self-report and behavioral assertion in an offender population. *Journal of Behavior Therapy and Experimental Psychiatry, 10,* 283-286.

Heimberg, R. G., Montgomery, D., Madsen, C. H., & Heimberg, J. S. (1977). Assertion training: A review of the literature. *Behavior Therapy, 8,* 953-971.

Heiser, P. & Gannon, L. R. (1984). The relationship of sex-role stereotypy to anger expression and the report of psychosomatic symptoms. *Sex Roles, 10,* 601-611.

Heisler, G. H. & McCormack, J. (1982). Situational and personality influences on the reception of provocative responses. *Behavior Therapy, 13,* 743-750.

Heisler, G. H. & Shipley, R. H. (1977). The ABC model of assertive behavior. *Behavior Therapy, 8,* 509-512.

Helzel, M. F. & Rice, M. E. (1985). On the validity of social skills assessment: An analysis of role-play and ward staff ratings of social behavior in a maximum security setting. *Canadian Journal of Behavioral Science, 17,* 400-411.

Henderson, M. (1983). Self-reported assertion and aggression among violent offenders with high or low levels of over-controlled hostility. *Personality and Individual Differences, 4*, 113-115.

Henderson, M. & Furnham, A. (1983). Dimensions of assertiveness: Factor analysis of five assertion inventories. *Journal of Behavior Therapy and Experimental Psychiatry, 14*, 223-231.

Henry, W. J. & Piercy, F. P. (1984). Assertive/aggressive ratings of women as a function of the raters' race and sex. *Journal of Non-White Concerns, 12*, 85-98.

Hersen, M. & Bellack, A. S. (Eds.) (1988). *Dictionary of behavioral assessment techniques*. New York: Pergamon Press.

Hersen, M., Bellack, A. S., & Turner, S. M. (1978). Assessment of assertiveness in female psychiatric patients: Motor and autonomic measures. *Journal of Behavior Therapy and Experimental Psychiatry, 9*, 11-16.

Hersen, M., Eisler, R. M., & Miller, P. M. (1974). An experimental analysis of generalization in assertive training. *Behaviour Research and Therapy, 12*, 295-310.

Hersen, M., Eisler, R. M., Miller, P. M., Johnson, M. B., & Pinkston, S. G. (1973). Effects of practice, instructions, and modeling on components of assertive behavior. *Behaviour Research and Therapy, 11*, 443-451.

Hersen, M., Kazdin, A. E., Bellack, A. S., & Turner, S. M. (1979). Effects of live modeling, covert modeling, and rehearsal on assertiveness in psychiatric patients. *Behaviour Research and Therapy, 17*, 369-377.

Herzberger, S. D., Chan, E., & Katz, J. (1984). The development of an assertiveness self-report inventory. *Journal of Personality Assessment, 48*, 317-323.

Hess, E. P. & Bornstein, P. H. (1979). Perceived sex role attitudes in self and other as a determinant of differential assertiveness in college males. *Cognitive Therapy and Research, 2*, 155-159.

Hess, E. P., Bridgewater, C. A., Bornstein, P. H., & Sweeney, J. M. (1980). Situational determinants in the perception of assertiveness: Gender-related influences. *Behavior Therapy, 11*, 49-58.

Hewes, D. D. (1975). On effective assertive behavior: A brief note. *Behavior Therapy, 6*, 269-271.

Higgins, R. L., Alonso, R. R., & Pendleton, M. G. (1979). The validity of role-play assessments of assertiveness. *Behavior Therapy, 10*, 655-662.

Higgins, R. L., Frisch, M. B., & Smith, D. (1983). A comparison of role-played and natural responses to identical circumstances. *Behavior Therapy, 14*, 158-169.

Hirsch, S. M., von Rosenberg, R., Phelen, C., & Dudley, H. K. (1978). Effectiveness of assertiveness training with alcoholics. *Journal of Studies on Alcohol, 39*, 89-97.

Hobbs, S. A. & Walle, D. L. (1985). Validation of the Children's Assertive Behavior Scale. *Journal of Psychopathology & Behavioral Assessment, 7*, 145-153.

Hobbs, S. A., Walle, D. L., & Hammersly, G. A. (1984). Assessing children's social skills: Validation of the Behavioral Assertiveness Test for Children (BAT-C). *Journal of Behavioral Assessment, 6*, 29-35.

Hodgson, R. & Rachman, S. (1974). II. Desychrony in measures of fear. *Behaviour Research and Therapy, 12*, 319-326.

Hoffmann, M., von Kalkstein, H., & Volger, I. (1978). An empirical study of training programs for overcoming anxiety about speaking. *Zeitschrift fur Klinische Psychologie und Psychotherapie, 26*, 23-33.

Hollandsworth, J. G. (1977). Differentiating assertion and aggression: Some behavioral guidelines. *Behavior Therapy, 8*, 347–352.

Hollandsworth, J. G. (1985). Social validation of a construct for differentiating assertion and aggression. *The Behavior Therapist, 8*, 136-137.

Hollandsworth, J. G. & Cooley, M. L. (1978). Provoking anger and gaining compliance with assertive versus aggressive responses. *Behavior Therapy, 9*, 640-646.

Hollandsworth, J. G. & Wall, K. E. (1977). Sex differences in assertive behavior: An empirical investigation. *Journal of Counseling Psychology, 24*, 217-222.

Hong, K. & Cooker, P. G. (1984). Assertion training with Korean college students: Effects on self-expression and anxiety. *Personnel and Guidance Journal, 62*, 353-358.

Hops, H. & Greenwood, C. R. (1988). Social skill deficits. In E. J. Mash & L. G. Terdal (Eds.) *Behavioral assessment of childhood disorders* (2nd edn). New York: Guilford Press.

Horan, J. J., D'Amico, M. M., & Williams, J. M. (1975). Assertiveness and patterns of drug use: A pilot study. *Journal of Drug Education, 5*, 217-221.

Horan, J. J. & Williams, J. M. (1982). Longitudinal study of assertion training as a drug abuse prevention strategy. *American Educational Research Journal, 19*, 341-351.

Hrop, S. & Rakos, R. F. (1985). The influence of race in the social evaluation of assertion in conflict situations. *Behavior Therapy, 16*, 478-493.

Huey, W. C. & Rank, R. C. (1984). Effects of counselor and peer-led group assertive training on Black adolescent aggression. *Journal of Counseling Psychology, 31*, 95-98.

Hull, D. B. & Schroeder, H. E. (1979). Some interpersonal effects of assertion, non-assertion, and aggression. *Behavior Therapy, 10*, 20-29.

Hung, J. H., Rosenthal, T. L., & Kelley, J. E. (1980). Social comparison standards spur immediate assertion: 'So you think you're submissive?'. *Cognitive Therapy and Research, 4*, 223-234.

Hupkens, C. E., Verhoeven, L. T., & Boon Van Ostade, A. H. (1975). Assertive behavior among staff psychologists in Indonesia and Holland. *Tijdschrift voor Psychologie, 3*, 1-10.

Hwang, P. O. (1977). Assertion training for Asian-Americans. In R. E. Alberti (Ed.) *Assertiveness: Innovations, applications, issues.* San Luis Obispo, CA: Impact.

Irani, K. D. (1986). Introduction: Modes of rationality. In M. Tammy & K. D. Irani (Eds.) *Rationality in thought and action.* New York: Greenwood Press.

Ivey, A. E. (1988). *Intentional interviewing and counseling: Facilitating client development.* Pacific Grove, CA: Brooks/Cole.

Jackson, D. J. & Huston, T. L. (1975). Physical attractiveness and assertiveness. *Journal of Social Psychology, 96*, 79-84.

Jacobs, M. K. & Cochran, S. D. (1982). The effects of cognitive restructuring on assertive behavior. *Cognitive Therapy and Research, 6*, 63-76.

Jacobson, N. S. (1982). Communication skills training for married couples. In J. P. Curran & P. M. Monti (Eds.) *Social skills training: A practical handbook for assessment and treatment.* New York: Guilford Press.

Jacobson, N. S (1989). The politics of intimacy. *The Behavior Therapist, 12*, 29-32.

Jakubowski, P. & Lange, A. J. (1978). *The assertive option.* Champaign, IL: Research Press.

Jakubowski-Spector, P. (1973). Facilitating the growth of women through assertive training. *The Counseling Psychologist, 4*, 75-86.

Janda, L. H. & Rimm, D. C. (1977). Type of situation and sex of counselor in assertive training. *Journal of Counseling Psychology, 24*, 444-447.

Jansen, M. A. & Meyers-Abell, J. (1980). Assertion training for battered women: A pilot program. *Social Work, 25*, 1964-1965.

Jansen, M. S. & Litwack, L. (1979). The effects of assertive training on counselor trainees. *Counselor Education and Supervision, 19*, 27-34.

Jaspers, K. (1957). *Socrates, Buddha, Confucius, Jesus.* Munich: R. Piper and Co.

Jenkins, J. O., Adams, H. E., & Rahaim, S. (1981). Investigation of personal investment in behavioral role-playing tasks used to assess assertiveness. *Psychological Reports, 49*, 567-574.

Johnson, W. G., Gross, A. M., & Wildman, H. E. (1982). Developing coping skills in adolescent diabetics. *Corrective & Social Psychiatry & Journal of Behavior Technology, Methods and Therapy, 28*, 116-120.

Joiner, J. G., Lovett, P. S., & Hague, L. K. (1982). Evaluation of assertiveness of disabled persons in the rehabilitation process. *Rehabilitation Counseling Bulletin, 26*, 55-58.

Jones, R. G. (1969). *The Irrational Beliefs Test.* Wichita, KS: Test System.

Jones, S. L. (1984). Assertiveness training in Christian perspective. *Journal of Psychology and Theology, 12*, 91-99.

Jordan, C. S., Davis, M., Kahn, P., & Sinnott, R. H. (1980). Eidetic-imagery group methods of assertion training. *Journal of Mental Imagery, 4*, 41-48.

Kaflowitz, N. G. (1986). Testing a self-presentational model of assertive behavior. *Dissertation Abstracts International, 47*, 2618-B.

Kahn, L. S. (1984). Group process and sex differences. *Psychology of Women Quarterly, 8*, 261-281.

Kahn, S. E. (1981). Issues in the assessment and training of assertiveness with women. In J. D. Wine & M. S. Smye (Eds.) *Social competence.* New York: Guilford Press.

Kanfer, F. H. (1985). Target selection for clinical change programs. *Behavioral Assessment, 7*, 7-20.

Kanfer, F. H. & Grimm, L. G. (1977). Behavioral analysis: Selecting target behaviors in the interview. *Behavior Modification, 1*, 7-28.

Kanfer, F. H. & Grimm, L. G. (1980). Managing clinical change: A process model of therapy. *Behavior Modification, 4*, 419-444.

Kanfer, F. H. & Phillips, J. S. (1970). *Learning foundations of behavior therapy.* New York: Wiley.

Kanfer, F. H. & Saslow, G. (1969). Behavioral diagnosis. In C. M. Franks (Ed.) *Behavior Therapy: Appraisal and Status.* New York: McGraw-Hill.

Kanfer, F. H. & Schefft, B. K. (1988). *Guiding the process of therapeutic change.* Champaign, IL: Research Press.

Kaplan, D. A. (1982). Behavioral, cognitive, and behavioral-cognitive approaches to group assertion training therapy. *Cognitive Therapy and Research, 6*, 301-314.

Katz, I., Cohen, S., & Glass, D. (1975). Some determinants of cross-racial helping behavior. *Journal of Personality and Social Psychology, 32*, 964-970.

Kazdin, A. E. (1974). Effects of covert modeling and model reinforcement on assertive behavior. *Journal of Abnormal Psychology, 83*, 240-252.

Kazdin, A. E. (1975). Covert modeling, imagery assessment, and assertive behavior. *Journal of Consulting and Clinical Psychology, 43*, 716-724.

Kazdin, A. E. (1976a). Effects of covert modeling, multiple models, and model reinforcement on assertive behavior. *Behavior Therapy, 7*, 211-222.

Kazdin, A. E. (1976b). Assessment of imagery during covert modeling of assertive behavior. *Journal of Behavior Therapy and Experimental Psychiatry, 7*, 213-219.

Kazdin, A. E. (1977). Assessing the clinical or applied importance of behavior change through social validation. *Behavior Modification, 1*, 427-452.

Kazdin, A. E. (1979a). Situational specificity: The two-edged sword of behavioral assessment. *Behavioral Assessment, 1*, 57-75.

Kazdin, A. E. (1979b). Effects of covert modeling and coding of modeled stimuli on assertive behavior. *Behaviour Research and Therapy, 17*, 53-61.

Kazdin, A. E. (1979c). Imagery elaboration and self-efficacy in the covert modeling treatment of unassertive behavior. *Journal of Consulting and Clinical Psychology, 47*, 725-733.

Kazdin, A. E. (1980). Covert and overt rehearsal and elaboration during treatment in the development of assertive behavior. *Behaviour Research and Therapy, 18*, 191-201.

Kazdin, A. E. (1981). Behavioral observation. In M. Hersen & A. S. Bellack (Eds.)

Behavioral assessment: A practical handbook (2nd edn). New York: Pergamon.

Kazdin, A. E. (1982a). Symptom substitution, generalization, and response covariation: Implications for psychotherapy outcome. *Psychological Bulletin, 91*, 349-364.

Kazdin, A. E. (1982b). The separate and combined effects of covert and overt rehearsal in developing assertive behavior. *Behaviour Research and Therapy, 20*, 17-25.

Kazdin, A. E. (1989). *Behavior modification in applied settings* (4th edn). Pacific Grove, CA: Brooks/Cole.

Kazdin, A. E., Esveldt-Dawson, K., & Matson, J. L. (1982). Changes in children's social performance as a function of preassessment experiences. *Journal of Clinical Child Psychology, 11*, 243-248.

Kazdin, A. E., Esveldt-Dawson, K., & Matson, J. L. (1983). The effects of instructional set on social skills performance among psychiatric in-patient children. *Behavior Therapy, 14*, 413-423.

Kazdin, A. E. & Krouse, R. (1983). The impact of variations in treatment rationales on expectancies for therapeutic change. *Behavior Therapy, 14*, 657-671.

Kazdin, A. E. & Mascitelli, S. (1982a). Covert and overt rehearsal and homework practice in developing assertiveness. *Journal of Consulting and Clinical Psychology, 50*, 250-258.

Kazdin, A. E. & Mascitelli, S. (1982b). Behavior rehearsal, self-instructions, and homework practice in developing assertiveness. *Behavior Therapy, 13*, 346-360.

Kazdin, A. E., Matson, J. L., & Esveldt-Dawson, K. (1981). Social skill performance among normal and psychiatric inpatient children as a function of assessment conditions. *Behaviour Research and Therapy, 22*, 129-139.

Kazdin, A. E. & Wilson, G. T. (1978). *Evaluation of behavior therapy: Issues, evidence, and research strategies*. Cambridge, MA: Ballinger.

Keane, T. M., Martin, J. E., Berler, E. S., Wooten, L. S., Fleece, E. L., & Williams, J. G. (1982). Are hypertensives less assertive? A controlled evaluation. *Journal of Consulting and Clinical Psychology, 50*, 499-508.

Keane, T. M., St. Lawrence, J. S., Himadi, W. G., Graves, K. A., & Kelly, J. A. (1983). Blacks' perception of assertive behavior: An empirical evaluation. *Behavior Modification, 7*, 97-111.

Keane, T. M., Wedding, D., & Kelly, J. A. (1983). Assessing subjective responses to assertive behavior: Data from patient samples. *Behavior Modification, 7*, 317-330.

Kelly, C. (1979). *Assertion training: A facilitator's guide*. LaJolla, CA: University Associates.

Kelly, G. A. (1955). *The psychology of personal constructs (Vol. II)*. New York: Norton.

Kelly, J. A. (1982). *Social skills training: A practical guide for interventions*. New York: Springer.

Kelly, J. A. (1985). Group social skills training. *The Behavior Therapist, 8*, 93-95.

Kelly, J. A., Frederiksen, L. W., Fitts, H., & Phillips, J. (1978). Training and generalization of commendatory assertiveness: A controlled single subject experiment. *Journal of Behavior Therapy and Experimental Psychiatry, 9*, 17-22.

Kelly, J. A., Kern, J. M., Kirkley, G. B., Patterson, J. N. & Keane, T. M. (1980). Reactions to assertive versus unassertive behavior: Differential effects for males and females and implications for assertiveness training. *Behavior Therapy, 11*, 670-682.

Kelly, J. A., St. Lawrence, J. S., Bradlyn, A. S., Himadi, W. G., Graves, K. A., & Keane, T. M. (1982). Interpersonal reaction to assertive and unassertive styles when handling social conflict situations. *Journal of Behavior Therapy and Experimental Psychiatry, 13*, 33-40.

Kelly, J. D. & Winship, B. J. (1979). *I am worth it*. Chicago: Nelson-Hall.

Kelly, W. J. (1983). The effects of role-playing and self-monitoring on the generalization of vocational skills by behaviorally disordered adolescents. *Behavior Disorders, 9*, 27-35.

Keltner, A. A., Marshall, P., & Marshall, W. L. (1981). The description of assertiveness in a prison population. *Corrective and Social Psychiatry and Journal of Behavior, Technology Methods, and Therapy, 27*, 41-47.

Keltner, A., Scharf, N., & Schell, R. (1978). The assessment and training of assertive skills with sexual offenders. *Corrective and Social Psychiatry and Journal of Behavior Technology, Methods, and Therapy, 24*, 88-92

Kern, J. M. (1982a). Predicting the impact of assertive, empathic-assertive, and non-assertive behavior: The assertiveness of the assertee. *Behavior Therapy, 13*, 486-498.

Kern, J. M. (1982b). The comparative external and concurrent validity of three role-plays for assessing heterosocial performance. *Behavior Therapy, 13*, 666-680.

Kern, J. M., Cavell, T. A., & Beck, B. (1985). Predicting differential reactions to males' versus females' assertions, empathic assertions, and nonassertions. *Behavior Therapy, 16*, 63-75.

Kern, J. M. & MacDonald, M. L. (1980). Assessing assertion: An investigation of construct validity and reliability. *Journal of Consulting and Clinical Psychology, 48*, 532-534.

Kern, J. M., Miller, C., & Eggers, J. (1983). Enhancing the validity of role-play tests: A comparison of three role-play methodologies. *Behavior Therapy, 14*, 482-492.

Kidder, L. H., Boell, J. L., & Moyer, M. M. (1983). Rights consciousness and victimization prevention: Personal defense and assertiveness training. *Journal of Social Issues, 39*, 153-168.

Kiecolt, J. K. & McGrath, E. (1979). Social desirability responding in the measurement of assertive behavior. *Journal of Consulting and Clinical Psychology, 47*, 640-642.

Kiecolt-Glaser, J. K. & Greenberg, B. (1983). On the use of physiological measures in assertion research. *Journal of Behavioral Assessment, 5*, 97-109.

Kienhorst, I., Van Ijzendoorn-Schmitz, R. M., & Diekstra, R. (1980). Assertiveness training: A survey study. *Tijdschrift voor Psychotherapie, 6*, 159-171.

Kimble, C. E., Yoshikawa, J. C., & Zehr, H. D. (1981). Vocal and verbal assertiveness in same-sex and mixed-sex groups. *Journal of Personality and Social Psychology, 40*, 1047-1054.

Kincaid, M. B. (1978). Assertiveness training from the participants' perspective. *Professional Psychology, 9*, 153-160.

King, L. W., Liberman, R. P., Roberts, J., & Bryan, E. (1977). Personal effectiveness: A structured therapy for improving social and emotional skills. *European Journal of Behavioural Analysis and Modification, 2*, 82-91.

Kinney, C. D. (1985). A reexamination of nursing role conceptions. *Nursing Research, 34*, 170-176.

Kipper, D. A. (1988). Role-playing techniques: Locus of control and the attraction to behavior simulation interventions. *Journal of Clinical Psychology, 44*, 810-816.

Kipper, D. A. & Jaffe, Y. (1976). The College Self-Expression Scale: Israeli data. *Psychological Reports, 39*, 1301-1302.

Kipper, D. A. & Jaffe, Y. (1978). Dimensions of assertiveness: Factors underlying the College Self-Expression Scale. *Perceptual and Motor Skills, 46*, 47-52.

Kirchner, E. P., Kennedy, R. E., & Draguns, J. G. (1979). Assertion and aggression in adult offenders. *Behavior Therapy, 10*, 452-471.

Kirkland, K. & Caughlin-Carver, J. (1982). Maintenance and generalization of assertive skills. *Education and Training of the Mentally Retarded, 17*, 313-318.

Kirkland, K. D., Thelen, M. H., & Miller, D. J. (1982). Group assertion training with adolescents. *Child & Family Behavior Therapy, 4*, 1-12.

215

Kirschner, N. M. (1976). Generalization of behaviorally oriented assertive training. *Psychological Record, 26*, 117-125.

Kirschner, S. M. & Galassi, J. P. (1983). Person, situational, and interactional influences on assertive behavior. *Journal of Counseling Psychology, 30*, 355-360.

Klass, E. T. (1981). A cognitive analysis of guilt over assertion. *Cognitive Therapy and Research, 5*, 283-297.

Klein, S. B. (1987). *Learning: Principles and applications.* New York: McGraw-Hill.

Kleinke, C. L. (1986). Gaze and eye contact: A research review. *Psychological Bulletin, 100*, 78-100.

Knapczyk, D. R. (1989). Generalizaton of student question asking from special class to regular class settings. *Journal of Applied Behavior Analysis, 22*, 77-83.

Knapp, M. L. (1972). *Nonverbal communication in human interaction.* New York: Holt, Rinehart & Winston.

Kolotkin, R. A. (1980). Situational specificity in the assessment of assertion: Considerations for the measurement of training and transfer. *Behavior Therapy, 11*, 651-661.

Kolotkin, R. A. & Wielkiewicz, R. M. (1984). Effects of situational demand in the role-play assessment of assertive behavior. *Journal of Behavioral Assessment, 6*, 59-70.

Kolotkin, R. A., Wielkiewicz, R. M., Judd, B., & Weiser, S. (1984). Behavioral components of assertion: Comparison of univariate and multivariate assessment strategies. *Behavioral Assessment, 6*, 61-78.

Kraut, A. M. (1982). *The huddled masses: The immigrant in American society, 1880-1921.* Arlington Heights, IL: Harlan Davidson.

Kumaraiah, V. (1979). Behavioral treatment of drug addiction: A multiple approach. *Indian Journal of Clinical Psychology, 6*, 43-46.

Kuperminc, M. & Heimberg, R. G. (1983). Consequence probability and utility as factors in the decision to behave assertively. *Behavior Therapy, 14*, 637-646.

Kwiterovich, D. K. & Horan, J. J. (1977). Solomon evaluation of a commercial assertiveness program for women. *Behavior Therapy, 8*, 501-502.

Labov, W. & Fanshel, D. (1977). *Therapeutic discourse: Psychotherapy as conversation.* New York: Academic Press.

LaFramboise, T. D. (1983). The factorial validity of the Adult Self-Expression Scale with American Indians. *Educational and Psychological Measurement, 43*, 547-555.

LaFramboise, T. D. & Rowe, W. (1983). Skill training for bicultural competence: Rationale and application. *Journal of Counseling Psychology, 30*, 589-595.

LaFrance, M. & Mayo, C. (1976). Racial differences in gaze behavior during conversations: Two systematic observational studies. *Journal of Personality and Social Psychology, 33*, 547-552.

Landau, P. & Paulson, T. (1977). Group assertion training for Spanish speaking Mexican-American mothers. In R. E. Alberti (Ed.) *Assertiveness: Innovations, applications, issues.* San Luis Obispo, CA: Impact.

Lande, S. D. (1980, November). An evaluation of exposure and assertiveness training in the fear of scrutiny. Paper presented at the annual convention of the Association for Advancement of Behavior Therapy, New York.

Lang, P. J. (1968). Fear reduction and fear behavior: Problems in treating a construct. In J. M. Schlien (Ed.) *Research in psychotherapy (Vol. 3).* Washington, DC: American Psychological Association.

Lang, P. J. (1977). Physiological assessment of anxiety and fear. In J. D. Cone & R. P. Hawkins (Eds.) *Behavioral Assessment: New directions in clinical psychology.* New York: Brunner/Mazel.

Lange, A. J. (1979). *What could I say? An assertion training stimulus program.* Champaign, IL: Research Press.

Lange, A. J. & Jakubowski, P. (1976). *Responsible assertive behavior*. Champaign, IL: Research Press.

Lange, A. J. & Jakubowski, P. (1978). *Responsible assertion: A model for personal growth*. Champaign, IL: Research Press.

Langer, E. & Abelson, W. (1974). A patient by any other name: Clinical group differences in labeling bias. *Journal of Consulting and Clinical Psychology, 42*, 4-9.

Langevin, R., Paitich, D., Hucker, S., Newman, S., Ramsey, G., Pope, S., Geller, G., & Anderson, C. (1979). The effects of assertiveness training, provera and sex of therapist in the treatment of genital exhibitionism. *Journal of Behavior Therapy and Experimental Psychiatry, 10*, 275-282.

Langone, M. (1979). Assertiveness and Lewinsohn's theory of depression: An empirical test. *Behavior Therapist, 2*, 21.

Lao, R. C., Upchurch, W. H., Corwin, B. J., & Grossnickle, W. F. (1975). Biased attitudes toward females as indicated by ratings of intelligence and likeability. *Psychological Reports, 37*, 1315-1320.

Latimer, P. R. & Sweet, A. A. (1984). Cognitive vs. behavioral procedures in cognitive behavior therapy: A critical review of the evidence. *Journal of Behavior Therapy and Experimental Psychiatry, 15*, 9-22.

Layne, R. G., Layne, B. H., & Schoch, E. W. (1977). Group assertive training for resident assistants. *Journal of College Student Personnel, 18*, 393-398.

Lazarus, A. A. (1973). On assertive behavior: A brief note. *Behavior Therapy, 5*, 549-554.

Lea, G. & Paquin, M. (1981). Assertiveness and clinical depression. *The Behavior Therapist, 4*(2), 9-10.

Leah, J. A., Law, H. G., & Snyder, C. W. (1979). The structure of self-reported difficulty in assertiveness: An application of three-mode common factor analysis. *Multivariate Behavioral Research, 14*, 443-462.

Lee, C. (1983). Self-efficacy and behavior as predictors of subsequent behaviour in an assertiveness training program. *Behaviour Research and Therapy, 21*, 225-232.

Lee, C. (1984). Accuracy of efficacy and outcome expectations in predicting performance in a simulated assertiveness task. *Cognitive Therapy and Research, 8*, 37-48.

Lee, D. Y., Hallberg, E. T., Slemon, A. G., & Haase, R. F. (1985). An Assertiveness Scale for Adolescents. *Journal of Clinical Psychology, 41*, 51-57.

Lefevre, E. R. & West, M. L. (1984). Expressed priorities of assertiveness trainees. *Canadian Counsellor, 18*, 168-173.

Lehrer, P. M. & Leiblum, S. R. (1981). Physiological, behavioral, and cognitive measures of assertiveness and assertion anxiety. *Behavioral Counseling Quarterly, 1*, 261-274.

Lemanek, K. L., Williamson, D. A., Gresham, F. M., & Jensen, B. J. (1986). Social skills training with hearing impaired children and adolescents. *Behavior Modification, 10*, 55-71.

Lerner, M. J. (1970). The desire for justice and reactions to victims. In J. R. Macaulay & L. Berkowitz (Eds.) *Altruism and helping behavior*. New York: Academic Press.

Lesser, E. (1976). Behavior therapy with a narcotics user: A case report: A ten-year follow-up. *Behaviour Research and Therapy, 14*, 381.

Lethermon, V. R., Williamson, D. A., Moody, S. C., Granberry, S. W., Lemanek, K. L., & Bodiford, C. (1984). Factors affecting the social validity of a role play test of children's social skills. *Journal of Behavioral Assessment, 6*, 231-245.

Lethermon, V. R., Williamson, D. A., Moody, S. C., & Wozniak, P. (1986). Racial bias in behavioral assessment of children's social skills. *Journal of Psychopathology and Behavioral Assessment, 8*, 329-337.

Levenson, R. W. & Gottman, J. M. (1978). Toward the assessment of social competence. *Journal of Consulting and Clinical Psychologyy, 46*, 453-462.

Levin, R. B. & Gross, A. M. (1984). Reactions to assertive versus nonassertive behavior: Females in commendatory and refusal situations. *Behavior Modification, 8*, 581-592.

Levin, R. B. & Gross, A. M. (1987). Assertiveness style: Effects on perceptions of assertive behavior. *Behavior Modification, 11*, 229-240.

Lewinsohn, P. M. (1975). The behavioral study and treatment of depression. In M. Hersen, R. M. Eisler, & P. M. Miller (Eds.) *Progress in behavior modification (Vol. 1)* (pp. 19-64). New York: Academic Press.

Lewis, P. N. & Gallois, C. (1984). Disagreements, refusals, or negative feelings: Perception of negatively assertive messages from friends and strangers. *Behavior Therapy, 15*, 353-368.

Lewittes, H. J. & Bem, S. L. (1983). Training women to be more assertive in mixed-sex task-oriented discussions. *Sex Roles, 9*, 581-596.

Liberman, R. (1976). *Actualization through assertion: A behavioral approach to personal effectiveness*. Los Angeles: Neuropsychiatric Institute (UCLA)/Behavioral Science Media Lab. (Distributed by Media Guild, Solana Beach, CA.)

Liberman, R. P., DeRisi, W. J., & Mueser, K. T. (1989). *Social skills training for psychiatric patients*. Elmsford, NY: Pergamon Press.

Liberman, R. P., Neuchterlein, K. H., & Wallace, C. J. (1982). Social skills training and the nature of schizophrenia. In J. P. Curran & P. M. Monti (Eds.) *Social skills training: A practical handbook for assessment and treatment*. New York: Guilford Press.

Lindquist, C. U., Lindsay, J. S., & White, G. D. (1979). Assessment of assertiveness in drug abusers. *Journal of Clinical Psychology, 35*, 676-679.

Lineberger, M. H. & Beezley, D. (1980). Components of assertive behavior: Are there black–white differences? Paper presented at the annual meeting of the American Psychological Association, Montreal, Canada, September.

Lineberger, M. H. & Calhoun, K. S. (1983). Assertive behavior in black and white American undergraduates. *Journal of Psychology, 113*, 139-148.

Linehan, M. M. (1984). Interpersonal effectiveness in assertive situations. In E. A. Blechman (Ed.) *Behavior modification with women*. New York: Guilford Press.

Linehan, M. M. & Egan, K. J. (1979). Assertion training for women. In A. S. Bellack & M. Hersen (Eds.) *Research and practice in social skills training*. New York: Plenum.

Linehan, M. M., Goldfried, M. R., & Goldfried, A. P. (1979). Assertion therapy: Skill training or cognitive restructuring. *Behavior Therapy, 10*, 372-388.

Linehan, M. M. & Siefert, R. F. (1983). Sex and contextual differences in the appropriateness of assertive behavior. *Psychology of Women Quarterly, 8*, 79-88.

Linehan, M. M. & Walker, R. O. (1983). The components of assertion: Factor analysis of a multimethod assessment battery. *British Journal of Clinical Psychology, 22*, 277-281.

Linehan, M. M., Walker, R. O., Bronheim, S., Haynes, K. F., & Yevzeroff, H. (1979). Group versus individual assertion training. *Journal of Consulting and Clinical Psychology, 47*, 1000-1002.

Little, K. B. & Schneidman, E. S. (1959). Congruencies among interpretations of psychological tests on anamnestic data. *Psychological Monographs, 73*, No. 6 (whole no 476).

Lohr, J. M. & Bonge, D. (1982). Relationships between assertiveness and factorially validated measures of irrational beliefs. *Cognitive Therapy and Research, 6*, 353-356.

Lohr, J. M. & Nix, J. (1982). Relationship of assertiveness and the short form of the Bem Sex-Role Inventory: A replication. *Psychological Reports, 50*, 114.

Lohr, J. M., Nix, J., Dunbar, D., & Mosesso, L. (1984). The relationship of assertive behavior in women and a validated measure of irrational beliefs. *Cognitive Therapy and Research, 8*, 287-297.

London, P. (1984). *The modes and morals of psychotherapy* (2nd edn). Washington: Hemisphere Publishing Corp.

Longin, H. E. & Rooney, W. M. (1975). Teaching denial assertion to chronic hospitalized patients. *Journal of Behavior Therapy and Experimental Psychiatry, 6,* 219-222.

Lowe, M. R. & Storm, M. A. (1986). Being assertive or being liked: A genuine dilemma? *Behavior Modification, 10,* 371-390.

Ludwig, L. D. & Lazarus, A. A. (1972). A cognitive and behavioral approach to the treatment of social inhibition. *Psychotherapy: Theory, Research and Practice, 9,* 204-206.

McCampbell, E. & Ruback, R. B. (1985). Social consequences of apologetic, assertive, and aggressive requests. *Journal of Counseling Psychology, 32,* 68-73.

McCormick, I. A. (1982). New Zealand student norms for the Rathus Assertiveness Schedule. *New Zealand Psychologist, 11,* 27-29.

McCormick, I. A. (1985). A simple version of the Rathus Assertiveness Schedule. *Behavioral Assessment, 7,* 95-99.

McCormick, I. A., Hahn, M., & Walkey, F. H. (1984). Reliability and normative data for the Simple Rathus Assertiveness Schedule. *New Zealand Journal of Psychology, 13,* 69-70.

McCullagh, J. G. (1982a). The modified Rathus Assertiveness Schedule—Short Form: Factor-analytic data. *The Behavior Therapist, 5,* 135-136.

McCullagh, J. G. (1982b). Assertion training for boys in junior high school. *Social Work in Education, 5,* 41-51.

MacDonald, M. L. (1978). Measuring assertion: A model and method. *Behavior Therapy, 9,* 889-899.

MacDonald, M. L. (1982). Assertion training for women. In J. P. Curran & P. M. Monti (Eds.) *Social skill training: A practical guide for assessment and treatment.* New York: Guilford Press.

MacDonald, M. L. & Tyson, P. (1984). The College Women's Assertion Sample (CWAS): A cross-validation. *Educational and Psychological Measurement, 44,* 405-412.

McDowell, J. J. (1982). The importance of Herrnstein's mathematical statement of the law of effect for behavior therapy. *American Psychologist, 37,* 771-779.

McFall, R. M. (1982). A review and reformulation of the concept of social skills. *Behavioral Assessment, 4,* 1-33.

McFall, R. M. & Lillesand, D. B. (1971). Behavior rehearsal with modeling and coaching in assertion training. *Journal of Abnormal Psychology, 77,* 313-323.

McFall, R. M. & Marston, A. R. (1970). An experimental investigation of behavior rehearsal in assertive training. *Journal of Abnormal Psychology, 76,* 295-303.

McFall, R. M. & Twentyman, C. T. (1973). Four experiments on the relative contribution of rehearsal, modeling and coaching to assertion training. *Journal of Abnormal Psychology, 81,* 199-218.

McFall, M. E., Winnett, R. L., Bordewick, M. C., & Bornstein, P. H. (1982). Nonverbal components in the communication of assertiveness. *Behavior Modification, 6,* 121-140.

McGovern, T. V., Tinsley, D., Liss-Levinson, N., Laventure, R., & Britton, G. (1975). Assertion training for job interviews. *Counseling Psychologist, 5,* 65-68.

McGuire, D. & Thelen, M. H. (1983). Modeling, assertion training, and the breadth of the target assertive behavior. *Behavior Therapy, 14,* 275-285.

McIntyre, T. J., Jeffrey, D. B., & McIntyre, S. L. (1984). Assertion training: The effectiveness of a comprehensive cognitive-behavioral treatment package with professional nurses. *Behaviour Research and Therapy, 22,* 311-318.

McKinlay, T., Kelly, J. A., & Patterson, J. (1978). Teaching assertive skills to a passive homosexual adolescent: An illustrative case study. *Journal of Homosexuality, 3,* 163-170.

Macklin, G. F. & Matson, J. L. (1985). A comparison of social behaviors among non-handicapped and hearing impaired children. *Behavior Disorders, 1,* 60-65.

McNamara, J. R. & Blumer, C. A. (1982). Role playing to assess social competence: Ecological validity considerations. *Behavior Modification, 6,* 519-549.

Maeda, M. (1985). The effects of combinations of vicarious reinforcement on the formation of assertive behaviors in covert modeling. *Japanese Journal of Behavior Therapy, 10,* 34-44.

Mahoney, M. J. (1977). Some applied issues in self-monitoring. In J. D. Cone & R. P. Hawkins (Eds.) *Behavioral assessment: New directions in clinical psychology* (pp. 241-254). New York: Brunner/Mazel.

Mansdorf, I. J. (1986). Assertiveness training in the treatment of a child's tics. *Journal of Behavior Therapy and Experimental Psychiatry, 17,* 29-32.

Maretzki, T. (1981). The cultural paradigm. In C. Eisdorfer, D. Cohen, A. Kleinman, & P. Maxim (Eds.) *Models for clinical psychology.* New York: Spectrum.

Margalit, B. A. & Mauger, P. A. (1984). Cross-cultural demonstration of orthogonality of assertiveness and aggressiveness: Comparison between Israel and the United States. *Journal of Personality and Social Psychology, 46,* 1414–1421.

Margalit, B. A. & Mauger, P. A. (1985). Aggressiveness and assertiveness: A cross-cultural study of Israel and the United States. *Journal of Cross-Cultural Psychology, 16,* 497–511.

Markham, D. J. (1985). Behavioral rehearsal vs group systematic desensitization in assertiveness training with women. *Academic Psychology Bulletin, 7,* 157-174.

Marlatt, G. A. (1972). Task structure and the experimental modification of verbal behavior. *Psychological Bulletin, 78,* 335-350.

Marlatt, G. A. (1985). Situational determinants of relapse and skill training intervention. In G. A. Marlatt & J. R. Gordon (Eds.) *Relapse prevention.* New York: Guilford Press.

Marlatt, G. A. & Gordon, J. R. (Eds.) (1985) *Relapse prevention: Maintenance strategies in addictive behavior change.* New York: Guilford Press.

Marshall, P. G., Keltner, A. A., & Marshall, W. L. (1981). Anxiety reduction, assertive training, and enactment of consequences: A comprehensive treatment study in the modification of nonassertion and social fear. *Behavior Modification, 5,* 85-102.

Martin, G. & Pear, J. (1988). *Behavior modification: What it is and how to do it.* Englewood Cliffs, NJ: Prentice-Hall.

Martin-Laval, H. M. (1983). The training of social skills in deaf adolescents: II. Behavioral changes, generalization, and attitude changes. *Revue de Modification du Comportement, 13,* 1-14.

Masters, J. C., Burish, T. G., Hollon, S. D., & Rimm, D. C. (1987). *Behavior therapy: Techniques and empirical findings* (3rd edn). New York: Harcourt Brace Jovanovich.

Materi, M. (1977). Assertiveness training: A catalyst for behavioral change. *Alcohol Health and Research World, 1,* 23-26.

Matson, J. L. & Ollendick, T. H. (1988). *Enhancing children's social skills: Assessment and training.* New York: Pergamon Press.

Matson, J. L. & Stephens, R. M. (1978). Increasing appropriate behavior of explosive chronic psychiatric patients with a social-skills training package. *Behavior Modification, 2,* 61-76.

Mednick, M. T. (1989). On the politics of psychological constructs: Stop the bandwagon, I want to get off. *American Psychologist, 44,* 1118-1123.

Meehan, E. F. & Goldkopf, D. A. (1982). Effects of attitudinal restructuring on multifaceted assertiveness training for women. *Journal of Urban Psychiatry, 2,* 38-44.

Megargee, E. I. (1966). Undercontrolled and overcontrolled personality types in extreme antisocial aggression. *Psychological Monographs, 3* (whole no. 611).

Meichenbaum, D. H. (1972). Examination of model characteristics in reducing avoidance behavior. *Journal of Behavior Therapy and Experimental Psychiatry, 3*, 225-227.

Meichenbaum, D. (1977). *Cognitive-behavior modification: An integrative approach*. New York: Plenum.

Meichenbaum, D. (1985). *Stress inoculation training*. New York: Pergamon.

Meichenbaum, D., Butler, L., & Gruson, L. (1981). Toward a conceptual model of social competence. In J. Wine & M. Smye, (Eds.) *Social competence*. New York: Guilford Press.

Meichenbaum, D. H. & Goodman, J. (1971). Training impulsive children to talk to themselves: A means of developing self-control. *Journal of Abnormal Psychology, 77*, 115-126.

Meichenbaum, S. & Turk, D. C. (1987). *Facilitating treatment adherence: A practitioner's guidebook*. New York: Plenum.

Melnick, J. & Stocker, R. B. (1977). An experimental analysis of the behavioral rehearsal with feedback technique in assertiveness training. *Behavior Therapy, 8*, 222-228.

Merluzzi, T. V. & Biever, J. (1987). Role playing procedures for the behavioral assessment of social skill: A validity study. *Behavioral Assessment, 9*, 361-378.

Merluzzi, T. V., Glass, C. R., & Genest, M. (1981). *Cognitive assessment*. New York: Guilford Press.

Meyers-Abell, J. E. & Jansen, M. A. (1980). Assertive therapy for battered women: A case illustration. *Journal of Behavior Therapy and Experimental Psychiatry, 11*, 301-305.

Michelson, L., Andrasik, F., Vucelic, I., & Coleman, D. (1981). Temporal stability and internal reliability of measures of children's social skill. *Psychological Reports, 48*, 678.

Michelson, L., DiLorenzo, T. M., Calpin, J. P., & Ollendick, T. H. (1982). Situational determinants of the behavioral assertiveness role-play test for children. *Behavior Therapy, 13*, 724-734.

Michelson, L., Molcan, K., & Poorman, S. (1986). Development and psychometric properties of the Nurses' Assertiveness Inventory (NAI). *Behaviour Research and Therapy, 24*, 77-81.

Michelson, L. & Wood, R. (1980a). A group assertive training program for elementary school children. *Child Behavior Therapy, 2*, 1-9

Michelson, L. & Wood, R. (1980b). Behavioral assessment and training of social skills for children and adolescents. In M. Hersen, P. M. Miller, & R. M. Eisler (Eds.) *Progress in behavior modification: Vol. 9*. New York: Academic Press.

Michelson, L. & Wood, R. (1982). Development and psychometric properties of the Children's Assertive Behavior Scale. *Journal of Behavioral Assessment, 4*, 3-13.

Miglins, M. L. (1985). An investigation of assertion-relevant attributions. *Dissertation Abstracts International, 46*, 4022-B.

Miller, J. B. (1983). The construction of anger in women and men. *Stone Center for Developmental Services and Studies*. Wellesley College, No. 83-01.

Miller, P. M. & Eisler, R. M. (1977). Assertive behavior of alcoholics: A descriptive analysis. *Behavior Therapy, 8*, 146-149.

Miller, P. M., Hersen, M., Eisler, R. M., & Hilsman, G. (1974). Effects of social stress on operant drinking of alcoholics and social drinkers. *Behaviour Research and Therapy, 12*, 67-72.

Miller, T. W. (1982). Assertiveness training for coaches: The issue of healthy communication between coaches and players. *Journal of Sport Psychology, 4*, 107-114.

Minor, B. J. (1978). A perspective for assertiveness training for Blacks. *Journal of Non-White Concerns in Personnel and Guidance, 6*, 63-70.

Mischel, W. (1968). *Personality and assessment*. New York: Wiley.

Mischel, W. (1986). *Introduction to personality: A new look* (4th edn). New York: Holt, Rinehart & Winston.

Mishel, M. H. (1978). Assertion training with handicapped persons. *Journal of Counseling Psychology, 25*, 238-241.

Mitchell-Jackson, A. (1982). Psychosocial aspects of the therapeutic process. In S. M. Turner & R. T. Jones (Eds.) *Behavior modification in black populations: Psychosocial issues and empirical findings*. New York: Plenum.

Mizes, J. S. (1989). Assertion deficits in bulimia nervosa: Assessment via behavioral, self-report and cognitive measures. *Behavior Therapy, 20*, 603-608.

Mizes, J. S., Morgan, G. D., & Buder, J. (1989). Global versus specific cognitive measures and their relationship to assertion deficits. *Educational and Psychological Measurement, 49*, 177-182.

Montgomery, D. & Heimberg, R. G. (1978). Adjunctive techniques for assertiveness training: Overcoming obstacles to change. *Professional Psychology, 9*, 220-227.

Monti, P. M., Corriveau, D. P., & Curran, J. P. (1982). Social skills training for psychiatric patients: Treatment and outcome. In J. P. Curran & P. M. Monti (Eds.) *Social skill training: A practical handbook for assessment and treatment*. New York: Guilford Press.

Monti, P. M., Curran, J. P., Corriveau, D. P., DeLancey, A., & Hagerman, S. (1980). Effects of social skills training groups and sensitivity training groups with psychiatric patients. *Journal of Consulting and Clinical Psychology, 48*, 241-248.

Monti, P. M., Fink, E., Norman, W., Curran, J. P., Hayes, S., & Caldwell, A. (1979). Effects of social skills training groups and social skills bibliotherapy with psychiatric patients. *Journal of Consulting and Clinical Psychology, 47*, 189-191.

Moon, J. R. & Eisler, R. M. (1983). Anger control: An experimental comparison of three behavioral treatments. *Behavior Therapy, 14*, 493-505.

Morgan, B. & Leung, P. (1980). Effects of assertion training on acceptance of disability by physically handicapped university students. *Journal of Counseling Psychology, 27*, 209-212.

Morrison, R. L. (1988). Social dysfunction in relation to other schizophrenic symptoms: New findings, new directions. *The Behavior Therapist, 11*, 139-142.

Morrison, R. L. & Bellack, A. S. (1981). The role of social perception in social skill. *Behavior Therapy, 12*, 69-79.

Morrison, R. L. & Bellack, A. S. (1984). Social skill training. In A. S. Bellack (Ed.) *Schizophrenia: Treatment, management and rehabilitation*. New York: Grune & Stratton.

Morrison, R. L., Bellack, A. S., & Manuck, S. B. (1985). Role of social competence in borderline essential hypertension. *Journal of Consulting and Clinical Psychology, 53*, 248-255.

Morrison, R. L., Van Hasselt, V. B., & Bellack, A. S. (1987). Assessment of assertion and problem-solving skills in wife abusers and their spouses. *Journal of Family Violence, 2*, 227-238.

Moss, R. A. (1985). The role of learning history in current sick-role behavior and assertion. *Behaviour Research and Therapy, 24*, 681-683.

Moy, A. C. (1980). Assertive behavior in a New Testament perspective. *Journal of Psychology and Theology, 8*, 288-292.

Muehlenhard, C. L. (1983). Women's assertion and the feminine sex-role stereotype. In V. Franks & E. D. Rothblum (Eds.) *The stereotyping of women: Its effects on mental health*. New York: Springer.

Muehlenhard, C. L., Julsonnet, S., Carlson, M. I., & Flarity-White, L. A. (1989). A cognitive-behavioral program for preventing sexual coercion. *The Behavior Therapist, 12*, 211-214.

Muehlenhard, C. L. & McFall, R. M. (1983). Automated assertion training: A feasibility study. *Journal of Social and Clinical Psychology, 1*, 246-258.

Mullinix, S. B. & Galassi, J. P. (1981). Deriving the content of social skills training with a verbal response components approach. *Behavioral Assessment, 3*, 55-66.

Neale, J. M. & Liebert, R. M. (1986). *Science and behavior: An introduction to methods of research* (3rd edn). Englewood Cliffs, NJ: Prentice-Hall.

Nelson, J. E. & Howell, R. J. (1982-83). Assertiveness training using rehearsal and modeling with male alcoholics. *American Journal of Drug and Alcohol Abuse, 9*, 309-323.

Nelson, R. O. (1977). Methodological issues in assessment via self-monitoring. In J. D. Cone & R. P. Hawkins (Eds.) *Behavioral assessment: New directions in clinical psychology.* New York: Brunner/Mazel.

Nelson, R. O. (1983). Behavioral assessment: Past, present, and future. *Behavioral Assessment, 5*, 195-206.

Nelson, R. O., Hay, L. R., & Hay, W. M. (1977). Comments on Cone's 'The relevance of reliability and validity for behavioral assessment'. *Behavior Therapy, 8*, 427-430.

Nelson, R. O. & Hayes, S. C. (1979). Some current dimensions of behavioral assessment. *Behavioral Assessment, 1*, 1-16.

Nelson, R. O. & Hayes, S. C. (1981). Nature of behavioral assessment. In M. Hersen & A. S. Bellack (Eds.) *Behavioral assessment: A practical handbook* (2nd edn) (pp. 3-37). New York: Pergamon.

Nesbitt, E. B. (1981). Use of assertive training in teaching the expression of positively assertive behavior. *Psychological Reports, 49*, 155-161.

Ness, M. K., Donnan, H. H., & Jenkins, J. (1983). Race as an interpersonal variable in negative assertion. *Journal of Clinical Psychology, 39*, 361-369.

Nietzel, M. T. & Bernstein, D. A. (1976). Effects of instructionally mediated demand on the behavioral assessment of assertiveness. *Journal of Consulting and Clinical Psychology, 44*, 500.

Nietzel, M. T., Martorano, R. D., & Melnick, J. (1977). The effects of covert modeling with and without reply training on the development and generalization of assertive responses. *Behavior Therapy, 8*, 183-192.

Nisbet, R. (1976). *Sociology as an art form.* London: Oxford University Press.

Nisbett, R. & Wilson, T. (1977). Telling more than we can know: Verbal reports on mental processes. *Psychological Review, 84*, 231-259.

Nisonoff, L. (1977). Assertion and its relationship to marital satisfaction and communication. *Dissertation Abstracts International, 38*, 1518-1519.

Nix, J., Lohr, J. M., & Mosesso, L. (1984). The relationship of sex-role characteristics to self-report and role-play measures of assertiveness in women. *Behavioral Assessment, 6*, 89-93.

Novotny, H. R. & Enomoto, J. J. (1976). Social competence training as a correctional alternative. *Offender Rehabilitation, 1*, 45-55.

Numerof, R. E. (1978). Assertiveness training for nurses in a general hospital. *Health and Social Work, 3*, 79-102.

O'Banion, K. & Arkowitz, H. (1977). Social anxiety and selective memory for affective information about the self. *Social Behavior and Personality, 5*, 321-328.

O'Leary, K. D. & Curley, A. (1984). Assertion and family violence: Correlates of spouse abuse. *Journal of Marital and Family Therapy, 12*, 281-290.

O'Leary, K. D., Curley, A., Rosenbaum, A., & Clarke, C. (1985). Assertion training for abused wives: A potentially hazardous treatment. *Journal of Marital and Family Therapy, 11*, 319-322.

O'Leary, K. D. & Wilson, G. T. (1987). *Behavior therapy: Application and outcome* (2nd edn). Englewood Cliffs, NJ: Prentice-Hall.

Olinger, L. J., Shaw, B. F., & Kuiper, N. (1987). Nonassertiveness, dysfunctional attitudes, and mild levels of depression. *Canadian Journal of Behavioural Science, 19*, 40-49.

Ollendick, T. H. (1981). Assessment of social interaction skills in school children. *Behavioral Counseling Quarterly, 1*, 227-243.

Ollendick, T. H. (1983). Development and validation of the Children's Assertiveness Inventory. *Child & Family Behavior Therapy, 5*, 1-15.

Ollendick, T. H., Hart, K. J., & Francis, G. (1985). Social validation of the Revised Behavioral Assertiveness Test for Children (BAT-CR). *Child & Family Behavior Therapy, 7*, 17-33

Ollendick, T. H. & Hersen, M. (1979). Social skills training for juvenile delinquents. *Behaviour Research and Therapy, 17*, 547-554.

Ollendick, T. H., Meador, A. E., & Villanis, C. (1986). Relationship between the Children's Assertiveness Inventory (CAI) and the Revised Behavioral Assertiveness Test for Children (BAT-CR). *Child & Family Behavior Therapy, 8*, 27-36.

Orosz, S. B. (1982). Assertiveness in recovery. *Social Work with Groups, 5*, 25-31.

Osborn, S. M. & Harris, G. G. (1975). *Assertive training for women*. Springfield, IL: Charles C. Thomas.

Pachman, J. S. & Foy, D. W. (1978). A correlational investigation of anxiety, self-esteem and depression: New findings with behavioral measures of assertiveness. *Journal of Behavior Therapy and Experimental Psychiatry, 9*, 97-101.

Palmer, P. & Shondeck, B. (1977a). *Liking myself*. San Luis Obispo, CA: Impact Publishers.

Palmer, P. & Shondeck, B. (1977b). *The mouse, the monster and me*. San Luis Obispo, CA: Impact Publishers.

Paul, G. L. (1969). Outcome of systematic desensitization. II: Controlled investigations of individual treatment, technique variations, and current status. In C. M. Franks (Ed.) *Behavior therapy: Appraisal and status*. New York: McGraw-Hill.

Paul, G. L. (1981). Social competence and the institutionalized mental patient. In J. D. Wine & M. D. Smye (Eds.) *Social competence*. New York: Guilford Press.

Paulson, T. (1975). Short term group assertion training with token feedback as an adjunct to ongoing group psychotherapy. *Counseling Psychologist, 5*, 60-64.

Pedersen, P. (Ed.) (1985). *Handbook of cross-cultural counseling and therapy*. Westport, CT: Greenwood Press.

Pentz, M. A. (1980). Assertion training and trainer effects on unassertive and aggressive adolescents. *Journal of Counseling Psychology, 27*, 76-83.

Pentz, M. A. (1981). The contribution of individual differences to assertion training outcome in adolescents. *Journal of Counseling Psychology, 28*, 529-532.

Pentz, M. A. & Kazdin, A. E. (1982). Assertion modeling and stimuli effects on assertive behavior and self-efficacy in adolescents. *Behaviour Research and Therapy, 20*, 365-371.

Pepper, S. C. (1942). *World hypotheses: A study in evidence*. Berkeley, CA: University of California Press.

Peterson, J. L., Fischetti, M., Curran, J. P., & Arland, S. (1981). Sense of timing: A skill defect in heterosocially anxious women. *Behavior Therapy, 12*, 195-201.

Phelps, S. & Austin, N. (1975). *The assertive woman*. San Luis Obispo: Impact.

Phelps, S. & Austin, N. (1987). *The assertive woman: A new look*. San Luis Obispo, CA: Impact.

Phillips, L. W. (1986). Behavior analysis in a case of 'post partum depression'. *Journal of Behavior Therapy and Experimental Psychiatry, 17*, 101-104.

Phillips, S. D. & Bruch, M. A. (1988). Shyness and dysfunction in career development. *Journal of Counseling Psychology, 35*, 159-165.

Piccinin, S., McCarrey, M., & Chislett, L. (1985). Assertion training outcome and generalization effects under didactic vs. facilitative training conditions. *Journal of Clinical Psychology, 41*, 753-762.

Piliavin, J. A. & Martin, R. R. (1978). The effects of the sex composition of groups on style of social interaction. *Sex Roles, 4*, 281-296.

Pilla, B. A. (1977). Women in business. *Training and Development Journal, 31*, 22-25.

Pitcher, S. W. & Meikle, S. (1980). The topography of assertive behavior in positive and negative situations. *Behavior Therapy, 11*, 532-547.

Plax, T. G., Kearney, P., & Beatty, M. J. (1985). Modeling parents' assertiveness: A retrospective analysis. *Journal of Genetic Psychology, 146*, 449-457.

Polifka, J. A., Weissberg, R. P., Gesten, E. L., de Apodaca, R. F., & Picoli, L. (1981). *The open-middle interview manual.* (Available from R. P. Weissberg, Department of Psychology, Yale University, New Haven, CT.)

Powell, G. S. (1978). The effects of training wives in communication skills upon the marital satisfaction of both spouses. *Dissertation Abstracts International, 38* (8-B), 3857.

Powell, J. L. (1985). Intergenerational learning of assertive and aggressive behavior in rural Appalachian families. *Dissertation Abstracts International, 45*, 3628-3629.

Quinsey, V. L., Maguire, A., & Varney, G. W. (1983). Assertion and overcontrolled hostility among mentally disordered murderers. *Journal of Consulting and Clinical Psychology, 51*, 550-556.

Rachlin, H. (1970). *Introduction to modern behaviorism.* San Francisco: Freeman.

Rachman, S. & Hodgson, R. (1974). I. Synchrony and desynchrony in fear and avoidance. *Behaviour Research and Therapy, 12*, 311-318.

Rahaim, S., Lefebvre, C., & Jenkins, J. O. (1980). The effects of social skills training on behavioral and cognitive components of anger management. *Journal of Behavior Therapy and Experimental Psychiatry, 11*, 3-8.

Raich i Escursell, R. M. & Vila i Vidal, J. R. (1985). Study of the Inventory of Assertiveness of Gambrill and Richey in a sample of psychology students from the Autonomous University of Barcelona. *Cuadernos de Psicologia, 9*, 127-141.

Rakos, R. F. (1979). Content consideration in the distinction between assertive and aggressive behavior. *Psychological Reports, 44*, 767-773.

Rakos, R. F. (1980). Toward cooperative behavior between pragmatic behaviorists and Marxist behaviorists: Philosophical, empirical, and social action considerations. *Behaviorists for Social Action Journal, 2*, 10-16.

Rakos, R. F. (1986). Asserting and confronting. In O. Hargie (Ed.) *A handbook of communication skills* (pp. 407-440). London: Croom Helm.

Rakos, R. F. & Hrop, S. (1983). The influence of positive content and mode of presentation on the social evaluation of assertive behavior in conflict situations. *Behavioral Counseling and Community Interventions, 3*, 152-164.

Rakos, R. F., Mayo, M., & Schroeder, H. E. (1982). Validity of role-playing tests and self-predictions of assertive behavior. *Psychological Reports, 50*, 435-444.

Rakos, R. F. & Schroeder, H. E. (1976). Fear reduction in help-givers as a function of helping others. *Journal of Counseling Psychology, 23*, 428–435.

Rakos, R. F. & Schroeder, H. E. (1979). Development and empirical evaluation of a self-administered assertiveness training program. *Journal of Consulting and Clinical Psychology, 47*, 991-993.

Rakos, R. F. & Schroeder, H. E. (1980). *Self-administered assertiveness training*. New York: BMA Audio Cassettes.

Rathus, S. A. (1973a). A 30 item schedule for assessing assertive behavior. *Behavior Therapy, 4*, 398-406.

Rathus, S. A. (1973b). Instigation of assertive behavior through videotape-mediated assertive models and directed practice. *Behaviour Research and Therapy, 11*, 57-65.

Rathus, S. A. & Nevid, J. S. (1977). Concurrent validity of the 30 item Assertiveness Schedule with a psychiatric population. *Behavior Therapy, 8*, 393-397.

Reardon, R. C., Hersen, M., Bellack, A. S., & Foley, J. M. (1979). Measuring social skill in grade school boys. *Journal of Behavioral Assessment, 1*, 87-105.

Rehm, L. P., Fuchs, C. Z., Roth, D. M., Kornbluth, S. J., & Romano, J. M. (1979). A comparison of self-control and assertion skills treatments of depression. *Behavior Therapy, 10*, 429-442.

Resick, P. A., Jordan, C. G., Girelli, S. A., Hutter, C.K., & Marhoefer-Dvorak, S. (1988). A comparative outcome study of behavioral group therapy for sexual assault victims. *Behavior Therapy, 19*, 385-402.

Rich, A. R. & Schroeder, H. E. (1976). Research issues in assertiveness training. *Psychological Bulletin, 83*, 1084-1096.

Riedel, H. P., Fenwick, C. R., & Jillings, C. R. (1986). Efficacy of booster sessions after training in assertiveness. *Perceptual and Motor Skills, 62*, 791-798.

Rijken, H. & de Wildt, A. (1978). Structured therapy groups for women with social/assertiveness problems. *Tijdschrift voor Psychotherapie, 4*, 155-163.

Rimm, D. C., Hill, G. A., Brown, N. N., & Stuart, J. E. (1974). Group-assertive training in treatment of expression of inappropriate anger. *Psychological Reports, 34*, 791-798.

Rimm, D. C. & Masters, J. C. (1979). *Behavior therapy: Techniques and empirical findings* (2nd edn). New York: Academic Press.

Rimm, D. C., Snyder, J. J., Depue, R. A., Haadstad, M. J., & Armstrong, D. P. (1976). Assertive training versus rehearsal, and the importance of making assertive response. *Behaviour Research and Therapy, 14*, 315-321.

Ringer, R. J. (1977). *Looking out for # 1*. New York: Fawcett Crest.

Riso, W. (1984). Social perception of assertive behavior. *Revista de Analisis del Comportamiento, 2*, 285-295.

Rist, F. & Watzl, H. (1983). Self-assessment of relapse risk and assertiveness in relation to treatment outcome of female alcholics. *Addictive Behaviors, 8*, 121-127.

Robinson, W. L. & Calhoun, K. S. (1984). Assertiveness and cognitive processing in interpersonal situations. *Journal of Behavioral Assessment, 6*, 81-96.

Rodriguez, R., Nietzel, M. T., & Berzins, J. I. (1980). Sex role orientation and assertiveness among female college students. *Behavior Therapy, 11*, 353-366.

Rogers, C. R. (1959). A theory of therapy, personality and interpersonal relationships, as developed in the client-centered framework. In S. Koch (Ed.) *Psychology: A study of a science, Vol. 3*. New York: McGraw-Hill.

Romano, J. M. & Bellack, A. S. (1980). Social validation of a component model of assertive behavior. *Journal of Consulting and Clinical Psychology, 4*, 478-490.

Rose, S. D. (1977). Assertive training in groups: Research in clinical settings. *Scandinavian Journal of Behaviour Therapy, 6*, 61-86.

Rose, S. D. (1978). The effect of contingency contracting on the completion rate of behavior assignments in assertion training groups. *Journal of Social Service Research, 1*, 299-305.

Rose, S. D., Roessle, A., & Solomon, R. H. (1980). Effects of a post-group newsletter and phone calls on the maintenance of changes achieved in an assertion training group program. Paper presented at the annual convention of the Association for Advancement of Behavior Therapy, New York, November.

Rose, Y. J. & Tryon, W. W. (1979). Judgements of assertive behavior as a function of speech loudness, latency, content, gestures, inflection and sex. *Behavior Modification, 3*, 112-123.

Roseby, V. & Deutsch, R. (1985). Children of separation and divorce: Effects of a social role-taking group intervention on fourth and fifth graders. *Journal of Clinical Child Psychology, 14*, 55-60.

Rosen, G. M. (1987). Self-help treatment books and the commercialization of psychotherapy. *American Psychologist, 42*, 46-51.

Rosenbaum, A. & O'Leary, K. D. (1981). Marital violence: Characteristics of abusive couples. *Journal of Consulting and Clinical Psychology, 49*, 63-71.

Rosenthal, T. L. & Reese, S. L. (1976). The effects of covert and overt modeling on assertive behavior. *Behaviour Research Therapy, 14*, 463-469.

Rotheram, M. J. (1984). Therapeutic issues in assertiveness training. *Psychology: A Quarterly Journal of Human Behavior, 21*, 28-33.

Rotheram, M. J. & Armstrong, M. (1980). Assertiveness training with high school students. *Adolescence, 15*, 267-276.

Rotheram, M. J., Armstrong, M., & Booraem, C. (1982). Assertiveness training in fourth- and fifth-grade children. *American Journal of Community Psychology, 10*, 567-582.

Rozelle, R. M., Druckman, D., & Baxter, J. C. (1986). Nonverbal communication. In O. Hargie (Ed.) *A handbook of communication skills* (pp. 59-94). London: Croom Helm.

Ruben, D. H. (1983). Methodological adaptations in assertiveness training programs designed for the blind. *Psychological Reports, 53*, 1281-1282.

Ruben, D. H. (1984). Comparison of two analogue measures for assessing and teaching assertiveness to physically disabled elderly: An exploratory study. *Gerontology and Geriatrics Education, 5*, 63-71.

Rudy, T. E., Merluzzi, T. V., & Henahan P. T. (1982). Construal of complex assertion situations: A multidimensional analysis. *Journal of Consulting and Clinical Psychology, 50*, 125-137.

Russell, A. & Winkler, R. (1977). Evaluation of assertive training and homosexual guidance service groups designed to improve homosexual functioning. *Journal of Consulting and Clinical Psychology, 45*, 1-13.

Russell, R. A. (1983). Cognitive barriers to assertiveness for the Christian. *Counseling and Values, 27*, 83-89.

Ryan, K. A. (1976). Assertive training: Its use in leisure counseling. *New Outlook for the Blind, 70*, 351-354.

Ryan, W. (1971). *Blaming the victim.* New York: Pantheon Books.

Ryba, K. A. & Brown, R. I. (1979). An evaluation of personal adjustment training with mentally retarded adults. *British Journal of Mental Subnormality, 25*, 56-66.

Safran, J. D. (1982). The functional asymmetry of negative and positive self-statements. *British Journal of Clinical Psychology, 21*, 223-224.

Safran, J. D., Alden, L. E., & Davidson, P. O. (1980). Client anxiety level as a moderator variable in assertion training. *Cognitive Therapy and Research, 4*, 189-200.

Salter, A. (1949). *Conditioned reflex therapy.* New York: Farrar, Straus & Giroux.

Sanchez, V. & Lewinsohn, P. M. (1980). Assertive behavior and depression. *Journal of Consulting and Clinical Psychology, 48*, 119-120.

Sanchez, V. C., Lewinsohn, P. M., & Larson, D. W. (1980). Assertion training: Effectiveness in the treatment of depression. *Journal of Clinical Psychology, 36*, 526-529.

Sanders, R. K. & Malony, H. N. (1982). A theological and psychological rationale for assertiveness training. *Journal of Psychology and Theology, 10*, 251-255.

Sanders, S. H. (1983). Component analysis of a behavioral treatment program for chronic low-back pain. *Behavior Therapy, 14*, 697-705.

Santas, G. X. (1979). *Socrates: Philosophy in Plato's early dialogues.* London: Routledge & Kegan Paul.

Saunders, D. G. (1984). Helping husbands who batter. *Social Casework, 65,* 347-353.

Scanlon, E. M. & Ollendick, T. H. (1985). Children's assertive behavior: The reliability and validity of three self-report measures. *Child & Family Behavior Therapy, 7,* 9-21.

Schefft, B. K. & Kanfer, F. H. (1987). The utility of a process model in therapy: A comparative study of treatment effects. *Behavior Therapy, 18,* 113-134.

Scherer, S. E. & Freedberg, E. J. (1976). Effects of group videotape feedback on development of assertiveness skills in alcoholics: A follow-up study. *Psychological Reports, 39,* 983-992.

Schloss, P. J., Espin, C. A., Smith, M. A., & Suffolk, D. R. (1987). Developing assertiveness during employment interviews with young adults who stutter. *Journal of Speech & Hearing Disorders, 52,* 30-36.

Schlundt, D. G. & McFall, R. M. (1987). Classifying social situations: A comparison of five methods. *Behavioral Assessment, 9,* 21-42.

Schneider, B. H., Ledingham, J. E., Poirier, C. A., Oliver, J., & Byrne, B. M. (1984). Self-reports of children in treatment: Is assertiveness in the eyes of the beholder? *Journal of Clinical Child Psychology, 13,* 70-73.

Schroder, H. M., Driver M. J., & Streufert, S. (1967). *Human information processing.* New York: Holt, Rinehart & Winston.

Schroeder, H. E. & Black, M. J. (1985). Unassertiveness. In M. Hersen & A. S. Bellack (Eds.) *Handbook of clinical behavior therapy with adults.* New York: Plenum.

Schroeder, H. E. & Rakos, R. F. (1978). Effects of history on the measurement of assertion. *Behavior Therapy, 9,* 965-966.

Schroeder, H. E. & Rakos, R. F. (1983). The identification and assessment of social skills. In R. Ellis & D. Whitington (Eds.) *New directions in social skill training.* London: Croom Helm.

Schroeder, H. E., Rakos, R. F., & Moe, J. (1983). The social perception of assertive behavior as a function of response class and gender. *Behavior Therapy, 14,* 534-544.

Schulman, J. A. & Bailey, K. G. (1983). An information feedback program for the development of assertive behavior. *Psychotherapy: Theory, Research & Practice, 20,* 220-231.

Schur, E. (1971). *Labeling deviant behavior.* New York: Harper & Row.

Schur, E. (1976). *The awareness trap.* New York: Quadrangle/New York Times Book Co.

Schwartz, R. D. & Higgins, R. L. (1979). Differential outcome from automated assertion training as a function of locus of control. *Journal of Consulting and Clinical Psychology, 47,* 686-694.

Schwartz, R. M. & Gottman, J. M. (1976). Toward a task analysis of assertive behavior. *Journal of Consulting and Clinical Psychology, 44,* 910-920.

Scott, R. R., Himadi, W., & Keane, T. M. (1983). A review of generalization in social skills training: Suggestions for future research. In M. Hersen, R. Eisler, & P. Miller (Eds.) *Progress in behavior modification (Vol. 15).* New York: Academic Press.

Scott, W. O., Baer, G., Christoff, K. A., & Kelly, J. A. (1984). The use of skills training procedures in the treatment of a child-abusive parent. *Journal of Behavior Therapy and Experimental Psychiatry, 15,* 329-336.

Searle, J. R. (1969). *Speech acts: An essay in the philosophy of language.* Cambridge: Cambridge University Press.

Segal, Z. V. & Marshall, W. L. (1985). Self-report and behavioral assertion in two groups of sexual offenders. *Journal of Behavior Therapy and Experimental Psychiatry, 16,* 223-229.

Seligman, M. E. P. (1975). *Helplessness*. San Francisco: Freeman.

Senatore, V., Matson, J. L., & Kazdin, A. E. (1982). A comparison of behavioral methods to train social skills to mentally retarded adults. *Behavior Therapy, 13*, 313-324.

Shapiro, E. S., Lentz, F. E., & Sofman, R. (1985). Validity of rating scales in assessing aggressive behavior in classroom settings. *Journal of School Psychology, 23*, 69-79.

Shaw, M. E. & Rutledge, P. (1976). Assertiveness training for managers. *Training and Development Journal, 30*, 8-14.

Shelton, J. L. & Levy, R. L. (Eds.) (1981). *Behavioral assignments and treatment compliance: A handbook of clinical strategies*. Champaign, IL: Research Press.

Shelton, J. L. & Mathis, H. V. (1976). Assertiveness as a predictor of resident assistant effectiveness. *Journal of College Student Personnel, 17*, 368-370.

Sigal, J., Braden-Maguire, J., Hayden, M., & Mosley, N. (1985). The effect of presentation style and sex of lawyer on jury decision-making behavior. *Psychology: A Quarterly Journal of Human Behavior, 22*, 13-19.

Sirkin, M. I. & Mosher, D. L. (1985). Guided imagery of female sexual assertiveness: Turn on or turn off? *Journal of Sex and Marital Therapy, 11*, 41-50.

Skatsche, R., Brandau, J., & Ruch, W., (1982). Development of a multidimensional test battery for the diagnostic assessment of the construct 'self-assuredness (assertivity)'. *Zeitschrift fur Klinische Psychologie, Forschung und Praxis, 11*, 292-314.

Skillings, R. E., Hersen, M., Bellack, A. S., & Becker, M. P. (1978). Relationship of specific and global measures of assertion in college females. *Journal of Clinical Psychology, 34*, 346-353.

Skinner, B. F. (1974). *About behaviorism*. New York: Knopf.

Smith, M. G. (1985). The use of hypnosis to accelerate assertiveness training. *Australian Journal of Clinical Hypnotherapy and Hypnosis, 6*, 99-107.

Smith, M. J. (1975). *When I say no, I feel guilty*. New York: Bantam.

Smolen, R. C., Spiegel, D. A., Bakker-Rabdau, M. K., Bakker, C. B., & Martin, C. (1985). A situational analysis of the relationship between spouse-specific assertiveness and marital adjustment. *Journal of Psychopathology and Behavioral Assessment, 7*, 397-410.

Solomon, L. J., Brehony, K. A., Rothblum, E. D., & Kelly, J. A. (1982). Corporate managers' reaction to assertive social skills exhibited by males and females. *Journal of Organizational Behavior Management, 4*, 49-63.

Stake, J. E., DeVille, C. J., & Pennell, C. L. (1983). The effects of assertive training on the performance self-esteem of adolescent girls. *Journal of Youth & Adolescence, 12*, 435-442.

Stake, J. E. & Pearlman, J. (1980). Assertiveness training as an intervention technique for low performance self-esteem women. *Journal of Counseling Psychology, 27*, 276-281.

Starke, M. C. (1987). Enhancing social skills and self-perceptions of physically disabled young adults: Assertiveness training versus discussion groups. *Behavior Modification, 11*, 3–16.

Starker, S. (1988). Psychologists and self-help books: Attitudes and prescriptive practices of clinicians. *American Journal of Psychotherapy, 42*, 448-455.

Stefanek, M. E. & Eisler, R. M. (1983). The current status of cognitive variables in assertiveness training. In M. Hersen, R. M. Eisler, & P. M. Miller (Eds.) *Progress in behavior modification (Vol. 15)*. New York: Academic Press.

Sterling, B. S. & Owen, J. W. (1982). Perceptions of demanding versus reasoning male and female police officers. *Personality and Social Psychology Bulletin, 8*, 336-340.

Sternberg, B. (1985). Relapse in weight control: Definitions, processes, and prevention stategies. In G. A. Marlatt & J. R. Gordon (Eds.) *Relapse prevention*. New York: Guilford Press.

St. Lawrence, J. S. (1981). Efficacy of a money deposit contingency on clinical out-patients' attendance and participation in assertive training. *Journal of Behavior Therapy and Experimental Psychiatry, 12,* 237-240.

St. Lawrence, J. S. (1982). Validation of a component model of social skills with a clinical outpatient population. *Journal of Behavioral Assessment, 4,* 15-27.

St. Lawrence, J. S. (1986). Assessment and treatment of social dysfunction in chronic schizophrenics. *The Behavior Therapist, 9,* 85-86.

St. Lawrence, J. S. (1987). Assessment of assertion. In M. Hersen, R. M. Eisler, & P. M. Miller (Eds.) *Progress in behavior modification. Vol. 21.* Newbury Park, CA: Sage Publications.

St. Lawrence, J. S., Bradlyn, A. S., & Kelly, J. A. (1983). Interpersonal adjustment of a homosexual adult. *Behavior Modification, 7,* 41-55.

St. Lawrence, J. S., Hansen, D. J., Cutts, T. F., Tisdelle, D.A., & Irish, J. D. (1985a). Situational context: Effects on perceptions of assertive and unassertive behavior. *Behavior Therapy, 16,* 51-62.

St. Lawrence, J. S., Hansen, D. J., Cutts, T. F., Tisdelle, D. A., & Irish, J. D. (1985b). Sex role orientation: A superordinate variable in social evaluation of assertive and unassert-ive behavior. *Behavior Modification, 9,* 387-396.

St. Lawrence, J. S., Hughes, E. F., Goff, A. F., & Palmer, M. B. (1984). Assessment of role-play generalization across qualitatively different situations. *Journal of Behavioral Assessment, 5,* 289-307.

St. Lawrence, J. S., Kirksey, W. A., & Moore, T. (1983). External validity of role play assessment of assertive behavior. *Journal of Behavioral Assessment, 5,* 25-34.

Stokes, T. F. & Baer, D. M. (1977). An implicit technology of generalization. *Journal of Applied Behavior Analysis, 10,* 349-367.

Stokes, T. F. & Osnes, P. G. (1989). An operant pursuit of generalization. *Behavior Therapy, 20,* 337-356.

Stoppard, J. M. & Henri, G. S. (1987). Conceptual level matching and effects of assertion training. *Journal of Counseling Psychology, 34,* 55-61.

Sturgis, E. T. & Adams, H. E. (1976). The right to treatment: Issues in the treatment of homosexuality. *Journal of Consulting and Clinical Psychology, 44,* 165-169.

Sturgis, E. T., Calhoun, K. S., & Best, C. L. (1979). Correlates of assertive behavior in alcoholics. *Addictive Behaviors, 4,* 193-197.

Sue, D. W. (Ed.) (1981). *Counseling the culturally different: Theory and practice.* New York: Wiley.

Sue, D., Ino, S., & Sue, D. M. (1983). Nonassertiveness of Asian Americans: An in-accurate assumption? *Journal of Counseling Psychology, 30,* 581-588.

Swan, G. E. & MacDonald, M. L. (1978). Behavior therapy in practice: A national survey of behavior therapists. *Behavior Therapy, 9,* 799-807.

Swimmer, G. I. & Ramanaiah, N. V. (1985). Convergent and discriminant validity of selected assertiveness measures. *Journal of Personality and Social Psychology, 49,* 243-249.

Talbert, E. E., Lawrence, P. S., & Nelson, R. O. (1980). The relationship between posi-tive and negative assertive behavior. *Behavioural Analysis and Modification, 4,* 36-47.

Taubman, B. (1976). *How to become an assertive woman: The key to self-fulfillment.* New York: Pocket Books.

Thelen, M. H., Fry, R. A., Dollinger, S. J., & Paul, S. C. (1976). Use of videotaped models to improve the interpersonal adjustment of delinquents. *Journal of Consulting and Clinical Psychology, 44,* 492.

Thelen, M. H. & Lasoski, M. C. (1980). The separate and combined effects of focusing information and videotape self-confrontation feedback. *Journal of Behavior Therapy and Experimental Psychiatry, 11*, 173-178.

Thorpe, G. L. (1975). Desensitization, behavior rehearsal, self-instructional training and placebo effects on assertive-refusal behavior. *European Journal of Behavioural Analysis and Modification, 1*, 30-44.

Thorpe, G. L., Freedman, E. G., & Lazar, J. D. (1985). Assertiveness training and exposure in vivo for agoraphobics. *Behavioural Psychotherapy, 13*, 132-141.

Thurman, C. W. (1985a). Effectiveness of cognitive-behavioral treatments in reducing Type A behavior among university faculty. *Journal of Counseling Psychology, 32*, 74-83.

Thurman, C. W. (1985b). Effectiveness of cognitive-behavioral treatments in reducing Type A behavior among university faculty: One year later. *Journal of Counseling Psychology, 32*, 445-448.

Tiegerman, S. & Kassinove, H. (1977). Effects of assertive training and cognitive components of rational therapy on assertive behaviors and interpersonal anxiety. *Psychological Reports, 40*, 535-542.

Trower, P. (1980). Situational analysis of the components and processes of behavior of socially skilled and unskilled patients. *Journal of Consulting and Clinical Psychology, 48*, 327-339.

Trower, P. (1982). Toward a generative model of social skills: A critique and synthesis. In J. Curran & P. Monti (Eds.) *Social skills training: A practical handbook for assessment and treatment*. New York: Guilford Press.

Turner, S. M. & Adams H. E. (1977). Effects of assertive training on three dimensions of assertiveness. *Behaviour Research and Therapy, 15*, 475-483.

Turner, S. M., Beidel, D. C., Hersen, M., & Bellack, A. S. (1984). Effects of race on ratings of social skill. *Journal of Consulting and Clinical Psychology, 52*, 474-475.

Turner, S. M., Hersen, M., & Bellack, A. S. (1979). Social skills training to teach prosocial behavior in an organically impaired and retarded patient. *Journal of Behavior Therapy and Experimental Psychiatry, 9*, 253-258.

Turner, S. M. & Jones, R. T. (Eds.) (1982). *Behavior modification in black populations: Psychosocial issues and empirical findings*. New York: Plenum.

Twentyman, C. T., Gilbralter, J. C., & Inz, J. M. (1979). Multimodal assessment of rehearsal treatments in an assertion training program. *Journal of Counseling Psychology, 26*, 384-389.

Twentyman, C. T., Greenwald, D., Greenwald, M., Kloss, J., Kovaleski, M., & Ziburg-Hoffman, P. (1982). An assessment of social skills deficits in alcoholics. *Journal of Behavioral Assessment, 4*, 317-326.

Twentyman, C. T., Pharr, D. R., & Connor, J. M. (1980). A comparison of three covert assertion training procedures. *Journal of Clinical Psychology, 16*, 520-525.

Twentyman, C. T., Zimering, R. T., & Kovaleski, M. E. (1981). Three studies investigating the efficacy of assertion training techniques. *Behavioral Counseling Quarterly, 1*, 302-316.

Unger, R. K., Raymond, B. J., & Levine, S. M. (1974). Are women a 'minority' group? Sometimes! *International Journal of Group Tensions, 4*, 71-81.

Vaal, J. J. & McCullagh, J. (1977). The Rathus Assertiveness Schedule: Reliability at the junior high school level. *Adolescence, 12*, 411-419.

Valerio, H. P. & Stone, G. L. (1982). Effects of behavioral, cognitive, and combined treatments for assertion as a function of differential deficits. *Journal of Counseling Psychology, 29*, 158-168.

Van Dijk, W. J. (1977). Assertive training for physical complaints. *Tijdschrift voor Psychotherapie, 3*, 189-191.

Van Hasselt, V. B., Hersen, M., & Bellack, A. S. (1981). The validity of role play tests for assessing social skills in children. *Behavior Therapy, 12*, 202-216.

Van Hasselt, V. B., Hersen, M., & Bellack, A. S. (1984). The relationship between assertion and sociometric status of children. *Behaviour Research and Therapy, 22*, 689-696.

Van Hasselt, V. B., Hersen, M., & Milliones, J. (1978). Social skills training for alcoholics and drug addicts: A review. *Addictive Behaviour, 3*, 221-233.

Van Hasselt, V. B., Kazdin, A. E., & Hersen, M. (1985). A behavioral-analytic model for assessing social skills in blind adolescents. *Behavior Research and Therapy, 23*, 395-425.

Vecsi, L. L. (1984). The relation of mothers' knowledge of assertion and expectations of its probable outcomes to their levels of assertiveness in responding to mother–adolescent daughter problem situations. *Dissertation Abstracts International, 45*, 689B-690B.

Viala, H. & Riviere, B. (1976). Assertive therapy in out-patient clinic and psychiatric hospital. *Perspectives Psychiatriques, 53*, 313-317.

Vlastos, G. (1971). Introduction: The paradox of Socrates. In G. Vlastos (Ed.) *The philosophy of Socrates*. Notre Dame, Indiana: University of Notre Dame Press.

Vogrin, D. & Kassinove, H. (1979). Effects of behavior rehearsal, audiotaped observation, and intelligence on assertiveness and adjustment in third-grade children. *Psychology in the Schools, 16*, 422-429.

Voss, J. R., Arrick, M. C., & Rimm, D. C. (1978). Behavior rehearsal, modeling, and coaching in assertive behavior. *Behavior Therapy, 9*, 970-971.

Waas, G. A. & French, D. C. (1989). Children's social problem solving: Comparison of the Open Middle Interview and Children's Assertive Behavior Scale. *Behavioral Assessment, 11*, 219-230.

Wadia, P. S. (1986). Reasoning, believing, and willing or the voluntarist paradox. In M. Tamny & K. D. Irani (Eds.) *Rationality in thought and action*. New York: Greenwood Press.

Waksman, S. A. (1984a). Assertion training with adolescents. *Adolescence, 19*, 123-130.

Waksman, S. A. (1984b). A controlled evaluation of assertion training with adolescents. *Adolescence, 19*, 277-282.

Waksman, S. A. & Messmer, C. L. (1979). *Social skill training: A manual for teaching assertive behaviors to children and adolescents*. Portland, OR: Enrichment Press.

Wallace, C. J. (1982). The social skills training project of the Mental Health Clinical Research Center for the Study of Schizophrenia. In J. P. Curran & P. M. Monti (Eds.) *Social skills training: A practical handbook for assessment and treatment*. New York: Guilford Press.

Wallston, B. S., Wallston, K., DeVellis, B. M., McLendon, E., & Percy, J. (1978). Modification of question asking behavior in high and low assertive women through modeling and specific instructions. *Social Behavior and Personality, 6*, 195-204.

Warehime, R. G. & Lowe, D. R. (1983). Assessing assertiveness in work settings: A discrimination measure. *Psychological Reports, 53*, 1007-1012.

Warren, N. J. & Gilner, F. H. (1978). Measurement of positive assertive behaviors: The Behavioral Test of Tenderness Expression. *Behavior Therapy, 9*, 178-184.

Warrenfeltz-Rodney, B. (1981). Social skills training of behavior disordered adolescents with self-monitoring to promote generalization to a vocational setting. *Behavior Disorders, 7*, 18-27.

Watson, D. L. & Tharp, R. G. (1988). *Self-directed behavior: Self-modification for personal adjustment* (5th edn). Pacific Grove, CA: Brooks/Cole.

Wehr, S. H. & Kaufman, M. E. (1987). The effects of assertive training on performance in highly anxious adolescents. *Adolescence, 22*, 195-205.

Weist, M. D. & Ollendick, T. H. (1989, May). Empirical validation of assertive behaviors in boys. Paper presented at the annual convention of the Association for Behavior Analysis, Milwaukee.

Wessberg, H. W., Mariotto, M. J., Conger, A. J., Farrell, A. D., & Conger, J. C. (1979). Ecological validity of role play for assessing heterosocial anxiety and skill of male college students. *Journal of Consulting and Clinical Psychology, 47*, 515-535.

Westefeld, J. S., Galassi, J. P., & Galassi, M. D. (1980). Effects of role-playing instructions on assertive behavior: A methodological study. *Behavior Therapy, 1*, 271-277.

Wildman, B. G. (1986). Perception of refusal assertion: The effects of conversational comments and compliments. *Behavior Modification, 10*, 472-486.

Wildman, B. G. & Clementz, B. (1986). Assertive, empathic assertive, and conversational behavior: Perception of likeability, effectiveness, and sex role. *Behavior Modification, 10*, 315-332.

Williams, J. M., Hadden, K., & Marcavage, E. (1983). Experimental study of assertion training as a drug prevention strategy for use with college students. *Journal of College Student Personnel, 24*, 201-206.

Williams, J. M. & Stout, J. K. (1985). The effect of high and low assertiveness on locus of control and health problems. *Journal of Psychology, 119*, 169-173.

Williams, M. T., Turner, S. M., Watts, J. G., Bellack, A. S., & Hersen, M. (1977). Group social skills training for chronic psychiatric patients. *European Journal of Behavioural Analysis and Modification, 1*, 223-229.

Williamson, D. A. & McKenzie, S. J. (1988). Social skills tests for children. In M. Hersen & A. S. Bellack (Eds.) *Dictionary of behavioral assessment*. New York: Pergamon Press.

Williamson, D. A., Moody, S. C., Granberry, W. W., Lethermon, V. R., & Blouin, D. C. (1983). Criterion-related validity of role play social skills test for children. *Behavior Therapy, 14*, 466-481.

Wills, T. A., Baker, E., & Botvin, G. J. (1989). Dimensions of assertiveness: Differential relationships to substance use in early adolescence. *Journal of Consulting and Clinical Psychology, 57*, 473-478.

Wilson, E. R. (1975). Women and assertive training in the Australian scene. *Australian Psychologist, 10*, 333-338.

Wilson, F. E. & Evans, I. M. (1983). The reliability of target-behavior selection in behavioral assessment. *Behavioral Assessment, 5*, 15-32.

Wilson, L. K. & Gallois, C. (1985). Perceptions of assertive behavior: Sex combination, role appropriateness, and message type. *Sex Roles, 12*, 125-141.

Wine, J. D. (1981). From defect to competence models. In J. D. Wine & M. D. Smye (Eds.) *Social competence*. New York: Guilford Press.

Wing, J. K. (1978) Clinical concepts of schizophrenia. In J. K. Wing (Ed.) *Schizophrenia: Toward a new synthesis*. London: Academic Press.

Winship, B. J. & Kelly, J. D. (1976). A verbal response model of assertiveness. *Journal of Counseling Psychology, 23*, 215-220.

Wojnilower, D. A. & Gross, A. M. (1984). Assertive behavior and likeability in elementary school boys. *Child and Family Behavior Therapy, 6*, 57-70.

Wojnilower, D. A., & Gross, A. M. (1988). Knowledge, perception, and performance of assertive behavior in children with learning disabilities. *Journal of Learning Disabilities, 21*, 109-117.

Wolf, M. M. (1978). Social validity: The case for subjective measurement or how applied behavior analysis is finding its heart. *Journal of Applied Behavior Analysis, 11*, 203-214.

Wolfe, J. L. & Fodor, I. G. (1975). A cognitive/behavioral approach to modifying assertive behavior in women. *Counseling Psychologist, 5*, 45-52.

Wolfe, J. L. & Fodor, I. G. (1977). Modifying assertive behavior in women: A comparison of three approaches. *Behavior Therapy, 8*, 567-574.

Wolpe, J. (1982). *The practice of behavior therapy* (3rd edn). New York: Pergamon Press.

Wolpe, J. & Lazarus, A. A. (1966). *Behavior therapy techniques: A guide to the treatment of neuroses.* Oxford: Pergamon Press.

Wood, P. S. & Mallinckrodt, B. (1990). Culturally sensitive assertiveness training for ethnic minority clients. *Professional Psychology: Research and Practice, 21*, 5-11.

Woolfolk, R. L. & Dever, S. (1979). Perceptions of assertion: An empirical analysis. *Behavior Therapy, 10*, 404-411.

Woolfolk, R. L. & Richardson, F. C. (1984). Behavior therapy and the ideology of modernity. *American Psychologist, 39*, 777-786.

Worell, J. (1988). Women's satisfaction in close relationships. *Clinical Psychology Review, 8*, 477-498.

Wortmann, H. & Paluck, R. J. (1979). Assertion training with institutionalized severely retarded women. *The Behavior Therapist, 2*, 24-25.

Yamasaki, K. (1985). The social skills training for a school refusal. *Japanese Journal of Behavior Therapy, 11*, 34-41.

Yanagida, E. H. (1979). Cross-cultural considerations in the application of assertion training: A brief note. *Psychology of Women Quarterly, 3*, 400-402.

Young, E. R., Rimm, D. C., & Kennedy, T. D. (1973). An experimental investigation of modeling and verbal reinforcement of assertive behavior. *Behaviour Research and Therapy, 11*, 317-319.

Youngren, M. A. & Lewinsohn, P. M. (1980). The functional relationship between depression and problematic interpersonal behavior. *Journal of Abnormal Psychology, 89*, 333-341.

Zeiss, A. M., Lewinsohn, P. M., & Munoz, R. F. (1979). Nonspecific improvement effects in depression using interpersonal skills training, pleasant activity schedules, or cognitive training. *Journal of Consulting and Clinical Psychology, 47*, 427-439.

Zielinski, J. J. (1978). Situational determinants of assertive behavior in depressed alcoholics. *Journal of Behavior Therapy and Experimental Psychiatry, 9*, 103-107.

Zielinski, J. J. & Williams, L. J. (1979). Covert modeling vs. behavior rehearsal in the training and generalization of assertive behaviors: A crossover design. *Journal of Clinical Psychology, 35*, 855-863.

Zollo. L. J., Heimberg, R. G., & Becker, R. E. (1985). Evaluations and consequences of assertive behavior. *Journal of Behavior Therapy and Experimental Psychiatry, 16*, 295-301.

Zuker, E. (1983). *Mastering assertiveness skills.* New York: American Management Association.

Name index

Abelson, W. 98, 113
Adams, H.E. 104, 127, 130, 193
Adejumo, D. 102
Adinolfi, A.A. 154
Aiduk, R. 129, 131, 132
Alberti, R.E.: Failure: Winning at the
 losing game 1, 22, 146, 172–3, 177,
 188, 195; *Making yourself heard* 189;
 Stand up, speak out, talk back, 189;
 Your perfect right, 4, 8, 10, 15, 23, 45;
 Your perfect right (the professional
 edn) 145–6, 163, 172, 187–8; *Your
 perfect right* (5th edn) 15, 174, 177,
 189, 191
Alden, L. 51–2, 55, 58, 77, 105, 132, 133
American Psychological Association 90
Ammerman, R.T. 196
Andrasik, F. 1, 103, 114, 141
Argyle, M. 13, 58, 59, 143, 191
Arisohn, B. 60, 193
Arkowitz, H. 10, 99, 101, 110, 111, 131
Arnold, B.R. 170
Arrindell, W.A. 191
Ary, D.V. 167
Augsberger, D. 82
Austin, N. 71, 189

Baer, D.M. 131, 135, 136, 144
Baer, J. 1, 71, 189
Bailey, K.G. 128, 148
Bair, J.P. 171
Baldwin, J.D. 121
Bander, R.S. 148
Bandura, A.: Self-efficacy 54, 85; *Social
 learning theory* 54, 58, 61, 63, 127–8,
 134, 143
Barbaree, H.E. 52, 155

Bates, P. 170
Beach, L.R. 54, 105
Beck, J.G. 102, 103
Beck, S. 31, 79, 80
Becker, R.E.: Assessment of social skills
 104; Cognitive and behavioral models
 9, 51, 60; Cognitive mediation of
 assertive behavior 52, 105, 114;
 Evaluations and consequences of
 assertive behavior 31, 192;
 Personalized versus standard role plays
 110; Relations of specific and global
 measures 33; *Social skill training
 treatment for depression* 99, 111, 137,
 155–6, 189
Beidleman, W.B. 152
Beil-Warner, D. 13, 102
Bellack, A.S.: Assessment of assertion
 and problem-solving skills 158;
 Assessment of assertiveness 33;
 Behavioral assessment of social skills
 12, 99, 103, 106–7, 109, 111–12, 118;
 A critical appraisal of strategies 110;
 Effects of live modelling 127; Effects
 of race 78; Group social skills training
 159; Measuring social skill 103;
 Recurrent problems 111; The
 relationship between assertion and
 sociometric status of children 168;
 Relationship of role playing 104, 110;
 Relations of specific and global
 measures 33; Role playing tests 104,
 110; Role of social competence 166;
 The role of social perception 12, 49,
 58; Social skill training 159; Social
 skill training treatment for depression
 99; Social skills training for highly

Irani, K.D. 2
Ivey, A.E. 98, 113, 182

Jackson, D.J. 162
Jacobs, M. 58, 133
Jacobs, M.K. 106, 132, 137, 138, 140, 145
Jacobson, N. 164
Jaffe, Y. 13, 102
Jakubowski, P. *see* Lange
Jakubowski-Spector, P. 71
Jansen, M.A. 159
Jansen, M.S. 171
Jarrett, R.B. 124
Jason, L.A. 155, 168
Jaspers, K. 5
Jenkins, J.O. 14, 78, 79, 104, 136, 152
Jensen, B. 101
Johnson, M.B. 126
Johnson, W.G. 108, 167, 168
Joiner, J.G. 168
Jones, R.G. 105, 114
Jones, S.L. 82
Jordan, C.S. 145

Kaflowitz, N.G. 54
Kahn, L.S. 163, 164, 183
Kahn, S.E. 72, 73, 162, 163, 164, 165
Kanfer, F.H.: Behavioral analysis 97,
   101; Behavioral diagnosis 22, 94, 101;
   *Guiding the process of therapeutic
   change* 49, 60, 94, 99, 131, 135–6, 147,
   176; *Learning foundations of behavior
   therapy* 94; Managing clinical change
   141; Target selection 95, 97, 98; The
   utility of a process model 140, 149
Kaplan, D.A. 132
Karoly, P. 129, 131, 132, 167
Kassinove, H. 58, 133, 168
Katz, I. 79
Kazdin, A.E.: Assertion modeling 127,
   128, 142, 152, 168; Assessing the
   importance of behavior change 10;
   Assessment of imagery 129, 138, 142;
   *Behavior modification in applied
   settings,* 107, 135, 182; A behavioral–
   analytic model 169; Behavioral
   observation 107–8; Behavior rehearsal
   130, 132, 136, 137; Changes in
   children's social performance 109, 138;
   A comparison of behavioral methods
   170; Covert and overt rehearsal 128,
   129, 130, 138, 142; Covert and overt

rehearsal and homework practice 128,
   129, 130, 136, 138; Covert modeling
   128, 129, 138, 142; Effects of covert
   modeling 128, 138; Effects of covert
   modeling and coding 128, 129, 138,
   142; Effects of covert modeling and
   model reinforcement 128, 138; The
   effects of instructional set 109; Effects
   of live modeling 127; *Evaluation of
   behavior therapy* 125, 194; Imagery
   elaboration 128, 129, 138; The impact
   of variations in treatment rationales 66,
   176, 196; The separate and combined
   effects 128, 130; Situational specificity
   93, 102; Social skill performance 109;
   Symptom substitution 95, 147
Keane, T.M. 58, 69, 72, 79, 166, 192
Kelley, J.E. 50
Kelly, C. 1
Kelly, G.A. 3, 64
Kelly, J.A.: Assessing subjective
   responses 69, 192; A behavioral
   approach 8; Blacks' perception 72,
   192; Corporate managers' reaction 31;
   Group social skills training 144–6, 172;
   I am worth it 189; Interpersonal
   adjustment 161, 180, 182; Interpersonal
   reaction 79; males' and females'
   reaction 192; *Social skills training* 180,
   182, 189; Teaching assertive and
   commendatory social skills 125;
   Teaching assertive skills 161; Training
   and generalization 180, 195; The use of
   skills training procedures 152; A verbal
   response model 31
Kelly, J.D. 31, 189
Kelly, W.J. 140
Keltner, A. 152, 153, 157
Kern, J.M. 30–1, 72–3, 77, 84–5, 103,
   110–11, 121, 192, 193
Kidder, L.H. 162
Kiecolt, J.K. 104
Kiecolt-Glaser, J.K. 109, 112
Kienhorst, I. 5
Kimble, C.E. 180, 181
Kincaid, M.B. 161
King, L.W. 107
Kinney, C.D. 171
Kipper, D.A. 13, 102, 175
Kirchner, E.P. 152
Kirkland, K. 170
Kirkland, K.D. 168

Subject index